NEUROLOGICAL EXAMINATION OF CHILDREN

Clinics in Developmental Medicine
Double volume 20/21

NEUROLOGICAL EXAMINATION OF CHILDREN

by

Richmond S. Paine

Professor of Paediatric Neurology, The George Washington University.
Neurologist, Children's Hospital of the D.C., Washington, D.C.

Thomas E. Oppé

Director, Paediatric Unit, St. Mary's Hospital Medical School.
Consultant Paediatrician, St. Mary's Hospital, London.

Foreword by Lord Brain

£3.00   1966

Published by the Spastics Society Medical Education and Information Unit in Association with William Heinemann Medical Books Ltd., London; J. B. Lippincott Co., Philadelphia.

ISBN 0433-246-50-2

Printed in England at THE LAVENHAM PRESS LTD., Lavenham, Suffolk.

Acknowledgements

This volume would never have been written were it not for the inspiration of Dr. Ronald Mac Keith and the editorial talents of Dr. Martin Bax. The illustrations were photographed by Mr. Robert Clark of the George Washington University School of Medicine, Mr. Ferdinand Harding, F.B.P.A., at the Children's Medical Center, Boston, Massachusetts, and Mr. J. Rytina at St. Mary's Hospital Medical School, London. Dr. Joseph M. LoPresti, Radiologist to the Children's Hospital in Washington, furnished most of the x-rays from which reproductions were made. Our secretaries, Miss Nelly Ledesma, Miss Mary England and Mrs. Howard West, typed successive versions of the text skilfully, patiently, and incredibly swiftly.

A final word of appreciation is due to the Cunard Steam-Ship Company, whose vessels have often provided for one of us the rare opportunity of four uninterrupted days to write and to think, and whose Purser's Assistants typed part of the revision of the manuscript.

Thanks are due to the following publishers for permission to reproduce certain illustrations in this book:

Harvard University Press for Fig. 1, Chap. XI and Fig. 4, Chap. XII (previously published in 'The Natural History of Cerebral Palsy' by Crothers and Paine, 1959);

'Pediatric Clinics of North America' for Figs. 2, 3, 4 and 7, Chap. VIII, Figs. 2 and 3, Chap. IX, Figs. 1 and 2, Chap. X, and Figs. 5, 6 and 9, Chap. XII;

'Pediatrics' for Fig. 10, Chap. IX.

Details of the Graham-Kendall memory design test may be obtained from the Psychological Corporation, 304 East 45th Street, New York, N.Y. 10017.

Contents

Foreword .. .. *Lord Brain*

Preface .. .. *Richmond S. Paine, Thomas E. Oppé*

CHAPTER I. **The History** 1
The Informant 1
The Framework 2
Details of History 2
Past Medical History 2
The Developmental History 3
Family History 4
Social and Environmental History 9
Detailed Review of Present Condition 9

CHAPTER II. **Some Particular Symptoms** 10
Clumsiness 10
Involuntary Movements 11
Weakness 11
Floppiness (Hypotonia) 12
Headache 14
Seizures 16
Enuresis 20
Pica 21
Deafness 22

CHAPTER III. **The General Physical Examination** 25
Principles of Paediatric Examination 25
The Routine Physical Examination 26

CHAPTER IV. **Neurological Examination — General Comments** .. 30
Outline of Recording Neurological Examination .. 31

CHAPTER V. **Mental State** 33
Consciousness 33
Intelligence 38
Affect 46

CHAPTER VI. **Speech** 47

Methods of Examination 47
Evaluation of the Child's Spontaneous Speech .. 47
Further Objective Testing 48
Related Functions to be Evaluated in Cases of Abnormal
Speech 49

Interpretation 52
Standards of Normal for Age 52
Defects of Voice 54
Dysarthria 54
Secondary Speech Disorders 55
'Specific Developmental Speech Disorders' 55
Dysrhythmia 56
Speech which is Deficient in Quantity 56
Diagnostic Clues 57
The Need for Periodic Re-evaluation 65

CHAPTER VII. **Special Tests of Cerebral Function** 66
The Purpose of the Tests 66
Methods of Examination 68
Gnosis 69
Praxis 71
Irregularities on Psychometric Tests 83
Interpretation 84

CHAPTER VIII. **Head, Neck and Spine** 85
Head 85
Neck 95
Spine 97

CHAPTER IX. **Cranial Nerves** 98

Cranial Nerve 1: *Sense of Smell* 98
Methods of Examination 98
Interpretation 98

Cranial Nerve 2: *Vision* 99
Determination of the Presence of Vision 99
Visual Acuity 100
Colour Vision 101
Visual Fields 101
Examination of the Eyes 104
Eyegrounds 108

Cranial Nerves 3, 4, 6: *Eye Movements* 110
Position of the Eyes at Rest 110
Movements of the Eyes 112
Pupils 120
Ptosis 121
Exophthalmos 122
Syndromes 122

Cranial Nerve 5: *Trigeminal Nerve* 124
Examination of Motor Function 124
Examination of Sensory Function 124
Interpretation 126

Cranial Nerve 7: *Facial Nerve* 127
Examination of Motor Function 128
Examination of Sensory Functions 129
Autonomic Functions 130
Interpretation 130

Cranial Nerve 8: *Auditory Nerve* 132
    Methods of Examination 132
    Interpretation 136

Cranial Nerves 9, 10: *Glossopharyngeal and Vagus Nerves* .. 136
    Examination and Interpretation of Motor Functions .. 137
    Examination and Interpretation of Sensory Functions .. 138
    Examination of Autonomic Functions 138
    Syndromes 138

Cranial Nerve 11: *Spinal Accessory* 138
    Methods of Examination 138
    Interpretation 139

Cranial Nerve 12: *Hypoglossal* 140
    Methods of Examination 140
    Interpretation 141

CHAPTER X. **Posture and Gait** 142
    Station 142
    Postures other than Standing 143
    Gait 143

CHAPTER XI. **Motor Function** 150
    Muscular Mass 150
    Muscular Power 152
    Muscular Tone 158
    Coordination 163
    Abnormal Movements 165
    Associated Movements 168
    Topographical Classification of Motor Disturbances .. 170

CHAPTER XII. **Reflexes, Responses and Infantile Automatisms** 171
    Deep Reflexes 171
    Clonus 175
    Superficial Reflexes 178
    Pyramidal Signs 180
    Abnormal Spinal Reflexes 183
    Infantile Automatisms 184

CHAPTER XIII. **Sensory Function** 196
    Superficial or Exteroceptive Sensation 196
    Deep or Proprioceptive Sensation 201
    Cortical Sensory Functions 204

CHAPTER XIV. **Autonomic Function** 207
    Methods of Examination 207
    Interpretation 208

CHAPTER XV. **Special Investigations** 213
    Introduction 213
    Electroencephalography 214
    Electromyography 216
    Studies of Nerve Conduction 220

Electroretinography 222
Special Studies of the Blood 222
Chromosomal Studies 225
Special Studies on Urine 226
Cerebrospinal Fluid 231
Subdural Taps 235
X-Ray and Contrast X-Ray Studies 236
Other Special Procedures which are Substitutes for Contrast
   X-Rays 241
Pharmacologic Tests 241
Caloric Nystagmus 249
Cerebral Circulation Time 249
Psychometric Tests 250
Audiometry 251
Cystometrograms 253
Biopsies of Muscle 256
Biopsies of Skin 260
Biopsies of Nerve 260
Biopsies of Rectum 260
Biopsies of Brain 261
Anaesthesia for Contrast X-Ray and Biopsy Procedures .. 262

References 263

Index 268

Foreword

The neurology of childhood has much in common with that of adult life but it also has distinctive features. It has to take into account the stages of development of the mind and the nervous system, and the examination of a child patient presents special problems. Moreover, there are a number of neurological disorders which are peculiar to childhood, and neurological disorders in childhood may be closely related to mental subnormality. The recent discoveries of chromosomal and biochemical abnormalities in relation to disease in childhood have opened up new fields for the paediatric neurologist. There is, therefore, an obvious need for textbooks of paediatric neurology to deal with the special problems of investigation of nervous disease in childhood and to survey recent additions to knowledge in this field. This book seems to me to serve both these purposes admirably, and I can unhesitatingly recommend it.

Brain

Preface

Many paediatricians and neurologists find that the examination and evaluation of the nervous system in the child presents particular difficulties. The central nervous system in the child is a developing and changing system while that of the adult is a relatively unchanging system. The effect of pathological processes occurring on such a background is bound to be different from the effects seen in adults.

Certain diseases such as Werdnig-Hoffmann's infantile progressive spinal muscular atrophy occur only in childhood, and others such as Alzheimer's disease are limited to adult life. It is self-evident that congenital anomalies, either anatomical or metabolic, occupy a larger part of the spectrum of disease of the nervous system in childhood than in adulthood. When diseases of adults such as disseminated sclerosis do occur in children, they are frequently atypical and difficult to recognise. It was not, however, our intent to write a textbook of paediatric neurology. Such texts are available (e.g. Ford 1960) and the physician who can make a diagnosis for one of his patients can usually find a discussion of the disease and of whatever treatment is available, either in one of these texts or in one of the standard multiple-volume publications which cover the entire field of neurology (e.g. Baker 1962). We hope however that this book will give the clinician help with the actual neurological examination. We have not dealt with the neurological examination of newborn babies as this has been the subject of a number of recent texts (e.g. Prechtl 1964).

There are obvious practical difficulties in the examination. Perimetric examination of the visual fields and similar tests are impossible to apply to very young, mentally retarded or uncooperative children. Some ingenuity and knowledge of special tricks may be required to adapt even the standard observations on motor and sensory function and reflexes to many children. This volume will not, however, be merely an exposition of techniques of examination and of a few of our own special 'tricks'. In addition, we have devoted space to the interpretation of findings, in the hope of bridging the gap between mere techniques of examination and the making of an anatomical and aetiological diagnosis.

We have done this because it is more difficult to decide whether or not a particular finding is abnormal in children than it is in adults. The range of variation of normal is greater among children, and the number of standards which must be learnt in order to evaluate the function of the nervous system at all the ages from the newborn period to adolescence is far greater than the changes which occur from adolescence to old age. Many special responses and automatisms are peculiar to early childhood and these responses are constantly changing with increasing age, as some disappear and others become demonstrable for the first time. Successful examination of young children depends on understanding these sequences of evolution and assessing the significance of deviations from them. In discussing the special features of the developmental neurological examination, we have tried to consider the interpretation of various possible findings as normal or abnormal, their relative importance, their implications about the possible locations of the responsible lesion and the nature of the disease process involved.

In bringing up these interpretations of clinical findings, it has seemed wise to include a certain amount of material on the underlying anatomy and physiology which is unfamiliar to many paediatricians (or has become so by the time they complete training in their speciality). We hope that the neurologist who only occasionally examines children will find useful the special methods and interpretations for young patients.

Richmond Paine
Thomas Oppé

CHAPTER I

The History

Comprehensive assessment and good management of a child with neurological disease is impossible without a full history. The history is often a better signpost to a correct diagnosis than the physical examination or special investigations. Often physical signs and investigations will reveal the need for further history-taking, so that it is mistaken to believe that the complete history must be elicited once and for all at the first interview. The initial history is aimed at obtaining rapport and confidence between physician, patient and informant, and providing sufficient information for the further management of the case to proceed at the right speed and in the right direction. Taking a history should rarely be a systematic cross-examination, but a series of structured conversations with the physician guiding but not dictating the process of communication.

The paediatric history differs from an adult history not so much in general design as in the different emphasis placed upon some aspects of the history. The developmental history of the child, including both the genetic and environmental fields, largely replaces the questions asked routinely of adults which are designed to throw light on degenerative processes. In discusssing history-taking here emphasis has been placed upon these features of the process.

Many of the problems which bring children to the physician are directly associated with emotional disturbances in the child or his family. The description of history-taking outlined will in general be found adequate for the initial exploration of organic neurological disease and for providing clues which suggest the probability of psychosomatic or psychogenic disorder. The more specialised methods of history-taking which are needed for the full elucidation of psychiatric problems in the child or his parents are not discussed, but it should be remembered that any history-taking is an intense emotional interaction which is never neutral and may be either of helpful or harmful therapeutic effect.

The Informant

The amount of information which the patient will contribute directly depends upon age, intelligence and cooperation. He should always have the opportunity to give his own account and most children of three years old and upwards can describe their symptoms well. However, children may mislead through a desire to please or the denial of symptoms which make them feel ashamed or guilty. The inability of a child to give clear or consistent information may be of diagnostic value. In most cases much of the history will be obtained through an informant, usually the mother, and care must be taken when talking to the informant in the patient's presence, for children understand — and misunderstand — much of overheard speech. Sometimes there are advantages in interviewing the patient and informant separately, but it is usually helpful for the child and mother to be together for most of the interview. Subsequent cooperation is increased if the child has witnessed friendly communication between physician and mother, and the doctor has opportunities for indirect observation of the child. It may be necessary, however, to exclude him from the interview if he distracts his mother or would be upset by what he hears.

The informant is rarely a detached, objective witness, so that her evidence must continually be interpreted by the physician in the light of what emerges revealing the informant's own personality and relationships with the child. Symptoms may be distorted, denied, invented, exaggerated or minimised, the presenting complaint may be a camouflage to conceal the real purpose of the consultation. Most mothers have good memories and are skilful witnesses. However, it is important to take and document the history in such a way that verifiable facts can be checked later. The child's place of birth, the names and addresses of physicians, and clinics and hospitals which the child has attended previously should be carefully recorded.

The informant will answer questions more readily and accurately if she understands their meaning, believes them to be relevant and feels that she will not be criticised if her replies do not meet with the physician's approval. The physician should appear to be unhurried and ample opportunity should be given to the informant for her to discuss the problem from her own point of view.

The Framework

The essentials of a paediatric neurological history must include (1) the identity of the patient, (2) the informant's presentation of the problem, (3) the past medical history, (4) the developmental history, (5) the family history, (6) the social and environmental history, (7) detailed review of present condition.

Rigidity regarding the order in which these items are taken is not necessary, and the extent and depth to which a particular area is explored will vary from patient to patient, especially at the initial interview. Some information from each of these areas should be obtained and recorded in every case.

Details of History

The Identity of the Child

The patient's names and address are recorded and a note is also made of the forename by which he prefers to be called. His age and date of birth are noted, as are his sex and ethnic group. The name and address of the informant and her relationship to the patient should be ascertained and if the informant is not the guardian of the child the name and address of the parents or guardians are noted.

The Informant's Presentation of the Problem

This should be recorded as briefly as possible in the informant's own words. Usually it will itemise the chief complaints and give the reason for the consultation.

Past Medical History

(a) The dates of all previous illnesses, accidents or operations are detailed, including the alleged diagnosis and treatment given,

(b) Enquiries are made about minor ailments, and details of non-prescribed medication such as laxatives, teething powders, vitamins and sedatives are sought.

(c) The number and type of immunising procedures undergone by the child are noted together with the age at which they were given and any reactions which followed.

(d) A review of the major systems is made, including questions referable to main symptoms associated with each system. This should bear in mind that symptoms encountered in adults with widespread degenerative disease are not found in childhood or have a different significance.

The Developmental History

This is designed to indicate the child's physical and mental potential and to identify factors which may have caused deviations from the child's expected progress. The amount of detail required will vary but a developmental assessment is part of every paediatric consultation. Antenatal, perinatal and postnatal development must be surveyed. The mother should be asked about her health during pregnancy, the course of confinement and mode of delivery. The neonatal history is important and a note should be made of the birth weight and estimated maturity.

It is often convenient at this stage to enquire into early feeding or sleeping difficulties before proceeding to survey the milestones of development during infancy and the pre-school years.

The experienced mother who has other children with whom the patient may be compared can be asked 'Do you think he is as forward as his brothers and sisters?' or 'In what ways is he growing up differently fron the others?' Only if there is doubt about the reply need a systematic exploration of the milestones be made; however, if there is any suspicion or if the mother lacks experience, a fuller developmental history must be taken.

The best milestones to check are those which mothers tend to remember clearly (smiling, sitting, standing, walking, first words, feeding himself and becoming clean and dry); those that cover several fields of development (following with eyes, attention to sounds, meaningful communication, building bricks); and those that have been shown to have reasonable predictive validity (not dentition or gross motor function). Discrepancies may have diagnostic value as delay in a single field nearly always indicates a localised rather than a generalised defect. Apparent inconsistencies raise doubts regarding the informant's memory or veracity, and should lead to further questions designed to show up these or perhaps indicate that the informant has interpreted the meaning of some questions differently from the physician.

The developmental progress of older children is often best evaluated by a consideration of school performance. Scholastic achievement, games ability and social behaviour are all important aspects of school life, and if there is any difficulty in obtaining information from the family the first-hand opinions of the school teachers should be obtained.

Family History

The family history may have aetiological significance in suggesting the presence of a specific genetic disorder or the inheritance of a constitutional susceptibility to certain disorders. It may reveal the prevalence of infective or other acquired disease which is concentrated in certain families because of environmental or cultural similarities and contacts. It may also give a hint that the basic reason for the consultation is underlying fear that the early signs of some family affliction are appearing in the patient. The place of the child within the family and the nature of the family group are important factors in development which must be elucidated in taking the history.

Initially the following basic information is desirable:

(a) Patient's sibs (names, ages and health) including miscarriages, stillbirths and early deaths. If an inherited disorder is suspected the age of onset of the disease in affected sibs should be noted.

(b) Parents (ages, health, consanguinity).

(c) Have any known members of the family on either side suffered from a condition in any way similar to the patient's?

(d) On the whole have the immediate members of the family enjoyed good health?

If the answers to these questions are in any way suggestive of genetic disorders, or if the patient is known to be suffering from a known genetic disease, a detailed pedigree should be prepared. When systematically taking and recording the pedigree it is usually convenient to follow the accepted symbols. The patient (propositus) is placed first and the siblings are then enumerated in birth order. Conventionally the propositus is indicated by an arrow and the sibs may be numbered in chronological order or their actual ages (or birth dates) indicated. Males are symbolised by squares or the sign ♂, females by circles or the sign ♀. Affected members of a family have their symbols blacked in. Thus in a family afflicted with muscular dystrophy the pedigree might start

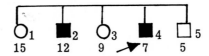

The health of the parents is then enquired about, and they are represented above their offspring on the chart, joined by a single marital bar if they are unrelated, double lines if there is consanguinity and interrupted lines if they are unmarried.

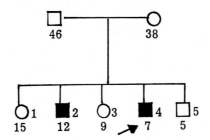

4

The aunts and uncles of the patient are next considered, taking the father's siblings first. If they are numerous it is allowable to give the numbers of normal or affected siblings of each sex. The offspring of these are documented but normals need not be detailed unless a complete genetic analysis is to be undertaken.

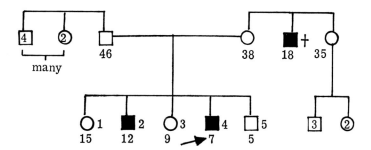

The pedigree now shows that the father has 4 normal brothers and 2 normal sisters who have had many normal children; on the other hand the mother had an affected brother who died aged 18 years, and has a surviving sister with 5 normal children (3 male and 2 female). It is now worthwhile to enquire into the previous generation, and assuming the information were available the complete pedigree might appear

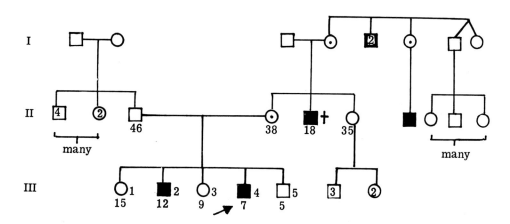

The patient's (III 4) mother can now be presumptively diagnosed as the heterozygous carrier of an X-borne (sex-linked) trait and has been given the conventional symbol for heterozygosity ⊙ . Furthermore, inspection of generation I shows additional evidence of X-borne transmission and two females can be assigned as

probable heterozygotes. The twins symbolised ╱╲ are obviously dizygotics;

monozygotic twins would have been given the symbol ╱─╲

5

Interpretation

The construction of such a chart is not time or space consuming and is necessary for even the simplest analysis of inheritance. Many neurological disorders are due to single-gene defects and it is worth recalling the characteristics of the classical modes of Mendelian transmission.

Autosomal Dominant Inheritance. When the clinical characteristics of a condition are found in individuals possessing the responsible gene on one only of a pair of autosomes, the pattern of inheritance is said to be dominant. The condition will be inherited from generation to generation as one affected parent will pass the gene to approximately half the offspring. The defective gene is carried on one chromosome of the pair and there is an even chance of the child receiving the chromosome bearing the abnormal gene. Therefore in a sufficiently large pedigree it will be expected that affected and unaffected sibs occur in about equal numbers.

Except in the case of new mutations, affected individuals will be found to have an affected parent. Unaffected parents should not have affected children. However it is characteristic of many dominantly inherited conditions that the gene effect (hence the severity of the clinical state) varies considerably. If the clinical evidence of the condition is only minimally apparent in an individual, the gene is said to be weakly 'expressed.' Variations in 'expression' may be due to the interaction of other modifying genes or be determined by environmental influences. Dominant autosomal inheritance is not affected by sex and a pedigree shows no inequality between males and females. However in several conditions the gene seems to be modified in the intensity of its expression by sex. Sometimes an individual who on genetic grounds must possess the abnormal gene, e.g. an apparently normal parent of affected children, shows no evidence of the trait. In such a case the gene is said to be non-penetrant. While non-penetrance may exist it is probable that often times it is due to inability to detect minor gene effects rather than a true biological phenomenon.

Conditions showing dominant inheritance tend to be of minor clinical importance, for if they were severe enough to cause death regularly in childhood or prevent reproduction the condition would disappear. There are a few exceptions in which disabling conditions may appear in the affected offspring before the parent is clinically affected, and there are also a few diseases which are severe but do not prevent reproduction. Examples from neurology are Huntington's chorea, Charcot-Marie-Tooth disease and myotonic dystrophy.

Autosomal Recessive Inheritance. A recessively inherited condition is only clinically apparent in individuals homozygous for the causative gene. They must therefore inherit the gene from both parents. The parents themselves may be heterozygous (carriers) or homozygous (affected) but it is unusual to find either parent homozygous, so most affected offspring have clinically normal parents. Given two heterozygous parents the expected distribution of affected offspring is, irrespective of sex, one-half normal but heterozygous (carriers), one quarter normal (homozygous normal), and one quarter affected (homozygous affected). This may be illustrated:

6

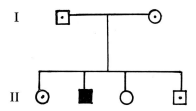

As at each mating the chances of the offspring being affected or unaffected are 1:4, it is only in large sibships that the expected distribution actually appears. Parents clinically normal but carriers of a recessive gene may have several children all unaffected so that presence of the gene is never suspected; on the other hand less fortunate parents may have an affected first child and limit their family because of this. Ascertainment of recessive inheritance by the analysis of pedigrees is therefore a complicated matter because only families with affected children will be included and many of these families will have an undue proportion of affected children.

There are two other ways of detecting autosomal recessive inheritance. If the recessive gene is a rare one it will be found with much greater frequency among related individuals than in the general population. The likelihood of a child having both parents heterozygous for the gene is much increased if the parents are themselves related, so it is found that the occurrence of consanguineous matings is a feature of families affected by the rarer harmful recessive genes. In the case of some of the commoner disorders due to recessive genes, parental consanguinity is less helpful but the heterozygous state can be detected directly by appropriate tests, e.g. phenylalanine tolerance in phenylketonuria, phospho-ethanolamine excretion in hypophosphatasaemia. The development of these special tests for showing up the effects of 'recessive' genes in apparently normal individuals demonstrates clearly that dominance and recessiveness are terms of clinical usefulness rather than expressions of biological laws, but they still have validity for genetic prognosis.

X-borne Inheritance. Certain traits are due to mutant genes on the X chromosomes and these may be either dominant or recessive. The essential feature of inheritance of these so-called sex-linked conditions is that males cannot pass the condition to their sons for the single X chromosome of the male is inherited only by daughters. Females having two X chromosomes may be heterozygous or homozygous for the gene and will show clinical effects depending upon this and on whether the gene is dominant or recessive in its behaviour. The male however can only be hemizygous for X-borne genes and will always have the gene expressed.

The majority of X-borne diseases are inherited as recessives and show transmission by normal carrier females to affected males. Dominant inheritance of X-borne genes is not so easily demarcated from autosomal dominant transmission because both males and females are affected and the condition appears in each generation. The crucial distinction between X-borne dominant and autosomal dominant inheritance is that in the former an affected male transmits the gene to all his daughters but to none of his sons, whereas in autosomal dominant inheritance affected males and females transmit the gene equally to half their offspring irrespective of sex.

It is unusual in practice to find that the family history immediately reveals that the condition is due to a single gene defect regularly transmitted in characteristic Mendelian fashion. More often suggestive fragments of history are obtained which arouse suspicion, and of course if the clinical diagnosis points strongly towards one of the known genetic diseases, further exploration and investigation is indicated.

Many neurological disorders are familial in that they tend to occur with greater frequency in some families than in the random population without having clear evidence of regular genetic transmission. Some types of epilepsy and some varieties of mental subnormality are examples. The severe congenital malformations of the central nervous sustem (anencephaly, meningomyelocele) also appear to run in families and there is a greater than random risk of recurrence in siblings. Whether these conditions or predisposition to them are due to combinations of genes, or the gene effect is strongly modifiable by undetermined environmental factors, is as yet uncertain.

Chromosome Anomalies. Several syndromes are now known to be caused not through defects of single genes but through major additions or deletions of whole chromosomes or chromosome fragments. Most of these are associated with mental retardation and some affect the nervous system in other ways. Chromosome anomalies may affect the autosomes or the sex chromosomes and are most often sporadic in occurrence. Of the autosomal defects Down's syndrome (mongolism) is the most common. Most cases of Down's syndrome are caused by uncomplicated trisomy for chromosome 21, which is associated with advanced maternal age, both parents having normal chromosomes. Familial forms of Down's syndrome exist and these are due either to various types of translocation or to chromosome mosaicism. Three other not uncommon autosomal chromosomal defects are now well-established. In 13/15 or group D trisomy there is cleft lip, cleft palate, eye defects, polydactyly and congenital heart disease; trisomy 16/18 or group E trisomy is associated with micrognathos, small mouth, low-set ears and short webbed fingers. In both these syndromes delayed development and early death are the rule. The fourth major defect of autosomal chromosome material is the Cri du Chat syndrome, which is due to deletion of the short arm of chromosome 5. Affected infants have characteristic facies with hypertelorism, prominent epicanthic folds and downward slanting eyes. They are hyptotonic and in infancy have a peculiar cry. Dwarfism and mental retardation are features of older children with the syndrome. As in mongolism, familial cases associated with translocation are known.

The sex chromosome anomalies (Turner's syndrome, Klinefelter's syndrome, XXY and other syndromes) are less likely to come to the attention of the neurologist although several are associated with mental defect. Cases are mainly sporadic and are associated with a mean maternal age greater than normal, though familial cases are recorded.

When the family history reveals other similar cases or the mother is under 30 years, it is important to request chromosome analysis of the patient when a chromosome disorder is suspected and also of the parents if the patient's karyotype is abnormal (see page 225).

Social and Environmental History

The essential features of this part of the history must include:

(a) The child's behavioural characteristics as shown by his relationships with his parents, siblings and other children and adults. This will necessarily include some developmental items concerning his use of language, ability to feed himself, dress himself and manage his toilets needs, the choice and use of play materials and cooperativeness with others in play situations.

(b) The personality, education, occupation and socio-economic status of his parents and other members of the immediate household.

(c) The physical environment, including housing, nutrition, opportunities for sociability and exposure to physical health risks.

(d) Present or past episodes such as separations, hospitalisations which may have impaired his ability to form normal relationships or hindered social development.

Detailed Review of Present Condition

This is the most important part of the history, as the informant perceives it as the most relevant. Sometimes it is logical to proceed directly with this after the statement about the main complaint. On other occasions it may be better to assemble preliminary parts of the history before analysing the present complaint in detail.

The approach to the history of the present condition is varied. In acute illness or disease of recent onset it is logical to enquire when the child was last well and to trace the development of symptoms and signs in the order of their appearance.

If the problem is one of recurrent attacks, as in convulsive disorders and migraine, it is often helpful to detail the last attack and work backwards, noting previous episodes and how these differ from the comprehensively described and presumably best remembered attack. Recurrent disease requires evidence regarding:

(a) Frequency of attacks

(b) Duration of attacks

(c) Changes in character of attacks

(d) Possible precipitating causes, alleviating and aggravating factors.

Disorders of long standing and those with an insidious onset need extremely careful history-taking. It is often difficult to get clear evidence as to whether a lesion was present at birth (congenital), or was acquired in early infancy; whether apparent progression of disability is due to pre-existing disease becoming revealed as development proceeds or is due to the presence of progressive disease. It is often difficult to assign correct relationships between symptoms and possible aetiological events.

The analysis of the presenting symptoms will usually suggest enquiries about pertinent symptoms which have not been spontaneously mentioned. Finally the informant should always be questioned about the child's appetite, sleep, elimination, personality, behaviour and human relationships at home and at school.

CHAPTER II

Some Particular Symptoms

Clumsiness

The statement of parents, teachers or referring physicians that a particular child is excessively awkward or clumsy is one of the most difficult of all presenting complaints to evaluate. It is often equally difficult for the physician to decide from his own examina · tion whether there is any abnormality of coordination, assuming that he has not been able to define spastic paresis, hypotonic paresis or some involuntary movement such as choreoathetosis.

It is well to recognise in the beginning that there are three different types of coor · dination, which need to be appraised separately since they may be abnormal in different proportions in different children. These concern: (1) movements based on large muscles, such as walking, running or climbing; (2) finer coordination for individual finger movements (or for movements of the bulbar musculature); (3) visual motor coordination as in drawing or writing with pencil and paper or catching a ball. The ages at which the major infantile developmental milestones are passed relate chiefly to coordination of the activity of the large muscles. The examiner must assess, by questioning or by his own observations, whether the child is able to use pencil and paper, tie his shoes and perform similar functions at the appropriate age and as well as other children of the same age. Standards of normal for this are not at all well established, although one can say in general that a child of six or at latest seven should be able to tie his shoe laces. It must be borne in mind that standards expected by the parents (or by teachers or even physicians) may be unrealistic.

Visual motor coordination and coordination of fine finger movements are often selectively impaired in children with minimal chronic brain syndromes (minimal cerebral dysfunction, minimal brain damage and special educational difficulties are other terms which have been applied to this very heterogeneous syndrome); but it should be remembered that many highly intelligent and neurologically unimpaired children are not good at games and may even be generally clumsy. Clumsiness must be distinguished from the effect of muscular weakness, recent illness and particularly of prolonged inactivity or confinement to bed. The differentiation rests chiefly on astute close observation and on the presence or absence of objective evidence of paresis, although the latter is difficult to appraise in young or uncooperative subjects who do not exert maximal effort against the examiner's resistance. Clumsiness must not be labelled a form of cerebral palsy unless there is more definite supporting evidence in the form of spastic paresis, involuntary adventitious movement, or one of the other recognised forms. Further, clumsiness should not be equated with ataxia, since ataxia implies incoordination based on sensory deficit or on impaired cerebellar function. Objective signs consistent with one or the other of these two categories must be demonstrated in order to apply the term ataxia properly.

If a definite but non-specific clumsiness has been observed, and more definitive diagnoses have not been established by further evaluation, the examiner must then consider whether the picture is a long-standing one which is undergoing some evolution with increasing age (and with the increasing expectations of those who deal with the child), or whether it is evidence of some progressive disease. Mentally retarded children are generally clumsier than children of normal intelligence (although some are quite agile), and children who suffer from almost any recognised type of the progressive diseases of the cerebral grey or white matter are likely to show impaired coordination as one of the early features. The examiner who is thinking along these lines should consult one of the various complete textbooks of paediatric neurology or refer the patient for neurological consultation, but a number of further suggestions may be found in Chapter XI on Motor Function.

Involuntary Movements

It has already been mentioned that mere abnormal clumsiness must be differentiated from abnormal movements such as in chorea, athetosis, dystonia and tremor. These latter terms have fairly specific meanings and implications in neurological tradition, and are only useful to communicate the concept of an abnormality if they are used in these restricted senses. The situation is sometimes confused by obscure neurological terminology and by the fact that some of the terms may have more than one definition or refer to individual diseases as well as to generic disorders of movement.

Classifying involuntary or adventitious movements requires experience of many patients with various combinations of such movements, or close observation of the relatively few useful teaching motion pictures which are available. The various specific abnormal movements may be closely simulated by general clumsiness, by tics and by certain other conditions, and the reader is referred to the definitions and discussion in the chapter on Motor Function (page 165).

A traditional question is whether or not the apparently involuntary movement ceases during sleep. This is actually not of much specific differential diagnostic value, for almost any of the categories of involuntary movement should be expected to cease during sleep, except in the case of myoclonus or epilepsia partialis continua. In extremely severe cases of dystonia or chorea, the persistence and violence of the involuntary movement may prevent sleep or interrupt it at frequent intervals, but even under these circumstances the movement usually ceases when the deep sleep of exhaustion is finally reached.

Weakness

'Weakness' properly means diminished muscular power compared with the standard of normal for age, whether or not the power is in proportion to muscular bulk. However, comparison of power with bulk is important in trying to establish a specific diagnosis. Weakness must be distinguished from disinclination to perform muscular activity in the case of the child who is uncooperative, mentally retarded, has been recently ill or is feeling out of sorts, or is simply very young. Conventional methods of testing muscular strength are described in Chapter XI on Motor Function, but this type of examination is frequently very limited with young or uncooperative subjects is unreliable if they are fatigued, and is also very time-consuming. It is often possible to get a more satisfactory impression of muscular power indirectly, by observing the child when he is left to himself in the examining room or during the course of other items of examination. In some instances, parental descriptions are more reliable than the physician's observations.

One wants to inquire specifically about weakness related to certain types of activity, such as going up and down flights of stairs; special difficulty in this case is a clue to weakness of the musculature about the pelvic girdle and frequently a clue to muscular dystrophy. Weakness may also be greatest in the distal musculature, and questions should also be put concerning the strength of movements of the wrists, hands, fingers and feet. Respiratory embarrassment, even if only in the presence of bronchial or other infections, may reflect weakness of the musculature of the trunk, particularly the intercostals, and the examiner should ask whether or not the child is able to cough normally and vigorously. Weakness of the bulbar musculature can be approached by a variety of questions concerning the function of the lower cranial nerves, but this section is concerned chiefly with weakness in the trunk and limbs.

Weakness, like clumsiness, should be evaluated as to whether it is progressive, stationary, or becoming milder. A progressive neurological disease with paresis, or a progressive myopathy, opposes the tendency of normal children to increase in muscular bulk and power as they become older and larger. Thus the existence of a progressive condition may not be apparent in its early stages, and the progressive nature of the problem may become evident only after a period of relatively stationary function. Actually, stationary function is rarely normal in growing children, and a paediatric patient is more often than not 'going backward' if he is not demonstrably 'going forward'.

If there is serious suspicion of weakness, the question of fatigue should then be investigated. Distinction between normal and pathological fatigue is admittedly difficult, and the history may be more valuable than observation or attempts at objective testing. The variability of the weakness from day to day should also be ascertained and whether or not the child is substantially normal in between episodes. The interpretation of the results of this sort of questioning is too complex for complete discussion at this point. In general, excessive fatigue raises the question of myasthenia gravis, but greater than normal fatigue is characteristic of almost any neuromuscular disease involving impaired power. Episodic severe weakness with normality in between attacks may suggest such diagnoses as hyperkalaemic or hypokalaemic periodic paralysis, porphyria, etc., according to the length of the attacks and interval between them, and other associated findings or complaints. Weakness may be simulated to a considerable extent by emotional disturbances, depression, and habitual inactivity. One should thus inquire about a possible discrepancy between the child's apparent power to do what is requested of him, and what he can accomplish in a sudden emergency or fight or when he particularly wants to do something himself.

Floppiness (Hypotonia)

In clinical experience, floppiness is infrequently a presenting chief complaint, or at least is mentioned only secondarily. The immediate problem which brings the patient to the physician's attention is usually some acute impairment of coordination in an older child, or delayed developmental motor milestones in the case of infants. The 'floppy baby' is usually brought to the physician because of failure to sit or walk at the expected age, and the hypotonia is then detected when physical examination is carried out. It is sometimes mentioned, however, that the patient is excessively floppy, or he may be compared to a bag of jelly or a limp dishrag or some other such object.

Whatever the circumstances in which hypotonia is detected, the examiner will want to find out whether it is increasing or decreasing and whether its relative distribution in the upper and lower limbs, or in the limbs as opposed to the trunk and neck, is changing in any way. Hypotonia restricted to upper or lower limbs may reflect a spinal lesion. In general, hypotonia, like weakness, is more suggestive of a myopathy if the greatest involvement is proximal, and of a neuropathy if the greatest involvement is distal in the limbs. However, most of the neuropathies of infancy, as well as Werdnig-Hoffmann disease, affect chiefly the proximal muscles.

Cerebral hypotonias are one of the commonest categories encountered in infancy, although they are not always recognised as such. Historical cerebral insults may or may not be defined in the available history and many cases are based on developmental anomalies of the brain. Absent tendon reflexes are always suggestive of a neuropathy or myopathy or other involvement of the lower motor unit, but areflexia may also accompany cerebral hypotonia in some cases. A more frequent finding is that reflexes are difficult to demonstrate and are obtainable only if the limb is got into exactly the right posture. In cases of this sort, it is worth questioning the parents as to whether other physicians have ever been able to obtain reflexes in the past, or whether it has always been difficult. Cerebral hypotonia is often associated with abnormally imposable tonic neck reflexes, microcephaly, mental retardation, electroencephalographic changes, or other evidence of cerebral involvement. These may be lacking, however, whether or not the eventual outcome will be a persistent hypotonic cerebral palsy, evolution to spasticity or some kind of dyskinesia, or simply general developmental retardation.

It is pointed out in Chapter XI (Motor Function) that examination of muscular tone depends chiefly on various approaches to the stretch reflex. The examiner studies separately the rapid response to stretch when a segment of a limb is suddenly mobilised ('flappability' or 'passivité'), and the resistance to slow flexion or extension of a joint considering a possible sudden give-way of resistance, cogwheel phenomenon, or limitation of available range of motion. Parents sometimes make surprisingly revealing spontaneous statements related to these phenomena, but in general the appraisal of muscular tone is a matter for physical examination more than for history-taking.

Hypotonia acquired in later childhood may reflect a large variety of diseases of the muscles, the neuromuscular junction, peripheral nerves or nerve roots, the lower motor neurones in the spinal cord, or a variety of affections of the cerebellum, central grey matter (as in Sydenham's chorea), or higher cerebral levels. The differential diagnosis of infantile hypotonia is somewhat different and the following table may be a useful guide.

Causes of Congenital Hypotonia

Level of Lesion	Most Important Disease Entities
Muscle	Congenital muscular dystrophy Polymyositis Non-progressive myopathies (central core disease, rod (nemaline) myopathy)
Neuromyal Junction	Myasthenia gravis
Nerve	Hypertrophic interstitial polyneuritis (Déjérine and Sottas) Other polyneuritides
Spinal Cord	Progressive spinal muscular atrophy (Werdnig-Hoffman) Traumatic myelopathy (usually injury at birth) Tumours, vascular anomalies, malformations
Brain	Cerebral dysgenesis Anoxic, traumatic, etc. encephalopathies Hypotonic stage of cerebral palsies which will later develop spasticity, or more frequently, choreoathetosis or dystonia Hypotonic cerebral palsy ('Atonic diplegia') Degenerative diseases (Tay-Sachs, etc.) Mental retardation (mongolism; other types, some classifiable and others unclassified)
Unknown	'Benign congenital hypotonia'
Other	Many chronic non-neurological diseases Repeated infections or illnesses Acute illness

Headache

The majority of children who complain of headache have no ascertainable organic disease, but its importance should not be under-estimated because it is sometimes the symptom of crucial significance which leads to the early diagnosis of an organic lesion which is still in the curable stage. Infants and young children are unable to verbalise the complaint of headache and its presence must be guessed at by changes in behaviour such as irritability and photophobia. Psychosomatic or tension headaches are more prevalent in the older school-age child, and it is therefore circumspect to treat with greater seriousness a well authenticated account of headache in younger children.

Acute Headache

Many acute febrile illnesses in childhood are accompanied by headache, especially at onset or during the prodromal phase. Headache if severe and protracted will suggest an intracranial infection such as meningitis, encephalitis or cerebral abscess, but enteric fever, infectious mononucleosis, malaria and many viral infections (e.g. influenza, winter vomiting disease) may be accompanied by severe headache in the absence of central nervous system complications.

Acute severe headache without fever may indicate intracranial haemorrhage and is encountered in meningeal involvement in leukaemia.

When acute headache is present there are usually sufficient other symptoms and signs to indicate the diagnostic possibilities.

Intermittent, Recurrent and Periodic Headache

Children whose complaint is primarily that of headache should be allowed to talk freely of their symptom with the minimum of direct questioning. When possible the child's account should be compared with that of the adult informant. In organic headache it is generally found that the histories are consistent, whereas in psychogenic headache there are often remarkable differences.

If the headache is recurrent it is useful to obtain a history of a typical attack and then ascertain the frequency and periodicity of the episodes of headache. Most children are limited in their ability to describe the character and localisation of their headaches, and the intensity of the pain must be judged more by the child's behaviour during an attack than the descriptive words used either by the child or the informant.

Headache due to raised intracranial pressure or to hypertension is rarely constant but may occur daily. It may also be present at night and interfere with sleep. Tension headaches are apt to occur regularly for a spell and then be followed by irregular periods of remission; on the other hand, classical migraine is episodic with a periodicity rarely more frequent than every two to three weeks.

Characteristically the headache of raised intracranial pressure is most severe on rising in the morning and wears off during the day; this is also true of headache associated with school phobia. Tension headaches not due to school phobia are usually more prominent in the evenings, as are headaches associated with eye-strain, excessive reading and television viewing.

The duration of episodes of headache is important. Transient headache lasting a few moments is often an attention-seeking symptom, organic headaches last for hours, while psychogenic attacks may be complained of for days on end.

It is useful to enquire about possible precipitating factors and any factors which exacerbate or relieve the headache. In adults the headache of raised intracranial pressure and to a lesser extent that of sinusitis is made worse by bending, coughing and sneezing. This feature is rarely present in childhood. Light exacerbates the headache of migraine, as does movement, so migraine headache is relieved by lying down in a darkened room. Simple analgesics serve to relieve most headaches and their efficiency is little guide to the aetiology of childhood headaches.

The presence or absence of associated symptoms and signs furnishes valuable clues. Vomiting in association with headache raises the suspicion of increased intracranial pressure, but is sometimes a feature of psychogenic headache and migraine. If the vomiting is not accompanied by nausea raised intracranial pressure is more likely.

Visual disturbances, subjective sensory disturbances and a preceding aura are typical of migraine, but in many children the classical pattern of migraine is incomplete and the headache is not always hemicranial in distribution. It is often difficult to differentiate migraine from the so-called 'periodic syndrome'. The latter is also periodic but the headache lacks the classical features of migraine and is more apt to be accompanied by vomiting, abdominal pain, pallor and pyrexia.

Headache is frequent during the post-ictal phase of a seizure and may sometimes be the only manifestation of epilepsy.

The family history should always be investigated when headache is a main complaint. A genetic basis for headache is problematical but the family history commonly reveals that near relatives suffer from headache, and occasionally it will be found that a relative has had severe intracranial disease which has made the family unduly concerned about the possible significance of headache.

In general paediatric practice it is rare for physical examination of the child with headache to reveal anything abnormal, and the physician satisfied that no urgent organic problem is present will proceed to look for psychogenic or psychosomatic disturbance as a basis for the child's complaints.

Excessive physical investigations may be harmful and lead to further problems even if the reassurance based on negative investigations is apparently accepted. However, the comparative rarity of organic headache should lead neither to negligence over the physical examination nor to lack of follow-up, until organic disease can be safely ruled out. While it may be assumed that examination of the eye-grounds is carefully done, it is surprising how often the measurement of blood pressure is omitted and the diagnosis of hypertension delayed until blurring of vision or hypertensive encephalopathy occurs.

Seizures

Most cases of seizures in childhood, whether idiopathic or secondary to some identifiable disease or lesion, are not associated with any abnormalities on neurological examination. Chiefly for this reason, the differential diagnosis depends almost entirely on a careful history (together with the evidence of the electroencephalogram) unless the physician is fortunate enough to witness an actual fit. Further, the description of the episodes by parents or other observers is often inaccurate because of the fright and confusion which the seizure generates in all concerned. In spite of these difficulties, a careful history must be taken from anyone available who has witnessed an attack. This often requires considerable guidance of the interview by the physician, who must nevertheless avoid asking too many leading questions which might distort the true description (and particularly, the description of any future episodes).

It is wise to let the parents (or other observers) describe the episode in their own words without interruption, but to follow this by careful re-tracing of the entire episode from beginning to end, being sure to get items in chronological order. The first important point is whether or not the child had any sort of aura or advance warning of impending seizures. Both child and parent should be asked about this, since their stories may differ. Frequently, the only evidence of an aura is that the child seemed frightened, or 'looked funny', or called out or ran to his mother immediately before the attack.

One next wants to know whether the loss of consciousness or fall took place immediately or whether it followed the onset of abnormal movements. A minute description of the involuntary movements and of their evolution in time is obviously of the greatest importance, and particular attention should be directed to any focal features or any suggestions of spread ('march') from one area to another and the directions and sequences involved. A focal fit which begins simultaneously in all of the areas involved and does not spread should be differentiated from one beginning, for example, in the hand and then spreading up the arm. Whether a focal seizure eventually became generalised is an obvious point to determine, particularly in connexion with the question of loss of consciousness. Focal seizures are consistent with retention of consciousness, but one would view with some suspicion a generalised seizure without unconsciousness. As exact a description as possible is particularly important concerning abnormal movements of the face, mouth, tongue, or pharyngeal musculature, and whether there were any repeated movements such as smacking of the lips or gulping or swallowing. Seizures may terminate (less often begin) with a belch or with the passage of flatus, events usually resulting in the mother attributing the attack to 'gas on the stomach' or in the bowels.

The position of the head and eyes is of special importance since deviation to one side during the fit implies an irritative discharge in the contralateral cerebral hemisphere. Any late asymmetry of involuntary movements or any predominance of involvement in one side or one limb is important information even in the case of generalised fits of simultaneous onset in all areas. In the case of possible petit mal fits, one also wants a careful description of the events involved. These attacks are sometimes unobserved by parents or unrecognised, and under such circumstances, or if adequate information cannot be obtained otherwise, it is well for the physician to attempt to imitate a petit mal attack and ask whether the child has ever done anything of the sort. The particular features to ask about are possible upward or other deviation of the eyes, a blank stare, rhythmic blinking, and the degree of loss of contact with the environment, as well as its duration. Valuable clues may often be gained by asking what happens when the child has an attack in the course of various types of daily activities. If he is engaged in a conversation or in the middle of a sentence, does he pick up where he left off or is there a lapse? Does he sway or even seem as if about to fall? If he is pouring milk from a pitcher* into a dish of breakfast cereal, does he continue pouring so that the milk overflows the dish, or does he drop the pitcher? In the case of akinetic ('drop') seizures, it is desirable but difficult to ascertain whether the attack is actually a sudden loss of muscular tone with the child dropping in his tracks, or whether it is a massive flexor spasm of the anterior musculature of the trunk so that he is thrown forward. In the case of the latter, history and perhaps inspection of the head are more likely to document repeated traumata.

The examiner should also inquire about possible autonomic changes, particularly toward the latter part of a seizure. Traditional questions concern incontinence of urine or faeces, biting of the tongue, retching or vomiting. Another highly important question is the presence or absence of sleep or depression of sensorium after the stage of involuntary movement, the apparent depth of any sleep and its duration. When the

*A jug to an Englishman is a pitcher to an American—Ed.

17

child 'came to' or at the end of the period of sleep, did he complain of headache, seem nauseated or confused, have any apparent post-ictal weakness or aphasia, and how much if anything did he remember of each stage of the episode?

Particular difficulties arise in the case of unobserved possible seizures in which the child was seen only at the end of the episode or in what might be a post-ictal state, and equally in those attacks which appear to consist simply in loss of consciousness without any abnormal or involuntary movements. A simple black-out involving nothing more than loss of consciousness and a fall is a possible form of seizure, but this problem requires very careful consideration of the differential diagnosis from other forms of syncopal attacks. The latter include vasodepressor syncope, orthostatic hypotension, reflex heart block, Stokes-Adams syndrome, cerebrovascular disease (less important in children than in adults), anoxia, hypoglycaemia, paroxysmal tachycardia or other cardiac disease, and simple fainting (which while heavily involving psychogenic factors may be based on fall in blood pressure).

Differentiation must also be made from the various causes of vertigo. Information as to blood pressure is virtually never obtainable unless another physician has examined the child at the time, and even information about the pulse rate is rarely available unless a parent can be taught to check this at a future attack and to give an accurate count rather than merely to say that the child's pulse was pounding or terribly fast (leaving one unable to decide whether the tachycardia was moderate and the consequence of the seizure, or extreme and possibly the immediate cause of syncope). A report of giddiness or light-headedness or of feeling sick or weak should not be equated with true vertigo, which is an hallucination of movement.

It is important to remember that vasodepressor and other forms of syncope may be associated with urinary incontinence or even result in a few clonic movements if the victim is maintained upright by a by-stander so as to prevent the increased flow of blood to the brain which follows falling (see discussion by Engel 1950). If one is fortunate enough to obtain an EEG during a period of time including an actual faint, this can usually be differentiated from a seizure since with simple syncope there is no electroencephalographic change until the loss of consciousness, and then merely generalised slowing with prompt recovery when consciousness is regained. Aside from this possibility, the differentiation of syncope from a seizure is difficult and rests entirely on an accurate history or on the opportunity to witness an actual attack. The lack of post-ictal sleep is one of the best diagnostic points in favour of syncope, but the distinction is not absolute and a certain amount of confusion or nausea often follows fainting.

After getting as complete a description as possible of the initial suspected seizure, the physician will then go on to ask about other possible or recognised prior or subsequent attacks. If the seizures are nocturnal, occasional and irregular bed-wetting may be a clue to an earlier time of onset or to unrecognised subsequent fits. As a minimum, information must be obtained as to the frequency of the attacks, their variation in duration or character, their spacing in time, and any trend to become more or less frequent, longer or shorter, or more or less severe. It is usually wise to get an accurate listing by dates if this is possible.

18

It is customary to inquire whether the fits have tended to occur at a particular time of day, in any consistent relationship to time of meals, or on waking in the morning. Preprandial fits may be suggestive of possible hypoglycaemia, as may attacks occuring two hours or so after meals, if a glucose load is followed by an abnormal secondary depression of glucose in the blood. Early morning fits may be hypoglycaemic in nature, but this timing is also typical of many cases of idiopathic epilepsy or of epilepsy symptomatic of a diversity of organic cerebral lesions.

Photogenic epilepsy is rare but a recognised entity. One may be told that the child typically has seizures on going out of the house on a bright day or while watching T.V.

The distinction between breath-holding spells and seizures, and the possibility that breath-holding may be followed by a fit, are difficult points. In typical breath-holding, the child, who is usually 6 months to 4 years of age, cries out, holds his breath in expiration long enough to become cyanosed, and then loses consciousness, falling limply to the floor. Consciousness returns promptly in a minute or less, and the child is then almost normal, lacking the headache, nausea, confusion or desire to sleep which characterize post-ictal states. Involuntary micturition may accompany either breath-holding or fits, but clonic movements or rigidity suggest the latter diagnosis. There is probably a second type of breath-holding spell in which the patient holds his breath in inspiration and loses consciousness with a Valsalva manoeuvre, usually without a cry and without cyanosis. The first type of breath-holding may precipitate a seizure by means of anoxia, but the second is less likely to do so. Breath-holding is typically precipitated by frustration (by people or by inanimate objects), but may follow sudden pain or fright. It usually but not invariably occurs in the presence of an audience.

Possible precipitating factors must be inquired about and parental statements about this listened to with respect, even though these are frequently inaccurate or even absurd. Fright, anxiety, fatigue, lack of sleep, over-exercise, apprehension or worry, pain or injury, and even such things as constipation or intake of certain foods deserve respectful consideration. In the case of adolescent girls one should inquire about any possible timing of seizures in relation to menstrual periods.

If the patient has had prior medication for seizures, it is mandatory but frequently difficult to get a detailed chronology of what drugs and what combinations of drugs have been given in what dosages, and for what periods of time, together with any changes which took place in the seizures in association with this medication, any possible changes in behaviour or personality, or any recognised side effects.

The foregoing recommendations doubtless seem a formidable task, and it is indeed true that a seemingly disproportionate amount of time must be spent on history-taking in the evaluation of seizure problems. Repeated review of the history, or taking it over again, fresh from the beginning, may bore both parents and physician, but may reveal new information in obscure cases or in those not responding to treatment. It is almost superfluous to point out, but frequently neglected, that accurate detailed history-taking is more important in the evaluation and management of seizures than in any other common neurological problem.

19

Enuresis

The majority of children who wet the bed (noctural enuresis), having reached the age at which they may be expected to be dry, do not have any demonstrable neurological or urological pathology. Emotional disturbance is more often a consequence of the unfortunate symptom and the reaction of their parents, siblings and peers to it than a cause. The minority of children whose enuresis is caused by or associated with major organic disease can usually be detected by means of a carefully taken history, thorough physical examination and urinalysis.

It is first necessary to establish that the act of voluntary micturition can be performed normally. If the history indicates continual wetting or dampness, inability to start a good flow of urine or dribbling at the end of micturition, a structural anomaly of the renal tract or major defect in the neuro-muscular apparatus of the bladder must be suspected.

The distinction between 'life-long' and 'onset' enuresis should be made. The former implies that bladder control has never been achieved during sleep and the mother complains that the child has 'always been wet', whereas in 'onset' enuresis there is clear evidence of failure to maintain dryness at night after nocturnal continence has been fully established. The distinction does not differentiate between functional and symptomatic enuresis but does give clues to the possible mechanisms involved. Lifelong enuresis with normal voluntary micturition is most often due to simple delay in the acquisition of bladder control, and of course the younger the child the more likely is this explanation. The true incontinence of spina bifida cystica is unlikely to be missed during early life, but the dribbling incontinence of obstructive uropathy at or distal to the bladder neck may pass unnoticed during the diaper age, as also may the effects of an ectopic ureter draining into the vagina.

In the 'onset' group without evidence of organic disease it is impossible to accept that the symptom is due to delayed maturation or to a learning difficulty, and attention must be given to a precipitating emotional cause. Onset enuresis may be due to acquired disease (e.g. urinary infection, diabetes mellitus) or to manifestation of a previously occult congenital malformation such as diastematomyelia.

Careful enquiry must be made about day-time symptoms. It is not unusual for functional enuretics to have some frequency and urgency during the day-time and in girls actual wetting may happen. However, really uncontrollable acts of micturition are more likely to signify epilepsy, or, if precipitated by laughter, anxiety or running and jumping, stress incontinence. Sudden micturition associated with giggling is a rare but well-defined entity. Bed-wetting with completely normal day-time micturition is usually functional, and if due to organic disease is caused either by polyuria or irritation of the bladder by infected urine or vesical calculus.

Any association with other disorders of eliminatory function should be evaluated. The involuntary passage of stools (encopresis) may exist with enuresis. Soiling is most commonly the result of faecal retention (psychogenic megacolon) with overflow incontinence. When this condition is fully established the child ceases to pass normal stools and the only faecal material evacuated is that which exudes from the over-distended rectum and anal canal. As stool-withholding frequently arises during a disturbed toilet-training period it is not surprising that enuresis often co-exists. Rarely, faecal retention is so massive that the over-filled rectum occupies the pelvic cavity so that the bladder and bladder neck are distorted, producing frequency and occasionally retention of urine.

The involuntary passage of normal stools is associated most often with severe emotional disturbance or neglectful toilet training. Day and night wetting occurs with disordered bowel function, as is found in severely retarded children from institutions or poor homes.

In the absence of the above findings, loss of bowel and bladder control in a child not acutely ill or disturbed should raise the question of a lesion involving the spinal cord (e.g. tumour, multiple sclerosis, Friedreich's ataxia) or pelvic nerves.

The family history is of importance. Functional enuresis is familial in that there is an excess of enuresis among the relatives of enuretic children compared with the general population. There is no good explanation for this.

Elucidation of enuresis requires a comprehensive approach to the child and his family, but the important points which are most useful in giving clues to the possibility of underlying neurological disease have been emphasised. Should the history suggest such a disorder, a careful neurological and urological examination should be undertaken and appropriate investigations initiated.

Pica

Pica is the repeated ingestion of materials normally considered inedible. Clay, earth, plaster, paint, paper, textiles and coal may all be included in the diet of the child with pica. Mothers are reluctant to volunteer the information that their child has such a perverted appetite and it is usually admitted only after direct questioning. Neither the real prevalence nor the cause of pica is accurately known. It is common among pre-school children in the 18 months to 3 year age group, and is probably more common in retarded, maladjusted and deprived children, among whom the symptom may persist beyond the usual age. Children with pica are frequently found to be anaemic and it has been thought that pica may represent a physiological craving for iron, but this is certainly not a complete explanation.

Pica is dangerous because of the likelihood that harmful substances may be ingested. The most important is lead, and in areas where paint containing lead is still found, children with pica are at considerable hazard. The ova of dog and cat tapeworms may be ingested by dirt-eating children, and there is some evidence that massive ingestion of earth and clay impairs iron absorption. Children with pica often dislike or refuse more conventional foods and may as a result be more prone to deficiency of protein and vitamins.

A history of pica may signpost the diagnosis of lead intoxication, and this should be investigated by examination of the red cells for punctate basophilia, the urine for coproporphyrins and x-rays of the long bones. Estimation of the blood and urine lead will confirm the diagnosis. The possibility of anaemia, visceral larva migrans, retardation or emotional disturbance must also be considered in cases of pica.

Deafness

The term 'deafness' is applied most appropriately to hearing loss of such severity that a gross functional handicap results. Lesser degrees of hearing loss, so-called partial deafness, may be due to generalised diminution of auditory acuity or to hearing loss localised to only certain frequencies of sound. Loss of hearing may affect either or both ears; unilateral hearing loss, even if profound, rarely causes much handicap, and may in childhood pass undetected for many years.

Clinically, hearing loss is categorised as conductive, nerve, or central, depending on the site of the pathological lesion. Conductive deafness is due to diseases or defects of the external and middle ear, while nerve deafness arises from lesions of the cochlea or eighth nerve. Central deafness is due to disease or damage affecting the auditory centres in the brain or their central connections. The term 'sensori-neural' is often used to describe nerve and central deafness.

Hearing can be tested clinically only by observing the patient's response to a sound stimulus. The sound stimuli used, and the methods of observing the response, vary according to the age, intelligence and anticipated degree of hearing loss. Absence of response is held to imply loss of hearing, but this interpretation is not always correct because response to sound is dependent on several factors such as attention as well as on the reception of sensory information. Minor or even moderately severe hearing losses are difficult to detect in ordinary clinical practice owing to background noise, so the services of an audiologist should be sought whenever there is suspicion of deafness.

The traditional distinction between congenital and acquired deafness has little practical usefulness. It is, however, important to distinguish between bilateral deafness, whatever its origin, existing before the acquisition of speech (deafness of early onset), and deafness occurring after normal speech has been learned (deafness of late onset).

In deafness of early onset it is unusual for the child to present with this complaint, and the diagnosis is unfortunately often delayed until there is evidence of retarded speech development or signs of backwardness. It is thus important to test the hearing of all infants who have a history suggesting any of the known antecedents of deafness or who show signs of malformations associated with the possibility of deafness. Partial deafness of early onset is difficult to detect at an early stage because infants respond only to loud or interesting sounds. Formal audiometry is necessary to complete the study of suspect children, and also identify those suffering from unilateral deafness.

Deafness of late onset, if profound and coming on suddenly, is easy to detect. The child himself may complain of hearing loss, or his parents and teachers note a diminished response to sound. Partial deafness may exist for a long time, and if progressive, reach a severe degree before the hearing is questioned. The child's unresponsiveness to sounds and commands may be ascribed to naughtiness, lack of concentration, or excessive preoccupation with his play.

Deafness is also a sequel of several neurological disorders such as meningitis and encephalitis, and may also appear during the later stages of some chronic progressive diseases. It is important therefore to assess auditory function at an early stage in childhood neurological disease so that any impairment of hearing occurring later can be detected quickly.

It is useful to have in mind a classification of the causes of deafness, both as a diagnostic aid and also as a reminder of the conditions known to be associated with deafness which demand careful assessment of hearing.

A. *Genetically Determined Deafness*

  1. Deafness prominent:
    (a) Deafness alone
    (b) Deafness with pigmentary anomalies of the retina
    (c) Deafness with goitre; deafness with nephritis
    (d) Deafness with white forelock
    (e) Undifferentiated syndromes.

  2. Deafness associated:
    (a) Muco-polysaccharoidoses
    (b) Neuro-fibromatosis
    (c) Heredo-familial degenerations of the central nervous system.

B. *Congenital Malformations Involving Hearing*
    (a) Malformations of external, middle or inner ear, often with ear-pits
    (b) Mandibulo-facial dysostosis
    (c) Klippel-Feil syndrome.

C. *Acquired*

  1. Prenatal:
    (a) Maternal rubella
    (b) Intra-uterine toxoplasmosis
    (c) 'Thalidomide' induced embryopathy.

  2. Perinatal:
    (a) Immaturity
    (b) Perinatal hypoxia and birth injury
    (c) Hyperbilirubinaemia
    (d) Ototoxic drugs.

  3. Postnatal:
    (a) Meningitis
    (b) Meningo-encephalitis
    (c) Otitis media
    (d) Ototoxic drugs
    (e) Trauma
    (f) Neoplasms: (i) benign, (ii) malignant.

The investigation of deafness must include a careful history to determine the probable duration of the handicap, its severity and possible causes. The family history is most important and it should be remembered that many of the varieties of hereditary deafness are of late onset and increased severity in later life. A review of prenatal factors, including maternal infections and drugs taken by the mother as well as obstetric events such as threatened abortion, should be made. The perinatal history is also important and should note the length of gestation, the birth weight, the details of labour and delivery, and a summary of the early postnatal progress. Possible postnatal factors should be checked. The symptoms associated with deafness must be elucidated, and an attempt made to ascertain whether the hearing loss is static or progressive.

A multiplicity of physical signs may be associated with deafness. The ears will of course be carefully examined, note being taken of vestigial auricles or ear-pits, as well as more obvious diseases or defects of the external ear, auditory meati and tympanic membranes. The tests described in Chapter XV will usually enable the deafness to be designated as conductive or sensori-neural. Young children who are apprehensive or uncooperative should be examined by the audiologist (often with a skilled psychologist and teacher of the deaf) before being submitted to painful or uncomfortable physical procedures or investigations.

The paediatric neurologist is likely to encounter a higher proportion of the rarer hereditary syndromes causing deafness than the otologist. Examination of the fundi is important, for several syndromes of retinitis pigmentosa with deafness are described, and such acquired conditions as rubella syndrome, toxoplasmosis and syphilis leave retinal abnormalities. Retinal abnormalities are seen also in disorders involving raised intracranial pressure with compression or distortion of the cranial nerves, e.g. craniostenosis, subdural haematoma, and hydrocephalus.

The so-called 'first-arch' syndromes with a variety of facial and cranial nerve abnormalities may be associated with deafness, and the white forelock of hair is the major sign of Waardenburg's syndrome. In the muco-polysaccharoidoses (Hurler's syndrome, gargoylism) typical facies may be present and corneal clouding noted. Deafness is more characteristic of the sex-linked form of the disease, and corneal clouding of the autosomal recessive.

The neurologist will see mostly cases of nerve and central deafness, but the otologist finds deafness most commonly due to localised disease of the middle ear, often on a basis of adenoid hypertrophy.

Unilateral nerve deafness is a not uncommon sequel of mumps; it may occur following head injuries, with brain tumour, or with neurofibromatosis.

A neurological examination may give evidence of such syndromes as cerebral palsy, progressive degenerative neurological disease, or minimal cerebral dysfunction. Café-au-lait patches may indicate neurofibromatosis and the cutaneous manifestations of tuberose sclerosis may be seen.

Following a complete physical examination it is important to test the urine of any deaf child for evidence of nephritis if the cause of deafness is not apparent. Further investigations will usually be suggested by any abnormalities found on history or physical examination.

CHAPTER III

The General Physical Examination

Physical examination of cooperative, intelligent children of school age can usually be done in the same way as the adult physical examination provided that due regard is paid to the feelings of the child. Pre-school children, and children of all ages who are un-cooperative, retarded or disturbed, are much less easy to examine and it is with them that the special skills and experience of the paediatrician may be needed.

The routine paediatric examination is based on careful observation of the whole child, followed by the physical examination of bodily regions rather than systems. Often it is far less rigidly structured than an adult physical examination, but it should be as comprehensive. The correct interpretation of the signs elicited depends upon familiarity with the range of normal in children at various ages, and the neurologist who sees few paediatric patients should refer to a good paediatric text or ask the help of a paediatrician if concerned about the significance of doubtful signs.

Principles of Paediatric Examination

The aim of the examiner is to complete his physical examination without resistance on the patient's part and preferably with full cooperation. It is important to remember that future medical examinations or procedures may be much more difficult if the child has bitter memories of the present occasion. Failures due to patients, resistance are minimised if the following general principles are kept in mind.

1. Time spent in establishing a friendly relationship with the mother helps gain the child's confidence and makes the mother a helpful assistant later.

2. Time taken on unhurried observation of the child's appearance, demeanour and behaviour will often give clues as to the best manner of approach as well as providing important diagnostic information. This should be done before the patient is undressed.

3. Defer until the closing stages of the examination the manoeuvres likely to cause fear, discomfort or pain.

4. Omit looking for signs which have little validity in the age group concerned or which are superfluous to other more pathognomic signs.

5. Avoid the temptation to elicit signs repeatedly once having been satisfied that they are unequivocally present, especially those signs provocative of discomfort or pain.

6. Endeavour to examine a child in the position in which he is most happy and comfortable, remembering that small children dislike being placed flat on their backs.

7. Silence disturbs children and friendly conversation makes them happier and more interested in the examiner.

8. Many physical examinations are unsuccessful because the physician has cold hands, cold instruments and a cold manner.

The Routine Physical Examination

A. Measurements

The child's height, weight, and head circumference should be measured and recorded at some stage and a note made of the degree of deviation from the normal for the child's age, and, in the case of head circumference, from the normal for his weight.

B. General Appearance

(1) If the child is ambulant and not acutely distressed he should be observed initially while fully clothed and indulging in normal, spontaneous activity. An estimate of his size, stature, build, bodily proportions can be made together with the appropriateness of his behaviour for his chronological age. The quality of his attachment to the parent is noted. When he is encouraged to explore the room and its furnishings, note is taken of the gait and the purposefulness, precision and coordination of manipulation. When the patient sits quietly the amount of spontaneous movement, grimaces, or involuntary movements can be seen. The configuration of the face, mobility of expression and quality of mood are assessed best by indirect observation. The response to the request to undress reveals his developmental status and degree of dependence on the mother; his ability to undo buttons and shoe-laces gives clues as to coordination and performance of fine movements. A great deal of useful information is lost if the physician attempts to save time by arranging for child patients to be undressed and placed on the examination couch by a nurse in readiness for examination. Infants and young children are often best examined on the mother's lap, where they feel more secure.

(2) The acutely ill or distressed child will usually be in bed and the initial approach must be different. The vital signs — body temperature, pulse rate, and respiratory frequency — are noted. State of consciousness is assessed by applying auditory and tactile stimuli and noting the patient's response. The posture of the patient is noted and the position and spontaneous movements of the limbs observed. The general body build, state of nutrition and hydration are noted, as is the facial expression. Pallor, cyanosis and jaundice are looked for.

C. Regional Examination

The order in which this is done will vary according to the nature of the complaint and the age and cooperation of the child. As far as possible the items of examination specifically referable to the nervous system are combined with the general examination.

(1) *Head and Neck*. The facies are carefully inspected and special note is taken of the facial expression, colour and texture of the skin. Cutaneous lesions such as angiomata, adenoma sebaceum or butterfly erythema are noted. The distribution and length of eyebrows and eyelashes are observed. The size and shape of the cranium is noted and the fontanelles and sutures palpated. At the same time the condition of the scalp and the distribution, growth and quality of hair is examined. The occipital region is palpated for lymphadenopathy and nodules, and if indicated (as it is in neurological cases) the skull is percussed for the 'cracked-pot' sign and auscultated for bruits.

Integrated with examination of the cranial nerves the buccal cavity, lips, teeth, tongue, palate, tonsils, fauces and pharynx are inspected, and the conjunctivae and mucous membranes examined for pallor, telangiectasia and pigmentation. With a light the nares are inspected, and the patency of the nasal air-way checked by observation of the condensation of the patient's exhaled air on a metal tongue depressor. The position, size, shape and symmetry of the ears are noted and the meati and tympanic membranes examined with an otoscope.

The position of the head upon the neck is noted and the neck itself carefully looked at. Any deformities, webbing, swellings or abnormal pulsations are noted and investigated. The cervical lymph nodes and the thyroid gland are systematically palpated, preferably with the examiner stationed behind the patient. Finally the position of the larynx and trachea is checked.

(2) *Thorax and Arms.* The child should be undressed to the waist and the front and back of the chest inspected, noting the symmetry or otherwise of the thoracic cage and the rate, rhythm and character of the respiratory movements. In older children the breasts should be examined both for abnormalities and for assessment of pubertal status. The cardiac impulse is often visible and its position should be checked by palpation. Percussion of the thoracic contents should always be light and can usually be omitted unless there is other evidence of abnormality of the heart or lungs. Auscultation is done in the accepted manner. When the child is asked to sit up so that the back can be examined, note is taken of the freedom of movement, ability to balance the head upon the trunk and the position of the spine and scapulae.

The axillae are palpated for the presence of lymphadenopathy and the skin of the arms inspected for rashes, café-au-lait patches and other cutaneous lesions (Figs. 1 and 2). The radial pulses are felt and the hands minutely examined. The shape of the hands and the fingers are noted, bearing in mind the broad palm of Down's syndrome with the concomitant dysplasia of the middle phalanx of the 5th finger and the abnormalities of palmar creases and prints. Long, slender fingers may indicate arachnodactyly (Marfan's syndrome) and short, stubby fingers pseudo-hypoparathyroidism or achondroplasia. Whether the hands feel warm or cold, and are dry or moist, gives some indication of the circulatory and emotional state of the child. The finger nails are looked at for evidence of clubbing, nail-biting or exceptionally koilonychia; dystrophic nails are found with chondro-ectodermal and ectodermal dysplasia.

(3) *The Abdomen.* The abdomen should be inspected while the child is either standing or lying supine, as abdominal distension and the abdominal excursions of respiration are less easily evaluated when the child is sitting. Note should be taken of abnormally dilated abdominal veins and abnormal pulsations. Inspection of the abdomen is often sufficient to show whether abdominal distension is due to enlarged viscera:— hepatomegaly, splenomegaly, renal swellings or distended bladder, or gaseous or faeculent enlargement of the gastro-intestinal tract, or ascites, or the presence of tumour. These impressions can be confirmed by palpation and special tests for ascites ('shifting dullness', fluid thrill). Less obvious enlargements of viscera will be elucidated by routine palpation.

Genitalia should be inspected; in boys the normality of the penis and urethral

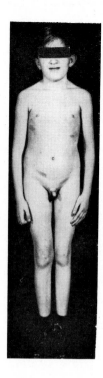

Fig. 1. Café-au-lait spots of neurofibromatosis. These are of smooth outline, usually oval in shape and arranged with the long axis of the ovals parallel to the dermatomes.

Fig. 2. While café-au-lait spots are the commonest lesion on the trunk in tuberose sclerosis, young children often have white spots of similar directional orientation.

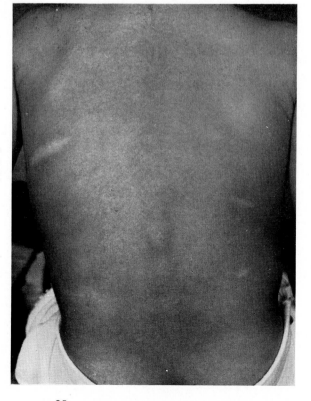

orifice, followed by palpation of the scrotum and groins. This together with the presence, distribution and character of pubic hair indicates not only abnormalities, if any, but indicates whether the child is infantile, pubescent or adolescent in sexual development. The pubis of girls is similarly examined, and the vulva, vaginal and urethral orifices inspected.

The anus is inspected and, if indicated, sensation in the perineal region tested. Examination of the genitalia and rectum are disturbing procedures and should only be carried out if indicated, and then with the utmost regard for the child's feelings and with some suitable explanation and perhaps a reassuring remark.

The groins should be palpated carefully for evidence of hernia, inguinal lymph-adenopathy and the presence of normal femoral artery pulsations. The back of the child should be examined and careful note taken of any swellings, dimples or tufts of hair in the mid-line. The position and mobility of the spine should be checked before proceeding to examination of the legs.

The lower limbs are examined generally in the same way as the arms. Special attention should be paid to the colour and temperature of the skin because circulatory disorders are often more pronounced in the legs.

For purposes of routine physical examination the procedures used in the neurological testing of muscle tone and power are sufficient to exclude major pathology in joints. However, when pain, tenderness or deformity lead to a suspicion of joint disease, the joints should be examined in detail. In children who are not yet walking the hip joints should be routinely examined to exclude dislocation.

CHAPTER IV

Neurological Examination—General Comments

The following chapters describe the methods and techniques of neurological examination in children, and the interpretation of these findings. There are, of course, many additional methods of examination which may be indicated from time to time, according to the nature of the problem suspected, or on the basis of the findings from more conventional testing. Relatively little special equipment is required for the examination as described in this volume, and it is possible to do most of what is needed with little equipment beyond an ophthalmoscope and a reflex hammer, together with supplies usually to be found in hospitals and clinics. A few special items which are useful are shown in Figure 1.

Fig. 1. Useful instruments for examination of nervous system of children. From left to right: reflex hammers (those with flexible handles may be preferable to the variety with the triangular rubber head), tuning fork, tracing wheel for sensory mapping, flashlight fitted with rubber adaptor for transillumination of head, coloured blocks which are also rattles, bell, squeaking rubber toy, cricket for testing hearing, pinwheel of type sold for July 4th (for testing eye movements and to hold gaze while eye grounds are examined), white-headed pins for testing visual fields or sense of pain, collection of common objects for testing sterognosis, two-point discriminator, bent paper clip which can also be used for two-point discrimination, steel tape measure for measuring heads and limbs (this can also be used as a dangling object to test visual fields or grasp).

With young children or those likely to be uncooperative or mentally retarded, it is most important to begin the examination by observation alone, without any attempt to handle the child or to ask him to do anything. Apparent intelligence, affect, relationship with parents, vision and hearing, function of cranial nerves, coordination or ataxia, and muscle power can be examined to a large extent by the observant physician while he is taking the case history. This unique opportunity for observing the child from the corner of one's eye while he is unaware of critical observation should not be missed (see page 26).

The order in which the examination is carried out will inevitably depend to some extent on the child's probable degree of cooperation and his span of attention. It is wise to leave the less pleasant items to the last and begin with those which are more agreeable, seem most important in the light of the history, or demand greater freshness and concentration. It is preferable to record the examination in a standard outline form; this ensures that nothing is left out, and makes it easier to see the implications of the findings and whether they can be explained by localised anatomical lesions. As a minimum, all positive findings should be recorded, together with those negative findings which are obviously pertinent in the context of the positive findings and the medical history. There are many ways of recording a neurological examination; the example offered below follows the outline of the chapters in this book.

Outline of Recording Neurological Examination

Mental State
> State of consciousness
> Orientation in place and time
> Apparent intelligence
> Emotional state
> Serial 7's, digit repetition, etc.
> Special tests of cerebral function

Language Functions
> Speech
> Understanding of commands, etc.
> Reading
> Writing
> Gestures—use and comprehension

Head
Neck and Spine
Cranial Nerves
> 1.
> 2.
> 3.4.6.
> 5.
> 7.
> 8.
> 9.10.
> 11.
> 12.

Station and Gait
Motor Function
> Muscular mass
> Muscular power

Muscular tone
Coordination
Associated movements
Involuntary movements

Reflexes BJ TJ Abdominals Cremasteric KJ AJ Ankle Clonus Plantars Others
record right and left
record as O, + (hypoactive), + + (normal), + + + (exaggerated), + + + +
(exaggerated + clonus)
Infantile automatisms and postural reflexes

Sensation
Touch, pain, temperature
Passive movement, position
Stereognosis, graphaesthesia
Discrimination of 2 points, texture
Vibration

Autonomic Function

When a child is especially ill, uncooperative or tired, it may be necessary to return on another occasion to complete the examination. In evaluation of doubtful cases, the child can be re-examined after a month or two, to determine whether the condition is a progressive one and to see how the normal anticipated development of the child has been distorted by the disease process. Detailed records are necessary in order to compare findings. In some cases motion pictures may be very helpful, provided the physician selects those physical findings (usually disorders of movement) which most lend themselves to this type of recording. Really useful motion pictures, whether as a case record or for teaching purposes, are seldom obtained unless the patient is sent to the photographer with a very clear description of what is wanted. Preferably, the physician or one of his assistants should actually be present while the film is being made, to assist in demonstrating the physical signs and to make certain that what is desired is actually being recorded.

CHAPTER V

Mental State

In the fully developed adult mental functioning is such a complexity of attributes that it is difficult to devise specific measures of each component. The situation is no easier in childhood, and this discussion will be primarily concerned with those rather obvious disturbances in mental state which are frequent concomitants of organic disease. In practice it is much easier to detect deviations from the normal by seeking evidence of change from the pre-existing state rather than by comparison with absolute criteria of normality or abnormality. The three main parameters of mental state which will be discussed are (a) consciousness, (b) intelligence, and (c) affect.

Consciousness

This will be defined as the state of awareness of the individual, his responsiveness to stimulation and his ability to recall past events. It will not be considered in terms of the deeper, almost metaphysical meaning given by psychiatry to denote a unique attribute providing an inside view of certain psychological processes within the individual. Clinically, consciousness can be somewhat arbitrarily divided into normal consciousness, sleep states (light and deep), stupor, and coma, based upon the ease with which the patient can be aroused. Infants and young children in deep sleep are sometimes difficult to wake up, thereby giving an impression of a pathological disorder of consciousness which may be misleading in such conditions as the post-ictal phase of convulsive disorder, head injuries, or diabetic acidosis.

Unconsciousness

Sudden transient loss of consciousness is nearly always a manifestation of convulsive disorder, and differentiation between epilepsy and other forms of actual or apparent loss of consciousness such as syncope and breath-holding attacks is discussed in Chapter II, pp. 18-19.

Prolonged loss of consciousness (coma) is a paediatric emergency. If it is profound the child is unrousable and responds only by withdrawal from painful stimuli. With lesser degrees of coma and in stupor the child may respond to auditory (calling his name, making loud noises), visual (reaction of pupils to light) and tactile (touch) stimuli, but will not become fully roused.

The size and reactivity of the pupils are a guide to the plane of consciousness but may be affected by the cause of the coma, as in head injury, intoxication or cerebral tumour. Similarly, the superficial and deep tendon reflexes are usually diminished or lost in profound coma of systemic origin, but may be increased in coma due to primary intracranial disease. Changes in the character and frequency of the pulse and respirations were formerly thought to be regularly related to depth of consciousness; however, they are more often altered by the causative pathology or by secondary effects such as cardio-respiratory insufficiency or airway obstruction.

Immediate management of the comatose child is designed to restore and maintain adequate oxygenation of the brain. Often the establishment of a clear airway and restoration of ventilatory function will cause an immediate lightening of the coma. Once resuscitation and initial aid have been given the cause of the coma should be ascertained and specific treatment started.

Unless the history gives a clear indication of the likely cause of the coma it is wise to consider first the possible lesions which demand immediate treatment. Hypoglycaemia, drug ingestion, lead encephalopathy, acute bacterial meningitis, middle meningeal haemorrhage, and haemorrhagic or bacteraemic shock are examples. Once these possibilities have been eliminated a more systematic approach can be made. The commonest cause of coma is epilepsy (often the seizure is not witnessed), but unless the patient is a known epileptic the possibility that the seizure was symptomatic must be considered. In the following schema of the causes of coma many of the pathological processes noted may be accompanied by seizures.

Causes of Coma

A. *Coma due to primary intracranial disease:*

1. Infection
   (a) bacterial; acute bacterial meningitis; tuberculous meningitis; cerebral abscess
   (b) viral; acute lymphocytic meningitis, viral meningoencephalitis
   (c) rickettsial
   (d) protozoal; cerebral malaria

2. Acute disseminated meningo-encephalitis (neuro-allergic encephalitis)
   (a) exanthematous (measles, chicken pox)
   (b) post-vaccinal (and following other immunising agents)
   (c) 'idiopathic'

3. Head injury
   (a) accidental
   (b) deliberately inflicted (maltreatment)

4. Cerebro-vascular accidents (non-traumatic)
   (a) cerebral haemorrhage (vascular lesions, haemorrhagic diathesis)
   (b) cerebral thrombosis (including sickle-cell crisis)
   (c) cerebral embolism
   (d) uncertain (acute infantile hemiplegia)

5. Intra-cranial tumour
   (a) cerebral tumour
   (b) leukaemia

6. Epilepsy
   (a) idiopathic
   (b) symptomatic

34

7. As a terminal event in progressive degenerative diseases of the central nervous system.

B. *Coma due to exogenously administered poisons:*

1. Drugs and medications: commonly aspirin and other salicylates, barbiturates, tranquillisers and anti-depressants, anti-histaminics, and ferrous sulphate.

2. Domestic, horticultural and agricultural chemicals

3. Lead encephalopathy

4. Alcohol

5. Bites of poisonous reptiles, fish and arthropods

C. *Coma due to endogenous metabolic disorder:*

1. Disorders of carbohydrate metabolism
   (a) diabetes mellitus
   (b) hypoglycaemia

2. Disturbances of acid-base metabolism
   (a) acidosis (i) hypercapneic, (ii) hypoxic, (iii) metabolic
   (b) alkalosis (i) respiratory, (ii) metabolic

3. Disturbances of water and electrolyte metabolism
   (a) water intoxication
   (b) hypernatraemia
   (c) profound dehydration

4. Renal failure: 'uraemic' coma

5. Hepatic failure; 'hepatic' coma

6. Disturbances of amino-acid metabolism

7. Hypothyroidism

D. *Coma due to physical agents:*

1. Temperature
   (a) hypothermia
   (b) hyperpyrexia

2. Electric shock

E. *Coma in 'shock' whether due to asphyxia, infection, trauma or hyper-sensitivity and as a terminal event in many diseases.*

Differential Diagnosis

The diagnosis of the cause of coma is greatly simplified if the circumstances preceding unconsciousness are known and if an accurate past medical history is obtainable. Any informants likely to be helpful must be detained or summoned and kept available until it is clear that no further information is needed. Vomitus, urine and faeces should be collected, labelled and retained for subsequent analysis, as should samples of any medications or suspected intoxicants.

Immediate physical examination indicates the need for resuscitation and furnishes diagnostic clues as to the likely cause. Signs of external injury must be looked for and their significance interpreted. The coma may be the result of head injury or the head injury inflicted by the sudden loss of consciousness. Vital signs are checked and recorded; tachycardia may indicate infection or haemorrhage, bradycardia may be a sign of raised intracranial pressure, cerebral depression or severe hypoxia. The character of the respirations is often dictated more by the state of the airways and mechanics of breathing than the depth of the coma. Evident hypoxia and respiratory insufficiency must be relieved. Hyperventilation of Küssmaul type suggests acidosis (diabetic ketosis, salicylate intoxication), while periodic breathing is a feature of cerebrovascular accidents.

The body temperature is below normal in many comatose states and the absence of pyrexia does not rule out infection. Cerebral depression, peripheral circulatory failure and exposure may all provoke hypothermia. Hyperpyrexia can indicate infection, irritation of the thermo-regulatory centres, or merely the unwise application of excessive external warmth. Hyperpyrexia is often a feature of sub-arachnoid haemorrhage and is said in these circumstances to be a grave prognostic sign.

Careful observations of the patient's posture and spontaneous movements should be made. Asymmetry may indicate localised disease or injury of a limb or a localised intracranial lesion giving rise to focal signs. Specific postures are seen in decerebrate and decorticate states, and in meningitis there may be hyper-extension of the neck or the trunk.

The head and neck are examined with care, the scalp and cranium being examined for evidence of disease or injury. The ears are inspected and any bleeding or signs of infection noted. When the eyes are examined the degree of visual awareness, direction of gaze, and size and symmetry of the pupils are noted. Haemorrhages of the conjunctivae, in the hyaloid or beneath the retina are indicative of trauma, the latter frequently of subdural haematoma. Asymmetry of the pupils, whether of position, size, shape, or reaction, unless congenital, should always raise the question of primary intracranial disease of a localised nature. The fundi should be inspected for the signs of general disease such as hypertensive retinopathy, albuminuric retinitis and diabetic retinopathy, as well as signs of neurological significance — papilloedema, optic atrophy, chorioretinitis, and retinitis pigmentosa. Choroidal tubercles are sometimes seen in miliary tuberculosis. The carotid arteries should be palpated.

The nasal and buccal cavities should be cleared of secretions, vomit and foreign materials at an early stage and later re-examined for signs of disease or injury.

Inspection of the total body surface is important; major exanthemata are unlikely to be missed but petechiae may be scanty in meningococcal meningitis, and 'rose-pink' spots few in enteric fever. Puncture marks may reveal injection sites which give a clue to diabetes mellitus or narcotic addiction. Wounds or skin sepsis are possible foci for the development of septicaemia or bacteraemia.

Although neurological examination of the comatose patient is not comprehensive, as those elements requiring cooperation cannot be properly done, it is nevertheless of great value. Apart from the abnormalities of posture, movement and eyes already noted, examination of muscle tone and the reflexes gives important information. In general, when asymmetry of tone and reflexes is found, localised intracranial disease, especially a space-occupying lesion or cerebrovascular accident, should be suspected. Generalised symmetrical loss of power, tone and reflexes is more characteristic of coma due to generalised systemic disease, intoxication or injury. Only in extremely profound coma or anaesthesia are the limbs completely flaccid and without reflexes, or the pupils fixed and dilated. If such signs are found, especially if they are asymmetrical, a paralytic lesion in the brain must be considered.

General physical examination must never be omitted in cases of coma. This examination may reveal the cause, as in cerebral abscess complicating bacterial infections of the heart or lungs, or indications of a primary neoplasm in cerebral tumour. Not uncommonly an intercurrent infection will precipitate coma in the juvenile diabetic and unless the infection is treated promptly the diabetic ketosis is less easily controlled. The physical examination may also indicate a disease process which is being treated with potentially toxic drugs such as digitalis, salicylates, aminophylline or anti-histamines.

Necessary special investigations are likely to be suggested from the history and physical examination. Rarely they will be required to elucidate the diagnosis when the cause of the coma remains unknown, more often they will be useful to confirm the provisional diagnosis and provide a clearer basis for management. As far as any investigations may be said to be routine the following are generally required.

1. Urine: test for glucose, acetone, albumen, coproporphyrins, examine deposit for cells and casts. Retain sample for special analytical tests.

2. Blood: *haematology*, haemoglobin, total white and differential count, examination of red cells, white cells and platelets, erythrocyte sedimentation rate.
   bacteriology, blood cultures, serum for virus studies.
   chemistry, blood sugar, blood urea (B.U.N.), serum bilirubin, blood pH, electrolytes (Na, Cl, K, Ca, P, HCO_3). Retain some of sample for special analytical tests and for possible grouping and cross-matching.

3. Lumbar Puncture: if there is any evidence of raised intracranial pressure care must be taken to withdraw cerebrospinal fluid slowly or to consider the advisability of neurosurgical approach. In cases of coma the cerebrospinal fluid glucose should be estimated routinely irrespective of the cell count and protein concentration.

4. Radiology: Skull x-rays should be taken for evidence of trauma, raised intracranial pressure, intracranial calcification or abnormalities of the pituitary fossa. A skeletal survey may be indicated if there is cranial trauma, possibility of lead intoxication ('lead lines' in bones), or malignancy.

5. Electroencephalography: a good deal of information both in respect of generalised disturbances and focal lesions may be obtained although it is rare for the precise nature of the lesion to be revealed by E.E.G.

Alterations in consciousness not amounting to coma may be found in the early stages or less severe forms of most of the pathological processes enumerated under coma. Clouding of consciousness or stupor will prompt the same sort of diagnostic enquiries as coma, but the situation is less urgent and immediate resuscitation is not required. The progressive degenerations of the central nervous system may be associated with more or less subtle deterioration in consciousness. These include the genetically-determined inborn errors of metabolism such as the neurolipidoses, hepatolenticular degeneration, and metachromatic leukodystrophy, and the demyelinating diseases and subacute inclusion body encephalitis. Subacute or chronic intoxication is rare except for lead poisoning, and excessive dosage with drugs such as phenobarbitone in the treatment of convulsive disorder.

Alterations in consciousness (awareness and orientation) may be encountered in various toxic and confusional states. Most of these occur in acute illness and are associated with fever (febrile delirium), or are the result of drug toxicity. The antihistamine drugs may cause drowsiness and some children react to barbiturates by becoming agitated and confused. The corticosteroids rarely produce mental changes in children.

Intelligence

Intelligence can perhaps be most usefully defined as the mental skills with which the individual relates to his environment. These skills allow him to solve problems and situations in his environment, and perform special tests or tasks involving the grasping of relationships — the degree of intelligence being proportional to the complexity or the abstractness or both of the relationships. The quantitative assessment of intelligence utilising standardised tests is the proper sphere of the psychologist, and the physician will be well-advised to consult his colleague rather than attempt such evaluations himself. He must, however, make some estimate of intelligence, particularly in the younger child when the techniques evolved by the psychologists are often not applicable but when the parents are anxious for a diagnosis. At this age it is often impossible to give a precise prognosis of the outlook for the child's intelligence, and sometimes one can only make a statement of the situation as it is at the time. The term 'backwardness' conveniently covers this general situation, and discussion of intelligence in this chapter is therefore conducted in these terms.

Backwardness or retardation exists when a child fails to reach the developmental status appropriate to his or her chronological age; it may be presumed sooner when a child presents physical features or biochemical evidence of a disorder regularly associated with mental defect. Conventionally, 'backwardness' or 'retardation' is applied to delayed development of physical and intellectual skills. Physical growth deficit is usually termed 'failure to thrive' or dwarfism, and delayed emotional development is categorised as 'immaturity.' Backwardness should not be used to designate the loss of functions which have once been attained, a condition more correctly termed 'regression.'

Backwardness may first be suspected by the parents, sometimes incorrectly as in the case of highly intelligent parents to whom an offspring of average ability may seem abnormally dull. Often, however, the physician discovers backwardness which is previously unsuspected, either as a result of routine examination or the evaluation of some other presenting condition.

Few paediatricians or neurologists have sufficient training, experience or time to administer and interpret the many excellent standardised tests of development, intelligence and other abilities used by the psychologist, nor is the medical consultation an appropriate setting for obtaining reliable results from such tests. It has been shown, however, that the more or less intuitive estimates of experienced physicians correlate well with expert psychometry at the more extreme deviations from the normal range.

The most severe degrees of backwardness (severe subnormality) are usually due to organic brain disease which may be of genetic, prenatal, perinatal, or postnatal origin, or combinations of these. Many children with organic brain disease have abnormal physical features which make a specific medical diagnosis possible, sometimes at an early and treatable stage. More difficulty, both in the recognition of backwardness and its precise pathological diagnosis, exists with children whose intellectual function and potential lie at the lower levels of the normal range of intelligence — so-called 'normal deviants' or children who have an intellectual potential of around average which is grossly impaired by maternal or social deprivation, or children with emotional difficulties. Such children have a normal appearance. Another important group of retarded children are those with a normal intellectual potential which is suppressed because of an isolated physical handicap such as deafness, poor vision, or locomotor defect.

Evaluation of backwardness after its initial detection is a complex problem involving specific medical diagnosis, medical, social and educational prognosis, and the formulation of a plan of management for the child and his family. Emphasis in this chapter is placed on detection and diagnosis, as it is these aspects which fall to the lot of the paediatrician and paediatric neurologist.

General Assessment of Intelligence

Developmental or intellectual testing of an uncooperative child in unfamiliar surroundings is often an exercise more of the physician's intuition than his scientific prowess. However the developmental examination of infants and young children need not be a fruitless procedure. Many of the well-standardised scales for the assessment of normal development which were developed as research procedures by Gesell, Griffiths and others have now been adapted and modified for clinical use. These procedures are designed to test the overall pattern of development of which 'intelligence' is a major parameter. Recent texts such as Illingworth (1966) and Sheridan (1960) give information on the basic developmental examination, and a suitable screening test is provided here (Table I).

It is important to remember that the norms are based largely upon white American and British children and may be considerably affected by cultural and child-rearing differences. When assessing development the background of the child must always be taken into account, and items which can be objectively tested are usually more reliable than those obtained by history. Developmental diagnosis and prognosis are more

TABLE I

Check List for Assessment by Observation of Developmental Level of Pre-school Child

Age	Historical (or Observed) Items	Items to be Tested
2 years	Runs well Walks up and down stairs — one step at a time Opens doors Climbs on furniture Puts 3 words together Handles spoon well Helps to undress Listens to stories with pictures	Builds tower of 6 cubes Circular scribbling Copies horizontal stroke with pencil Folds paper once
2½ years	Jumps Knows full name Refers to self by pronoun 'I' Helps put things away	Builds tower of 8 cubes Copies horizontal and vertical strokes (not a cross)
3 years	Goes upstairs, alternating feet Rides tricycle Stands momentarily on one foot Knows age and sex Plays simple games Helps in dressing Washes hands	Builds tower of 9 cubes Imitates construction of bridge with 3 cubes Imitates a cross and circle
4 years	Hops on one foot Throws ball overhand Climbs well Uses scissors to cut out pictures Counts 4 pennies accurately Tells a story Plays with several children Goes to toilet alone	Copies bridges from a model Imitates construction of a gate with 5 cubes Copies a cross and circle Draws a man with 2 to 4 parts - other than head Names longer of two lines
5 years	Skips Names 4 colours Counts 10 pennies correctly Dresses and undresses Asks questions about meaning of words	Copies a square and triangle Names 4 colours Names heavier of 2 weights

reliable with extreme deviations than border-line situations, and repeated examinations at intervals provide a better picture than a single session.

The pre-verbal child can be tested for his locomotor skills, his manipulative ability and his efforts at communication. Most paediatricians rely on such unstandardised and subjective qualities as the child's apparent awareness of, and interest in, his surroundings and his reactions to the expression and gestures of the examiner. The main pitfall here is that many retarded infants are alert visually and may respond happily to the examiner's advances (but often in an inappropriate and undiscriminating manner).

Older children who speak can be quickly screened by observing their replies to appropriate questions. It is the interest in the procedure, rapidity and aptness of response that is more revealing than the knowledge or ignorance of facts. The more or less standardised questions used to test for dementia in adults, e.g. 'What is the name of the President of the U.S.A.?' or 'Who is the leader of the House of Commons?' are usually unsuitable for children, but most physicians have favourite questions which they put to children at various ages. Such questions should not be exclusively those used in every day social conversation, e.g. 'How old are you?', 'Where do you live?', 'What are the names of your brothers and sisters?' because some well-trained retarded children are adept at social conversation in spite of severe deficiency in reasoning powers, while some children of normal ability from impoverished environments may appear extremely stupid. Many of the tests in the chapter on Special Tests of Cerebral Function (Chap. VII), may be used, and retarded children will in general perform them poorly.

After a single or repeated examination the examiner may be convinced that the child is backward or may still be in some doubt. Referral to a skilled psychologist will usually settle the question when there is doubt. It is better for the untrained physician to refer at an early stage rather than try to use tests or parts of tests which belong properly to the psychologist.

Backwardness Associated with Organic Disease

Detection of mental retardation in the child who appears abnormal is not difficult provided that the physician is acquainted with the physical syndromes associated with brain disease or damage. Often the child's abnormal appearance is the presenting feature and he is brought for advice before backwardness is apparent or suspected, or the significant physical findings may first be observed during routine paediatric examination. Conversely, the child may be seen because of backwardness and the abnormal physical features may provide the clues to the pathological cause.

Examination of the head is most informative. The size, shape and conformation of the skull should be noted and the maximum circumference measured with a steel measuring tape. (A table of head circumferences is given on page 86). A large head is found with hydrocephalus and hydranencephaly, both of which may be associated with backwardness, and in achondroplasia and cleidocranial dysostosis, which are not. A small head is indicative rarely of microcephalia vera, but more often the restriction of cranial growth is consequent upon maldevelopment or damage to the

41

underlying brain. Deformities of the skull due to premature fusion of the sutures (cranio-stenosis) which may be associated with retardation must be distinguished from postural plagiocephaly, which is only associated with retardation because defective infants are slow in sitting up, and is also common in very immaturely born infants. Characteristic facies are seen in Down's syndrome (mongolism), hypothyroidism, gargoylism (Hurler's syndrome), the severe type of infantile hypercalcaemia, Cornelia de Lange syndrome and some cases of cranio-facial disorders.

The facial skin may reveal significant abnormalities such as the unilateral naevi of the Sturge-Weber syndrome and the 'butterfly' eruption of tuberose sclerosis. Eye signs of diagnostic importance in some mental deficiency states include: microphthalmia in congenital toxoplasmosis and trisomy 13-15 disease; absence of tears in familial dysautonomia; glaucoma in Lowe's syndrome. Conjunctival telangiectasia are seen eventually in the ataxia-telangiectasia syndrome, corneal clouding is a feature of gargoylism and the Kayser-Fleischer ring pathognomonic of Wilson's disease. In the iris Brushfield's dots are indicative of mongolism. Cataracts of central type may be due to rubella syndrome or toxoplasmosis; lamellar cataracts are seen in galactosaemia, hypoparathyroidism and babies born extremely prematurely. Retinoscopy is of value in the diagnosis of toxoplasmosis (chorioretinitis), Laurence-Moon-Biedl syndrome (retinitis pigmentosa) and amaurotic family idiocy (cherry-red spot).

The lips, mouth and buccal cavity may provide diagnostic clues. Hare-lip with or without cleft palate is compatible with normal intelligence but some affected individuals are mentally subnormal. In babies a thick tongue should arouse suspicion of hypothyroidism and it may be the most important physical sign; by contrast a broad, or flat, often furrowed tongue is found in Down's syndrome. A high-arched palate is traditionally associated with feeble-mindedness, and it is a component of several embryopathic states, but it is quite compatible with normality. Contrary to popular belief the timing of dentition bears little or no relation to mental development, but retarded children often have carious teeth caused by poor dental hygiene and inadequate nutrition.

Abnormalities of the shape and position of the ears are associated with several rare syndromes, some of which include mental retardation.

The trunk and limbs furnish fewer evidences of mental retardation syndromes than the head. As a group the mentally retarded grow poorly and are frequently infantile. However, some syndromes are associated with obesity, such as the Laurence-Moon-Beidl syndrome, and Prader's syndrome of obesity, infantilism and mental retardation. Growth failure of extreme degree is a sign of hypothyroidism, and disproportionate dwarfism is seen in gargoylism. Short stature, shield-shaped chest and webbing of the neck with cubitus valgus is typical of gonadal agenesis (Turner's syndrome). Generalised hypotonia is often a feature of severe mental deficiency, but the reverse is seen in the commonest type of cerebral palsy—spastic tetraparesis. Cutaneous lesions are found on the trunk in tuberose sclerosis, and café-au-lait patches may indicate neuro-fibromatosis (Von Recklinghausen's disease), which is sometimes associated with retardation.

Sexual maturation is delayed or imperfect in several of the syndromes which are due to anomalies of the sex-chromosomes. Most of these are frequently associated with mental retardation.

Congenital heart disease is associated with mongolism (usually ventricular septal defect or persistent atrio-ventricular canal), and with gonadal agenesis (coarctation of the aorta). Hepato-splenomegaly is a feature of gargoylism, lipid histiocytosis (Niemann-Pick Disease) and cerebroside lipidosis (Gaucher's disease).

Broad hands with a single transverse crease are characteristic of mongolism, as is the dystrophic middle phalanx of the 5th digit. Polydactyly is a component of the Laurence-Moon-Beidl syndrome and syndactyly is sometimes associated with cranio-stenosis (Apert's syndrome).

Physical findings which are specific for identifiable types of mental retardation have been emphasised because an exact diagnosis enables the course of the disease to be predicted with more certainty and is of value in counselling the parents. Nearly all the conditions are rare (with the exception of mongolism) and few can be ameliorated by therapy.

Of much greater therapeutic importance are the syndromes of mental deficiency which can be identified before irreparable brain damage has occurred and for which treatment is available. At the present time only galactosaemia, phenylketonuria and hypothyroidism (cretinism) come into this category. Hypothyroidism can only be detected by recognition of its earliest signs — prolonged neonatal jaundice, lethargy, constipation, thick tongue, failure to thrive, and characteristic facies. Phenylketonuria and galactosaemia can be diagnosed by mass screening before the appearance of physical signs, and programmes for this are being set up in many areas.

Backwardness Without Abnormal Physical Features

The proportion of backward children (backwardness defined as limitation of intellectual functioning of such a degree as to preclude or make unlikely education at a normal school) who have demonstrable cerebral disease or damage is small, so the physician is most often confronted with the detection and assessment of retardation in children who have no associated abnormal physical features. Suspicion of backwardness therefore depends upon the familiarity of the parents or paediatrician with the developmental norms at various ages, and the extent to which the child deviates from them. Deviations are shown up more as increasing demands are made upon higher cerebral functioning, so moderate degrees of backwardness may not be suspected until schooling begins. Similarly, many retarded children who seem to be only mildly dull in infancy appear to be much more backward when their difficulties in learning to read and write are exposed at school age.

The developmental history shows either that there has been consistent and generalised delay from an early age or that development proceeded normally until a certain age when abnormal development appeared. The essential information is the times at which the child passed the 'milestones' of development and to what extent he has now failed to reach the expected developmental level appropriate to his chronological age. Some parents fail to give accurate information for many reasons; they may be unfamiliar with the normal course of development, unobservant of the progress of their own child or have unconscious defences leading to delusions about their child's abilities. For this reason the testimony of others who know the child well, such as relatives and teachers, may be of great value. It is unusual for parents to be able to give absolute dates for the times at which various 'milestones' were passed unless they have been alerted by doubts, or are of the type that records meticulously the events of childhood. However, experienced mothers are apt at comparing their own children and can usually state reliably whether a certain child was more 'forward' or 'backward' than his sibs. A complaint from a mother that one of her children is developing more slowly than his sibs or neighbourhood contemporaries should always be taken seriously.

Apart from the specific developmental history, enquiry should be made about the general behaviour and personality of the child, especially during the first year or so of life. Feeding, problems, sleeping difficulties, undue irritability or placidity are often indicators of mental retardation although by no means specific for it. If the history and examination support the probability of retardation, further historical information should be obtained in order to establish whether the disorder is progressive or non-progressive. This is often difficult, for a static disorder may not be at all obvious in early infancy and may appear to progress rapidly at time when new and greater demands are made upon the growing child. Similarly, slowly progressive disease, whether organic or functional, may be mistakenly regarded as a non-progressive disorder which is becoming more manifest. This difficulty is mostly encountered with infants and pre-school children, for by school age the basic potential and achievements of a child are known with reasonable accuracy.

At this stage in assessment it is probably best to evaluate the child's present state (see page 39) before investigating the history further, because the examination frequently shows the area in which information of aetiological importance must be sought.

Some Causes of Backwardness

Once a child has been categorised as retarded, it is essential to determine the probable cause of the handicap. Unfortunately a specific treatable disorder is rare, although deafness, environmental deprivation, visual defects and emotional difficulties are entities amenable to treatment. Causal analysis is worthwhile because it leads to better management of the child, more comprehensive assessment of other possible handicaps and more helpful parent counselling including genetic advice.

Further review of the history is designed to reveal possible causative factors. The family history must be investigated not only for the possible occurrence of chromosomal and single gene anomalies but also for the general level of intelligence and abilities. The influences of prenatal insults to the brain may be indicated by a history of rubella or other maternal illness during early pregnancy. Threatened abortion (spontaneous or induced) with a history of vaginal bleeding may be significant. At the end of pregnancy and in early neonatal life many brain-threatening hazards occur. Prematurity, asphyxia neonatorum, neonatal convulsive disorder (due to hypoglycaemia or birth injury), and severe neonatal jaundice are all pertinent and sometimes predictive of future neurological impairment.

In later infancy the occurrence of meningitis, undiagnosed febrile illness (especially with convulsions), lightning spasms or reactions to immunising procedures may indicate the source of brain damage. The toddler is at risk of encephalopathic toxic agents such as lead as well as of intracranial infections and cerebral trauma. Major defects in child rearing are associated with backwardness, so the history must include an estimation of the quality and quantity of maternal care and stimulation offered to the child. Often it is found that the child has been subjected to many adverse factors: for instance, the immature infant weighing less than 3 lb. at birth who had hyperbilirubinaemia and was brought up in several poor-quality foster homes because his mother is of too low intelligence to rear him successfully. Because it is frequently difficult to make a precise diagnosis on history and physical examination it is now the usual practice to do certain routine investigations when retardation is established. These include:

Urine: tests for reducing substances, abnormal aminoaciduria.

X-rays: skull for intracranial calcification, evidence of past trauma, confirmation of premature fusion of the sutures, evidence of raised intracranial pressure.

Electroencephalogram: rarely helpful except where retardation is associated with convulsive disorder.

Special tests such as cerebral angiography, pneumoencephalography, brain biopsy should be done only if indicated (see Chapter XV). Cytogenetic analysis is useful to confirm a doubtful diagnosis of a condition such as mongolism and in searching for the origin of hitherto unclassified entities.

Regression

Loss of already established skills (regression) may easily be confused with retardation as a regressed child falls short of the expected developmental status for his age. The distinction is important for the diagnosis of some progressive degenerative cerebral diseases. Regression is held by some to be characteristic of the autistic child. Regression may be permanent, as in the case of progressive degenerative disease, or temporary, as in some instances of encephalitis, head injury or severe psychological disturbance.

Beyond infancy, that is when a degree of reasoning power and memory has become apparent, the term 'regression' is used mainly to indicate reversion to an emotionally more infantile form of behaviour. Progressive loss of intellectual function is described as dementia. The diagnosis of dementia implies that a normal degree of thought, learning and memory existed before the onset of the illness and that impairment of these abilities can be demonstrated (see Chapter VII).

Apparent dementia as shown by falling off of school performance is often psychogenic but this is usually a failure to maintain the previous rate of school progress rather than a demonstrable loss of already acquired abilities. The early stages of some slowly progressive dementing diseases may however be difficult to distinguish from this.

The most important causes of organic dementia are the progressive degenerative brain diseases, especially those involving the grey matter, cerebral tumours, and poisoning with drugs either therapeutic, addictive or accidental. It is controversial whether convulsive disorder *per se* is ever associated with dementia. Many brain diseases are associated with both fits and dementia, and the treatment of epilepsy with drugs such as phenobarbitone, phenytoin and primidone may induce intoxication.

The investigation of dementia is obviously complex and must include a careful history and complete physical examination. Psychometry is always indicated in those cases where apparent dementia exists as an isolated complaint. In most instances other symptoms or signs will give a clue to the nature of the disease process, and provide a guide to the directions of further enquiries. In nearly all cases of dementia an electroencephalogram will be called for, and cerebral tumour ruled out by early investigations for this possibility. Provided that no remediable lesion remains undiagnosed it may be wise for a period to observe the evolution of the disease before making hazardous or painful investigations such as brain biopsy.

Affect

Affect refers to the child's emotional relationship with his environment and the way he reacts by demonstration of spontaneous feelings to the people around him. The distinction between the child with a disorder of affect and one with mental retardation is extremely difficult unless there is unequivocal evidence of normality prior to the onset of the complaint, and the physician may have to proceed on hints, perhaps from the history rather than his own observations. Where there is doubt he should obtain a psychiatric consultation at an early stage. The following are some of the clues which might alert one to the possibility of primary affective disorder:

1. Development proceeded quite normally during the first year of life and perhaps some talking was established, but a deterioration not traceable to an organic defect has occurred since.
2. Some evidence of flashes of intellectual functioning which are very much higher than the general level of functioning.
3. Reports, accompanied by observation, that the child avoids looking at people and does not become involved in play activities with other children.
4. Reports that normal mother/child affective ties have always been one-sided. The mother might describe the child as 'an uncuddly baby.'

A British Working Party chaired by Dr. Mildred Creak formulated 9 diagnostic criteria which they felt described a schizophrenic syndrome in childhood (Creak 1961) but the whole subject is still one of considerable controversy.

The terminology of affective disorders in childhood is confused. The word 'autism' has been used increasingly in recent years since Kanner introduced it (1943). Unfortunately the children to whom this label has been attached do not form a homogeneous group; some of them have simple mental retardation, but others certainly seem to have a psychotic illness, and in a few there is evidence of organic degenerative brain disease.

Emotional lability, poor concentration, distractibility and perseveration are behavioural signs indicating a disturbance of mental state which is held by some to be characteristic of chronic brain syndromes of childhood. These mental attributes are indeed often found with children who have minor neurological abnormalities, learning difficulties and discrepancies between verbal and performance I.Q. tests. They are also familiar in many epileptic children.

CHAPTER VI

Speech

METHODS OF EXAMINATION

Evaluation of the Child's Spontaneous Speech

It is almost self-evident that what the child says casually to himself, to his mother, or to the physician during the early part of the visit is likely to be the truest sample of his speech. Much can often be learned by judicious listening to this, during the course of the taking of the medical history and initial discussions with the mother, while the child is not aware that his vocalising is being appraised. To do this usefully requires considerable experience on the part of the physician, and also careful listening and constant attention to the various components of function involved in the production of spoken language. It may be appropriate to consider these qualities under the headings of quantity of speech, its qualities, and its content.

Quantity of Speech

The child may be completely mute, may make sounds only but no spoken words, may speak little or a normal amount, or excessively so as to chatter constantly. All these points are worth noting, although the implications of the quantity of spontaneous speech on the part of the child are often more important in regard to psychiatric aspects of his situation than to neurological ones. The physician's office or clinic is a strange place, and it is probable that a majority of children react by speaking less, or occasionally more, than they normally do at home or in familiar surroundings. Nevertheless this information should be taken into account for whatever it may be worth.

Qualities of Speech

These should be thought of in connexion with the component functions involved in producing spoken language. Respiration is the first and simplest essential, to produce a flow of air to the larynx at a controlled rate, and—equally importantly as McDonald (1964) has pointed out—to assist in the formation of syllables by releasing and arresting the flow of air by action of the intercostal muscles, for those syllables which are not begun or terminated by consonants.

Phonation is usually considered the next step, in which the moving air is disturbed and set into vibration by the vocal cords and other laryngeal structures. This process determines the pitch and the intensity of the sound and whether it is voiced or unvoiced (one may investigate the difference by palpating one's own larynx for the presence or absence of vibration during the saying of the different consonant sounds). Actually, in some English sounds, the air passes the larynx undisturbed.

Articulation, the next and most difficult step, involves the transformation of the moving or vibrating stream of air into a continuous and highly coordinated series of vowel and consonant sounds. McDonald (1964, p. 87) defines articulation as 'a process

47

consisting of a series of overlapping ballistic movements which place varying degrees of obstruction in the way of the outgoing air stream and simultaneously modify the size, shape and coupling of resonating cavities.' This resonation has much to do with the character of the sound produced: for example, *t* is exploded with the tip of the tongue largely out into the free air, whereas *k* is exploded from contact of the posterior tongue and the palate into a large oral cavity. There is growing evidence of the importance of sensation and discrimination of what the speaker hears and of the integration of this auditory feedback in the coordination of speech and particularly in its rhythm.

Obviously, a defect of speech can exist at any step in this sequence, and frequently at several. The listening examiner must attempt to gain an impression of how the child produces each of the vowel and consonant sounds of the language and whether these are produced correctly as the beginning of a syllable, between vowels, as the termination of a syllable, or in combinations ('blends' such as *st*, *br*, etc.). In conventional terminology these individual vowel and consonant sounds are called phonemes. Actually, the phoneme may be an artificial concept, as McDonald (1964) has suggested, pointing out that it is impossible to speak an isolated consonant unless it is followed (or preceded) by some sort of vowel; thus, the syllable is perhaps more appropriately considered the basic unit of speech. Nevertheless, the examiner will do well to write down which vowel and consonant sounds the patient is able to produce correctly, and in the case of the others, whether they are omitted, substituted with other sounds, or distorted. Many children with defects of articulation do not mispronounce the same sound on every occasion, and some approximate idea of the percentage of the time this happens is worth noting.

Content of Speech

This refers to what the child says, considered separately from how he says it. This is inevitably a highly subjective and approximate evaluation when done by a physician, and can include little more than an impression of the size of the child's vocabulary for nouns and verbs, whether adverbs and adjectives are used, and how many, and particularly the variety and appropriateness of use of pronouns, prepositions and conjunctions. De Renzi and Vignolo (1962) have described a 'type-token test' which compares the number of different prepositions (or conjunctions) used in a few paragraphs of spoken or written speech with the total number of that part of speech used. Adults or children with aphasias, and also probably deaf children, show a paucity in variety in these small parts of speech.

The syntax of what the child says should also be thoughtfully considered, listening particularly for a possible telegraphic style and for grammatical correctness. The child's grammar, and also his pronunciation, must be judged in the light of what he hears at home, and some attention to the speech of the parents may be enlightening. Whether or not the child asks questions is an important point. Also, are these merely 'where?' or 'what?' or do they include a more mature type of inquiry such as 'why?' or 'how?'.

Further Objective Testing

All the features just described may be appraised during casual listening, and this is the best evaluation obtainable if the child vocalises freely. If he does not, it may be useful to get his mother to engage him in conversation, but the conversation should not be a triangular one, but rather between child and mother or between child and physician. Asking him to name a collection of common objects, or the examiner's actions or gestures, may draw out speech if the child is shy, but this of course tests for possible aphasia as well as for dysarthria. Sets of square cards approximately 4" x 4" may be purchased, each bearing the outline drawing of some common object, the whole set being arranged so as to demonstrate when properly named an alphabetically arranged series of phonemes, at the beginning of the word, in the middle, or at the end. This provides a systematic test and insures against omissions or errors of interpretation. This separation of pronunciation of a sound according to its initial, central, or terminal position may be less discriminatory than whether it occurs in isolation, in a blend (as *bl* and *nd* in the word 'blend') or abutting another consonant in a separate syllable (as *d b* in 'red book'.)

Dysrhythmias are usually best detected in listening to casual speech or in conversation, but a number of test phrases are conventionally used, such as 'Royal Irish Constabulary', 'Methodist Episcopal', and 'Round the rugged rock the ragged rascal ran'. Other phrases more appropriate to childhood experiences can be developed, and every examiner has his own favourite.

Critical evaluation of a child's speech is often impossible or limited because of the child's non-cooperation, or because of the limited experience or time of the physician. The evaluation can be supplemented to a certain extent by direct questioning of the parent, assuming the latter to be a critical observer, as may not always be the case.

The physician will, of course, refer to the speech pathologist cases which are complicated or not immediately obvious, in order to obtain a full and comprehensive description of the child's speech. The physician — who has to correlate all of the findings and formulate a diagnostic impression — needs to be familiar with the therapist's methods of evaluation of speech in order to interpret them intelligently and, most importantly, needs to realise that what one usually gets from a speech pathologist is a description, not a diagnosis. To be aware that a child fails to speak in sentences, or that he omits prepositions and conjuctions, or that he omits, distorts or substitutes certain sounds, leaves one in a position comparable to having completed a neurological examination and recorded the physical signs. One must then try to fit the findings, together with the historical facts and any special investigations available, into a diagnosis of the neurological disturbance or other malfunction responsible.

Related Functions to be Evaluated in Cases of Abnormal Speech

Anatomical Considerations

Abnormal speech may result from a variety of abnormalities of the structures of speech, and it is superfluous to remind the examiner to look for cleft lip or palate, micrognathia, dental malocclusion, palatal or pharyngeal disproportion, enlarged tonsils and adenoids, etc. If the child breathes through the mouth constantly, it is important to find out whether he is in fact able to breathe through the nose with effort or whether there is nasal obstruction. Many children with mental retardation or with cerebral palsies or other defects of suprasegmental control tend to let the mouth hang open even if the nasal airway is clear. Movements of the face, lips, tongue and palate should be examined, both to command and in imitation of the examiner's expressions. Any weakness or disability must be considered as to whether it reflects abnormality of the lower or upper motor neurone (see Chapter IX). Voluntary control may be lacking even in the absence of paresis: for example, a child may be unable to elevate the palate to command when told to say 'aaah' but the palate may elevate normally in the gag reflex. Rapid alternating or sequential movements should also be tested, as many children who can put the tongue into any desired single position are unable to put it through small rapid alternating movements.

Hearing

The evaluation of hearing in at least a crude way is a proper part of every neurological examination, and the physician should not hesitate to do this because the patient has already been subjected to some form of audiometry. The examiner should ascertain whether children turn the head or eyes involuntarily toward sounds presented from unseen sources on either side of the head, or whether they can be induced to point to the source of sound.

Best results are obtained by using relatively faint sounds which are unusual enough to be interesting, and presenting each sound only a few times before going on to another one. Rattles, squeaking toys, clicking 'crickets', devices to imitate bird or animal sounds, or even rustling of the fingertips are usually effective if hearing is normal, although a louder sound or one often presented may be ignored. Particularly in the case of aphasic or autistic children, this method may document a certain level of hearing even in patients who are stated to be deaf by the audiologist (such patients often react to the sound inconsistently or only after a delay of several seconds). This is not to say of course that turning head or eyes or pointing to the source of a sound is any evidence that spoken language is normally perceived at a cerebral level, and it is equally possible for a person with normal hearing to have impaired ability to localise sounds. Testing with whispered voice is another conventional approach. In testing this, it is important to note any distortion in repetition of what is whispered. This may reflect diminished auditory acuity, or alternatively a difficulty in prompt and accurate production or reproduction of a particular sound (possibly in spite of ability to produce all the phonemes of the spoken language on one occasion or another even if not in appropriate places and combinations).

Both in testing by whispered voice and in conversation it is important to note whether the child answers questions or whether he repeats them verbatim (echolalia is perhaps most easily recognised from the response to questions). Children who are highly distractible or hyperactive or who have short spans of attention, and also some aphasics, are most satisfactorily tested if the eyes are covered. Many such children become so tied up in visual stimuli that they ignore auditory stimuli.

Comprehension of Spoken Language

Testing of comprehension is obviously of highest importance in the case of patients with abnormal speech, but fortunately it is usually readily tested in terms

50

of the child's response to commands and of his ability to point to the correct one of a group of common objects or pictures when the examiner speaks the name. Complex 2- or 3-step directions should be given to children of school age, including such things as 'put the penny on top of the block,' or 'give me the penny when I touch the block with my finger, but not before.' Many children who appear to have pure disabilities of expression will prove to have more subtle defects of comprehension when tested by these methods.

Finally, if there is any suspicion of a hearing loss or of a dysphasia, the child should be given this whole series of tests both while he has the opportuntity of watching the examiner's facial expression and lip movements, and again while the examiner is behind him and unseen.

Reading

A collection of children's books appropriate to various educational levels is essential examining equipment. The child's ability to read out loud and to read silently and repeat or paraphrase should be tested, with particular attention to possible omission of certain words, substitution of other words of comparable outline shape, and reversals such as 'tac' for 'cat' or 'god' for 'dog'. The accuracy of eye movements and the frequency of change of position of the eyes during silent reading are also worth observing but somewhat difficult to interpret, although it is generally recognised that children who are poor readers move the eyes far more frequently than do good readers.

Writing

The patient's ability to write to dictation and to write the names of objects shown or of actions of the examiner, and his ability to write something of his own composition, are the conventional tests. Special points to note include abnormal size of handwriting, abnormal formation of letters, letters written backwards or reversed in sequence or reversals of entire words comparable to those which may be observed when the child reads aloud. Obviously, the content of the handwriting and its neatness and the child's coordination in writing it are different considerations.

'Inner Language'

One of the best tests of 'inner language', a difficult subject to get at, is to ask the child to repeat in paraphrase the substance of what he has just read or had said to him aloud. All tests of mathematical ability involve some kind of symbolisation and are doubtless related to spoken or written symbols, but the practical application of this is difficult. The child's use of gestures and other non-verbal language, and his comprehension of the same type of symbols, is in contrast not difficult to evaluate qualitatively and is of high importance. A standardised objective test of imitation of gestures has been developed by Bergès and Lézine (1963). However, this involves the duplication by the child of various unfamiliar and non-meaningful gestures demonstrated by the examiner. It is more a test of perception, of concept of body image and spatial orientation, and of visual motor coordination than a test of anything related to symbolic language.

51

Special Tests for Aphasia

In practical work with children, the classification of the developmental aphasias depends chiefly on demonstrating discrepant disabilities in the language functions outlined above, and discrepancies between these functions and the child's intelligence and other abilities. A number of standard manuals, many of which contain their own test materials, are available for testing for aphasia. The best known is that of Eisenson (1954), although certain parts of this are difficult to apply to young children.

INTERPRETATION

Standards of Normal for Age

Production of Sounds

Murphy (1964) has tabulated some interesting data from tape recordings of the babbling and other vocalising of normal infants from birth up to 14 months of age. Briefly, combinations of guttural sounds with vowels are the earliest features, under 4 months of age, and followed by such combinations as ebe, epe, and ele at 4 to 6 months, and then at 7 or 8 months by the familiar tata, papa, dada, mama, etc., which are usually mistaken for actual words; 'dada' is related to adult males in general at 9 to 10 months but not to the father specifically until around a year of age, at which time the child also acquires such meaningful words as 'nana', 'teddy', 'ni-ni' (night-night) and whatever euphemism is used for bodily functions ('wee wee' etc.). As speech develops further, differentiation of the vowel sounds is acquired first and the consonants only considerably later. Some consonants are normally acquired much later than others.

Shank (1964) gives the following normal timetable, accepting that boys may normally be somewhat slower than girls:

$3\frac{1}{2}$ years: p, b, m, w, h
$4\frac{1}{2}$ years: t, d, n, g, k, ng, y
$5\frac{1}{2}$ years: f, v, s, z
$6\frac{1}{2}$ years: sh, zh, l, th
up to 8 years: ch, r, wh

The younger children typically deal with consonants they are unable to pronounce by omitting them. At later ages the normal mechanism is substitution, or subsequently distortion, with production of an incorrect but approximate imitation. Correspondingly, children with severe speech defects are more likely to omit or substitute sounds than to distort them. Whether the child is making a normal substitution for a sound not to be expected at his chronological or mental age, or whether he is making an abnormal substitution at a later age, the usual tendency is to substitute those consonants which are easy, simple and normally acquired early in life for those which are more difficult, complex or acquired later. For example, *t* is substituted for *k*, *g* for *d*, *w* for *r*, *w* for *l*, and *sh* for *th*. However there is considerable variation from one child to another.

Children with disarticulations are not all alike in their distortions or substitutions, nor is their speech comparable to the normal speech of a younger child in every respect even though it is sometimes strikingly reminiscent. McDonald (1964) has pointed out that, in addition to the normal sequence from omission to substitution to distortion to correct production of sound, there is a parallel sequence of always saying it incorrectly, then sometimes correctly and sometimes incorrectly, and finally always correctly. The position of the consonant in the syllable (initial, central, or terminal) is also of some significance, and in one survey (Amidon 1941) only 36 per cent of the errors detected in 100 first-grade children occurred in all three positions in words. Blends of two consonants are usually more likely to be incorrect than their individual components, but there is some evidence that the reverse may sometimes be true (Roe and Milisen 1942).

Vocabulary

Sheridan (1964) gives the following guidelines concerning the normal number and variety of spontaneously produced words for different ages:

15 months — 2 to 6 words.

18 months — 2 to 20 words; understands commands and points out named objects.

21 months — primitive sentences or phrases of 2 or 3 words.

24 months — 50 or more words. Asks questions in terms of what? where? who?

30 months — uses pronouns and prepositions and can repeat short simple nursery rhymes.

36 months — 250 words; forms plurals; asks questions of why? how? when?

48 months — tells stories and can describe his experiences. Asks the meaning of words, particularly abstract ones.

Every paediatrician is aware, however, of the enormous range of normal variation on this timetable and it seems probable that by no means all these variations can be attributed to the degree of verbal stimulation which the child receives at home. In the authors' experience, the ability to speak in short sentences by 2 years of age is almost always followed by normal intelligence or better, but the converse of this statement is not true. Elaborate investigation of children for failure to speak at the age of $2\frac{1}{2}$ is very often fruitless, leading to no definite diagnosis concerning a child who later proves to speak approximately normally 6 months or a year afterwards. However, failure to speak meaningful sentences would always have to be considered abnormal at $3\frac{1}{2}$ and probably at 3.

It is needless to point out that parental estimates of vocabulary are usually on the optimistic side, and may reflect what can be got out of the child by a parent who repeatedly says 'say kitty' until the child finally mimics a set of sounds which he fails to acquire and use spontaneously. The statement that the child says a word and then does not say it again for weeks or months is rather suggestive of mental retardation combined with over-strenuous efforts to teach speech. In any event, the evaluation of the quantity of a child's speech is extremely difficult for the paediatrician or neurologist, since he must attempt to judge a total vocabulary from a short interview. Certain standards are available such as those of Rochford and Williams (1964), but require periods of time and experience of the method which most physicians will lack.

Defects of Voice

Abnormal Phonation

Either aphonia (more properly, hypophonia) or stridor may be due to paralysis of the innervation of the larynx, particularly of the recurrent laryngeal nerve. Hysterical aphonia is well recognised but is one of the less common psychosomatic manifestations in childhood. Hypophonia must be distinguished from whispering, which a normal child may do more or less as a game, or because of shyness. Excessively loud speech often indicates a mild or moderate degree of hearing loss (usually conductive) in adults, but the tendency to shout occurs so frequently among normal children that this sign is of limited value. Autistic children are frequently mute but often go through a stage of loud screaming as their only vocalisation, usually after 2 or 3 years of age. Variation of pitch during speaking and variation in stress and rhythm (intonation and inflexion) are important clues, although not specific. Speaking or vocalising in a steady monotone is characteristic of deaf children, but is also encountered with some of the developmental 'aphasias'.

Abnormal Resonance

A nasal quality of speech is the principal abnormality of resonance which is encountered. Actually, there are two different types of nasal speech. Palatal paresis results in incomplete closure of the palate against the pharynx and in increased nasal escape, so that *d* is pronounced as *n* or *ng*. Anatomical obstruction, such as with a common cold or enlarged adenoids, results in diminished nasal escape and *n* and *ng* become *d* and *g*.

Dysarthria

Dysarthria is best defined as abnormal sound production due to local structural anatomical abnormalities, or due to neurological abnormalities which affect the functions of the lips, tongue and/or palate. There are thus two main types of dysarthria.

Structural Dysarthria

This is based on visible anatomical defects such as cleft lip or palate, missing or widely separated incisors (a common cause of lisp), disproportionate size of the palate, the tongue, or the pharynx, and very rarely on tongue-tie. Milder degrees of malformations may be compensated by an intelligent child who hears correct spoken language and whose other essentials for speech are normal. However, when a relatively mild anatomical variation is associated with a neurogenic, psychogenic or environmental problem, the two together may cause a greater degree of dysarthria than either would separately.

Neurogenic Dysarthria

This may originate in the lower motor neurone, as in palatal paralysis due to old poliomyelitis, diphtheria, Guillain-Barré syndrome, or injury to the palatal nerves at tonsillectomy. Nuclear agenesis (Moebius' syndrome) can also result in dysarthria if bulbar nuclei other than the facial are involved.

54

'Spastic speech' and 'athetoid speech' are the two principal dysarthrias resulting from affection of the upper motor neurones. These are difficult to describe, but those gifted at mimicry can produce characteristic versions, and the physician who has heard a sufficient number of cerebral palsied patients speak can make a tentative diagnosis even from a telephone conversation with the patient. The normally sluggish jawjerk is likely to be exaggerated if a speech defect is based on spasticity, but there is little other possibility of documenting spasticity as one would do in the case of the musculature of the limbs. Unilateral spasticity, as in hemiparesis, has relatively little and short-lasting effect on articulation. Most examples of so-called athetoid speech involve more than one disability. Dystonia of the trunk may interfere with the provision of a uniform flow of air to the larynx and with its initiation and checking by the intercostal muscles. This type of speech is usually contorted and relatively guttural, suggesting that dystonia of the pharyngeal musculature may be even more important than athetosis of the tongue and facial muscles, although all clearly contribute. A constantly open mouth and involuntary drooling are further indications of impaired control, yet there is no actual paralysis and the patient can keep his mouth shut on command and by concentration, so long as he is not trying to do anything else.

A supranuclear paresis of the bulbar musculature described by Worster-Drought (1956) as congenital suprabulbar paresis can result in a dysarthria very similar to that of athetotic cerebral palsy, but without any affection of musculature elsewhere in the body. Bosma (1965) has mentioned cases in which dysphagia and dysarthria have been associated with defective stereognosis and 2-point discrimination on the lips, tongue, and buccal mucous membranes. These cases are doubtless rare but investigation of sensation in patients with speech defect may prove illuminating in the future.

Secondary Speech Disorders

Ingram (1964) includes in this class abnormal speech which is based on mental retardation, hearing loss, the various developmental aphasias, psychological factors, unfavourable environment, very possibly habit, and more often than not on combinations of two or more of these factors.

'Specific Developmental Speech Disorders'

Ingram divides these into difficulties with the medium (vocalisation) and difficulties with language. The latter group obviously corresponds to the developmental aphasias to be discussed subsequently. Ingram designates as dyslalia one type of the former difficulty, in which the patient is able to imitate sounds and syllables more accurately than he can produce them on his own initiative. Disarticulation is more severe in respect to those sounds recently learned than to those acquired earlier, but early nursery rhymes are likely to be more primitive than texts which have been learned in later childhood.

There may be a second type of difficulty with the medium, as opposed to difficulty with language itself, in which the patient is unable to copy correctly a sound or word said to him, although he may produce all the sounds of spoken language

55

correctly at one time or another, frequently in the wrong word. Morley (1957) and Brain (1961) have called this 'developmental articulatory dyspraxia'. Other types of apraxia are sometimes, but not invariably, found on neurological examination of such patients. Some authorities deny the validity of this category of articulatory dyspraxia.

Dysrhythmia

Stuttering is by far the commonest dysrhythmia of childhood. Best current opinion does not differentiate stuttering, stammering, and related terms, but includes as 'stuttering' hesitation or difficulty in starting or stopping speech, usually with reduplication of the initial sound, or less frequently of an internal or terminal sound. This is probably based on defective coordination of the respiratory component of speech with other speech activities. The degree to which it is psychogenic is hotly debated, but stuttering can be stated to have very little organic neurological implication. The examiner will want to remember that a certain amount of normal non-fluency is to be expected in the case of pre-school children. This may occur in as many as 50 words per 1000. It is generally believed undesirable to direct particular attention at this.

Scanning speech is the other dysrhythmia which immediately comes to mind and which is most important as a cerebellar sign. It results from alternate acceleration and deceleration of speech, so that it first drags and then speeds up in an explosive fashion. This may be obvious from careful listening, but having a child recite the alphabet or count to 100 is frequently a better way of bringing it out.

Speech Which is Deficient in Quantity

Any of the defects of voice, articulation, or rhythm described are compatible with a normal quantity of speech in terms of vocabulary, syntax, and even of conversational ability with a patient and sympathetic listener. Other children, in contrast, may pronounce sounds or words normally but speak substantially less than normal children of the same age (often, but not invariably, the quality of speech is also atypical in some way). This is one of the commonest problems brought to a paediatric neurologist and also to many paediatricians, and its evaluation is one of the physician's most difficult tasks.

Causes of Abnormal Quantity of Speech

1. Deafness, either sensorineural or conductive. Hearing losses less than 30 decibels, or possibly even more, rarely have much effect on the quantity of speech.
2. Defects of central auditory transmission. As a hypothesis one may suggest that some patients have normal function of the middle ear, cochlea and acoustic nerve, but are abnormal at some more central level such as the cochlear nuclei, the superior olives, trapezoid bodies, inferior colliculi or medial geniculate bodies. Documentation of this hypothesis is almost entirely lacking, but one can conceive of an increased ratio of noise to signal, of distortion of the signal, or of temporal disarrangement of the series of signals, as well as of defective coding itself. Such patients would be expected to behave much like deaf persons, except perhaps in regard to inconsistency of audio-

metry by current methods and possible retention of some low level auditory responses.

3. Defect of central auditory perception. Again, as a hypothesis without documentation, there might plausibly be a disability of short-term memory, of analysis of temporal sequence, or of association of such sequences of sounds with objects, acts and ideas previously experienced. The suggestion has also been advanced that patients who do not perceive and associate auditory input normally, tend to shut it out by some process of descending central inhibition comparable to the ability of all of us to become unaware of the sound of an electric fan in the room, or of a mother to sleep through the noises of motor vehicles passing in the street, only to waken immediately to the much fainter crying of her baby.

4. Motor disabilities or anatomical defects. These would have to be extremely gross in order to abolish speech totally. The amount of speech may be considerably reduced, but dysarthria is usually the most severe manifestation.

5. Mental retardation.

6. Aphasias.

7. Autism, elective mutism, and other psychiatric disturbances.

8. Environmental and situational causes.

Diagnostic Clues

General Clues

Table II summarizes the historical statements and clinical observations which most frequently follow certain characteristic patterns among children whose deficit of speech is due to deafness, aphasia, mental retardation or psychiatric disease. It should be emphasized that many exceptions to these correlations exist and paradoxical findings are often encountered.

Specific Clues to Deafness

This is usually an easy diagnosis although frequently suspected by parents earlier than by paediatricans. The lack of response to sound is not absolute, for almost no-one is sufficiently deaf to ignore a telephone ringing 6 inches from his head, or a jet aeroplane breaking the sound barrier overhead. It is also worth asking whether the child responds to sounds which include vibration, such as the slamming of a door, because failure to respond to these implies some more central problem than sensori-neural deafness. The predilection of deaf children for watching the faces of others is well known and their alert expressions immediately impress one. Earliest infantile babbling is normal in time and quantity but soon deteriorates by 7 or 8 months of age if it is not converted to the next sequence in development. This may also be true of mentally retarded children, although the age of beginning to babble is often delayed in those circumstances. Experienced audiologists can usually obtain quantitative audiograms from peripherally deaf children with ease and consistency, by almost any of the current clinical methods.

TABLE II

Clues as to Causes of Delayed Speech

NORMAL	PERIPHERAL DEAFNESS	'CONGENITAL APHASIA'	'PSYCHIC DEAFNESS' (AUTISM)	MENTAL RETARDATION
Reactions to Sound				
turns toward or startles	only if loud	inconsistent: frequently delayed	inconsistent, delayed; responds to *absence* of sound	normal; rarely delayed
listens projectively	only if loud	no	no	may: short attention span
responds to imitation of own sounds	yes (unless severe)	yes	is disturbed, stops babbling	yes
no echolalia	no echolalia	variable	frequent, especially to whisper	sometimes
Reactions to Gestures				
responds	very much so	not usually	no	yes
uses gestures himself	very much so	may or may not	symbolises 'internally' only, if at all	yes
reacts to movement	excessively	not usually	insensitive	yes
watches faces and lips	very much so	less than deaf	avoids faces	only normally, or less
Sensory Reactions				
to visual cues, shadows	excessively	may ignore or delay response	may avoid, or delay	normal or diminished
to touch	excessively	relatively insensitive	ignores (even pain at times)	normal or diminished
to tapping or vibration	excessively	confused, erratic	ignores	often excessive

TABLE II   (Contd.)

Clues as to Causes of Delayed Speech

NORMAL	PERIPHERAL DEAFNESS	'CONGENITAL APHASIA'	'PSYCHIC DEAFNESS' (AUTISM)	MENTAL RETARDATION
Vocalisation				
spontaneous babble at 6 to 8 months	normal but soon lost	variable; none or soon lost	often none	normal or delayed
later babble for pleasure	none, but not mute	none, but not usually mute	none; may be totally mute	usually
vocalises for attention	yes	often not	no	yes
normal intonation and inflexion	no	variable	no	normal or partially reduced
jargon (appropriate for age only)	abnormal, monotonous	meaningless	no	usually
laughs and cries	diminished monotonous	diminished; whines	depressed to absent	yes
Motor Function				
coordination of hands	normal	usually clumsy	abnormal mannerisms	often clumsy
gait	shuffles feet (no auditory feedback) ataxic if vestibular damage	often delayed	not delayed; circling movements of body; walks on toes	often clumsy; milestones often late, not always
Social Responses				
normal maturity	immature	immature	immature to none	immature
normal personality	relatively normal	indiscriminate; not shy; lacks depth; perseveration; distractibility; inhibition poor	bizarre; lack of affect; fascination by spinning objects; prefers objects to persons; desire for ritual, routine, and 'sameness'	may be odd but less bizarre than in autism

Clues to Central Auditory Defects of Transmission or Perception

This group probably includes the majority of so-called aphasic children. Response to sound is abnormal, but less consistently so than with deafness of the type discussed in the preceding paragraph. The child is inconsistent in his reactions to sound, may ignore louder sounds but respond to faint ones, and is often described as seeming to hear more on some days than on others. Audiometry is difficult and frequently gives inconsistent results from one trial to another. If the electrodermal test is used, in which alterations in skin resistance are measured following presentation first of sounds followed by electric shocks, and then of the sounds alone, the child often proves difficult to condition and the wave form of the changes in skin resistance is distorted or difficult to interpret.

Even electroencephalographic audiometry has its limits. The elicitation of a startle reaction to movement or a K complex in response to a sound does not indicate that it is transmitted in normal quality and in a form 'recognisable' at a conscious level. This argument is equally true of study of electroencephalographic potentials evoked by clicks and other sounds, using techniques of computer averaging. An initial problem is that the evoked response is best demonstrable from the vertex of the head and only less well or usually not at all from the temporal regions (in contrast to the response to a flash of light which is readily obtained from the inion or from either occipital electrode). It has been variously suggested that the response to sound recordable from the vertex represents some sort of movement of the musculature of the scalp, setting of the ears, contraction of the stapedius muscles, or even movement of the ossicles of the middle ears. Thus, it may reflect some response to sound at a level far below the temporal cortex or below the level of consciousness. Preliminary work by one of us (R.S.P.) in testing a small number of children in a school for aphasics suggests that most of them have some recordable evoked electroencephalographic response to sound, although this may be qualitatively different from that of normal children.

Conditioning experiments in which pairs of stimuli of sound and light are presented at irregular intervals, and then followed by sound alone, have so far failed to demonstrate conditioning in the small number of aphasic children tested, but this is a difficult technique even with normals and much further work is required before it can be applied clinically. If such a defect of association can be demonstrated in terms of conditioning, this might however help to differentiate those 'aphasic' children who really have central auditory imperception or defects of transmission from those who cannot associate one modality of sensory input with another or perhaps with past experience or internal language.

Aphasias

The conventional classification of aphasias most often utilised is that of Weisenburg and McBride (1935) who recognised four types:

1. Predominantly receptive
2. Predominantly expressive

3. Amnesic (this would be the same as what is sometimes called nominative or nominal aphasia and is thought by some to be a subtype of 1)
4. Expressive and receptive.

Eisenson (1954) uses a more elaborate classification:
1. Evaluative
    a. Auditory aphasia
    b. Alexia
2. Defect of recognition (agnosia)
    a. Visual agnosia
    b. Auditory agnosia
    c. Musical agnosia
    d. Tactile agnosia (astereognosis)
3. Expressive
    a. Nominal aphasia
    b. Agraphia
    c. Defects of spelling
    d. Acalculia
    e. Paraphasia (multiple and often bizarre errors of omission or commission in grammar, word substitution, reversals of sounds or letters, spelling and usage of words in both speech and writing. These may have a counterpart in normal persons who are fatigued, emotionally disturbed or intoxicated)
    f. Dysprosody. Inability to sing or to produce a tune by humming or whistling
4. Related disturbances of expression
    a. Dysarthria
    b. Apraxia.

The two preceding classifications of aphasia may be applied with some modification to postnatally acquired aphasias in the case of children who have already learned some degree of speech. Hemiplegias of the dominant side are usually associated with aphasia in children as in adults, although the degree and speed of recovery are correspondingly greater the younger the age, unless global dementia accompanies. One often gains the impression that with children who begin with a fairly complete expressive aphasia (more often than not with a receptive component as well), this persists longest in regard to ready recall of nouns and assumes the character of a nominal aphasia at one stage of its recovery.

However, the classifications applicable to acquired aphasia in speaking people are extremely difficult to apply to the children who have never developed any speech. Some deny the existence of this syndrome (or perhaps more properly, syndromes), suggesting that so-called aphasic children are really deaf children who are also mentally retarded or brain damaged, but it is common clinical experience in all parts of the civilised world that there exists an admittedly heterogeneous group of children who are characterised by specific retardation of development of speech which is disproportionate to or not explicable by any accompanying anatomical, auditory, or motor disability (of the muscles of speech), or by mental retardation or psychiatric disturbance. Such

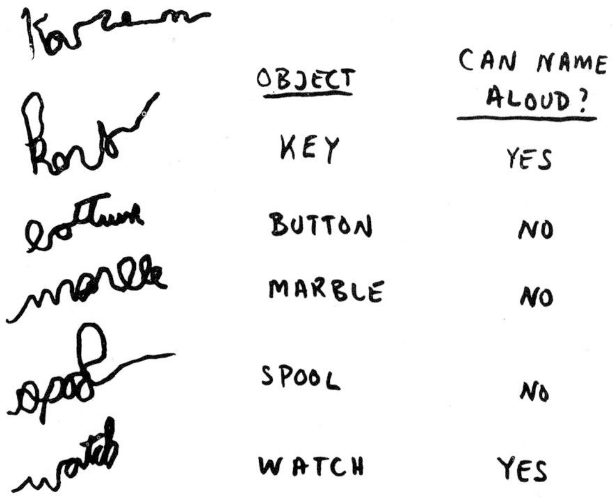

	OBJECT	CAN NAME ALOUD?
Karen	KEY	YES
Kont	BUTTON	NO
button	MARBLE	NO
marble	SPOOL	NO
spool	WATCH	YES
watch		

Fig. 1. Distorted handwriting of a seven-year-old girl with developmental aphasia. Note however that she is able to write the names of some objects shown her when she was unable to name them aloud.

patients almost always have difficulties of both expression and reception. Some difficulty in comprehension of two or three-step or of conditional verbal directions can almost universally be demonstrated on careful testing, but nearly normal understanding of what is said is sometimes encountered. Such patients may have defects of association at a cerebral level or in those regions of the brain involved in expressive speech. Difficulty in reading and writing almost always accompanies these developmental aphasias (Fig. 1).

Children of this type who have been taught by the 'associational method' are usually able to read and to write only those words which they have been taught by rote, and at least at younger ages they have difficulty in original composition of sentences. The frequent habit of drawing the object alongside its written name is evidence of experience with the technique of intersensory reinforcement of different modalities. Occasionally, such patients are able to write more than they are able to say. The reading problem in this case is, however, distinct from that of true dyslexias. Patients with developmental aphasias, as well as the larger group of children with minimal chronic brain syndromes of diffuse types, have such difficulties as right-left confusion, reversal of sequences of letters or of letters themselves, and substitution of words of similar outline shape but dissimilar meaning, such as 'which' for 'white', 'this' for 'thin', etc. However, this disability in recognising a word by sight and as a whole is most characteristic and most persistent in the case of what is usually referred to as 'developmental dyslexia' or 'specific reading disability.'

A child with a specific reading disability may be able to sound out a word by the phonic method if he has been taught this, but not unless he has received instruction or remedial reading work by this particular method. Herrman's (1959) concept of word blindness (or developmental dyslexia or specific reading disability) is that it is a constitutional disability in perception of the printed word as a whole (Gestalt), at sight, a problem which is almost entirely confined to boys and which is frequently present by history in male relatives of the patient. Some degree of difficulty with mental arithmetic and confusion of fingers or in right-left orientation is allowed, but Herrmann's view is that patients with word blindness fail to show other features of minimal chronic brain syndromes. Thus, they would be expected to lack the disproportionate depression of abilities at design copying, constructional praxis, maze tracing, etc., which stand out in comparison with overall intelligence in brain-injured subjects, and patients with a true specific reading disability ought not to show the pronounced hyperactivity, distractibility and shortness of attention span which characterise the brain-injured.

Actually, it is probable that the two syndromes (or, more properly, groups of syndromes) overlap to a degree. Perhaps the majority of children with minimal cortical encephalopathies show some initial difficulty in learning to read, because the disability in perception of designs in general carries over to the recognition of letters. Reversals of letters and the writing of letters backward are also disproportionately common in comparison with normal children. However in the majority of cases the child with a diffuse cortical syndrome will, if not also generally mentally retarded, learn to read and to write more satisfactorily than the child with specific reading disability by about the 3rd or 4th grade, at which time arithmetic and especially arithmetical problems are almost invariably his most difficult subject.

Writing is much more difficult to evaluate than reading because so much depends on the child's educational experience and the methods by which he has been taught. Children generally write better to dictation than when forced to compose the content themselves. What might appear to be a specific defect of writing ability should be accepted with caution, since true dysgraphia is rare in childhood unless as the result of cerebrovascular accidents; such cases usually reflect general mental retardation, educational backwardness because of poor or inconsistent teaching or failure of application, or else are a part of a more global disturbance of language functions. A few standards are available, such as those of Rochford and Williams (1964) for various linguistic parameters. The spelling test of Kinsbourne and Warrington (1964) was used for adults but might be adaptable for children.

Children who know or have been exposed to more than one language should be evaluated for each. In the case of acquired aphasias, it is generally accepted that the language most recently learned, a secondary tongue, is the one lost entirely or in greatest degree, and the last one to be regained. Young children exposed to two spoken languages usually learn each without difficulty and with perfect pronunciation, speaking one to their parents and the other to the family's servants (if living abroad) without confusion. However, any difficulty of whatever type, whether one of motor articulation, intellectual ability, hearing or perception, or emotional stability, usually results in failure to learn either language adequately, and in mixing them together. Thus, this tendency is not of any specific differential diagnostic value.

Psychiatric Disturbance

Infantile autism in the classical concept of Kanner is a recognised cause of failure to develop speech, but it is probable that this type of child is relatively rare and that one far more commonly sees children with mental retardation or other manifestations of cerebral abnormality who have a greater or lesser overlay of autistic behaviour. Differential diagnosis between the two is difficult, particularly at young ages, but both groups may come to the physician's attention because of failure to develop adequate speech. The experienced examiner is usually immediately struck by the child's remoteness, with his deficient or indiscriminate relationships with people and a preference for objects, and frequently by such individually non-diagnostic characteristics as a tendency to run round in circles, to walk on the toes, to arrange toys in a rigid ritualistic fashion, an obsession with spinning objects which elicit ecstatic mannerisms, or by a tendency of the child to take the examiner's hand and place it on a door knob or some other object as though it were a tool and detached from the individual.

Careful history-taking often elicits descriptions of similar behaviour, frequently with reports that the child was unaffectionate from the beginning or that he always preferred to be propped with his bottle as opposed to being held. He may have been totally mute and have failed to babble, or if he did babble, he typically stopped this type of vocalisation when anyone else imitated his sounds (normal children find this pleasurable and continue to vocalise almost as if in a wordless conversation). Later, if the autistic child speaks at all (and the presence of some degree of speech is probably correlated with a more favourable prognosis than that of the child who remains mute), his speech consists mostly of nouns. Characteristically, he asks no questions and does not use the word 'yes'. Pronominal inversion is common, with the tendency to refer to himself as 'you' or 'he' (in normal children, however, confusion of 'you' and 'I' is normal up to the age of about 3). Echolalia is often present and a word or an entire sentence may be repeated verbatim after a considerable period of time, even weeks. There may be a tendency to confuse the part with the whole, and a diversity of abnormal metaphors is sometimes present. A boy described by Rimland (1954, p.15) was once told 'Don't throw the dog off the balcony' when he was about to do this with a stuffed toy, and ever afterwards used this entire phrase as a substitute for 'No'. The experienced paediatrician or the neurologist accustomed to working with children can often become very astute at recognising autistic behaviour, but it is superfluous to mention that psychiatric consultation is always indicated.

Environmental and Situational Causes

It is generally recognised that the baby or young child who is institutionalised for a long period of time with a minimum of stimulation may fail to develop appropriate language. This possibility applies equally to the child who lives in an uncommunicative home where no-one speaks to him and in which he receives a minimum of personal attention and cultural stimulation. A different situational type of delayed speech may be encountered if the child has all his needs anticipated for him so that he has no need to ask, or if ill-advised pressure has been applied to teach him to speak. These situations are most often seen with the youngest child of a sibship, particularly if much younger, so that he is treated as a doll or as a baby by the others, gains certain benefits in this manner, and comes to act the part. This part, of course, includes not speaking and sometimes not being toilet-trained as well. It is probable, however, that anticipation of a child's needs by his parents has much less effect in delaying his own speech than the parents usually suppose. This type of situation doubtless forms the basis of many cases of 'simple delayed speech' in which no other neurological or psychological or audiological abnormality can be detected, and in which the child eventually learns to speak more or less normally, usually whether anything is done about it or not. Other cases remain unexplained and are due to causes presently unrecognised.

The Need for Periodic Re-evaluation

Definitive classification of children with defective acquisition of language is notoriously difficult, and the diagnostic acumen of even the most experienced examiner is limited. Every such patient should receive a thorough neurological examination with special attention to the more subtle signs of minimal cerebral dysfunction, a detailed psychological evaluation, audiometry by whatever methods are available and applicable and usually a psychiatric consultation.

With children of pre-school age, a definitive diagnosis is more often than not impossible. A trial of education in a special school setting for the deaf or for the aphasic (if this is available) may furnish important diagnostic evidence. Children who fail to respond to instruction by competent teachers over a reasonable period of time, using accepted methods, usually prove to have associated neurological handicaps or to have been misdiagnosed or misclassified. Thorough re-evaluation at intervals of a year or two is essential in the case of all children who are not coming along as expected in the educational setting in which they are placed. These therapeutic trials of special education may be in the long run the most useful diagnostic tools.

CHAPTER VII

Special Tests of Cerebral Function

The Purpose of the Tests

Many of these tests will be performed poorly by children with known neurological disorders. For example, most children with spastic cerebral palsy, although not the dyskinetic group, perform poorly on this group of tests, as do some epileptics. However, it is in the recognition of 'minimal cerebral dysfunction', 'minimal chronic brain syndromes' or 'minimal brain damage' that detection of the irregularities of higher cerebral functions is of paramount importance.

The major testable facets of cerebral function include motor activity, mental ability (thought and learning), cortical sensation, and electrical activity. The corresponding overt deficits are cerebral palsy, mental deficiency, cortical blindness or deafness, and epilepsy, respectively. Corresponding sub-clinical abnormalities may be conceived as existing in each area: general awkwardness, borderline or non-certifiable mental retardation or irregularity of learning ability of 'organic pattern,' perceptual irregularities, and EEG abnormality without actual fits. Clinical and sub-clinical abnormalities in the different spheres of cerebral function potentially exist in any combination, the number of permutations running into hundreds, each affected child being almost invariably in some way different from the others. As much as four or five per cent of the general school population may show some degree of this problem, which is frequently but not invariably severe enough to occasion referral for medical evaluation. The parents' or teachers' complaints are usually of poor performance at school in comparison with what might be expected from full-scale intelligence quotients, of inability to sit still or to concentrate in the class room, or of difficult behaviour. This group of symptoms may of course be psychogenic, but many such cases have an organic component, although nearly always with an emotional overlay. It is plausible that children with irregular or less than optimal cerebral function will cope less effectively with the difficulties of growing up, and thus be more subject to neurotic or other emotionally-determined behaviour problems. Children of this type are frequently encountered in child guidance clinics, juvenile courts, and school classes for the emotionally disturbed. It is often difficult to decide whether the emotional difficulties are an overlay or the origin of the problem.

The physician who tests only knee jerks and other conventional neurological signs will seldom find anything helpful, but testing higher cerebral functions in some depth will often be diagnostically useful, although a directly treatable cerebral lesion is seldom found. The clinical psychologist and electroencephalographer will probably find abnormality oftener than the clinical physician. Minimal chronic brain syndromes have been much discussed in the medical literature of recent years (Wigglesworth 1961,

Paine 1962), and irregularities of the type discussed have been found disproportionately frequently in groups of children with behaviour disturbances (Bender 1955, Laufer
and Denhoff 1957), child guidance clinic populations (Hanvik 1961), children with
special learning disorders at school (Boshes and Myklebust 1964), clumsy children
(Walton *et al.* 1962), and among high-risk groups such as premature infants (Knobloch
and Pasamanick 1959).

The relationship of these 'organic' irregularities to the developmental dysphasias
and to reading disabilities is difficult to define, but the various diagnostic entities overlap to a considerable extent. In the present authors' experience, most children with
developmental aphasias show abnormalities of cerebral function in a number of the
other areas outlined. 'Specific reading disability' may exist in some instances as almost
a 'pure culture' of poor reading without other difficulties, the condition then occurring
almost entirely in males and often with a dominant family history. Difficulty in reading
is, however, a component of many broader chronic brain syndromes, and even in the
hereditary male type is often associated with difficulty in mental arithmetic, in right-
left orientation, and in finger gnosis (Herrmann 1959).

Further research and study of minimal cerebral dysfunction and further collabora-
tion between physicians and psychologists is clearly needed. Nevertheless, the tests
described are clinically useful in the hands of examiners experienced enough to
interpret what is normal against what is not. It is true that a treatable condition is
seldom found and the diagnosis usually left as 'chronic brain syndrome' due to
(what ever cause is presumed) and manifest by (a listing of the disproportionate
deficits as compared with overall intellectual ability as measured by I.Q.). Even to
define the problem this far is often reassuring to parents and helpful to teachers in
planning the child's management. For more elaborate discussion of these difficult
problems, the reader is referred to the books by Strauss and Lehtinen (1947) and Birch
(1964).

Similar irregularities of perception, gnosis, coordination and behaviour are also
encountered in children with organic dementias or who have sustained cerebral injury
after the gestational or perinatal periods. Endless combinations and variations on the
different themes are encountered. The picture is further complicated by the process of
recovery, which may extend over a couple of years before the ultimate degree of
recovery is reached, although it may be arrested at any point. Repeated testing of
cerebral function is extremely distressing to these patients and also detracts from the
reliability of the tests. Testing should therefore be done by the most competent person
available and only when it is essential for making immediate plans or for following
the progress of the case.

The higher cerebral functions to be tested may be classified in categories such as
short-term memory and recall, the various linguistic functions, perception of design,
concept of body image, concept of extracorporeal space, directional orientation, praxis,
abstraction, and cerebral inhibition, although many other classifications would be possible. Most of the tests given overlap several of these functions, and the examiner must
identify the functions tested from his findings.

Methods of Examination

General

The neurological examination of a patient at any age should include an impression of the patient's alertness, his response to questions, apparent intelligence, etc. How far one pursues special tests of cerebral function depends principally on whether there is any reason to suspect abnormality on the basis of the chief complaint, past medical history, or other areas of the physical examination, and also on whether or not referral for detailed psychological evaluation is planned. If experienced clinical psychologists are readily available and such testing is contemplated, it is wiser for the physician not to attempt to do in a relatively inexperienced and subjective manner those tests which the psychologist will do better and in a quantitative way. Giving a child advance experience of subtest items from standard psychological tests detracts from the accuracy of their use as part of a complete Binet or WISC test. However, many of the tests to be described in this chapter overlap the areas of competence of physicians and psychologists, and clinicians may quite properly make use of them in the absence of resources for psychological referral, or in order to decide whether such referral is required. While the tests all study functions which are selectively and disproportionately depressed (in comparison with overall ability) in the presence of organic encephalopathies, particularly cortical lesions, a disproportionate depression can only be determined in comparison with the overall formal full-scale I.Q., which usually limits the use which physicians make of this type of test.

Orientation in Space and Time

Orientation in space and time may be tested in older children much as with adults, although impaired orientation is rarely seen as a major specific deficit in conscious children who are not demented generally. Also, it is difficult to state whether or not a child of a particular age should know the day of the week or month, or the name of the hospital.

General Information

General information may be evaluated by asking the child questions such as the name of the President or Monarch or various questions from history or geography as taught at school. Obviously the standard of normal response to be expected depends on the child's age, intelligence, home background and educational experience; this type of enquiry is seldom worth pursuing very far, since other tests described below are of greater diagnostic value.

Memory

Long-term (rote) memory is tested by asking for the patient's home address or telephone number, or for the names and ages of his siblings. Testing of short-term immediate memory is more important, and is done by asking the child to repeat a series of digits spoken to him, or a series of words of one syllable. Both forward and backward repetition should be tested, since the latter is disproportionately depressed in many organic brain syndromes. The standards of normal for children are not yet well worked out. As an approximation it may be stated that the average six-year-old can repeat five digits forwards and two or three backwards. A ten-year-old should be able to repeat at least six forwards and four backwards. Another test of immediate memory. which also tests comprehension of spoken language or printed material, is to ask the child to repeat or paraphrase the sense of a story or paragraph. Ability at paraphrasing depends greatly on the amount of experience and training which a child has had in this task.

Tests of Language Function

Testing of the child's ability to understand spoken language and evaluation of his speech are considered in the chapter on Speech. If abnormality of speech or of comprehension of spoken language is present, or if there is any reason to suspect difficulty in reading or writing from the history as given, the understanding of written language and the ability to write or print should also be compared and the degree of relative deficit in each area contrasted. Purely expressive aphasias are rarely, if ever, encountered in childhood, and there is practically always some deficit of comprehension of spoken speech and also some difficulty in reading and writing. Reading is best tested with a child's book appropriate to his age and level of intelligence, but another useful tool is a set of 'word-game' cards, half of which bear outline pictures of common objects and the other half the printed names. One can thus find out whether the child can read the printed words, whether he tends to substitute a word of similar outline 'shape,' and whether he may be better able to match word and picture than to read the word aloud.

Mental Arithmetic

Simple problems in addition, subtraction, multiplication or division may be given, but one must know in testing this whether the child has been taught to say 'six minus two' or 'six take away two', etc. One also finds nowadays that the majority of children are taught the multiplication table only through tens, not elevens or twelves.*
Arithmetical ability is selectively depressed compared with other intellectual functions in many chronic brain syndromes (also in some normal people!), and such patients show greater difficulty with problems than with sums and differences. Thus, a child may be able to say that four times five is twenty but be unable to tell what four pencils should cost at five cents each.

Other tests fall chiefly into two areas, those involving some type of gnosis (perception and recognition) and those involving praxis (the performances of acts involving either a learned skill or conscious planning).

Gnosis

Adaptation of Methods of Examination of Sensory Function

The chapter on sensory examination describes the method of testing for stereo-

---

*Most British children still learn the multiplication table up to twelves.

gnosis using small common objects to be manipulated by the patient in his hand. The naming of common objects as shown to the patient, or from more or less simplified pictures, is an adaptation of the same idea. Auditory gnosis may be tested by asking the child to identify such sounds as a rattle, whistle or bell. Very occasionally, this ability may be preserved in the presence of visual agnosia. In the case of children with developmental aphasias, auditory gnosis for sounds is relatively better than for words. Another applicable test which is really part of the sensory examination is that for graphaesthesia. The child is asked to identify arabic numerals 'written' with some blunt object on the palm of the hand or on some other part of the body. Tactile inattention, displacement and extinction should also be tested for, as described in the chapter on sensory examination (Chap. XIII).

Tests of Perception

Patients with cortical encephalopathies will usually have difficulty in recognising shapes or patterns, and recognising the relationship of the parts of a figure to one another and to the 'whole' (Gestalt) which the parts make up. Tests of design copying or of reproduction of designs from memory involve both Gestalt perception and praxis, and, particularly, visual motor coordination. Perception may be more specifically tested by asking the patient to indicate which of several closely similar geometric designs is different from the others or to match identical pairs in a duplicate set of such figures. Perceptual ability is more critically tested if two figures are presented simultaneously (Kinsbourne and Warrington 1962). Discrimination of figure from background may be especially difficult. The standard test plates for examination of colour vision may be used if the child is not colour blind. The H-R-H pseudo-isochromatic plates published by the American Optical Company, Buffalo, New York, contain circles, X's, and triangles which are identifiable by young children who do not know the arabic numerals of the Ishihara plates. Frostig (1961) has published a group of tests on perception of shape, of figures versus background, and of spatial relationships. Other tests requiring perception of hidden figures have been described by Werner and Strauss (1941) and by Teuber and Rudel (1962). Halstead's (1947) battery has been used more with adults than with children. Birch and Belmont (1964) have developed a test of perception of auditory Gestalten in the form of grouped tapping sounds.

Children with cortical encephalopathies often appear to fail tests of colour vision because of confusion of figure with background.

Concept of Body Image

Corporeal awareness or 'body image' as a concept is beyond the scope of a volume such as this, and lies more in the field of philosophy or experimental psychology. Nevertheless it is particularly poor (more often underdeveloped than distorted) in children with chronic brain syndromes and its testing is clinically useful. Perhaps the earliest evidence of a concept of body image is the child's manipulation of himself and his cooperation in being dressed by his mother. Later, at least by 21 months and frequently as young as a year, the child will point to various parts of his body when asked 'where is your nose?' etc. by his parents. In their initial form, these are probably conditioned tricks comparable to playing pat-a-cake and it is difficult to say when they evolve into a real concept of the body. With slightly older children, a simple method of testing is to ask the child to point to various parts of his body or face as the examiner names them, or to ask the child to name them himself as they are pointed at or touched by the examiner.

Identification of fingers is more difficult than that of other parts and a child under six or seven can rarely identify any digits other than the thumb and little finger. Having to point out the fingers of the examiner or of a glove rather than the child's own finger renders the test more critical. Finger agnosia is a part of the Gerstmann syndrome associated with lesions of the dominant parietal lobe, but this is rarely encountered in childhood. Herrmann (1959) reports finger agnosia in children with specific reading disability ('word blindness').

Orientation for Right and Left

Bergès and Lézine (1963) have published normative data on the ages at which normal children can be expected to distinguish right and left on themselves, on the examiner, etc. There is, as would be expected, considerable variation, but most paediatricians are aware that a normal child of six is doing well to differentiate his own right and left consistently and may not be able to do so for other persons for another one to three years. Drill sergeants in the army might even extend the upper limit to 18 or 20, but might not call this normal! Benton (1959) has published another widely used test of right-left discrimination. It is generally accepted that to identify correctly the right and left thumb or designated finger of a pair of gloves is the most critical test, but this, like other tests of right and left, also draws on the concept of body image.

Concept of Extracorporeal Space

Tests involving directions and relative positions of people or objects, such as to the right or left, behind or in front, above or below, all investigate concept of space, which in this context inevitably involves directional orientation. Tests of reproduction of geometrical designs or of constructional praxis, and any test of drawing involving planning and orientation of a figure on a piece of paper, also approach the same problem. To request the drawing of a map of a country or city is a particularly useful test, but difficult to apply to children below adolescence. Younger children may do better if asked to draw a plan of their bedroom. The result also depends considerably on the quality of the geography lessons which the child has received. Asking a child to describe the route by which he walks to school or by which he reaches his classroom once there, is another approach.

Praxis

The word praxis implies more than merely coordination or the absence of ataxia, and refers to skilled acts which have been learnt or which require conscious thought and planning. Skills in everyday acts such as cutting up food, eating with a spoon, dressing oneself, tying shoes, etc., all involve praxis even though they become subconscious

71

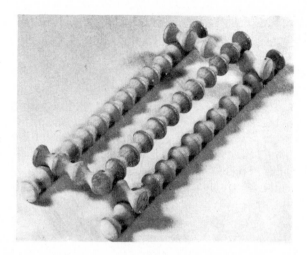

Fig. 1. Three-dimensional figure assembled from notched sticks of a child's building set. The figure is constructed without the child watching and he is then asked to make an identical one from a collection of assorted sticks, as a test of constructional praxis. This figure can be duplicated readily by the average normal six-year-old. (Some modern sets of this type have sticks of different colours for different lengths; these are not suitable since part of the task is for the child to select components of the correct length.)

with time. The examiner may evaluate the functions by direct observation or by questioning the parents.

Constructional Praxis

This may be tested by asking the child to construct a replica of a blockhouse or three-dimensional figure, using any of the sets of children's building sticks available (Fig. 1). Current versions of these sticks are made of plastic and are unfortunately colour-coded. This removes the element of selection of sticks of proper size and greatly detracts from the value of the test, so that the older uncoloured wooden version should be obtained if possible. (The Goldstein sticks used for the sorting test may also be used, as may Lincoln logs or other children's toys, but ability with playthings will vary greatly according to the past experience which the child has had with similar materials at home or at school.) This is essentially a three-dimensional version of the design copying test with pencil and paper, and involves the integration of Gestalt perception, concept of space, and of course visual motor coordination. Form boards, in which wooden squares, circles, stars, etc., are to be placed into corresponding holes in the board, are a familiar tool of clinical psychologists, but are more properly tests of perception of shape and visual motor coordination than of praxis in the strict sense. To a lesser degree this argument applies to the copying of designs (printed on cards) with the Kohs blocks. Surprisingly, assembly of jigsaw puzzles on which pictures are printed is relatively little affected in children who show marked difficulty in design perception, visual motor coordination, etc., and these do not prove to be suitable test objects. Other puzzles involving assembly of six or seven geometric shapes not bearing parts of pictures into various outline forms may be useful, however, but must be standardised by

Fig. 2. Octagon puzzle sold under name 'Euclid' (Tryne Games, Inc., Springfield Gardens, L.I., N.Y.) This can be assembled by an intelligent eight-year-old.

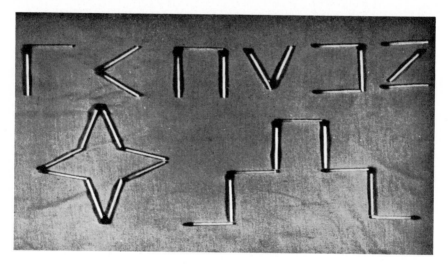

Fig. 3. Designs made with matchsticks which are used as tests of constructional praxis.

the examiner himself (see Fig. 2, the puzzle sold under the name of Euclid). Another method which may be used if no special materials are at hand is the construction of two-dimensional designs with matchsticks. Figure 3 contains examples of patterns which may be used.

Drawing

Drawing with pencil and paper is one of the most important tests to be carried out on children suspected of minimal cerebral dysfunction. The standard tests are to ask for a picture of a man or woman, and of a house; drawing an object of the child's

73

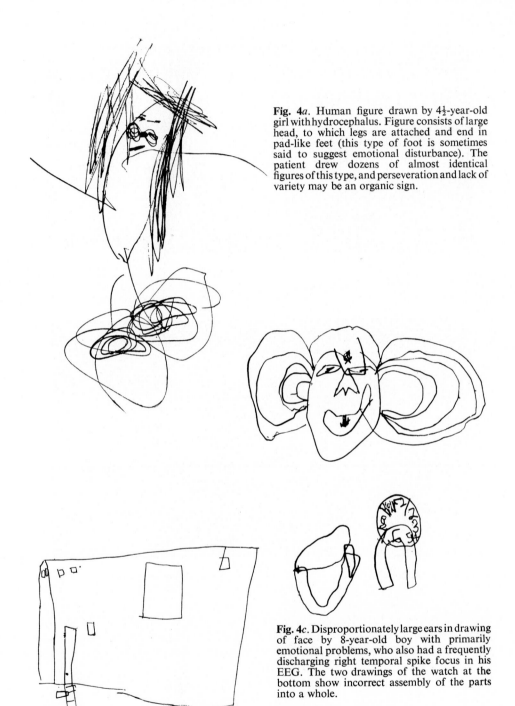

Fig. 4a. Human figure drawn by 4½-year-old girl with hydrocephalus. Figure consists of large head, to which legs are attached and end in pad-like feet (this type of foot is sometimes said to suggest emotional disturbance). The patient drew dozens of almost identical figures of this type, and perseveration and lack of variety may be an organic sign.

Fig. 4c. Disproportionately large ears in drawing of face by 8-year-old boy with primarily emotional problems, who also had a frequently discharging right temporal spike focus in his EEG. The two drawings of the watch at the bottom show incorrect assembly of the parts into a whole.

Fig. 4b. Disproportion in size of doors and windows in drawing of a house by 7-year-old with chronic brain syndrome.

74

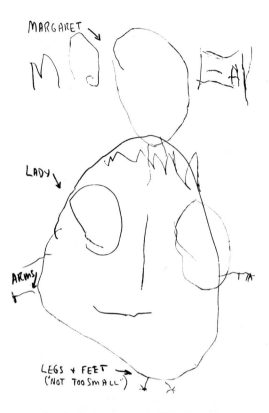

Fig. 4d. Human figure drawn by 7-year-old girl with chronic brain syndrome. Note arms and legs coming from head, with no body being drawn. The patient also attempted to write her name in a fashion reflecting difficulty in perception and reproduction of letters.

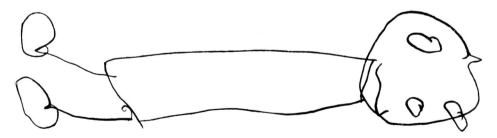

Fig. 4e. 90° rotation of human figure drawn lying on its side, but described by the patient as a drawing of a man walking upright along the street.

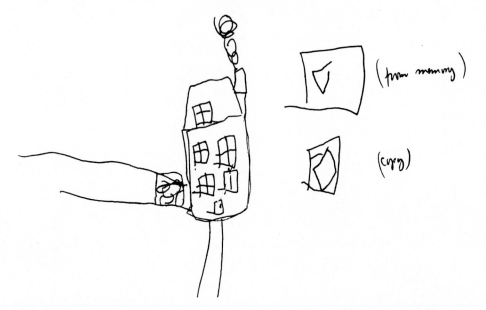

Fig. 4f. Drawing by intelligent 8-year-old with chronic brain syndrome. At right, note difficulty in reproducing diamond inside square, either from memory or by direct copy. Drawing of house reflects recent residence in France. Note also automobile lying on side in garage, with wheels up against the left hand wall.

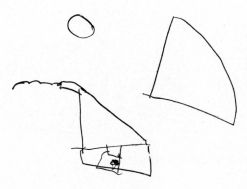

Fig. 4g. Abnormal drawing of house by 7-year-old with chronic brain syndrome. Note tendency to rotation 90° with chimney and smoke horizontal. Figure of man at top shows bifurcation of body at neck, a feature not found in normal drawings of younger chldren.

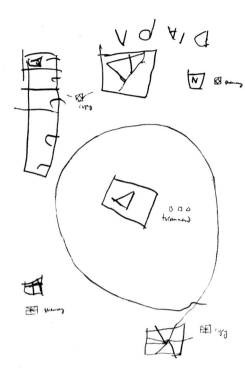

Fig. 4h. Seven-year-old boy with chronic brain syndrome writes his name 'David' with letters out of order, upside down, and backwards. There is also difficulty in reproduction of designs. A subway train is drawn standing on end at the upper left.

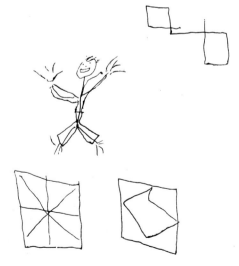

Fig. 4i. Primitive stick figure drawn by 13-year-old boy with chronic brain syndrome. Note also difficulty in reproduction of designs from memory.

Fig. 4*j*. Cartoon-like drawing of 10-year-old boy. He always chose black crayons from the set provided and consistently drew figures without arms. However, study of many drawings revealed that these were characters in an imaginary comic strip. No other abnormalities were detected and cartoon-like drawings should not be considered abnormal in themselves.

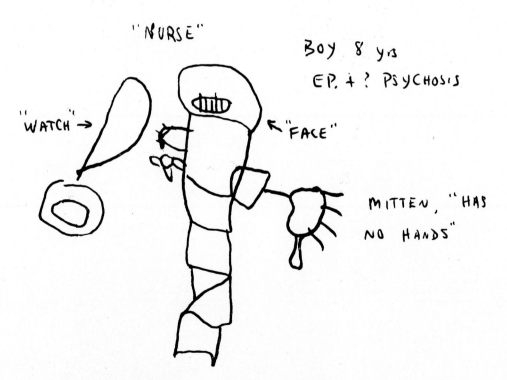

Fig. 4*k*. Bizarre drawing of figure of a nurse by epileptic boy of eight who is probably also psychotic. Note disassembly of parts of watch.

78

Fig. 4*l* (above). Drawing of human figure by schizophrenic 7-year-old boy. Lack of facial features and internal detail, and inclusion of the genitalia are features very suggestive of psychosis.

Fig. 4*m* (right). Drawings by 13-year-old schizophrenic girl. She refused to draw a human face and the two lower figures are her reluctant efforts to copy the upper sample drawn by the examiner. Note lack of facial features.

own choice is also often revealing. Drawing does not, of course, test any single function but depends on intelligence and experience, manual and visual motor coordination, and on the concepts of body image and of extracorporeal space. The 'draw-a-man' test of Goodenough has been standardised and scored as a test of intelligence, but it should be remembered that the drawing of a human figure is depressed out of proportion to overall intelligence in many children with cortical disease. Emotional disturbance and depression may also sharply reduce the number of scoreable elements of the figure, and bizarre distortions may result from either organic or functional affections of the brain (Figs. 4a-m). Children with organic brain syndromes commonly produce a drawing of a person or of a house which is closely comparable to the product of a normal child of younger age. Thus, familiarity with normal children's drawings is a prerequisite to interpretation of drawings of possibly abnormal children. On other occasions, children with organic encephalopathies will produce a type of drawing never encountered with normals, typically including features such as rotation of the whole by 90° or other angles, disproportion of parts, disassembly of the whole out of the parts, or erroneous arrangement or attachment of parts. However, the drawings of psychotic children are the most bizarre which the physician will encounter, often with such features as omission of internal detail, disassembly of the parts, or abnormal inclusion of features such as the genitalia (the umbilicus is normal) or of intestines or other internal viscera.

Design copying or reproduction of geometric designs from memory may bring to light the selective disability in visual perception of designs or Gestalten, and the deficit in visual motor coordination seen with organic cortical disease. The Graham-Kendall figures (Fig. 5) for reproduction from memory, and the Bender test of copying (Fig. 6), are standard methods of testing. If a detailed psychometric test is to be made by a clinical psychologist, the physician will do well not to give the child preliminary experience of these types of tests, but acquiring a sufficient familiarity with them to use selected parts of the tests for screening purposes may aid in determining which child ought to be sent for psychological work-up. Ability to draw is of course impaired by visual motor incoordination alone, even if this is an isolated handicap. Visual motor coordination may be tested by asking the child to make a pencil trace between converging lines without crossing them, or to place pencil dots in small circles, or to trace a figure placed under his sheet of paper.

Gestures

Gestures may also be used for a number of tests. Everyday gestures for 'yes,' 'no,' 'come here', pointing etc., are non-verbal symbols, but may or may not be misunderstood or misused in the case of developmental aphasias; they are typically ignored by autistic children, but are excessively utilised by the deaf. The test of imitation of gestures by Bergès and Lézine (1963) uses a standardised series of gestures made by the examiner and to be imitated by the child. The posture to be imitated is static, but the child has a visual observation of the manoeuvre by which the examiner puts his arms or hands into the posture desired. The test clearly depends not only on intelligence but on concept of body image and of space, and of right-left orientation as well as what may be called dexterity, coordination or praxis. It is supposed to be selectively depressed in 'brain damaged children' (probably another of the areas of especial difficulty usually involved in organic encephalopathies but without specific significance otherwise). Surprisingly, the Bergès test of imitation of gestures failed to correlate closely with the result of the Goodenough draw-a-man test or of the Grace Arthur mannequin assembly test on the same children (Bergès and Lézine 1963).

Lateral Dominance

Lateral dominance may be tested in terms of preference for the right or left hand, eye and foot. Hand preference may be tested by observation or writing or throwing a ball, or by questioning the parents. The simplest test of eye dominance is to give the child a sheet of paper with a hole in the centre, telling him to hold it with both hands simultaneously and to peep at the examiner through the hole, noting any consistent preference of one eye over the other on a number of trials. Kicking a ball is the best test of

Fig. 5. Figures to be reproduced from memory in the design memory test of Graham and Kendall. Each figure is scored on a scale from 0 to 3 according to the amount of distortion or especially of rotation or reversal. The figures are shown for 5 seconds and the child then asked to reproduce them from memory. Scoring is complicated and the test cannot be readily adapted for use as a screening instrument by non-psychologists.

81

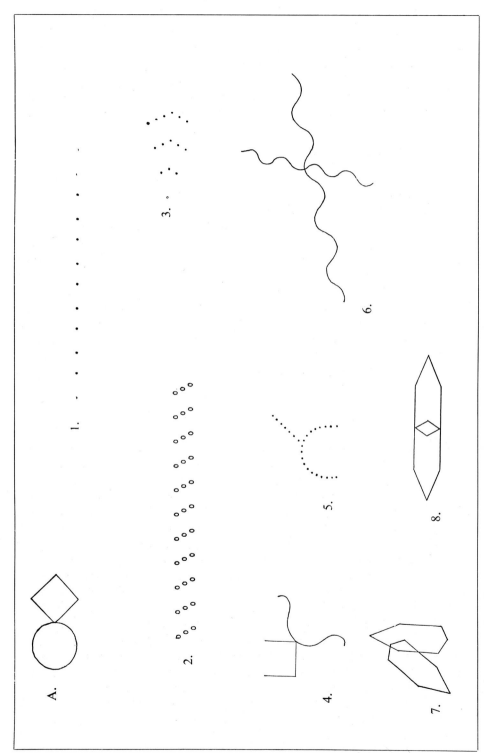

Fig. 6. Design copying test of Bender. The figures are reproduced with the original remaining in front of the patient (see discussion in text).

foot preference, but several trials of hopping on one foot (the examiner not indicating which) may be used instead. It is generally recognised that inconsistent (mixed) dominance or crossed dominance, in which one hand and the opposite foot are preferred, are commoner among children with developmental aphasias, specific reading disabilities, and almost any variety of organic brain syndrome. Thus the finding is non-specific and of limited practical importance in our present state of knowledge.

Other Tests, Especially for Younger Children

Coordination and praxis are usually evaluated together, chiefly by observation alone, in the case of very young, mentally retarded or uncooperative children. Particularly important functions to observe include walking, running, turning or changing direction, manipulation of objects in the examining room, dressing and undressing (especially buttons and shoes and socks), facial expressions, and use of gestures. Many of the standard tests of motor coordination really involve praxis as well. If testing for constructional praxis or with pencil and paper is unsuccessful or impossible, the examiner may wish to consider the child's ability to execute the finger-to-nose and similar tests, his finger movements to imitation and to command, face, mouth, and tongue movements (similarly to imitation and to command), hopping on one foot, and catching or kicking a ball. A bead-stringing game such as is sold for three-year-olds is a useful test for young children and a peg-board (a board with holes into which a number of small pegs are put) may be used for older children.

Irregularities on Psychometric Tests

Although this information may be obtained from a clinical psychologist, the physician will want to be aware of the pattern of irregularities typically shown by children with organic brain syndromes. The pattern may be superimposed on any level of formal I.Q. The scatter between different sub-tests and the discrepancy between verbal and performance I.Q.'s is enormously greater than the irregularities which may be encountered with normal people. The verbal I.Q. is typically twenty or more points higher than the performance. In other cases, the performance I.Q. may be much the higher of the two if there is some disproportionate language difficulty which falls short of an overt aphasia. The proportion of patients of these two types varies from one clinic to another, probably according to the interest of the physicians and psychologist in charge, and the nature of the population from which they draw. Abstract ability is poorer than performance on more concrete tasks. The sub-tests which involve design memory, block design, coding, numerical concepts, and classification are more poorly executed than those depending on memory. (Parents make similar reports, at least as regards memory, taking it as evidence of intelligence as a whole in all too many cases.) Short span of concentration and ready distractibility are often reported by the testing psychologist, who may also mention a childhood equivalent of the 'catastrophic reaction' of Goldstein (1942), in which the patient gives up in panic when confronted with a task at which he seems likely to fail.

83

Behavioural Features

The short span of attention and easy distractibility of the 'brain injured child' are well known. The basis of this is a subject for speculation, but it may depend in some way on a deficit of cerebral inhibition. Alternatively, the children affected may lack the subconscious ability to refer new stimuli or experiences to past experience, so determining without conscious thought whether a new stimulus is really menacing, new, or requiring exploration. The hyperactive 'brain damaged child' responds to every stimulus and moves constantly from one to another much in the manner of a normal two-year-old, but with the strength and potentiality for getting into trouble of his actual age. Span of attention, distractibility and hyperactivity may often be observed by the physician while the child is wrecking his office, or similar reports may be obtained from parents or school teachers. The ease with which such children become overstimulated, their low tolerance to frustration, and ready lapse into temper tantrums, are often obvious while the history is being taken. The pattern of behaviour is sufficiently similar in such children for its hectic quality to be recognised at a glance, and it is of major diagnostic importance. However, highly similar behavioural patterns may be chiefly or entirely psychogenic, and in any event the behaviour reflects to a considerable degree (often inversely) the efforts which have been made by parents, teachers and others to control it.

Interpretation

As was suggested in the first section of this chapter, abnormal performances on any single test in this section may well be very difficult to interpret. In making the diagnosis of chronic brain syndrome, the physician depends on the association of a number of minimal abnormal findings with (commonly) a history of past insult to the cerebrum.

CHAPTER VIII

Head, Neck and Spine

Head

Inspection

Careful observation of the child's head is one of the most important parts of the examination, although often neglected. The size is the first point to evaluate. The head should be measured along a circumference including the inion and the most prominent part of the forehead. A steel tape should be used, and several separate measurements made, of which the greatest is taken as the true value to be recorded. The table on page 86 gives head circumferences in children from 0-10 years.

Small Heads

Microcephaly is sometimes defined as a head circumference below the third percentile with a small-appearing cranial vault. What this actually means is that the examiner believes the weight of the brain to be abnormally small, and is using the circumference of the head as a parameter. Thus it is obviously of great importance whether the cranial vault is of normal outline or whether it narrows sharply toward the vertex in a 'pinhead' shape. Some authors have made a distinction between constitutional (and frequently familial) microcephaly or 'microcephalia vera', in which the head is obviously excessively small on the first day of life, and what might be considered an acquired microcephaly. The latter may be based on a failure of the brain to grow subsequent to some peri- or postnatal cerebral insult or may be a manifestation of some pathological process interfering with cerebral maturation after birth.

In very small children, the circumference of the head can be compared with that of the chest, bearing in mind that the chest should surpass the head at about twelve months of age. The heads of children who are underweight and undersized because of non-neurological diseases, or for unknown reasons, are usually closer to the normal size than are the other dimensions, if the brain within is normal. The experienced examiner will be reluctant to accept an abnormally small head as being due to anything other than an abnormally-sized brain within. An excessively small head may, as mentioned, be due either to prenatal underdevelopment of the brain or to the effect of some postnatal insult or disease process, but the large majority are in fact cases of 'primary microcephaly' in which the fundamental difficulty is undergrowth of the brain. The smallness of the skull, the early closure of the fontanelle, and the diminished prominence of the cranial sutures as discovered by palpation and by x-ray, are all secondary phenomena. Rarely, primary premature synostosis of all cranial sutures will produce a secondary microcephaly, but these cases are usually obvious because the fontanelle is closed to palpation at the time of birth, the cranial sutures are completely closed rather than merely diminished in prominence, and because papill-oedema or optic atrophy may be present. In most and perhaps in all cases of primary

TABLE III

Head Circumferences, in cm., in Children ½-10 Years of Age

BOYS Age	10%	25%	50%	75%	90%
6 mo.	42.7	43.3	43.9	44.8	45.4
9 mo.	44.5	45.1	46.0	46.5	47.1
12 mo.	45.5	46.5	47.3	47.8	48.4
15 mo.	46.3	47.1	48.0	48.5	49.2
18 mo.	47.3	48.0	48.8	49.4	50.1
2 yr.	48.1	48.7	50.0	50.4	51.2
3 yr.	48.9	49.7	50.4	51.3	52.0
4 yr.	49.5	50.3	50.9	51.7	52.6
5 yr.	49.8	50.6	51.3	52.2	52.6
6 yr.	50.4	51.0	51.7	52.7	53.5
8 yr.	51.0	51.7	52.4	53.7	54.5
10 yr.	51.6	52.2	53.0	54.1	54.7
GIRLS Age	10%	25%	50%	75%	90%
6 mo.	41.4	42.0	42.8	43.6	44.5
9 mo.	43.2	43.8	44.6	45.4	46.3
12 mo.	44.3	45.0	45.8	46.7	47.7
15 mo.	44.9	45.6	46.5	47.4	48.4
18 mo.	45.8	46.5	47.3	48.3	49.1
2 yr.	46.3	47.1	48.1	49.1	50.2
3 yr.	47.6	48.3	49.3	50.3	51.2
4 yr.	48.1	49.1	49.8	50.8	51.7
5 yr.	48.4	49.5	50.3	51.3	52.2
6 yr.	48.9	49.7	50.9	52.0	52.8
8 yr.	49.9	50.4	52.0	52.8	53.6
10 yr.	50.8	52.1	52.9	54.2	54.8

86

microcrania, the fontanelle will be completely closed at birth, but it is wise to make x-rays of the skull in every case in order to define the problem objectively.

Large Heads

Excessively large heads are also of obvious importance. Hydrocephalus, subdural haematoma, and intracranial tumour are the most important causes, but certain biochemically-determined progressive degenerations also produce enlargement of the head. The last-mentioned include the cerebral lipoidoses, the spongy cerebral degeneration of Canavan or of Van Bogaert and Bertrand (Zu Rhein *et al.* 1960) and an occasional case of metachromatic leucodystrophy. Differential diagnosis of the last group depends on special chemical investigations (see Chapter XV), but differentiation between tumour, subdural haematoma or effusion, and hydrocephalus depends more on other clinical findings. Comparison with previous serial measurements or with baby photographs may be helpful; enlargement of the head is pathological if the circumference is increasing at such a rate that it crosses the percentile lines on the normal graphs, or if it is above the ninety-seventh percentile and continues even parallel to this. However, one would be content to observe a child without taking drastic measures if the rate of increase in head circumference were decelerating.

The shape of the head as well as its size is again important: a large normal head appears quite different from the prominent forehead of hydrocephalus, with dilated veins in the scalp and frequently downward deviation of the eyes. The tension of the fontanelle, its size, and whether it is open excessively late (fifteen months is perhaps the upper limit of normal) are also important. Other information can be obtained from feeling the degree of separation of the cranial sutures and from transillumination of the head. Transillumination should be carried out as described on page 94.

Abnormally Shaped Heads

Abnormal shape or asymmetry of the head must be noted. Almost all babies in the first year of life have some degree of positional asymmetry (plagiocephaly) due to lying most of the time on one side of the head, perhaps initially to look towards the centre of the room or towards the light, rather than towards the wall. The soft infant skull soon becomes flattened on one occiput and it is then uncomfortable for the infant to lie in any other posture. Positional asymmetry is exaggerated in the case of infants who have failed to achieve sitting balance by the normal age, or in the presence of infantile torticollis. It is important to distinguish positional asymmetry (Fig. 1), in which one occiput is flatter and the ipsilateral frontal region more prominent but the two hemicrania are of equal volume, from the quite different situation in which one hemicranium is larger than the other, making one suspect intracranial haematoma or another expanding lesion on that side.

Premature primary synostosis of all the cranial sutures is rare, but synostosis of a single suture is much more common and results in an abnormal shape of the head which can be recognised very early. Premature closure of the coronal suture prevents growth of the skull in the anteroposterior direction but leaves lateral growth still possible, resulting in a foreshortened head of a shape called brachycephaly (Figures 2a, b). Conversely, closure of the sagittal suture prevents growth in the right to left

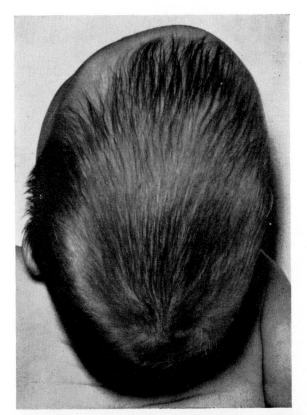

Fig. 1. Positional asymmetry or plagiocephaly.

Figs. 2a, b. Premature synostosis of coronal suture resulting in head which is short in the antero-posterior dimensions (brachycephaly).

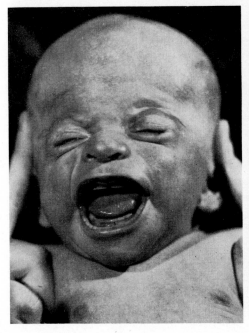

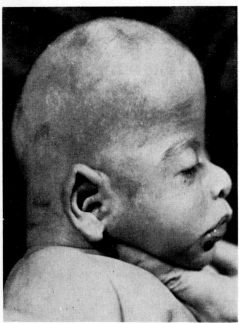

Fig. 2a

Fig. 2b

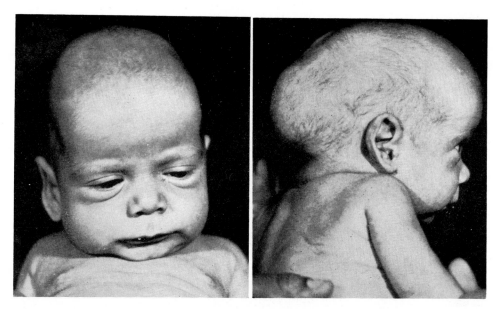

Fig. 3. Premature synostosis of the sagittal suture resulting in long, narrow head (dolichocephaly or scaphocephaly).

dimension, leaving anteroposterior growth still possible, and results in a long, narrow head, called dolichocephaly or scaphocephaly (Fig. 3). Synostosis of the metopic suture can result in a narrow anterior fossa with a prominent metopic ridge, but such findings probably more often reflect anomalous development of the frontal lobes of the brain. Premature closure of a single coronal suture produces an asymmetrical head which, however, is not difficult to distinguish from positional plagiocephaly, since in unilateral coronal synostosis the total volume of one hemicranium is obviously smaller than the other (Fig. 4).

There is currently some debate as to the necessity for neurosurgical craniectomy for the various types of craniosynostosis, but operations may at least produce an improvement in the patient's ultimate appearance and may in some cases prevent mental retardation. It is always wise, therefore, to have x-rays made of the skull and to obtain a neurosurgical consultation.

The Facies

The general appearance of the facies may in itself give the examiner his diagnosis. Many syndromes are recognisable at a glance by the experienced examiner, but ability to recognise them depends almost entirely on having seen comparable cases before. It is very difficult to take photographs which faithfully reproduce abnormal facies, but a number of attempts are given in Figs. 5a-f. Generally speaking, the 'odd-looking child' will either strike the examiner at once as being a particular syndrome, or else he will never be able to reach a firm conclusion by prolonged inspection or by trying to add up the different features to be observed. Comparison

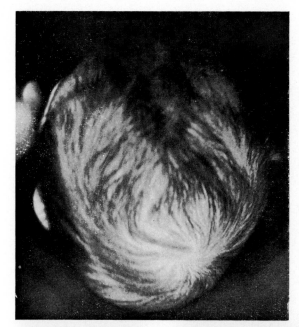

Fig. 4 (left).   Unilateral (right) coronal synostosis resulting in asymmetric head in which the whole right hemicranium is smaller than the left. This must be distinguished from positional asymmetry or plagiocephaly in which the two hemicrania are of equal content.

Fig. 5a.   Four-year-old with cretinism. Thyroid medication had been discontinued a year previously.

Figs. 5b, c.   Typical appearance of gargoylism with coarse facial features, bushy eyebrows which converge over the depressed bridge of the nose, thick lips, and enlarged liver and spleen.

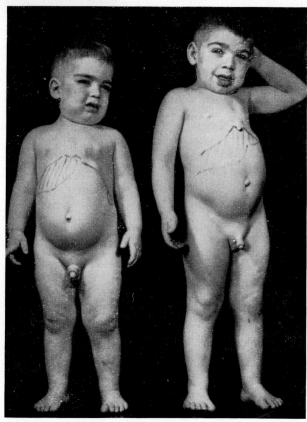

Fig. 5a

Fig. 5b

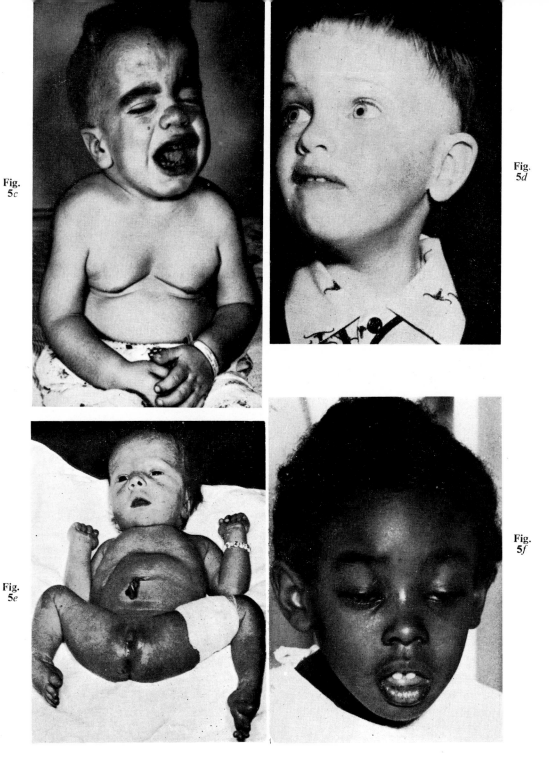

Fig. 5d. Typical case of phenylketonuria at age three, with blond hair, blue eyes, and eczema on face.
Fig. 5e. Immobile, inexpressive face of Moebius' syndrome. The facial appearance in later life is much the same as in the newborn period. Moebius' syndrome is often associated with other congenital anomalies, such as clubfeet and amyoplasia in this instance.
Fig. 5f. Bilateral ptosis and inexpressive face in five-year-old girl with myasthenia gravis.

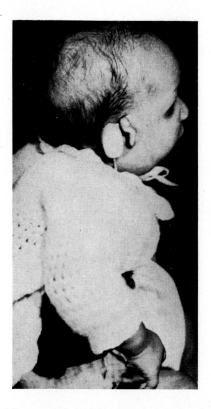

Fig. 6. Treacher Collins syndrome, with deformed external ears, conduction hearing loss, small mandible, anti-mongoloid slant of eyes, and sometimes coloboma of lower lids. Despite the odd appearance, these patients are usually of normal mentality.

with parents' facial appearances is always a wise precaution. Even if the external anomalies do not add up to a recognisable syndrome, single or multiple, they may be accompanied by an anomalous central nervous system. This is probably the basis of a considerable percentage of cases of unexplained mental retardation, but not every such combination is necessarily accompanied by mental retardation (e.g., Treacher Collins syndrome, Fig. 6), and the child may be odd-looking but bright. External ears which are abnormally low set, particularly if they are flabby to palpation and feel as though missing cartilage in their upper part, go most often with anomalies of the kidneys, but cerebral anomalies also accompany this type of ear with far greater than random frequency.

Children with unusual facies together with mental retardation or other symptoms referable to the central nervous system are obvious subjects for chromosomal studies. This procedure is time-consuming and expensive, and therefore impractical as a routine measure, but if suitable criteria are used in selecting patients for study the percentage of positive results should be much higher (see section on chromosomes in Chapter XV).

One occasionally sees local protrusions of the soft tissues of the scalp, areas of skin which look different from the skin surrounding them, cutaneous dimples or tufts of hair which appear anomalous. These seemingly innocuous lesions are often reflexions of dermoid or epidermoid tumours, dermal sinuses, encephaloceles or lipomata, and warrant the making of x-rays (which may however fail to show the possible abnormal communication between skin and subarachnoid space), and surgical consultation. These lesions may have intracranial extensions which are larger and more serious than the extracranial portion, and therefore they should in most instances be operated on by a neurosurgeon.

The prominence of the arteries and veins of the scalp varies so much from one normal individual to another that the examiner should not attribute too much importance to any but the most extreme cases. The scalp veins are often extremely prominent in cases of hydrocephalus or of intracranial vascular malformations. Considerable asymmetry of venous prominence can be normal, but asymmetry is exaggerated in the occasional hemiparesis which is due to thrombosis of the venous drainage rather than of the arterial supply (in such cases the lower limb is more severely affected than the upper, in contrast to the usual situation).

Palpation

The scalp and skull should be felt as well as looked at, although the usual findings from palpation are one or more bony prominences which eventually prove to be without significance. Bony depressions or actual openings in the skull may be felt, which may be old depressed fractures, congenital anomalies such as biparietal foramina (usually harmless unless very large), or a variety of other lesions. Local tenderness of the skull to pressure most often reflects a recent injury of some kind, but it is well to bear in mind that occipital tenderness, particularly if greater on one side than on the other, is a sign of a posterior fossa tumour which is frequently over-looked.

Auscultation

Even though important diagnostic information will only infrequently be obtained by auscultation of the head, this procedure should be carried out as part of every routine neurological examination. It should be done with a bell-type stethoscope, since the diaphragm-type does not fit closely against the child's head. A quiet room and a quiet patient are essential; the latter may require return visits to complete this part of the examination. The majority of bruits in children prove to be non-significant (Dodge 1956), and it is very difficult to give criteria for evaluation. Almost all true bruits are systolic in timing, but must be distinguished from transmitted cardiac murmurs as well as from the venous hum, which is more continuous and much influenced by a change in position of the head or by compression of one jugular vein. Systolic bruits, which are heard in the distribution of the superficial temporal artery, should be checked to determine whether they continue after digital compression of that artery.

The patient should also be asked to close his eyes, so that the stethoscope can be placed over the closed lids. At least a faint hum is normally heard, and it is not significant unless asymmetrical on the two sides (even then, this may be due to facial paresis). In evaluation of bruits which appear genuine and possibly significant, one also wants to determine whether they disappear on compression of the carotid artery on that side (although there may be sufficient collateral circulation from the opposite

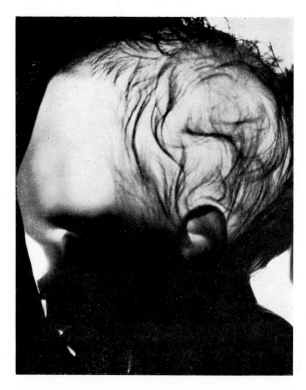

Fig. 7. Total transillumination of head in hydranencephaly. Flash-light is held behind child's head on other side and shines through to side nearest examiner. For purposes of making this photograph a small amount of light was allowed to leak to outline the head, but the test should be performed in total darkness with a close light-tight seal of the flashlight against the child's head. (Courtesy of Dr. Philip R. Dodge, Boston, Mass.)

side to minimise the effect of carotid compression). The quality of the bruit itself is one of the best criteria for the experienced examiner, since pathological bruits have a characteristic quality which is difficult to describe in words but is sometimes compared to 'footsteps in an empty church'. However, it is difficult and usually impossible to distinguish by auscultation alone the entirely innocuous bruit from that resulting from an intracranial vascular malformation or vascular tumour, or from bruits associated with hyperthyroidism, transmitted cardiac murmurs, and possibly with pyrexia alone.

Transillumination

Transillumination of the head should be a routine part of the neurological examination of all children under a year of age, and even up to two or three years of age if hydrocephalus, porencephaly, etc., are suspected. The procedure is valueless and deceiving unless the proper technique is rigorously observed. A totally dark room is essential, and it is a waste of time to attempt transillumination under other circumstances. A strong flashlight must be used, and must be fitted with a dark rubber or other light adaptor to make sealed contact with the infant's head. Finally, the examiner must wait long enough in the dark room with the child for his own

94

eyes to become adapted to the dark. Ability to transilluminate one's own hand between the distal ends of the metacarpal bones is a satisfactory criterion of dark adaptation. In transilluminating, the flashlight should be applied successively against the frontal, parietal, and occipital regions on either side, and possible total transillumination from right to left or from occiput to forehead should be checked. A small halo of light around the flashlight is normal, and the size of this depends to some extent on the power of the light. Up to half an inch may be normal in very young infants, and the normal halo is usually wider at the front of the head than at the back.

Total transillumination of the cranial vault may be due either to hydranencephaly (Fig. 7) or to extreme degrees of hydrocephalus. Porencephaly may be suspected from a large local area of illumination, but the appearance of an old subdural effusion is similar. A fresh subdural haematoma, in contrast, often reduces the normal halo on the affected side. Non-localised excessive transillumination over the frontal regions generally may reflect cortical atrophy with an excess of subarachnoid fluid, but this should be interpreted with caution. Any abnormal protruding area should also be transilluminated. Encephaloceles usually transilluminate, whereas cephal-haematomata and the moderate protrusion of the normal brain which may take place through large fused biparietal foramina do not. A final point to remember is that subdural puncture followed by leakage of subarachnoid fluid under the scalp or infiltration of fluid from an intravenous infusion in a scalp vein will produce dramatic 'transillumination', which may be largely confined to one side if the patient has been lying with that side dependent.

Neck

The neck is inspected for abnormal shortness, which may be due to an anomaly of the cervical spine or to Klippel-Feil syndrome. Webbing of the neck should also be looked for, since it suggests the syndromes of Turner and Bonnevie-Ullrich. Stiffness of the neck (see page 162, Chapter XI), with a tendency to retraction, and pain and resistance on flexion, is usually associated with meningitis or other meningeal irritation (subarachnoid haemorrhage can produce a neck just as stiff as will meningitis). Stiffness of the neck, with or without tenderness to pressure over some region of the cervical spine, may also be due to a bony lesion or an intraspinal tumour.

The posture in which the head is carried may appropriately be considered here, since this is determined by movement of the cervical spine. Turning of the head is to be distinguished from tipping. Turning properly means rotation to one side about a vertical axis without any other change in position of occiput relative to jaw. Lateral turning of the head may be due to the resultant suppression of diplopia, if caused by paresis of the lateral rectus muscle. The patient looks in the direction of a paretic muscle. Slight turning of the head may also be a compensation for homonymous hemianopia, often unknown to the patient. (Turning the head towards the hemianopic side does not, of course, actually increase the visual field, but it does place it more directly in front of the patient.)

Tipping of the head, with the chin elevated on the side towards which the face is turned, the contralateral occiput being slightly depressed, has a different significance

95

from turning. Infantile torticollis is probably the commonest cause in childhood, in which case the examiner's attempt to reverse the direction of tipping will immediately make obvious the tight sternocleidomastoid muscle on the side opposite that to which the patient keeps his face turned. Prolonged head tipping for any other reason would be followed by some secondary contracture, but the other causes of tipping rarely persist long enough for contracture to develop. Spasmodic torticollis of the type seen in adults is fortunately rare in childhood, but an occasional adolescent is encountered with spasmodic torticollis which may be psychogenic or may represent the beginning of dystonia musculorum deformans. Jerky, intermittent tipping of the head may be one form of psychogenic tic.

Head tilting or tipping is frequently not due to any type of torticollis. It may be a manoeuvre to eliminate the rotary diplopia associated with paralysis of the fourth cranial nerve or mixed diplopias due to involvement of the third and other cranial nerves. Under such circumstances there is no pain or resistance to the examiner's reversing the direction of tilt, a manoeuvre which will usually make the non-parallelism of the eyes obvious (they appeared parallel in the unreversed original tilt). Since head tilting or turning is often a response to diplopia associated with tumours in the posterior fossa, careful search for other cranial nerve signs, cerebellar signs, or signs referable to the long tracts of the brain stem is always indicated. One also sees head tilting in children with posterior fossa tumours who do not have any diplopia or disturbance of extra-ocular motility. The manoeuvre may in some way alter the hydrostatic pressures within the skull which produce headache, or reduce tension of pain-sensitive structures. Thus, unexplained head tilting should be considered a sign of posterior fossa tumour until otherwise explained, or until that diagnosis can be ruled out.

Sudden active or passive flexion of the head may cause a patient to complain of a sensation 'like an electric shock' running down his back. The phenomenon (the 'barber's chair sign' of Lhermitte) is probably based on a sudden alteration of blood supply to the spinal cord, but has a variety of causes including anomalies and injuries of the cervical spine, spinal tumours, and, in adults, a number of other diseases which are rare in childhood, such as disseminated sclerosis, spondylosis of the cervical spine, and subacute combined degeneration of the cord.

Norris and Fawcett have recently described (1965) a sign consisting of marked dilatation of the pupils during flexion of the neck with slow recovery of the previous size of the pupils afterwards. This sign was regarded as evidence of an expanding intracranial mass lesion with impending uncal herniation. In a variety of patients between the ages of 4 and 80 years the sign was found in 12 cases of proven mass lesion and in 1 case of fatal subarachnoid haemorrhage, although 18 other cases of proven mass lesions failed to give the sign, if the intracranial hypertension existed without impending herniation. The test was also negative in 105 patients with various neurological diagnoses without increased intracranial pressure, and in psychoneurotics.

Wadia (1960) has reported that manual obstruction of the internal or external jugular vein in the presence of an intracranial angioma may cause a rapid or excessive filling of these veins. This test might very well alert an examiner to the possibility of an angioma or vascular malformation causing increased venous return, but is less probable that the side of the lesion could be predicted. While the superior sagittal sinus usually drains mainly into the right internal jugular vein, and the deep cerebral circulation and the straight sinus mainly into the left internal jugular vein, there is so much normal anatomic variation that asymmetry of venous return should not be used as a definite indication of the site of any lesion.

Spine

Inspection and Palpation

Meningoceles, myelomeningoceles or the operative scars following their removal are immediately obvious. In the case of unoperated lesions, transillumination with a flashlight may help one estimate the extent to which nervous tissue is involved in the sac. The presence of a complete healthy-looking covering of skin over a sac on the thoracic, lumbar or sacral spine is somewhat in favour of a diagnosis of meningocele as opposed to myelomeningocele, and the latter is conversely more likely if there is no skin covering or if it is ulcerated, leaking, or incomplete. Demonstration of a deficit of motor or sensory function in the lower extremities of course proves the involvement of nervous tissue in the sac, and thus the presence of a myelomeningocele. However, neurological examination in the early weeks of life is very difficult to carry out in a complete quantitative way, and the lesser degrees of disability frequently escape recognition in the newborn period or even for many months afterwards.

Spina bifida occulta may be suspected from palpation and, if so, this warrants radiography, but it is not usually accompanied by neurological abnormalities. Cutaneous dimples, tufts of hair, or openings of sinus tracts overlying the spine warrant careful thought, since these are often accompanied by intraspinal anomalies. X-rays are indicated, and frequently spinal puncture with manometry or myelography, depending on the history and on other findings. This statement does not necessarily apply to the low sacral pilonidal dimples or sinuses, which are usually unaccompanied by other abnormality. Localised vertebral tenderness on palpation, particularly if the back is also carried stiffly, is an important clue to vertebral disease or to intraspinal lesions.

Posture of the Spine

Exaggerated kyphosis in the sitting posture may be due merely to muscular hypotonia, but the thought of gargoylism should cross the examiner's mind. Exaggerated lumbar lordosis in muscular dystrophy is also mentioned in Chapter X. Scoliosis is very likely to be idiopathic if it begins at adolescence: in the case of younger children a bony anomaly should be suspected and x-rays made. Scoliosis may also follow poliomyelitis (recognised or unrecognised) or any other disease producing muscular weakening. Scoliosis occurs sooner or later in most cases of Friedreich's ataxia, and is occasionally the earliest presenting sign. Finally, scoliosis should raise the question of neurofibromata of the intercostal nerves or of intraspinal tumour (although the last-mentioned far more often results in tenderness and stiffness).

CHAPTER IX

Cranial Nerves

CRANIAL NERVE 1: SENSE OF SMELL

Methods of Examination

The child is asked to occlude each nostril in turn with his finger (or the mother or examiner may do this for him) and test odours are presented first to one nostril and then to the other. The standard test odours used for adults are not familiar to most children, and special choices are limited as certain substances may irritate or induce a feeling of coolness by stimulating trigeminal endings (ammonia, preparations containing strong concentrations of alcohol, and also peppermint, menthol and camphor are thus unsuitable). Recommended test substances include oil of wintergreen, oil of roses, oil of cloves, oil of lavender, toothpaste, and asafoetida, but chocolate, oranges and chewing gum may be more useful. If the child is unable to name the odours but says he smells *something* this is sufficient evidence of sense of smell. In very young or uncooperative patients, changes in facial expression suggest the child can smell.

Interpretation

Anosmia in children is seldom significant, even if unilateral, and should not be taken as evidence of abnormality unless accompanied by other abnormalities. Apparent anosmia is usually due to a common cold, sinusitis, allergic or other rhinitis, or nasal obstruction by a polyp or deviated septum. Unilateral anosmia in adults has its greatest value in aiding the diagnosis of meningiomata of the olfactory groove, which are virtually unknown in children, or of gliomata of the frontal lobe, which are uncommon in childhood. More plausible causes of anosmia in children include fractures of the cribriform plate, old meningitis, proximal lesions of the anterior cerebral artery, lead poisoning, hydrocephalus, and hysteria. In hysterical anosmia, taste is usually unaffected, whereas reported ability to taste flavours is notoriously diminished in organic anosmia, since much of what we think of as 'taste' is actually 'smell'. In organic anosmia, irritating vapours such as from ammonia or acetic acid are readily recognised, but these are usually ignored in hysteria.

Hyperosmia is usually a manifestation of hysteria or psychosis but may be present (as also hyperacusis) in migraine and has been described in encephalitis. Parosmia (including kakosmia, the presence of a disagreeable odour) also occurs in psychic states and may follow head injuries, particularly to the region of the uncus. Olfactory hallucinations may be psychic in origin but often occur in the presence of irritative lesions in the central olfactory system. A disagreeable olfactory or gustatory hallucination is well known as the characteristic aura of an uncinate fit. Such phenomena may occur with lesions in the uncinate gyrus, in the hippocampus, amygdala, or in the neighbouring medial portion of the temporal lobe, and it is probably preferable to consider olfactory hallucinations as merely one possible component of psycho-motor or temporal lobe seizures. Such patients do not show objective loss of sensation of smell.

Central anosmia or olfactory agnosia is rare and requires bilateral lesions in the central olfactory pathways (because of partial decussation) or in their terminations in the para-olfactory area, inferior cingulate gyri, or in the uncus, hippocampal gyri or amygdaloid nuclei.

CRANIAL NERVE 2: VISION

Determination of the Presence of Vision

Proof of vision at ocular level depends chiefly on the absence on ophthalmoscopic examination (see page 108) of abnormalities inconsistent with vision, and on integrity of the pupillary reaction to light (see page 120). Constriction to light may be retained in the presence of partial (but not complete) optic atrophy but requires in addition some functional preservation of its reflex arc through the optic nerve, the ipsilateral or contralateral optic tract, a synapse at the pretectal nuclei at the level of the superior colliculi, and another synapse at the Edinger-Westphal nuclei of the third nerve, as well as of the third nerve itself. Integrity of both ocular and cortical vision is confirmed if the patient can pass one of the tests for visual acuity described in the next section, but there are also other criteria which are useful if the child is very young or mentally retarded or if visual acuity is markedly reduced.

The child can be asked to name common objects or by gesturing demonstrate their use, or locate accurately a small object in the visual field in order to touch it with the fingers. Following a light or moving object with the eyes is another easy test which requires cortical vision in man. This following reaction to light or objects may be absent because of extreme mental deficiency, but this is a problem in differential diagnosis chiefly in the case of babies, since it is absent or inconsistent only under a maturational level (for vision) of 8 weeks. This is also the case with the blink reflex to a menacing gesture such as a finger thrust at the eye (this test should not be executed with the open hand since a draught of air may then produce a blink via the corneal reflex).

Opticokinetic nystagmus may be obtained by rotating a striped drum (Fig. 1) in front of the patient's eyes, or by drawing a tape measure or strip of cloth mounted with coloured squares or figures across in front of the eyes. By use of these methods, the presence of opticokinetic nystagmus can confirm cortical vision. Opticokinetic nystagmus has been obtained in newborn infants by drawing a striped plastic canopy across the entire visual field (Gorman *et al.* 1957). It is frequently impossible to elicit opticokinetic nystagmus with uncooperative children or in cases of hysteria or malingering.

Congenital absence of vision, whether ocular or cortical, or blindness acquired in early life, is probably always associated with some abnormal eye movement at rest. Roving, large-scale and frequently disconjugate eye movements, not organised into a regular nystagmus, are typical of blindness acquired before the age of fixation

Fig. 1. Striped drum used for testing opticokinetic nystagmus.

(2 or 3 months, and may be seen in lesser degree if blindness is of later onset). Congenital nystagmus of recognised rhythmicity, whether of the jerk or pendulous type, is usually associated with diminished visual acuity, but in many cases it is difficult to decide whether the visual defect or the nystagmus is the primary abnormality. In any event, blindness acquired under the age of 2 or 3 years, and possibly up to 5 or 6, is usually accompanied by some degree of nystagmus. Nystagmus or roving movements are useful clues to visual deficits or blindness, and also in documenting early onset of visual deficit in the case of older children or adults. Uniocular blindness, acquired at any age, usually results in lateral deviation of the blind eye in the position of rest, but this must be distinguished from strabismus, whether with amblyopia ex anopsia or not. Deliberately simulated blindness is rare in children; hysterical blindness is almost always bilateral, and occurs chiefly in girls (Yasuna 1963).

Visual Acuity

The standard Snellen letter chart at a distance of 20 feet or 6 metres is appropriate for children who are familiar with the letters, and the alternative illiterate E chart can be used for others above the age of about 3. For the latter method it may be necessary for the mother to teach the child the 'game' of positioning his fingers to parallel the strokes of the E and then bring him back for definitive examination. Sheridan (1956, 1962) has pointed out some of the deficiencies of this test and has standardised a test in which the child matches letters. Visual acuity charts are also available with stylised figures of houses, boats, scissors, umbrellas, etc. Many children find it difficult to recognise these simplified figures but the test may be more successful if a small card is available containing the various possibilities, to which the child may point with his finger for identification.

Asking the child to name small common objects (marbles, dice, pennies, etc.) at various distances, or to count fingers, are less accurate but frequently useful methods. Another trick is to ask the child to locate a 2 mm. saccharine tablet which has previously been placed or is thrown, in the child's presence, onto a dark-coloured carpet. For a child three feet tall, ability to locate promptly a 2 mm. tablet corresponds to a visual acuity of approximately 20/40. In all tests of visual acuity it should be remembered that a physiological far-sightedness is normal in pre-school children and that a visual acuity of 20/20 should not be expected until 6 or 7 years of age. Even among young children of school age, the Jaeger tests for near vision are of limited usefulness, and ability to read J1 is not to be expected. Unilateral blindness or severe visual defect is very difficult to demonstrate in children not old enough to test with standard charts, but may sometimes be suspected if a child objects violently to having one eye covered but not the other.

Colour Vision

The standard tests for colour vision, such as the Holmgren test of matching coloured skeins of yarn or the Ishihara colour plates, may be applied to children. The Ishihara cards require knowledge of Arabic numerals, but through the American Optical Company one can obtain a set of pseudo-isochromatic plates in which the test figures are circles, triangles and X's. Even children as young as 3 can be got to trace these figures with the fingers if they cannot name them. Some degree of colour blindness, usually a partial defect for red-green discrimination, occurs in 5 or 6 per cent of the male population but only in 0·3 per cent of females. However, identification of a defect of colour vision is of rather limited importance in actual neurological work with children. A child with a severe defect of colour vision may need certain concessions and special handling at school to protect his morale and self respect, but such a defect is more serious in a child with some defect of learning or perception for which colour coding may be used as a reinforcing or associational cue in special educational methods.

Patients with day blindness (hemeralopia) see most effectively with the peripheral retina and of course have diminished perception of colour. Hemeralopia is uncommon in children, although it occurs with central scotoma of any cause, in the early stages of formation of nuclear cataract and in toxic amblyopias (chiefly due to tobacco and methanol and scarcely to be considered in paediatric practice), or as rare reaction to trimethadione medication.

Visual Fields

Methods of Examination

Crude testing of visual fields to rule out homonymous or bitemporal hemianopia is possible from a surprisingly early age. If a child or even a baby of about 9 months is seated in a chair or on its mother's lap opposite the examiner, the latter may then dangle two objects, one from either hand, behind the child's head and then bring one or the other forward into the field of vision, noting the point at which the child's eyes deviate towards and fix on the object (Fig. 2). This is the probable limit of the peripheral visual field. The steel case of a tape measure, dangling from its tape, may be used, but better test objects are ten-cent pieces or sixpences which have been pierced and suspended from black threads. A crude approximation of visual fields

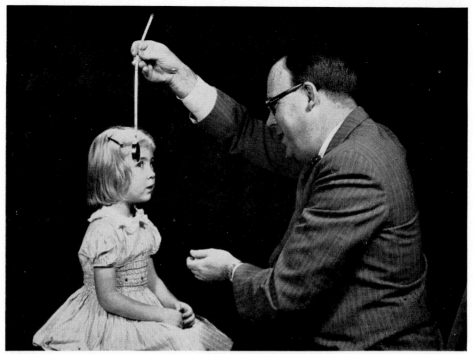

Fig. 2. Testing visual fields of four-year-old child. Patient has been looking directly at the examiner, but automatically turns her eyes towards a dangling object brought round from behind her head, as soon as it reaches the peripheral limit of the visual field.

Fig. 3. Another method of testing visual fields. The patient has been looking at the examiner and was told to point to whichever of his fingers moved (her eyes move from the midline position as soon as she points).

in very young, semi-stuporose or uncooperative patients can be obtained by suddenly thrusting a finger towards the eye from either peripheral field and noting whether the child blinks. (Use of the open hand may elicit a corneal reflex and give an erroneous impression of vision.)

A child of three years or older can sit opposite the examiner on the same eye level and fixate on a point between the examiner's eyes: the examiner then places his hands at the lateral limit of his own visual field, at a point halfway between himself and the patient, and quickly flexes one or the other (or both) previously extended forefingers, the child being asked to point to the one which moved (Fig. 3). This test has the advantage of requiring no special equipment and of detecting visual inattention (or extinction) as well as hemianopia, but it presents an unavoidably large test object and will sometimes give a falsely normal result when a hemianopia or quadrantanopia can be found by perimetry. Any of the several approximate methods of testing visual fields discussed in this paragraph can be adapted to test for bitemporal hemianopia, right or left homonymous hemianopia, as well as for homonymous quadrantic defects. The methods are most successful with both eyes open and thus do not test the fields of either eye separately, although this can sometimes be accomplished by having the child's mother or an assistant cover one of the patient's eyes.

The conventional method of testing the visual fields by confrontation, using a 2 mm. diameter white-headed pin, preferably stuck in the end of a pencil eraser to give it greater distance from the examiner's hands, can be carried out with a cooperative intelligent child of about 6 years and upward, to map approximately each visual field and also to measure crudely the normal blind spot. In the authors' experience, however, testing with a standard perimeter is seldom satisfactory before 8 or 9 years and with most models of perimeter one loses the major advantage which confrontation methods offer (that the examiner is directly opposite the child and will note immediately when the patient's eye deviates away from the desired fixation point). Tangent screen examinations and the mapping of central scotomata are still more difficult with children and usually require an age of 10 or 11. Perimetry and tangent screen examinations are usually unnecessary to find the common visual field defects of children, which are chiefly homonymous hemianopia (mainly accompanying spastic hemiparesis) and bitemporal hemianopia in the presence of tumours near the optic chiasma. However, craniopharyngiomata and tumours of the temporal lobes involving the optic radiation may initially produce only partial quadrantic defects. In cases where lesions of this type are suspected, every effort should be made to accomplish perimetry and tangent screen examination, which should include the use of red and green objects since the visual fields for these are 10 and 20 degrees smaller, respectively, than the fields for white and may show a definite abnormality somewhat earlier.

If hemianopia is suspected but cannot be definitely demonstrated, two further tests may help. In homonymous hemianopia of cerebral origin, the opticokinetic response is diminished when the stripes on the drum or figures on the cloth strip or tape move toward the cerebral hemisphere involved, and this may also be true in some cases of hemianopia of lower anatomical origin. A narrow beam of light shone into the eye diagonally from one peripheral visual field on to the opposite half of the retina only, will produce diminished pupillary constriction if presented from a hemianopic side as compared with the reaction from the normal side, *provided* the hemianopia is based on a lesion in the optic tract. This is not true, however, with lesions above the lateral geniculate, and the test is therefore of no value in the large majority of suspected hemianopias in children.

Interpretation

Regular concentric contraction of the visual fields is characteristic of optic atrophy, either primary or secondary, and also of some degenerative diseases of the retina such as retinitis pigmentosa. Extremely narrow tubular fields, which do not expand as one gets progressively farther away from the eye, are characteristic of hysteria. Hysteria is also classically held to produce spiral contraction of the visual fields with the peripheral limit of vision becoming progressively narrower as one goes round and round, but spiral fields are also highly characteristic of fatigue.

Enlargement of the normal blind spot, if the patient is old enough to be tested on a tangent screen, is typical of papilloedema and of optic neuritis. Optic neuritis more frequently produces a central scotoma, a defect also seen in toxic amblyopias and in multiple sclerosis. Caecocentral scotomata involving both the macular area and the blind spot, with loss of nearly all central vision, most frequently imply optic neuritis. Annular or ring scotomata are unusual and most frequently based on pigmentary degeneration of the retina. All the foregoing scotomata are negative in nature; i.e., unless very large, they are not perceived by the patient until the visual fields are mapped. With positive scotomata, in contrast, the patient perceives the blind spot as a dark or blind area. If not due to changes in the media, positive scotomata are usually due to choreoretinitis or colobomata of the retina or to old retinal haemorrhage or exudate. The typical scintillating scotoma of migraine is rarely described by children with this condition but a few may give a history of either spots or flashes.

Examination of the Eyes

Before examining the eye grounds the eyes themselves should be inspected for a large number of possible clues to neurological disease. Conjunctival telangiectasia (Fig. 4. Colour Fig. 3) may suggest ataxia telangiectasia as the basis for the child's ataxic git. (Telangiectasia also occur on the ears—Fig. 5). Kayser-Fleischer rings may be visible as a green-gold or muddy yellow-brown discolouration in the inner layer of the peripheral cornea (Colour Fig. 1) (the differential diagnosis from arcus senilis does not have to be considered in children) but slit lamp examination should be carried out if Wilson's disease is really suspected. Brushfield spots (Colour Fig. 2) are white or yellowish dots of less than a millimetre's diameter which are arranged in a ring around the irides, concentric with the pupil and located somewhat nearer the border of the irides than the pupils. They are seen in a fair percentage of normal children, but are particularly characteristic of mongolism, in which they appear in more than ninety per cent of cases, although they tend to disappear with age and are often not detectable above six years. Brushfield spots are either

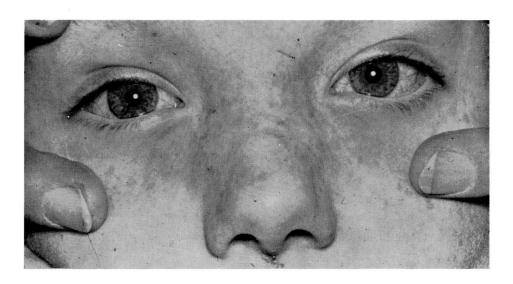

Fig. 4. Conjunctiva in ataxia telangiectasia.

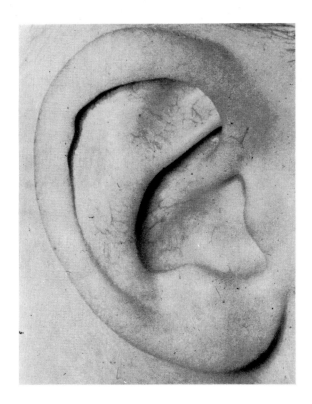

Fig. 5. Telangiectasia on ear, in a case of ataxia telangiectasia.

105

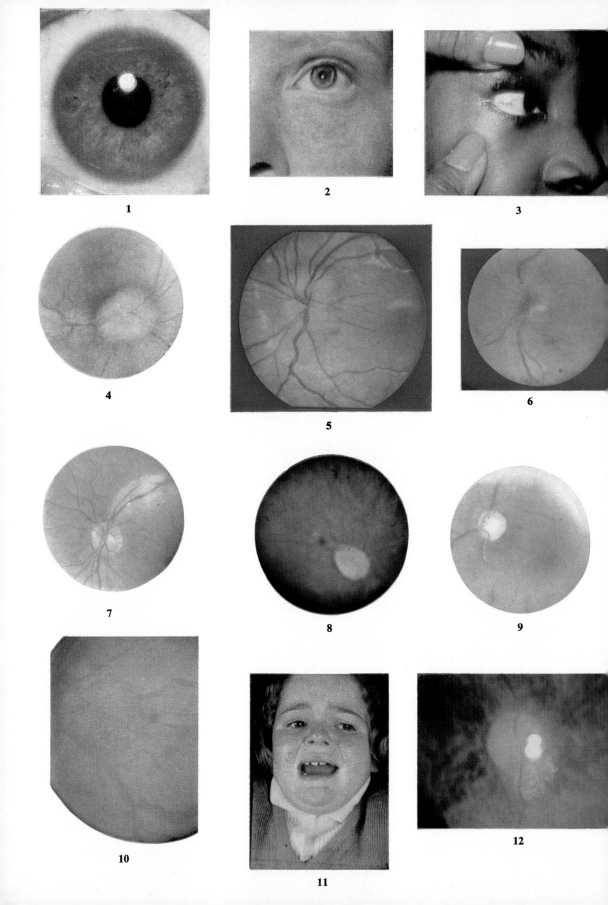

Colour Figures 1-12

1. Kayser-Fleischer ring at periphery of cornea in Wilson's disease.

2. Rings of Brushfield spots in the irides in mongolism.

3. Ataxia telangiectasia.

4. Papilloedema. (Supplied by Dr. D. A. Hiles, West Hyattsville, Md.)

5. Congenital pseudopapilloedema, anatomic blurring of the margin of the optic disc, a normal variation but one which can be diagnosed only by serial or prior examination of the eye grounds.

6. Optic neuritis. (Supplied by Dr. D. A. Hiles, West Hyattsville.)

7. Persistent myelinated nerve fibres radiating out from (actually towards) the optic disc at 2 o'clock. In other cases the fibres may not reach the periphery of the retina and may be present around the entire disc, giving a picture which could be confused with papilloedema at a superficial glance. (Supplied by Dr. D. A. Hiles, West Hyattsville.)

8. Macular degeneration and pigmentation in a cerebromacular degeneration. (This is the Spielmeyer-Vogt type and does not show the cherry red spot of Tay Sachs disease since the ganglioside does not accumulate in the ganglion cells as is necessary to render the retina white and to make the macula stand out as red.)

9. Optic atrophy. Note pallor of disc and narrowing of retinal vessels. (Supplied by Dr. D. A. Hiles, West Hyattsville.)

10. Retinal angiomatosis in Von Hippel-Lindau disease associated with haemangioblastoma of cerebellum.

11. Tuberose sclerosis (epiloia).

12. Papillary excrescence on optic disc in tuberose sclerosis.

more difficult to see or disappear earlier if the irides become brown rather than remaining blue.

A different colour of the two irides may be congenital heterochromia iridis and without significance. Heterochromia also results from an old paralytic lesion of the cervical sympathetic chain, (for example, in the lower (Klumpke) type of brachial palsy, the iris on the affected side remains blue while the other iris becomes grey, hazel or brown in colour with increasing age, unless the child is genetically blue-eyed). In Negro and Oriental races, pigmentation of the irides begins early in foetal life and injury to the cervical sympathetic even at birth results in only the minimal fading of iridic pigment which is encountered in the presence of sympathetic lesions acquired by brown-eyed persons in later childhood or adult life. Congenital cataracts may occur as an isolated anomaly but are commonly associated with maternal rubella in the first trimester of pregnancy, in which case they may be accompanied by mental retardation, microcephaly, congenital heart disease or other anomalies. Cataracts also develop early in galactosaemia and in Lowe's oculorenal dystrophy (buphthalmos or microphthalmos are commoner in the latter), and develop as a late complication in mongolism and in myotonic dystrophy.

Eyegrounds

Methods of Examination

An ophthalmoscope is used with children much as with adults, but a few special tricks are worth mentioning. While babies under 2 months of age require the use of mydriatic drops, sedation, and often lid retractors for adequate examination, babies up to a year or even 18 months will often permit examination without struggling, if the examiner is patient, and restrains them only minimally. Children up to the age of 3 years are usually best examined while they are supine, and older children most often resist least if seated. Young children tend to look directly at the light, and a sparkler-type wheel (see Fig. 1, p. 30) is useful to try to fix their gaze in the desired directions. With such methods, with patience and in a darkened room, one can examine the fundi of most children sufficiently for ordinary purposes. In the case of especially uncooperative or mentally retarded children, or if the maculae and peripheral retinae must be seen in detail, general anaesthesia may be required. Under these circumstances, the physician must decide whether or not the information to be gained warrants the slight risk of anaesthesia, and if so, whether he or an ophthalmologist is the best person to make the examination.

Interpretation

Examination of the retinae may disclose retrolental fibroplasia, choreoretinitis or other abnormalities. Choreoretinitis is particularly suggestive of old toxoplasmosis or cytomegalic inclusion disease, but can result from other infections and must be differentiated from congenital retinal colobomata. Retinal angiomatosis (Colour Fig. 10) may suggest Von Hippel-Lindau disease, and phakomatous lesions occur in some patients with tuberose sclerosis. (Colour Fig. 12.).

Retinal deposits of pigment may have many possible explanations. Black deposits of pigment in the peripheral retina of stellate (bone corpuscle) shape are typical of retinitis pigmentosa (more properly, pigmentary degeneration of the retina), which is a feature of Laurence-Biedl-Moon syndrome and of a considerable number of other familial affections of the nervous system. Retinitis pigmentosa must be distinguished from a marked degree of pepper and salt retina, from the flagstone-shaped blocks of melanosis retinae (a harmless congenital anomaly) and from the hyperpigmentation which often accompanies cerebromacular degenerations.

In Tay-Sachs disease, the deposition of ganglioside in the ganglion cells of the retina gives it a whitish appearance which is most conspicuous around the macula, which then appears as a cherry red spot. In other types of cerebromacular degeneration (Bielschowsky, Spielmeyer-Vogt and Kufs) the ganglioside is deposited chiefly in the inner and outer nuclear layers, and a cherry red spot does not appear, although there is later pigmentary degeneration of the macula (Colour Fig. 8). Cherry red spots also occur in some cases of Neimann-Pick's disease and have been described in one case of metachromatic leukodystrophy.

The optic disc is a focal point of interest in examining the eye grounds. Papilloedema is one of the most valuable indications of increased intracranial pressure in children as in adults; however, it may not develop if the increased pressure is very recent, or may be absent if the pressure is relieved by an open fontanelle, or by very prompt separation of the sutures in a young child. Papilloedema (Colour Fig. 4) is usually first evident in blurring of the nasal and superior borders of the disc, the temporal border being the last to become elevated with protrusion of the papilla into the globe of the eye. The examiner should attempt to measure the number of diopters of papilloedema from the difference between the power of the lens of the ophthalmoscope used to bring the disc itself into optimal focus, and that of the lens used to focus on the surrounding retina. The disc is initially hyperaemic, a feature then followed by dilatation of the veins, disappearance of normal venous pulsations, increasing tortuosity of the veins and contraction of the arteries, and the appearance of haemorrhages. The haemorrhages appear earliest in the areas around the disc, are frequently linear or flame-shaped and radiate out from the disc. Retinal haemorrhages also occur in hypertensive retinopathy, with haemorrhagic diatheses such as leukaemia, and in the presence of subdural haematoma. Papilloedema must be distinguished from a congenitally blurred and somewhat elevated disc with absence of the physiological cup (Colour Fig. 5). This is seen especial y in hypermetropic eyes. In such cases the disc is actually little raised, there is no dilatation of the veins or hyperaemia, and the blind spot is not enlarged. In doubtful cases one may need to re-examine the eyes after a short interval or compare findings with another physician who has seen them in the past.

The examiner must also distinguish papilloedema from optic neuritis, from the harmless persistence of embryonal myelinated nerve fibres radiating out from the disc (Colour Fig. 7), and from infiltration about the optic nerve head in leukaemia. Optic neuritis (Colour Fig. 6) is difficult to distinguish from papilloedema but there is usually greater exudation over the disc; while the physiological cup may be lost or the disc even elevated a few diopters the degree of actual oedema is not usually proportionate to the other changes (con-gestion, infiltration, exudation, and haemorrhages). However, in optic neuritis there is marked loss of visual acuity (this is slight in early papilloedema), and there is usually pronounced loss of the central visual field, often with a caecocentral scotoma in contrast to only modest enlargement of the physiological blind spot in early papilloedema.

Optic atrophy is the other major abnormality of the optic disc. The principal feature is excessive pallor, but experience is required to evaluate this in the case of infants who normally have paler discs than do adults. In optic atrophy (Colour Fig. 9), the disc margins stand out more sharply than normal. The physiological cup may be increased in depth and diameter and the lamina cribrosa may be increased in prominence and may extend to the edge of the disc. The capillaries supplying the disc are fewer and less prominent than normal and the retinal arteries may also be narrowed. It is often possible to count the number of vessels on the optic disc (as they cross its margin). Bland (1964) puts the normal number of vessels at 16 to 22. In optic atrophy the number of visible vessels is decreased, whereas the rising venous pressure which accompanies increased intracranial pressure distends the vessels and makes a larger number visible. Primary optic atrophy may have a wide variety of infectious, genetic or demyelinating (retrobulbar neuritis) causes. The appearance of secondary optic atrophy is similar, but as it usually follows papilloedema or optic neuritis, there are more often than not residual signs of these conditions. The disc margins may be blurred or the lamina cribrosa may be hidden by connective tissue or proliferation of glia. Optic atrophy is usually associated with considerable loss of visual acuity, and with concentric contraction of the visual fields.

CRANIAL NERVES 3, 4, 6: EYE MOVEMENTS

Position of the Eyes at Rest

Methods of Examination

Examination of the extraocular muscles and of their associated cranial nerves should begin by inspection of the position which the eyes assume at rest, when the patient looks straight ahead. Observation of the location of the points of reflexion of a distant flashlight (normally reflected almost from the middle of each pupil) aids in the detection of minor degrees of non-parallelism of the eyes. Conjugate deviation of the eyes or gaze directed largely towards one side must be confirmed by observation over a reasonable period of time or by several examinations. Subsequent testing of eye movements (page 112) to following, to command and reflexly, may of course bear out the examiner's suspicion by revealing paralysis of gaze in the opposite direction.

Interpretation

In paralysis of the *3rd nerve*, the affected eye deviates laterally and slightly downward. Complete paralysis of the 3rd nerve (if confirmed by further examination of eye movements in following and to command) is usually due, in children, to some affection of the nerve outside the midbrain and the ipsilateral eye is the one involved. If the paralysis is partial the interpretation is more difficult. There is a surprising amount of dispute and confusion about the anatomical arrangements, as to which fibres cross and which are uncrossed. Paralysis of the 3rd nerve also results in ptosis of the upper lid and dilatation of the pupil, which will be discussed in subsequent sections of this chapter.

Paralysis of the *4th nerve* produces relatively little change in the position at rest during forward gaze in the midline although there may be slight elevation of the eye. This becomes more obvious as the eye is adducted. The 4th cranial nerve leaves the brain stem by its posterior aspect and is completely decussated so that nuclear lesions produce contralateral paralysis, and lesions along the nerve, ipsilateral paralysis.

Paralysis of the *6th cranial nerve* produces medial deviation of the affected eye during midline forward gaze. In abducens paralysis of recent onset, the patient usually rotates the head slightly laterally toward the paretic side in order to suppress diplopia. This also makes the eyes more nearly parallel to inspection. Paralysis of the 3rd or 4th nerves is associated with tipping rather than turning of the head, the occiput being tipped toward one shoulder and the face directed toward the opposite side and slightly upward. If the examiner, noting the asymmetrical posture of the head, reverses it manually, the primary deviation resulting from the paralytic strabismus will immediately become much more obvious.

Conjugate deviation, or gaze largely directed to one side, may be due to either a contralateral irritative lesion or an ipsilateral paralytic lesion in one of the cortical centres for eye movements. The most important of these is the frontal centre which is in the posterior part of the 2nd and 3rd frontal convolutions, and is probably concerned with volitional control of conjugate movements of the eyes. A zone immediately anterior to the primary visual (striate) cortex, in areas 18 and 19 of Brodmann, subserves optically induced movements of the eyes and optical fixation reflexes. Other areas involved in movement of the eyes are located in the angular gyri and in the temporal lobe. Various areas in the diencephalon, brain stem, and cerebellum are also involved in ocular deviation. Deviation of the eyes to the opposite side is conceivable with small irritative mass lesions in the opposite hemisphere but, clinically, irritative deviation is associated chiefly with Jacksonian, focal, or simultaneous unilateral seizures. Under these circumstances it is usually accompanied by turning of the head in the same direction as the eyes. Destructive or paralytic cortical lesions cause deviation of the eyes toward the side of the lesion. Recovery from the deviation at rest usually takes place within a few weeks, although lateral gaze to command may be affected much longer (not following movements or reflex movements; see below). Irritative lesions are uncommon in the pons and midbrain but, if they occur, produce ipsilateral deviation of the eyes. Destructive lesions at this level are associated with contralateral deviation but this is usually slight. (Paresis of gaze toward the side of the lesion is more obvious in most cases.) Abnormal positioning of the head is not nearly so characteristic of brain stem lesions as of cortical ones.

The 'setting sun sign' of forced downward deviation of the eyes at rest (Fig. 6) with some paresis of upward gaze is an important sign of increased intracranial pressure in newborn and young infants. It is usually present in hydrocephalus and

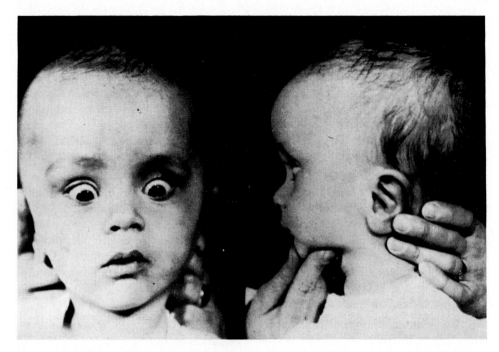

Fig. 6. Forced downward deviation of the eyes, the 'setting sun sign' in a case of hydrocephalus.

may persist after the increased pressure is compensated by some surgical procedure or by nature, perhaps due to a persistent deformity of the bony orbit in such cases. Increased intracranial pressure is not the only cause of downward deviation of the eyes, however, as the phenomenon is a constant one in kernicterus in early infancy. It can be seen in normal infants for brief periods of time. In kernicterus in later childhood, in contrast, the position of the eyes at rest is usually normal but instead there is paresis of conjugate upward gaze, to command or to command and following as well. This resembles the Parinaud syndrome which is associated with lesions in the vicinity of the quadrigeminal plate, but the mechanism in kernicterus remains obscure (see Stillhart 1954).

Skew deviation of the eyes in which one eye (usually the ipsilateral one) is turned downward and inward while the other deviates outward and upward is occasionally encountered in disease of the cerebellum or of other structures in the posterior fossa, but its anatomical basis is subject to debate.

Movements of the Eyes

Methods of Examination

Eye movements should be tested not only in following an object moved about by the examiner, but also by asking the child to look in different directions,

112

providing he is sufficiently mature and cooperative. If the patient is 4 years old or younger, it is best to have him sit opposite the examiner, on a chair or on his mother's lap. The examiner should then begin by testing conjugate movement of both eyes together, since young children often become upset when one eye is covered, even by the mother's hand. Following movements should be tested from side to side and up and down in the midline as well as on either side. These are usually fairly automatically elicited if the examiner moves a flashlight, a sparkler pinwheel, or some dangling object such as a coin on a string or the steel case of a measuring tape, into the appropriate positions. Movements of each eye should be tested with the other covered, but if the patient appears to object violently, this part of the examination may reasonably be omitted provided binocular conjugate gaze is normal in all directions.

During the testing of conjugate movements of the eyes, the question of diplopia should be investigated. The patient is asked if he sees double when a pencil or a small light is held in front of him and moved about. The position of the object and its relation to the eyes is noted if diplopia is present. One eye may then be covered and the patient asked which object has disappeared. Cooperative older children may be tested with a red glass or Maddox rod held at a distance of about 3 feet and moved into various quadrants of vision, to determine where the maximum separation of images is present. The relative positions of the two images may ideally be charted on a grid.

Interpretation

In attempting to attribute abnormalities of eye movement to possible anatomical locations, knowledge of the action of the individual nerves and muscles is essential.

The 3rd *cranial nerve* innervates the medial rectus (a pure adductor of the eye), the superior and inferior recti and the inferior oblique, as well as the levator palpebrae superioris and the constrictor pupillae muscles.

The 4th nerve supplies only the superior oblique and the *6th nerve* the external rectus. The external rectus is a pure abductor but the superior and inferior recti and oblique muscles have functions of both vertical movement and rotation. These are mixed in forward gaze in the midline; on abduction of the eye 23° the superior and inferior recti are pure elevators and depressors respectively. If adduction of the eye were carried to 51° the superior and inferior oblique muscles would be pure depressors and elevators respectively, but this degree of adduction may not be anatomically possible. Both vertical deviation and rotation are therefore tested together in appraising the oblique muscles, but for practical purposes upward and downward movement are tested with the eye adducted as far as possible. Rotatory action of the extraocular muscles may sometimes be detected by picking out a small defect in the iris and following it. A more accurate method is to anaesthetize the cornea and place a small sliver of filter paper at 12 o'clock, but in practical work it will seldom be necessary to go this far.

If weakness of a particular ocular muscle or of several muscles is detected, one must next attempt to decide whether the involvement is *nuclear* or *infranuclear*. Nuclear lesions of the *3rd nerve* often involve only one or more of its extraocular muscles, frequently without ptosis or internal ophthalmoplegia (that is, the pupillary reactions and accommodation remain normal). Infranuclear lesions usually result in complete paralysis unless the lesion is within the orbit itself.

There is no accurate basis for distinction between nuclear and infranuclear lesions of the *4th nerve* except that the former produce contralateral and the latter ipsilateral paralysis.

A *nuclear 6th nerve* palsy is almost always accompanied by involvement of the closely adjacent 7th nerve.

All four of these nuclei are close to the median longitudinal bundle and complicated syndromes are more commonly encountered than isolated nuclear palsies. Apparent paralysis of eye movement must also be distinguished from weakness associated with ocular or orbital disease, refractive errors, strabismus based on muscular imbalance or myasthenia gravis.

Supranuclear disturbances of eye movement affect conjugate gaze more than individual eye movements. Paralysis of conjugate upward gaze is associated with lesions at the level of the superior colliculi (Parinaud's syndrome) and may be encountered with pineal tumours as well as with encephalitis, vascular lesions, disseminated sclerosis, and other abnormalities in the same region. The internal cortico-tectal fibres from the occipital lobes are more superficially located posteriorly than are the cortico-bulbar fibres; thus reflex and following movements upward are usually lost earlier than voluntary movements in the case of extrinsic tumours pressing upon the quadrigeminal plate. Intrinsic infiltrating lesions in the midbrain may cause loss of voluntary movements first.

The common impairment of eye movements from lesions of the median longitudinal bundle is anterior (or superior) internuclear ophthalmoplegia, appearing on lateral gaze as paralysis of adduction of the contralateral eye (adduction is usually preserved in convergence), together with monocular nystagmus of the abducting eye and sometimes a degree of paresis in abduction. Convergence may also be affected if the lesion is in the midbrain. Posterior or inferior internuclear ophthalmoplegia is supposed to consist of paresis of abduction of the ipsilateral eye, which is more marked than the weakness of adduction of the contralateral eye, which may converge normally, but there is doubt as to the existence of this entity. A diversity of intrinsic lesions of the brain stem may produce internuclear ophthalmoplegia; disseminated sclerosis is by far the commonest, although one would entertain other diagnoses in young children.

Destructive cerebral lesions involving frontal centres for conjugate gaze result in deviation of the eyes toward the side of the lesion in the acute stage, but recovery is quick, within a month or so in most instances. During the same period, and frequently long afterwards, there is paresis or paralysis of contralateral conjugate gaze to command but reflex and following movements are spared. However, in the case of destructive lesions of the anterior occipital lobe, voluntary movements of the eyes are little affected, but there is loss of following or reflex movements to the opposite side.

Children are occasionally seen with a presumably congenital disability, characterised by loss of volitional control of eye movements, frequently with a 'catch' on following from side to side, nystagmus or other neurological abnormalities, but with preservation of random movements of the eyes. Cogan and Adams (1953) have termed this 'oculomotor apraxia'. The characteristic features are: some defect of voluntary horizontal eye movements and also of horizontal attraction movements of the eyes, together with normal and full random eye movements; characteristic jerking movements of the head, which may aid in positioning of the eyes when used voluntarily; defect of the quick phase of opticokinetic nystagmus; controversion or lag of the eyes on rotation of the head to the opposite direction on a vertical axis, a doll's-eye type of phenomenon; and difficulties in reading in most if not all patients who are old enough to be able to read. All of the early cases reported were males (Altrocchi and Menkes 1960). Most of the patients also had normal vertical eye movements but absent or defective following movements in the horizontal plane, and at least historical awkwardness of gait. All of the signs were usually symmetrical. The anatomical basis of the condition as well as the treatment are unknown.

MONOCULAR DIPLOPIA is usually hysterical but can occur with cataracts, subluxation of the lens, retinal detachment, and (rarely) in cerebral lesions with dissociation of visual projection. Double images of different size or shape but not different position (aniseikonia) result from some intraocular abnormality and not from dysfunction of the ocular muscles. Diplopia is not a feature of the usual concomitant squint of childhood because of suppression of the function of one eye (amblyopia-ex-anopsia), and even after freshly acquired paralytic strabismus diplopia is initially minimized by altering the position of the head (which the examiner should reverse if it is asymmetrical). This is usually followed by suppression of the diplopic image from the paretic eye, within a few weeks or months.

STRABISMUS (squint) is by far the commonest cause of non-parallelism of the ocular axes in children. The visual axes of the two eyes cannot be simultaneously fixed on the same point, but in the common non-paralytic strabismus of childhood either affected eye can be moved through nearly the complete range of motion if tested separately. With the other eye covered or with both eyes moving together, the involved eye can follow the fixating eye with a constant error even though it may be non-parallel at rest. The deviation may be divergent or convergent, upward or downward, unilateral or alternating (in the last mentioned, the patient can fix with either eye but the opposite eye then deviates).

The term heterotropia is used for manifest strabismus with non-parallelism obvious with both eyes open. Esotropia is convergent strabismus and exotropia divergent: hypertropia refers to vertical deviation. Heterophoria refers to a latent rather than manifest tendency to imperfect binocular balance. Again, hyperphoria is a tendency to vertical deviation, esophoria to inward and exophoria to outward deviation. Esophoria and exophoria are common in patients with hyperopia and myopia respectively.

Most cases of childhood strabismus are evident in routine examination of the extraocular muscles. In doubtful cases it may be helpful to ask the patient to fixate on a distant flashlight and then to check whether the pinpoint reflection in the pupils is central on each side. Latent strabismus is best brought out by the so-called 'cover test', in which first one eye and then the other is covered and slight movement of the non-covered eye looked for, as the cover is applied, or, more frequently, as it is removed.

Diplopia is not a feature of the common strabismus of childhood, owing to early suppression of the visual image of the squinting eye. This development of amblyopia makes early recognition of strabismus and referral to an ophthalmologist by at latest 2 years of age highly desirable. Non-paralytic strabismus is not necessarily of any further neurological significance but it should be mentioned that strabismus is considerably more common in children with organic brain syndromes than in the general population. 50 per cent of patients in cerebral palsy clinics are usually found to be affected, but strabismus has no specific diagnostic significance as it is not associated with any single abnormality.

NYSTAGMUS is an involuntary movement of the eyeball which may be either rhythmic or non-rhythmic and may be associated with disease of the cerebellum and its central connexions, the eye, or the inner ear. It may also be produced as a normal phenomenon under certain circumstances. The two types of nystagmus are rhythmic (or jerky, biphasic, or directed) with alternate slow and quick components resulting in a jerky, unequal repeated movement, and pendular nystagmus with more or less regular, equal to-and-fro movements to either side of a central point. Nystagmus is also classified as to direction: horizontal, vertical, oblique, rotatory or mixed. The approximate speed, which may vary from 10 to as many as 100 oscillations per minute, should be noted. The approximate amplitude should also be noted. (Movements of smallest amplitude are often brought to the examiner's attention only during ophthalmoscopic examination or by covering the eye with a +20 diopter lens which magnifies the nystagmus and eliminates fixation. Generally, 'fine nystagmus' is a term applied to excursions of less than 1 mm. and 'coarse nystagmus' to excursions over 3 mm.

The effect of the position of the eyes on the nystagmus should also be noted. The least intensity (first degree) is present only when the patient looks in the direction of the quick component; second degree nystagmus is present in the neutral position and third degree even when looking in the direction of the slow component. Latent nystagmus appears only when one eye is covered, there being no abnormal movement when both eyes are used together.

1. Nystagmus is never normally present at rest but can be induced in normal individuals under several circumstances:

(a) *Opticokinetic nystagmus*. This is the nystagmus of persons watching the landscape from a moving railway car or automobile and is sometimes referred to as railway nystagmus. The slow phase is in the direction of the moving field of vision or of the movement of stripes on a rotating drum, with the quick phase in the opposite direction. The slow phase appears to be a reflex pursuit of a moving object based on retinal stimulation but the origin of the quick phase of recovery is more obscure. Opticokinetic nystagmus is generally held to be proof of cortical vision, or at least of the presence of the cortical reflex involved, but tectal vision or reflexes at lower levels can probably produce the response in lower animals and possibly in newborn infants. Under the age of 2-4 months, opticokinetic nystagmus cannot be obtained to a rotating drum or to the moving figures on a tape measure drawn across in front of the patient, but it can be elicited in most normal full-term newborns by drawing a striped cloth or plastic canopy across the entire visual field. (Gorman *et al.* (1957) have developed an apparatus for this purpose.) The presence of opticokinetic nystagmus can be used as a criterion of cortical vision in infants and young children, but the response to a tape measure or striped drum is delayed for weeks or months in cases of general developmental retardation, so that its absence should not be accepted alone as sufficient proof of cortical blindness.

(b) *Labyrinthine nystagmus.* This is a normal physiological response to stimulation of the semicircular canals by rotation or by changes in temperature produced by irrigating the auditory canal with warm or cold water. The slow phase corresponds to the direction of movement of the endolymph and the rapid phase is in the opposite direction. This is primarily a test for function of the 8th cranial nerve and will be considered under that heading. The standard test, if the head is accurately positioned, stimulates the horizontal semicircular canal and produces a pure lateral nystagmus, but mixed nystagmus may result if more than one semicircular canal is simultaneously stimulated. The slow component is the significant one and is of labyrinthine origin, but by convention this type of nystagmus (like others) is described as to the right or to the left, according to the quick phase. The direction of labyrinthine nystagmus does not reverse with shift of gaze from left to right, an important difference from most other types of nystagmus.

(c) *Toxic nystagmus* can occur in normal individuals as a response to a diversity of drugs, including barbiturates or diphenylhydantoin (in which it is, together with ataxia, one of the major signs of over-dosage), lead, nicotine and quinine.

(d) *Occupational nystagmus*, induced by eye strain in deficient light, occurs chiefly in miners but sometimes in unusually diligent students who have poor light in which to work. It results from using the rods for vision in relative darkness, with failure of macular fixation and constant shifting of the axes of the eyes, since the maculae contain no rods but only cones.

(e) *Fixation and fatigue nystagmus* are observed when the patient achieves extreme deviation of the eyes, especially laterally, or when he holds this position for a sustained period. Fatigue nystagmus is sustained but fixation nystagmus ceases after 5 or 6 jerks. Another variety of endpoint nystagmus occurs on attempts to fixate the eyes beyond the limits of the binocular visual field, although this is not present in every normal individual. This nystagmus of eccentric fixation is increased by fatigue.

Unilateral lesions in the anterior occipital lobe (areas 18 and 19), or in the angular gyrus or posterior temporal lobe, produce respectively a directional preponderance of opticokinetic or labyrinthine nystagmus. In the former, opticokinetic nystagmus is depressed on rotation of the striped drum away from the side of the lesion. Caloric

117

nystagmus is diminished in duration and intensity if the ears are irrigated in such a manner as would normally produce nystagmus away from the lesion (a 'directional preponderance' towards the side of the lesion). Directional preponderance is difficult to test in children who are uncooperative, even under sedation. Methods are described in the section on the 8th cranial nerve.

2. Pathological nystagmus occurs in association with diseases of the eye:

(a) *'Ocular nystagmus'* is pendulous and may be either coarse or rapid. The coarse, slow searching movements are characteristic of blindness, either ocular or cortical, acquired before the age of fixation, and can be seen with congenital cataract, corneal opacities, etc. Searching movements of smaller amplitude or pendulous to-and-fro nystagmus may occur with any serious impairment of visual acuity acquired in early childhood or probably as late as the age of 6. Defective vision acquired in later childhood or adult life does not produce ocular nystagmus unless macular vision is specifically affected; the movements are then aimless and slower, and probably represent attempts at fixation rather than a true nystagmus.

(b) *'Congenital nystagmus'* is sometimes held to be present from birth, and is differentiated from ocular nystagmus, which is then said to be associated with attempts to develop fixation in the presence of abnormal vision. However, in families in which congenital nystagmus is a known autosomal or sex-linked recessive trait (or an irregular dominant) it is frequently not observed in the first month of life, and it is difficult to distinguish the two conditions. Congenital nystagmus may be pendulous or may have slow and rapid components, the latter being in the direction of gaze. It is generally held to be the result of some developmental anomaly in the central nervous system, possibly in the midbrain, but since it is associated with underdevelopment of central vision, it could be argued that ocular factors are primary. Also, congenital nystagmus associated with total or partial albinism is a recognised subgroup. Uniocular nystagmus in babies is almost always part of the syndrome called 'spasmus nutans', and is usually but not invariably accompanied by rhythmic nodding or shaking of the head. The classical view was that spasmus nutans developed in children raised in mines or in dark dwellings with inadequate sunlight, but this is certainly not the predominant cause today. At least the head movement, and usually the nystagmus as well, improve considerably or disappear with increasing age, although the percentage of babies with spasmus nutans who later prove to be mentally retarded or otherwise neurologically abnormal is probably greater than random chance.

The nystagmus of spasmus nutans, as well as congenital nystagmus, may be affected by position of the head and children sometimes learn to hold the head so as to minimize the nystagmus. The examiner should therefore test for the effect of different head positions.

3. Several types of nystagmus are associated with abnormality of the nervous system:

(a) *Vestibular nystagmus* is a pathological form of the normally inducible labyrinthine nystagmus. It can result from either exaggeration or depression of the function of semicircular canals, vestibular nerves, or vestibular nuclei. 'Labyrinthitis' is an uncommon cause of nystagmus in children, unless associated with acute infections of the middle ear. The slow phase of the nystagmus is towards the affected side. Labyrinthine nystagmus is soon compensated, however, and even after total destruction of one labyrinth or one vestibular nerve the nystagmus lasts only a few weeks. In the early acute stage, there should always be a degree of vertigo as well. Menière's syndrome, associated with hydrops of the semicircular canals, including paroxysms of vertigo and progressive hearing loss as well as nystagmus, is extremely rare in childhood if it occurs at all. Neoplasms, demyelinating processes and other lesions in the brain stem may produce nystagmus from involvement of the vestibular nuclei, the median longitudinal bundle or other structures. Vertical or rotatory nystagmus is particularly characteristic of these processes. Nystagmus may also be seen with lesions of the spinal cord, at least down to the 2nd cervical segment, and occurs with tumours, syringomyelia and other lesions, probably based on involvement of the median longitudinal bundle.

(b) *Cerebellar nystagmus.* In animals, but perhaps not in man, cerebellar nystagmus usually depends on involvement of vestibular connexions to and from the flocculonodular lobe and fastigial nuclei via the inferior peduncle, but cerebellar nystagmus also occurs with lesions of the hemispheres, at least in man. The eyes tend to be positioned slightly away from the affected side when at rest, and when the patient looks to either side nystagmus develops with the quick component in the direction of gaze (either to right or left) and the slow component toward the position of rest. The nystagmus is more pronounced when the patient looks toward the side of the lesion. Two useful points in distinguishing cerebellar from vestibular nystagmus are that nystagmus based on cerebellar disease depends on fixation and is reduced by holding a strong positive lens in front of the eye, and that the direction of cerebellar nystagmus depends on the position of the eyes and reverses on shifting from right to left gaze.

(c) *Positional nystagmus* may be present only when the head is in certain positions, and is best tested by having the patient lie on a bed or examining table with his head over the side, the head being then manoeuvred into a variety of postures. Positional nystagmus (Dix and Hallpike 1952) may be a post-traumatic phenomenon and associated with vertigo, but is not necessarily evidence of any progressive lesion of the nervous system and may be a benign paroxysmal phenomenon.

(d) *Hysterical nystagmus* is supposed to be brought on by emotional strain but it is doubtful whether this is a genuine entity. The examiner should bear in mind that any variety of pathological nystagmus is likely to be increased by anxiety, fatigue, or prolonged fixation.

Abnormal eye movements other than nystagmus chiefly comprise paroxysmal, involuntary conjugate deviation of the eyes, most often upward. These oculogyric crises are characteristic of postencephalitic Parkinsonism but sometimes occur in other postencephalitic states, at least in children. They must of course be distinguished from petit mal fits. Quick, jerky, violent shooting movements of the eyes in various directions, but particularly upward, are often seen in acute idiopathic cerebellar ataxia of childhood.

Pupils

Methods of Examination

The pupils should be examined in the conventional way by inspection of size, shape, equality and position and by their reflex responses to light and to accommodation. The reaction of the pupil to light is its most important reflex. This should be examined both directly and consensually (constriction of one pupil to light shone into the opposite eye). Reflex miosis to accommodation is tested by getting the child to look at some attractive object at a distance of several feet and then bringing the object towards the bridge of the nose in the midline.

Interpretation

Once the newborn period is passed, the pupils are usually larger than in adult life and react vigorously to light and to accommodation. Excessively small pupils are seen in the presence of deep coma, some cases of increased intracranial pressure, acute brain stem lesions involving interruption of dilator fibres, and during sleep. Very slight constriction normally occurs during the expiratory phase of respiration. Miosis occasionally results from irritative lesions of the 3rd nerve but this is rare. Paralytic lesions of the cervical sympathetic system or of the C8 and T1 roots produce miosis which is probably the most sensitive part of the Claude Bernard-Horner syndrome. The other features, which are uncommonly encountered without miosis include slight ptosis (much less than is seen with paralytic lesions of the para-sympathetic fibres in the 3rd nerve), suppression of perspiration on the affected side of the face, and enophthalmos.

In the case of babies who are born with blue eyes but later become brown or grey-eyed, the eye on the affected side has a lesser degree of pigmentation if the lesion is acquired at birth or in early infancy, as for example in stretch injuries of the cervical sympathetic during delivery. Interference with the integrity of the sympathetic pathway at a later age produces only minimal change in colour. This is also true with birth injuries to patients of Negro or Oriental extraction, since pigmentation begins around the 4th foetal month in these races. Heterochromia iridis as well as anisocoria may be harmless congenital anomalies.

Dilatation of the pupils (defining mydriasis in children as a pupillary diameter above 5 mm.) occurs with anxiety, fear, pain, hyperthyroidism, certain stages of coma, and with some lesions of the midbrain. Paralysis of the parasympathetic fibres in the 3rd nerve may result from small lesions in the orbit, or from involvement of the nerve in the superior orbital fissure, in the cavernous sinus or in its intracranial course. If the dilatation is unresponsive to light as well as marked in degree, this is a particularly important sign of increased intracranial pressure, which results in most cases from herniation of the hippocampal gyrus through the incisure of the tentorium, compressing the 3rd nerve.

Miosis and mydriasis are characteristic reactions to a great variety of drugs. Nearsighted eyes may be somewhat dilated just as farsighted eyes may be constricted, and anisocoria may be the result of a refractive error. The most important implication of mydriasis, however, is a possible paralytic lesion of the 3rd cranial nerve. What appears to be mydriasis may be aniridia, and cataracts may be associated with miosis. Hippus, a rhythmic dilatation and constriction of the pupils, is usually of no diagnostic significance.

Slightly oval or eccentric pupils may be a harmless normal variation, and are frequently also seen in the stage of recovery from induced mydriasis. Coloboma of the iris is a relatively innocuous congenital anomaly, dominantly inherited in most cases, and sometimes associated with coloboma of the retina.

With lesions of the 3rd nerve, both direct and consensual responses are absent on the affected side but both are intact in the opposite eye. The pupil of a blind eye (due to an ocular lesion or to one in the optic nerve) does not constrict to light, nor does that of the opposite eye consensually, but the blind eye may show consensual pupillary constriction when the opposite eye is stimulated. Before congenital syphilis became so uncommon, the Argyll-Robertson pupil was of considerable diagnostic importance. The combination of absent pupillary constriction to light with preservation of the response to accommodation is not entirely pathognomonic of syphilis of the central nervous system, but can occur in post-encephalitic states, syringobulbia, lesions in the region of the pineal body or superior colliculus, and in disseminated sclerosis. Absence of reflex miosis to light is also seen in Adie's syndrome, which may be associated with absence of tendon reflexes, leading to further confusion with syphilis of the central nervous system. However, the pupil is usually slightly dilated in average room light in Adie's syndrome, whereas the Argyll-Robertson pupil is small and relatively invariable in size. Also, the pupillary abnormality is unilateral in the majority of Adie cases. The myotonic pupil of Adie's syndrome is excessively sensitive to mecholyl—another differential test.

Other reflexes involving the pupils include dilatation in response to slightly painful stimulation of the skin of the back of the neck on the ipsilateral side, constriction (or constriction following initial dilatation) in response to painful stimulation of the eye itself, and Byrnes' reflex of dilatation of one pupil in response to painful stimuli to the opposite lower extremity. A loud noise produced suddenly may be followed by dilatation of the pupil. Reactions to certain drugs instilled in the eye, such as atropine, pilocarpine, mecholyl, neostigmine, nicotine and cocaine, may be used in the differential diagnosis of irritative versus paralytic lesions of the sympathetic versus parasympathetic fibres. (See Chapter XV, Special Investigations.)

Ptosis

Slight ptosis associated with paralysis of the superior tarsal muscle is present in paralytic lesions of the cervical sympathetic. However, the upper lid droops only to or slightly below the upper margin of the pupil, and the patient can usually raise the lid completely by voluntary effort. Complete ptosis with paralysis of the 3rd nerve and of the levator palpebrae superioris is more extreme and the palpebral fissure may be completely closed. Partial cases occur, and are sometimes more easily recognised if one watches the contraction of the frontalis muscle as the patient attempts to open his eye. This is supposed to be absent in hysterical ptosis. Cases of ptosis must be differentiated from an abnormally wide palpebral fissure on the opposite side due to paresis of the 7th nerve and the orbicularis oculi, and from lid lag in hyperthyroidism. Jaw-winking (the Marcus Gunn phenomenon) is actually a congenital ptosis with reflex elevation of the lid in response to movements of the jaw. Elevation of the lid is largely preserved in voluntary action and in upward gaze.

Congenital ptosis may be pronounced, and is usually dominantly inherited. The presence of ptosis should also suggest the possibility of myasthenia gravis. There are congenital cases or cases of very early onset (as distinct from the transient neonatal myasthenia of infants born to myasthenic mothers), which often go unrecognised until several years of age. Ptosis is almost a constant finding in myasthenia of early childhood but may be strikingly and even consistently asymmetrical. A diagnostic test should be carried out with edrophonium (tensilon R) in appropriate cases (see Chapter XV), although the response to tensilon may be atypical in childhood myasthenia.

Exophthalmos

Enophthalmos has already been discussed as a feature of the syndrome of paralysis of the cervical sympathetic, but it can also occur with atrophy of intra-orbital tissue. Bilateral exophthalmos is usually due to hyperthyroidism and, if marked, presents no difficulty in recognition, although a considerable degree of apparent exophthalmos is seen in many normal Negroes. Unilateral exophthalmos frequently has neurological significance. In doubtful cases, lid lag, depression of ability for convergence, increased width of the palpebral fissure, and an infrequency of spontaneous blinking may help the diagnosis. Unilateral exophthalmos can occur in hyperthyroidism but usually indicates localised intraorbital or intracranial disease. These include retrobulbar masses within the orbit, orbital cellulitis, deformities of the skull, thrombosis of the cavernous sinus (with paralysis of the 3rd, 4th, and 6th cranial nerves and of the first two divisions of the 5th), and with intracranial tumours of the anterior fossa.

Pulsating exophthalmos is often stated to be characteristic of arterio-venous fistula in the cavernous sinus, but in many such cases pulsation is absent. Exophthalmos may also pulsate if due to an intracranial aneurism or to a vascular malformation elsewhere. Auscultation of the eye and of the surrounding region for bruit is particularly important in such cases. Ex- and enophthalmos may be simulated by macrophthalmos and microphthalmos, respectively.

Syndromes

The syndromes involving the 3rd, 4th and 6th cranial nerves may be based on 3rd nerve affections of the cavernous sinus, hippocampal herniation, internuclear ophthalmoplegia (p. 114), and the syndromes of Horner (p. 120) and Parinaud (p. 114). Gradenigo's syndrome consists of paralysis of one lateral rectus with tenderness or swelling behind the ipsilateral ear, and indicates inflammatory disease in the petrous pyramid.

A number of syndromes are based on congenital anomalies. These are usually non-progressive and more or less innocuous to the patient, but their recognition is important in the exclusion of more serious disease. Parents are sometimes unaware of mild degrees of these conditions, in the case of partial congenital ptosis, and the alert physician will demand the family's baby photographs for comparison with the patient's present condition. Moebius' syndrome is paralysis of the external recti (rarely only on one side) associated with paresis or paralysis of the facial musculature. It has been debated whether this is due primarily to aplasia of the nuclei in the brain stem or aplasia of the muscles themselves. Other ocular muscles may be involved and many other congenital anomalies in various areas of the body may co-exist. Paralysis limited to both external recti is sometimes referred to as Gerhardt's syndrome. In Duane's syndrome the lateral rectus muscles are largely replaced by fibrous tissue, and the palpebral fissure widens as the patient attempts lateral gaze (which is limited) and narrows as he adducts. There is retraction and elevation of the globe on adduction. There may also be fibrosis of the levator palpebrae superioris.

Several acquired syndromes of ocular nerve paresis with involvement of the long tracts of the brain stem are recognised. Benedikt's syndrome includes ipsilateral oculo-motor paralysis with contralateral tremor, ataxia or some kind of hyperkinesis in the upper extremity, and reflects involvement of the 3rd nerve as it passes through the red nucleus. Weber's syndrome is based on involvement of the 3rd nerve as it passes through the cerebral peduncle, and includes paralysis of the 3rd nerve on one side and a contralateral hemiparesis. The syndrome of Millard and Gubler is ipsilateral 6th nerve paralysis (usually plus 7th) and contralateral pyramidal hemiparesis. The syndrome of Foville is possibly a variation of this. It consists of hemiparesis on one side with opposite facial paralysis, ipsilateral to the lesion, and a paresis of lateral gaze attributed by some to involvement of the paraabducens nucleus. There are probably several variations of the syndrome of Raymond-Cestan, including paresis of ipsilateral conjugate gaze on deviation of the eyes to the opposite side, contralateral hemiparesis, and sometimes contralateral sensory deficit for touch, passive movement, or position. The latter indicates involvement of the medial lemniscus, which is also occasionally affected in some of the other syndromes mentioned. All of these combinations reflect an intrinsic lesion of the brain stem.

In children this lesion is unfortunately most frequently an intrinsic glioma infiltrating the brain stem, and inoperable. (Such tumours usually produce papill-oedema only terminally, in contrast to most other tumours in the posterior fossa.) The onset is usually gradual over several weeks or months, but may be as short as a week in a few cases, even if well observed. Pneumoencephalography confirms the diagnosis by showing posterior displacement of the 4th ventricle and aqueduct. Infiltrating gliomata of the midbrain, pons, and medulla may also include a large number of other cranial nerve signs, chiefly crossed with respect to the long tract signs in the extremities, but there may be bilateral and very irregular spotty involvement.

Another syndrome with similar implications is that of Nothnagel — unilateral 3rd nerve paralysis with ipsilateral ataxia from involvement of the brachium conjunctivum and its connexions. The so-called syndrome of the Interpeduncular Space consists of bilateral 3rd nerve paresis with a spastic tetraparesis of the limbs. In the absence of other evidence of intrinsic involvement, this could be due to pressure from an extrinsic lesion on the cerebral peduncles and oculomotor nerves, and one might well attempt to outline the basal cisterns by pneumoencephalography in the hope of finding an operable lesion.

CRANIAL NERVE 5: TRIGEMINAL NERVE

Examination of Motor Function

The mass of the masseter and temporalis muscles are appraised by inspection and their tone palpated as the patient clenches his jaw. He is then asked to open the mouth and the examiner looks for deviation of the mandible, which is towards the side of any paresis. Paresis of the 7th nerve with weakness of the facial muscles may simulate deviation of the jaw to some extent, but its simulation of deviation of the tongue is more striking. In doubtful cases the patient should be asked to open the jaw against resistance from the examiner's finger and to move it from side to side against resistance. Another useful test is to ask the child to bite on a tongue depressor and test his ability to hold it against the examiner's efforts to withdraw it from between the teeth, and then to look for symmetry or asymmetry of the toothmarks on the stick.

The jaw jerk is tested by asking the child to open his mouth slightly (not fully) and to relax as much as possible. The examiner places his index finger on the midpoint of the child's chin and taps his finger with a reflex hammer (Fig. 7). An alternative method is to place a tongue depressor over the lower incisors and tap the blade just outside the lower lip. The normal response is a bilateral contraction of the masseter and temporalis muscles with sudden elevation of the mandible. Experience is required to decide whether the jaw jerk is exaggerated or depressed. There is some variation from one patient to another and the response is slight or even absent in some normal individuals. The reflex is enhanced by a degree of setting of the muscles of the jaw, voluntary or involuntary. Clonus of the jaw may be elicited in testing the jaw jerk if the latter is exaggerated, as with supranuclear lesions or in normal babies. A unilateral jerk may sometimes be obtained by tapping the angle of the jaw or by tapping the end of a tongue depressor which has been placed over the lower molar teeth (the examiner holds the protruding end between his forefinger and thumb). A head-retraction reflex may be demonstrable by tapping the centre of the upper lip, while the patient holds his head bent slightly forward. There is usually no reaction in normal patients, but a quick retraction of the head may be seen in the presence of bilateral pyramidal lesions above the cervical cord. Only the sensory arc of this reflex is carried in the trigeminal nerve; the efferent arc is through the upper cervical nerves.

Examination of Sensory Function

The sensory portion of the trigeminal nerve supplies the skin of the face in front of a line drawn approximately from the point of the jaw, passing just anterior to the

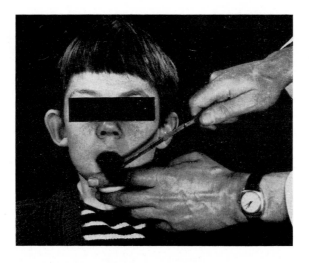

Fig. 7. Method of testing jaw-jerk.

angle of the mandible and to the ear, ending a little behind the vertex of the scalp. It also supplies the eyeball, the paranasal sinuses, the nasal cavity, the mucous membranes of the hard and soft palate (except the posterior border), the nasopharynx, the buccal mucous membranes, the gums, the teeth, the lips, and the tongue (for sensations other than taste). The conventional screening type of examination consists in testing appreciation of touch and pinprick over the distribution of the three sensory divisions of the nerve (Fig. 8). Examination of the oral cavity is required only in special instances. There is no satisfactory method of testing proprioception from trigeminal areas, but when indicated it is possible to test two-point discrimination (the threshold on the face is normally 1·0 to 2·0 cm. and on the lips 1 or 2 mm., the lips being at least as sensitive as the fingertips).

The corneal reflex is the most important sensory trigeminal response. The cornea should be touched lightly with a wisp of cotton wool, of which the tip should be at least larger than a fibre or two. The child should be asked to look to one side, and the examiner then approaches from the opposite side to avoid a visual blink reflex. The corneal reflex should always be present unless there is interruption of its nervous pathway, or drying of the cornea over some time. A comparable wink response can usually be obtained by stimulating the conjunctiva, but this is less consistent and may be absent in hysterical individuals or in those with a high tolerance for pain. Testing the corneal reflex may produce deviation of the mandible to the opposite side, the so-called winking-jaw or reverse Marcus Gunn phenomenon. This is supposed to reflect a supranuclear lesion of the cortio-bulbar tract. An alternative method of testing the corneal reflex is to blow a short puff of air into the patient's eye, from the examiner's mouth or preferably from a small rubber bulb. This is less upsetting to young children and may reduce the risk of ruining the remainder of the examination, though it may also stimulate the eyelashes, lids and surrounding facial skin.

125

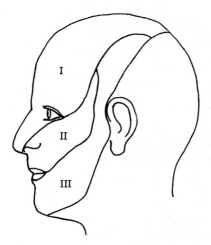

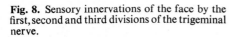

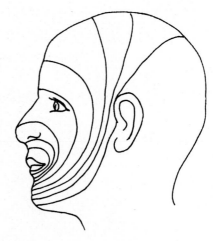

Fig. 8. Sensory innervations of the face by the first, second and third divisions of the trigeminal nerve.

Fig. 9. Segmental arrangement of the representation of pain and temperature from the face in the spinal tract of the fifth nerve and in its nucleus. The arrangement has been compared to onion peel. The area around the mouth, which is the most rostral, has the highest representation and the more posterior and inferior regions are lowest, in the upper segments of the cervical cord.

Interpretation

Obvious wasting of the masseter and temporalis muscles usually indicates a lesion affecting the lower motor neurone or peripheral nerve. This level of involvement can also be inferred from lateral deviation of the mandible on opening the mouth. (The motor function of the trigeminal nerve has largely bilateral cortical representation although in some individuals there may be definite deviation of the jaw with unilateral affections of the cortex or in the cortico-bulbar tract). Spastic hypertonus is rarely demonstrated, however, and the best evidence of supranuclear involvement is an exaggerated jaw jerk. In cases of spastic hemiparesis or tetraparesis, this is important in placing the level of abnormality above the foramen magnum and in eliminating the possibility of a spinal lesion.

Irritative motor phenomena are possible as well as paretic ones. These include Jacksonian or focal seizures, yawning or gaping movements sometimes associated with disease of the basal ganglia, and trismus. The last mentioned is characteristic of tetanus and rabies but can also be seen with encephalitis, meningitis, tetany, hysteria, and as a reaction to drugs of the phenothiazine group. Chewing movements and grinding of the teeth may merely be habit mannerisms of neurotic or of more or less normal children, but are disproportionately frequent in the mentally retarded.

It is not possible to discuss here all the anatomical localisation of tumours, vascular lesions, etc., affecting the intracranial trigeminal pathways, which depends on detailed knowledge of neuroanatomy and associated signs and symptoms. The

126

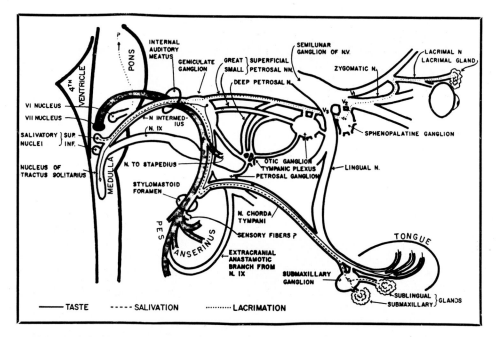

Fig. 10. Anatomical arrangement of facial nerve. The course of the motor fibres is shown in grey. Relative sizes have been somewhat distorted for clarity and to permit labelling. Minor anastomotic connexions and possible secondary sensory pathways have been omitted.

motor and main sensory nuclei are located in the upper pons at the level of emergence of the nerve itself. The mesencephalic nucleus subserves proprioception and also provides the afferent arc of the jaw jerk, which is thus not abolished by lesions of the Gasserian ganglion or its sensory pathway (McIntyre and Robinson 1959). Sensations of pain and temperature are transmitted through the descending spinal tract of the 5th nerve which passes down the brain stem as far as the second cervical segment, with a synapse to the cells of the nucleus of the descending root from which fibres then decussate and ascend in the contralateral quintothalamic tract. Thus, disturbance of facial sensation can be encountered with lesions of the upper cervical cord. One would expect these to be posteriorly on the face or over the inferior part of the mandible, since the conventional view is that the segmental distribution is in an 'onion peel' (Fig. 9) arrangement about the mouth with the areas nearest the lips having the highest representation in the descending tract and nucleus.

CRANIAL NERVE 7: FACIAL NERVE

The facial nerve has an extremely complicated anatomical arrangement which must be understood in order to examine its functions (see Fig. 10). Its larger portion is motor and supplies all the muscles of the face and ear, the platysma and stapedius muscles, the posterior belly of the digastricus and the stylohyoid muscles. The facial nerve transmits sensation, according to the conventional view, from the eardrum, from

127

the external auditory canal and from the pinna. Sensation of taste from the anterior part of the tongue passes from the lingual nerve to the facial via the chorda tympani but the fibres run in the nervus intermedius proximal to the geniculate ganglion. Autonomic efferent fibres also run in the facial nerve to the lacrimal gland (but leave at the geniculate ganglion via the greater superficial petrosal nerve) and via the chorda tympani to the submaxillary and sublingual salivary glands.

Examination of Motor Function

This must be accomplished by inspection alone in the case of young, mentally retarded or uncooperative children, and is best carried out while taking the case history from the mother, so that the patient does not know he is being closely observed. One should look not only for obvious weakness or for asymmetry, but for the mobility of facial expression, its exaggeration or depression, possible infrequency of blinking and for any changes which may be present in the degree of wrinkling of the skin normal for the age. Other useful tests are to ask the child to close his eyes against the resistance of the examiner's fingers, to grin, and to blow up his cheeks. The upper and lower face should be appraised separately in the examiner's mind and he should also try to distinguish emotional movements from those of voluntary effort. Abnormal movements should be looked for, which may include focal seizures, fasciculation, tics, grimacing, myoclonus, choreoathetosis, or facial spasms. Episodic hemifacial spasm reflects an irritative lesion of the facial nucleus or along the nerve. Persistent spastic paretic facial contracture has also been reported (Sogg et al. 1963) which is chronic and persistent and not episodic as in the case of hemifacial spasm. It also lacks the associated (mass) facial movements seen with contractures following Bell's palsy. The cases reported by the authors mentioned were associated with intrinsic pontine tumours.

If the upper face is included in a mild unilateral paresis, a wider palpebral fissure on the affected side may be the most subtle evidence on inspection. Other ways of detecting slight involvement are to ask the patient to close his eyes while the examiner attempts to hold the upper lid elevated and to palpate or auscultate with a stethoscope for a difference in vibration of the eyelids as they are held closed against some resistance (said by Wartenburg (1953) to be the most sensitive sign of an old or very mild facial paresis). Other signs which are seldom positive unless there is other evidence by simpler tests, include loss of the ability to whistle, and a tendency for liquids to leak from the paretic corner of the mouth when the patient attempts to retain them in the mouth (he swallows normally). Even if the tongue is protruded in the midline it may appear to deviate towards the side of the facial paresis and the position of the tip of the tongue should be carefully checked in relation to a pencil held vertically in front of the patient's nose. The presence of contractures with old facial paresis may make the examiner believe at first that the weakness is on the opposite side. A young child, or particularly a newborn, with a congenital anomaly of absence of the depressor anguli oris muscle on one side, fails to draw down that corner of the mouth during crying as babies usually do. Distinction from facial paresis depends on inability to demonstrate any other area of weakness and on relative thinness of the cheek just below the angle of the mouth. The latter is appraised by palpation with one finger in the child's mouth and one on the cheek.

There are several useful reflexes referable to motor function of the facial nerve. Reflex contraction of the orbicularis oculi with brief closure of the eye follows sudden percussion of the supraorbital ridge (McCarthy's reflex), the glabella, or the margin of the orbit. This is probably a stretch reflex, and is diminished or absent in lesions of the lower motor neurone and preserved or exaggerated with supranuclear varieties of facial paresis. It may also be absent in coma. Reflex closing of the eyes may be demonstrated in response to a sudden loud noise, to a bright light shone in the eyes, to sudden cutaneous stimulation of the face (especially if painful) or to stimulation of the palate. The eyeballs roll up during the contraction of the orbiculares oculorum on closure of the eyes, whether voluntary, reflexive, or in sleep. This is actually an associated movement rather than a true reflex. Its manifestation when a patient attempts to close the eye on the side of a facial paresis is referred to as Bell's phenomenon. Tapping the upper lip or the side of the nose produces reflex contraction of the quadratus labii superioris and levator anguli oris muscles, with elevation of the upper lip and corner of the mouth. The afferent arc of the reflex is mediated through the trigeminal nerve and the efferent through the facial. This response is normal during approximately the first year of life (and in early infancy usually extends to a rooting reflex). However, obtaining this type of reflex retraction after infancy suggests a supranuclear lesion above the level of the 7th nucleus; this may be pyramidal or possibly extrapyramidal. The response to percussing either the upper or lower lip may include spread to involve contraction of the orbicularis oris with a protrusion of the lips referred to as the 'snout reflex'. This occurs in bilateral supranuclear lesions and in a variety of degenerative cerebral diseases. The sucking reflex may also be present. In the palmomental reflex, scratching the thenar eminence of the hand is followed by ipsilateral elevation and retraction of the angle of the mouth. This reflex is also normal in infancy but at later ages suggests disease of the pyramidal tract or opposite frontal lobe. It may occasionally be obtained with normal individuals, however. The Chvostek sign of contraction of the facial muscles following percussion of the pes anserinus is not a true reflex but is based on increased irritability of the motor fibres to mechanical stimulation, in tetany or other conditions.

Examination of Sensory Functions

The auditory canal, tympanic membrane, and an uncertain cutaneous area on or about the external ear are usually stated to convey sensory fibres via the facial nerve. However, there is overlap with sensory innervation from the 5th, 9th and 10th cranial nerves and the 2nd and 3rd cervical roots. Thus, examination of the exteroceptive function of the facial nerve cannot be made.

Hyperacusis is exaggerated or unpleasant perception of loud sounds, especially if of a low pitch, and is attributed to paralysis of the facial nerve's motor branch to the stapedius. It is subjective and difficult to evaluate in children either by description or by observation of facial expression, but if hyperacusis can be documented it implies a lesion in the upper facial canal or more proximally. An exaggerated startle reaction to sound is well known as a characteristic of Tay-Sachs disease, but may also be seen with other progressive cerebral degenerations and in blind children.

Sense of taste is conveyed from the anterior 2/3 of the tongue via the chorda tympani and facial nerve. It is well known that sensation of taste is based to a large extent on smell, and patients with anosmia may complain of inability to taste their food instead. The four fundamental modalities of taste are sweet, sour, salty and bitter. These may be tested using strong solutions of sugar, 1% hydrochloric acid, strong sodium chloride solution, and quinine or chloramphenicol (but not the sweetened oral preparations sold for medication of children!). To detect more subtle differences one may use respectively 5% glucose solution, 1% citric acid, 3% sodium chloride and 0.1% quinine hydrochloride. Dropper bottles may be used to place drops on selected areas of the patient's tongue, or cotton-tipped applicator sticks may be dipped in the solution and applied to the tongue.

Whatever method is chosen the procedure should be explained to the child in detail before starting. He is asked to protrude his tongue, after which a drop of the solution or the cotton applicator will be placed on the right or left side of the tongue separately; he is then to keep the tongue protruded and to nod his head when the examiner reaches the appropriate point of the sequence of spoken words, 'sweet, sour, salty, bitter'. Older children who can read the words may point to them as written on a piece of paper. If the patient retracts his tongue into his mouth, he spoils the test, for both sides of the tongue and the gustatory function of the 9th cranial nerve are then tested simultaneously. The mouth should be rinsed out with water between these test substances, and bitter is preferably used last both because children dislike it and because it leaves the greatest after-taste. If diminished appreciation of taste is suspected (this is rarely complete unless there is also anosmia), the tongue should be inspected carefully for possible intrinsic disease.

Autonomic Functions

Increased lacrimation and involuntary flow of tears down the face (epiphora) are usual in a fresh facial paralysis of the lower motor unit. Diminished lacrimation on the side of a facial paralysis may be the result of drying of the eye but occasionally occurs with tumours near the geniculate ganglion (Tremble and Penfield 1936). Hanging a strip of filter paper on each lower lid may reveal a greater amount of moistening on one side than on the other. Examination of salivation is probably superfluous if taste is normal.

Interpretation

Lesions of various possible types located at different levels of the course of the facial nerve produce impairment of its functions in varying combinations (Table IV). Interpretation of these signs as regards the various possible pathological bases of facial paralysis is reviewed in standard textbooks of neurology and in the medical literature (especially in the case of children — Paine 1957). Partially recovered old facial palsies are particularly difficult to evaluate because of possible associated contractures and because the upper face may recover first in a peripheral facial palsy, then giving the impression of a supranuclear lesion. Also, while the upper part of the face usually has a more bilateral supranuclear innervation than the lower, the upper face

TABLE IV

Clinical Findings in Facial Paralyses due to Lesions of Various Anatomical Locations

Location of Lesion	Voluntary Movements Upper Face	Voluntary Movements Lower Face	Emotional Movements	Lacrimation	Salivation Submaxillary and Sublingual	Taste Anterior 2/3 of tongue	Hyperacusis
Supranuclear	Retained	Lost	Retained	Retained	Retained	Retained	Absent
Nuclear	Lost	Lost	Lost	Retained	Retained	Retained	Present
Intracranial (between pons and int. aud. meatus)	Lost	Lost	Lost	Usually Lost	Usually Lost	Usually Lost	Present
In canal at or above geniculate ganglion	Lost	Lost	Lost	Lost	Lost	Lost	Present
Between ganglion and nerve to stapedius	Lost	Lost	Lost	Retained	Lost	Lost	Present
Between stapedius and chorda tympani	Lost	Lost	Lost	Retained	Lost	Lost	Absent
Between chorda tympani and branching on face	Lost	Lost	Lost	Retained	Retained	Retained	Absent
In pes anserinus	Variable	Variable	Partly Lost	Retained	Retained	Retained	Absent

is not always entirely spared in unilateral supranuclear facial paresis. Emotional movements of the face are supposed to be relatively spared under the same circumstances.

With these limitations, however, the level of involvement may be more or less accurately localised by the criteria in Table IV. Impairment of emotional facial movements, particularly in smiling or crying, with retention of voluntary movements, is thought to be associated with disease of the extrapyramidal cortical projections, the basal ganglia or thalamus, or possibly the reticular part of the pons superior to the facial nucleus. A mask-like face, with paucity of movement and infrequent blinking, is characteristic of Parkinson's disease, but in the case of children it may reflect a post-encephalitic state, pseudo-bulbar palsy or involvement of the globus pallidus or putamen. The presence of vesicles on the eardrum or at the external auditory meatus suggests facial palsy associated with herpes zoster, but, in view of the multiple anastomoses of the lower cranial nerves, the herpetic involvement may not necessarily include the geniculate ganglion in the syndrome described by Ramsey Hunt (Denny-Brown *et al.* 1944). A bilaterally expressionless and hypotonic face may be a congenital defect, especially if combined with impaired abduction of the eyes in Moebius' syndrome. Acquired facial diplegia may reflect the several causes of cranial neuritis but should raise the question of Guillain-Barré syndrome. True involuntary facial spasm may result from irritation of the facial nucleus or of the nerve anywhere along its course. It must be distinguished from tic or habit spasm and from chorea, subjects discussed in the chapter on involuntary or unwanted movements.

After incomplete recovery from a traumatic or cryptogenic facial palsy there are usually phenomena of misdirected re-growth of fibres, with spread of 'mass movement' to muscles other than those appropriate and a loss of differentiation of finer degrees of facial expression. Misdirected regeneration of nerve fibres for salivation along the pathway to the lacrimal gland may result in the syndrome of 'crocodile tears' in which the patient cries when strongly flavoured foods are put into his mouth. Similar misdirected re-growth into the auriculotemporal nerve may produce the auriculotemporal syndrome of flushing and sweating over the cheek in response to food in the mouth. The last mentioned is rarely seen after non-traumatic facial palsies. Surgical incisions in the region of the parotid gland are the principal cause.

Distinction between facial paresis and congenital absence of the depressor anguli oris muscle has already been mentioned. Two other conditions which are not neurological in nature may more closely simulate facial paresis. One is progressive facial hemiatrophy (hemihypertrophy on the opposite side may give a similar impression) and the other is the myopathic facies of facioscapulohumeral muscular dystrophy (Landouzy-Déjérine).

Various procedures give prognostic information about recovery from acquired facial palsy. Failure to demonstrate an electrical reaction of degeneration after 2 weeks or so implies that complete denervation has not taken place and that at least a substantial partial recovery can be expected. These electrical tests have been largely superceded by determination of strength-duration curves of the threshold for electrical stimulation and, more recently, by electromyography to look for evidence of denervation (see Chapter XV).

CRANIAL NERVE 8: AUDITORY NERVE

Methods of Examination

Evaluation of Hearing

Up to the age of 3 or 4, testing of hearing is difficult and of necessity somewhat unrefined. If the child is unable to sit comfortably supported or has poor head control, it is best to place him supine and stand at the head of the bed above the child's head, producing an interesting noise with first one and then the other of two similar noisemakers (see below) held under either ear, out of the range of vision. With older children, a similar test may be better carried out by seating the child on the mother's lap facing the examiner, who then holds the objects at arm's length slightly behind either ear. The best test objects are those producing slightly unusual sounds, preferably not too loud, such as rattles, small bells, metal crickets, crinkling paper, or even the rustling of the examiner's finger against the thumb. The criterion of hearing is a change of expression or more frequently turning of the head or eyes toward the source of the sound. The test can only be carried out with a quiet, reasonably placid, but not too somnolent patient, and it should be remembered that turning of the head and eyes toward the sound is not normally consistently obtained until a developmental age of 4 months. Delay beyond this age is due in many cases to general developmental retardation rather than to hearing loss.

The startle reaction to sound is another criterion of hearing. This can be obtained at some stage in a series of trials even with most normal newborns, but the hand-clap, or whatever is used to make the sound, must not produce sensory stimulation of the face by a draught of air. Devices producing perceptible vibration in the room are also not suitable. Evaluation of hearing in normal infants or in retarded older children is often difficult and in the authors' opinion the various types of audiometry are sometimes unreliable under these circumstances. This objection also applies to the psychogalvanometric skin resistance (PGSR) test, a conditioned reflex study of sweating and skin resistance involving presentation of a sound followed by an electric shock and subsequently presentation of the sound alone. Even at much later ages, the establishment and extinction of conditioned reflexes are often abnormal in the case of children with cerebral abnormalities (see Chapter XV, section on Audiometry).

Information may sometimes be obtained by electroencephalography during the application of acoustic stimuli, of which a sharp click is the best. Evoked cortical activity may be recorded (from the vertex, not from the temporal leads) in a standard EEG from scalp electrodes, in the case of infants in the first month or so. At later ages, algebraic summation and averaging of 20 or more responses by a computer is required. EEG audiometry is really a research technique in the process of development, and its application to clinical work should be made with caution.

With older and reasonably cooperative children, the examiner can test hearing for screening purposes by rubbing his fingers together 4 inches from the child's ear and asking him to indicate the side from which the sound comes, or by noting how close a vigorously vibrating tuning fork must be brought before it is detected. (The last mentioned requires standardisation for each model of tuning fork and frequency.) Whispered voice can also be used as a test, the child being asked to repeat what the examiner whispers to him at a distance of a foot or so from either ear; the possibility of lip reading is avoided by screening the examiner's mouth from the patient's view. Otoscopic examination should precede or follow whatever tests of hearing are used.

The Rinné and Weber tests are less used now than formerly. In the Rinné, a tuning fork is normally heard longer by air conduction that it is by bone conduction. Both are diminished proportionately in nerve deafness, but bone conduction is retained and may be better than air conduction in cases of conduction deafness associated with disease of the middle ear or of the external auditory canal. In the Weber test the vibrating tuning fork is touched to the patient's forehead. It is normally heard equally in each ear. In conduction deafness the Weber test is lateralised to the abnormal side and in nerve deafness towards the normal side.

However, the Rinné, Weber, and other tests with tuning forks are probably not worthwhile if time is limited, since a patient suspected of abnormal hearing from other tests or the history should be referred for audiometry (q.v.).

Patients with hearing losses should be questioned about tinnitus. This is often difficult to do with children without asking leading questions, and distinction between tinnitus, a self-perceived bruit, auditory hallucinations, and psychogenic problems is difficult.

'Developmental Aphasias'

The difficult problem of evaluating delayed development of speech has been considered in Chapter VI. It is probable that all developmental aphasias (as well as the majority of acquired aphasias in older children or adults) include some degree of disability in the comprehension of spoken language as well as in the motor production of speech. Since this concept of combined receptive and expressive aphasia is so applicable to the developmental aphasias of childhood, these must be considered in the differential diagnosis of apparent defects of hearing. Documentation of normal hearing in the presence of developmental aphasias is difficult but certain cues from observation, testing or history may be evaluated as in Table II, Chapter VI. Responses to sounds may be inconsistent or delayed or there may be equal inconsistency or delay in responding to tactile or other stimuli. The child often reacts to relatively faint sounds, especially if new or interesting, and appears to ignore louder sounds. Questioning or observation as to whether the child reacts to the slam of a door, the ring of a telephone near him, or the passing of an airplane overhead is useful, because few if any patients are so deaf as not to perceive these very loud sounds. Failure to react suggests either some type of receptive aphasia or a psychiatric problem such as infantile autism.

In dealing with a child who might conceivably have some type of aphasia, the physician should view the audiogram with some suspicion. Even when a pure tone or speech reception threshold audiogram indicates a considerable hearing loss, the clinician may be able to document consistent or usual responses to rattles, bells and similar sounds presented in the manner for testing infants as outlined above. This does not mean that there is a normal appreciation of auditory input, but rather that the deficit, if any, is central rather than peripheral. Deprived or disturbed children may respond to any stimulus only after some delay, or variably.

Vestibular Function

There are several ways of testing integrity of the vestibular receptors in the semi-circular canals and in the utricle and saccule, and their central connexions. Such manifestations of abnormality as staggering gait, deviation of the eyes, and nystagmus are considered in other sections. Older children may be tested in a standard Barány chair or in a revolving office desk chair. With the patient sitting erect, the head should be tilted forward about 30° to place the horizontal semi-circular canals in the horizontal plane. The pupil of the eye and the external auditory meatus should lie in a plane parallel to the floor. The chair is rotated about 10 times in a 20-second period, the patient's eyes being closed to prevent development of opticokinetic nystagmus. Normally, when the patient is rotated to his right there is past-pointing and postural deviation to the right with vertigo towards the left. When the patient's eyes are opened, nystagmus is seen with the quick component to the right and the slow one to the left.

Directions are reversed on stopping rotation. Depending on the speed of rotation, the nystagmus may normally last 20 or 30 seconds. Rotatory or mixed (rotatory plus vertical) nystagmus results if the head is not optimally positioned.

Infants and young children who are not too heavy to lift with confidence may be picked up under the axillae and held vertically facing and slightly above the examiner's own head. The patient's head should again be inclined forward from the vertical axis. The examiner then rotates about his own axis by moving his feet on the spot making 3 or 4 rotations in a few seconds. With normal young infants, there is full and obligate deviation of the eyes in the direction towards which the examiner is rotating, with the quick phase of nystagmus backwards, these directions being reversed when the rotation stops. With older children, the nystagmus is more prominent than deviation of the eyes in the horizontal plane. It might at first appear that the direction of deviation and nystagmus in this manoeuvre is opposite to that of the Barány chair, but this is not the case because the patient held at arm's length actually rotates about his own axis in the same direction as does the examiner, and it is rotation about his own axis, as opposed to rotation about the examiner, which is physiologically significant.

One of the above rotational tests is sufficient for screening purposes unless one suspects abnormality of a single vestibular nerve rather than of both. The right and left sides are best tested separately by caloric stimulation. The ears should be examined for possible perforation of the eardrum or obstruction of the external auditory canal (which must then be cleaned out). If these features are satisfactory, the child should then lie on a bed or examining table in the supine position, with the head elevated about 30° above the horizontal on a pillow, placing the horizontal semicircular canal in the vertical position in space. The simplest test is made with a 10 millilitre syringe with a short length of polyethylene tubing attached to permit injection of the water directly against the tympanic membrane. Ten ml. of previously prepared ice water is injected slowly and steadily over about 1 minute, the usually struggling patient being held forcibly in the correct posture by assistants (two are often required). Nystagmus usually begins shortly before or shortly after the end of irrigation, but the test should be repeated at least twice before concluding that there is no reaction. Excessively rapid injection of the ice water will often fail to elicit nystagmus when it can be readily demonstrated by slower injection. Irrigation with cold water, which is preferable to hot water as the latter may irritate the auditory canal, produces deviation of the eyes towards the side of the irrigation with the quick phase of the nystagmus away from it. If the right ear is stimulated the quick phase of the nystagmus is to the left; past-pointing is towards the right and if the patient gets up from the bed he tends to fall towards the right and to have vertigo (hallucinated movement) towards the left.

Lesions of the cerebral hemispheres may affect caloric as well as opticokinetic nystagmus but evaluation of possible abnormality at a cerebral level requires testing for directional preponderance of the nystagmus. In the method of Carmichael *et al.* (1954), a minimum volume of 300 ml. of water at a temperature of 30° or 44°C is instilled in a 40-second period. The time is recorded from the beginning of irrigation to the end of visible nystagmus, ignoring the latent period. Lesions in the temporal lobe or in the angular or supramarginal gyri produce directional preponderance (longer persistence) of the fast component of the nystagmus toward the side of the lesion. This method is difficult to apply with children because their smaller auditory canals make it impossible to inject the required volume of water in the allotted time. The test could probably be done with smaller volumes but standards have not been published and need to be worked out. (A trial of 100 to 200 ml. is suggested.)

If vestibular abnormality is suspected or demonstrated, the acuity of hearing should always be adequately evaluated and specific enquiry should be made for presence of tinnitus or vertigo. The subjective symptom of vertigo is, of course, dizziness, but this is strictly speaking a true hallucination of movement in which the patient will, if he is old enough and intelligent enough to describe it, speak of a feeling of rotation or movement, usually horizontal, in some direction. True vertigo should be differentiated from nausea, faintness, and from drug effect, although nausea and vomiting often accompany genuine vertigo.

Interpretation

Possible causes of hearing loss include familial deafness, maternal rubella in pregnancy, neonatal hyperbilirubinaemia, encephalitis and a diversity of febrile illnesses, meningitis, congenital syphilis, trauma, drugs and toxins (especially streptomycin), and vascular or expanding mass lesions. However, consideration of the differential diagnosis is beyond the scope of this volume. Vertigo may also have many causes. Labyrinthitis is infrequent in childhood unless associated with infectious processes. A variety of irregular dissociations of responses to testing caloric nystagmus may be seen with lesions in the median longitudinal bundle, in the pons, or in the cerebellar peduncles or midbrain.

Menière's syndrome rarely if ever occurs in childhood. The syndrome of the cerebellopontine angle includes deafness and tinnitus, followed by episodic vertigo and development of a peripheral facial palsy, pain or depressed sensation in the face, a depressed corneal reflex, and involvement of the inferior cerebellar peduncle and frequently of the 6th, 9th and 10th cranial nerves. Nystagmus is common and is slower and coarser on looking towards the side of the lesion. This syndrome is usually due to a neuroma, neurofibroma or meningioma. These tumours are rare in childhood but acoustic neurofibromata do occur in children in association with generalised neurofibromatosis and are then usually bilateral. Another syndrome of progressive hearing loss followed by otorrhoea, tinnitus, vertigo, pain in the ear, and involvement of the lower cranial nerves occurs with glomus tumours. The tumour may be visible in the auditory canal on otoscopic examination.

CRANIAL NERVES 9, 10: GLOSSOPHARYNGEAL AND VAGUS NERVES

The glossopharyngeal and vagus nerves are closely associated in anatomical arrangement and in function. Both have motor and visceral efferent (autonomic) branches originating from nuclei in the medulla, and both convey exteroceptive and general and special visceral sensations to closely similar central structures. Both leave the skull through the jugular foramen, together with the 11th nerve. Thus, two or three nerves are often affected jointly, and it is frequently difficult to decide which is producing the abnormal signs and symptoms.

Examination and Interpretation of Motor Functions

The 9th cranial nerve supplies only the stylopharyngeus muscle, and its paralysis may be impossible to detect. At most, there may be slight drooping of the palatal arch at rest (although the two sides elevate equally in saying 'aah').

The motor fibres of the vagus which originate in the nucleus ambiguus (as do also those of the 9th nerve) supply all of the striated muscles of the soft palate, pharynx and larynx except the stylopharyngeus and the tensor veli palatini. Unilateral vagal paralysis produces drooping of the palatal arch on the affected side and the uvula and medial raphé deviate towards the normal side. Retraction of the uvula toward the normal side is increased on phonation. In some instances where 5th nerve function is normal, contraction of the tensor veli palatini will prevent obvious drooping of the palate. If the vagal paralysis is bilateral, the palate cannot elevate on phonation, although again the palate may not droop markedly. The palatal reflex is tested by stimulating the inferior surface of the uvula or soft palate with a tongue blade or cotton applicator, the normal response being elevation of the soft palate and retraction of the uvula. Eliciting this response by lateralised stimulation may produce greater elevation on the stimulated side. The sensory arc of this reflex is through the 9th nerve and the motor arc through the 10th.

Vagal lesions produce surprisingly little difficulty in articulation or swallowing, although in acute lesions there may be dysphagia, especially for liquids, and some regurgitation of fluids into the nose when swallowing. Acute unilateral lesions may give a nasal quality to the speech and this effect is greater with bilateral vagal paralysis. Phonemes such as *b*, *d* and *k*, tend to become *m*, *n* and *ng* respectively. The effect is quite similar to that of a cleft palate. The function of the pharyngeal muscles is tested by the quality of phonation, by observation of the patient's efforts to swallow solids and liquids, by the elevation of the larynx on swallowing and by the pharyngeal or gag reflex. The gag response can be elicited by applying a tongue blade or cotton-tipped applicator to the pharyngeal wall, tonsilar pillars or to the base of the tongue, testing each side separately. The normal response is elevation and constriction of the pharyngeal muscles with retraction of the tongue. As with the palatal reflex, the afferent arc is in the 9th nerve and the efferent in the 10th. The gag reflex is normally more active in some individuals than others and if it appears to be depressed one should question the child's parents as to whether it has ever been very active (most children have had frequent experience of this reflex on visits to paediatricians or general practitioners in the past). If the superior constrictor muscle of one side of the pharynx is paralysed one may observe a 'curtain movement' of the pharyngeal wall towards the normal side on testing the gag reflex.

The vagal innervation of the larynx is first appraised by directing attention to the character of the patient's voice, and to any difficulty with articulation or in breathing. If there is any suggestion of abnormality (other than hoarseness readily explicable by an acute infection of short duration) the vocal cords should be examined. Examination of the larynx with a mirror or direct laryngoscope is difficult and upsetting with children and is frequently impossible without anaesthesia, and the examiner must decide whether the findings will be important enough to warrant this. The paediatrician or neurologist carrying out laryngeal examination himself will presumably either be familiar with the various syndromes of paralysis of the different muscles involving the vocal cords, or will consult appropriate references before proceeding.

Examination and Interpretation of Sensory Functions

Glossopharyngeal nerve sensation can be tested to touch or pinprick on the pharyngeal walls around the tonsils, and on the posterior 3rd of the tongue. The overlapping supply by the vagus may make interpretation difficult. The palatal and gag reflexes have already been described. The exteroceptive distribution of the vagus to the eardrum, the external auditory meatus and the pinna cannot be reliably examined because of overlapping innervation by other cranial nerves. Sense of taste over the posterior tongue (glossopharyngeal nerve) can be examined by using cotton-tipped applicator sticks dipped in appropriate solutions, as described under the section on the facial nerve.

The afferent arc of the carotid sinus reflex is conveyed through the glossopharyngeal nerve. Digital stimulation of the carotid sinus or body at the bifurcation of the common carotid artery causes reflex bradycardia, fall in blood pressure, and vasodilatation on the skin. Hyperactivity of this reflex may produce vertigo, syncope or even convulsions. The efferent arc of this reflex is through the vagus. The vagus also carries the efferent path of the oculocardiac reflex, of which the afferent portion, however, is in the trigeminal nerve. Pressure on the eyeballs produces slight slowing of the cardiac rate but this varies from individual to individual, is unstandardised, and may be counteracted by emotionally induced tachycardia. The swallowing and cough reflexes also involve chiefly the 9th and 10th nerves. Reflex sneezing to stimulation of the nasal mucous membrane (5th nerve) involves efferent pathways chiefly through the vagus and phrenic nerves with some involvement of the 7th and 9th cranial and upper thoracic nerves.

Examination of Autonomic Functions

The vagus is the longest and most important parasympathetic nerve in the body but its automatic functions are not easily accessible to clinical examination. The oculocardiac and carotid sinus reflexes have already been mentioned. Few satisfactory methods are available for appraisal of the visceral function of the vagus, and pharmacological tests are complicated and usually impractical.

Syndromes

The 9th and 10th nerves are involved in a number of medullary syndromes which are discussed briefly in the section on the 12th nerve.

CRANIAL NERVE 11: SPINAL ACCESSORY

Methods of Examination

The distribution of this nerve is purely motor, to the sternocleidomastoid muscle and to the upper part of the trapezius. The bulk and power of the sternocleidomastoid are appraised by inspection and palpation as the patient attempts to rotate his head to one side against resistance. Reflex contraction of the sternocleidomastoid muscle may be obtained by percussing its clavicular origin. The mass of the trapezius may also be observed and its power tested by asking the patient to elevate the shoulder against resistance. If there is weakness of the trapezius the upper part of the scapula tends to fall laterally. When the arm is extended anteriorly there may also be some 'winging' of the scapula with medial deviation of its inferior angle, but this is much less marked than in the presence of paralysis of the serratus anterior. However, winging is most marked in the last mentioned when the arm is extended above the horizontal; with weakness of the trapezius it is more pronounced with the arm extended anteriorly but below the horizontal plane. Extension of the neck against resistance depends chiefly on action of both trapezii together.

The examiner should also watch carefully for possible abnormal movements. Fasciculations may be visible as fine rapid ripples in the muscle and overlying skin, although they may be hard to detect if the patient is obese. Focal seizures may include turning of the head to one side.

Interpretation

In attempting to examine and evaluate apparent abnormalities of this nerve, one should remember that it originates from a small cranial part which is accessory to the vagus and unites with a much larger spinal portion arising from the accessory nuclei in the anterior horn of the spinal cord from the lower medulla to the 5th cervical segment. Rootlets from the latter nuclei leave the cord and join in a single trunk which ascends within the dura and enters the skull through the foramen magnum. The combined accessory nerve then leaves the skull through the jugular foramen together with the 9th and 10th nerves. Obviously, then, all three may be affected together by lesions in this vicinity and by mass lesions in the upper neck.

Spasmodic or hyperkinetic deviation or other involuntary movement of the head may be seen in post-encephalitic states, in the dystonia accompanying so-called 'athetoid' cerebral palsies, in dystonia musculorum deformans and in spasmodic torticollis, although the last mentioned is rare in children. Psychogenic tics may produce rather similar movements. Maintained torticollis, in children, is most often the neonatal torticollis of which the physiological basis is doubtful. Distinction should also be made from the effect of tender cervical lymph nodes, retropharyngeal abscess, and other acute processes. Paralytic torticollis may be based on a lesion of either the upper or lower motor neurone. Head tilting without any actual tightness of the sterno-cleidomastoid muscle is also often designated by the term torticollis, but may have other causes. It may be maintained to compensate for and prevent the diplopia associated with paralysis of the extraocular muscles. With children, head tilting should suggest a tumour in the posterior fossa. Such tumours may produce head tilting to suppress diplopia, but the phenomenon occurs in other cases without diplopia and may in some obscure way alter the fluid dynamics within the posterior fossa to reduce headache.

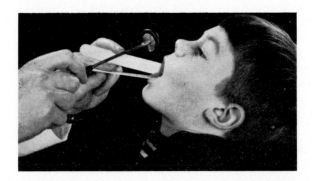

Fig. 11. Method of testing tongue for myotonia (see text).

CRANIAL NERVE 12: HYPOGLOSSAL

Methods of Examination

The position of the tongue at rest should be noted with the mouth open and the tongue lying naturally within it. Attention should be directed especially at any apparent atrophy or fasciculation. Fasciculations are visible as small furrow-like depressions which appear and disappear rapidly at irregular intervals. At times the whole surface of the tongue may have a rippling appearance, but this is not synchronous and must be distinguished from the synchronous tremor of the tongue as a whole which is normally observed in young children during crying. When a child is crying it is usually impossible to determine the presence or absence of fasciculation. Fasciculations are most easily visible through the relatively thin mucous membrane on the under-surface of the tongue.

The patient is then asked to protrude his tongue, to test whether it protrudes in the midline. In facial paresis there may be a false impression of lateral deviation of the tongue; this should be verified by comparing the position of the tip of the protruded tongue with the location of a pencil held vertically in the midline in front of the patient's nose. Slight degrees of deviation may be made more obvious by asking the child to protrude his tongue against the resistance of a tongue blade held in the examiner's hand. He should also be asked to push the extended tongue laterally against the blade, to compare the available power to the right and to the left. Although proprioceptive sensation from the tongue may conceivably travel in the hypoglossal nerve there is no available method for testing this. Other sensations from the tongue are carried in the 5th, 7th and 9th cranial nerves.

If myotonia congenita is suspected, the tongue is one area in which myotonia may be demonstrated by percussion. A tongue blade is placed between the under-surface of the tongue and the lower teeth to protect the under-surface of the tongue during the manoeuvre. Another tongue blade is then held by the examiner with its long axis running from him towards the patient, with the short dimension then vertical, the inferior edge being brought in contact with the upper surface of the patient's tongue (Fig. 11). The upper border of the tongue depressor is then percussed and the tongue blade withdrawn. A brief 'dimple' occurs with the normal myotatic response but promptly disappears. If there is myotonia, the subsidence of the dimple is much slower.

Interpretation

The 12th cranial nerve, the motor nerve for the tongue, originates in a long column of cells called the hypoglossal nucleus, of which the location resembles the upward extension of the anterior horns of the spinal cord. Its roots leave the skull through the hypoglossal canal and then unite into the nerve.

Diminished mass of the tongue may occasionally represent congenital hypoplasia but more often reflects atrophy, implying a lesion of the lower motor unit, since atrophy is minimal with supranuclear lesions. The bulk of the tongue may be increased in cretinism, mongolism, and some forms of glycogen storage disease as well as in amyloid disease. A wide variety of abnormalities of the appearance of the surface of the tongue are seen with many systemic diseases and in nutritional deficiencies. Deficiencies of the B group vitamins may also affect the nervous system; this may be a valuable diagnostic clue. Paretic lesions of the lower motor unit of the hypoglossal nerve cause not only unilateral or bilateral atrophy but affect protrusion of the tongue, which is generally weak if the lesion is bilateral. Unilateral paresis causes the tongue to deviate towards the affected side when protruded. Marked degrees of lateral deviation on protrusion of the tongue, in combination with unilateral atrophy, imply a lesion of the hypoglossal nucleus or nerve. If fasciculations are also present they imply a degenerative or progressive involvement of the hypoglossal nucleus.

Bilateral weakness, atrophy and fasciculation in infants is almost pathognomonic of Werdnig-Hoffmann's infantile spinal progressive muscular atrophy. In adults and rarely in older children such a combination may suggest motor neurone disease (amyotrophic lateral sclerosis or progressive bulbar palsy) or syringobulbia. It is sometimes suggested that fibrillations (spontaneous contractions of individual denervated muscle fibres), as opposed to fasciculation (irritative contraction of a group of muscle fibres innervated by a single lower motor neurone), can be seen on the tongue as a fine shimmering of the surface. However, the last mentioned appearance is probably merely low amplitude fasciculation; fibrillation is properly considered an electromyographic diagnosis not otherwise detectable.

Supranuclear lesions affecting the tongue produce relatively little atrophy and slight or no deviation on protrusion if unilateral. However, one does see children with long-standing cerebral hemiparesis who show some wasting of the tongue on the affected side, and some weakness of protrusion of the tongue to the opposite side or even deviation from attempted midline protrusion towards the affected side. Hypertonus and loss of voluntary control of movements of the tongue to command or to imitation may be conspicuous in cerebral tetraparesis as well as in pseudobulbar palsy. Patients with athetosis and dystonia frequently show comparable unwanted movement of the tongue, which is obvious chiefly on attempted movement to command or in attempted speech, chewing or swallowing. This loss of supranuclear control of movements of the tongue and oral musculature can be a major handicap with both spastic and so-called athetoid cerebral palsies, and is of major importance in connexion with speech, eating, and impression on the public.

141

CHAPTER X

Posture and Gait

Station

Methods of Examination

The term 'station' refers to the patient's attitude or posture in standing. An experienced examiner can usually observe the station satisfactorily with the child fully dressed, if the child resists undressing. However, many mistakes are made because of failing to undress patients adequately either because of lack of time or because of undue respect for their modesty; inspection of a more or less fully clothed child should always be followed later by some attempt to improve the examination by getting a better view of him without clothing. The standing child should be inspected for possible lordosis, kyphosis or scoliosis of the spine.

Normal children from 1 to 3 or 4 years of age have a considerable tendency to exaggerated lumbar lordosis and a pot-bellied appearance, but this stance is exaggerated in the presence of weakness of the muscles about the hip joints, as in muscular dystrophy. (Non-neurological causes should be considered, such as bilateral dislocation of the hips, enlarged abdominal organs, ascites, coeliac syndrome, etc.). The characteristic abnormal postures of the trunk and extremities in pyramidal and extrapyramidal syndromes may be detectable from observation of the standing patient, but become more obvious during appraisal of gait and are discussed under that heading.

The patient's ability to maintain the erect posture is more critically tested if he is asked to place the feet closely together. The examiner should not only look for a tendency to sway or fall, but note the direction of this movement. The patient is then asked to close his eyes, while the examiner observes whether ataxia is significantly increased by the removal of visual cues. Any apparent preference for standing on a broad base should be noted. Possible truncal tremor or titubation of the head and neck are other movements which should be noted.

Interpretation

An abnormality of station, closely resembling genuine ataxia, may be seen when muscular weakness alone is present from whatever cause, and whether primarily neuromuscular or not. The picture can include swaying from side to side, trembling, some flexion of the hips and knees, and a tendency to seek support on furniture. Painful falls may also occur.

Instability of standing posture inexplicable on the basis of muscular weakness (proven by objective testing), is usually due to cerebellar or sensory ataxia. Cerebellar ataxia is mildly increased by closing the eyes, but the change is much more spectacular in the case of sensory ataxia, when the inadequacy of proprioceptive information becomes more apparent as visual cues are withdrawn. The first appearance of ataxia of station or its marked exaggeration when the patient closes the eyes while standing with the feet close together is called the Romberg sign. Patients with midline cerebellar lesions, and very typically with medulloblastomata, tend to fall forwards or backwards. The direction of swaying is more variable with lesions of the cerebellar hemispheres but if these are unilateral the patient tends to fall towards the affected side. Hysteria may produce inability to stand or walk (astasia abasia) even though normal muscle power is present and there are no other organic signs to explain the disability. Apparent ataxia in standing with the feet together, especially with the eyes closed, may also be psychogenic (a 'false Romberg test'). There are several distinguishing clues, however: the hysteric sways from the hips instead of from the ankles; he rarely falls even though he may swing through a considerable arc, and does not injure himself even if he does fall; diverting his attention by asking him to execute the finger to nose test will sometimes diminish the ataxia or at least not increase it, while true organic ataxia will increase during this manoeuvre. Patients with organic ataxia often tend to steady themselves by touching the wall or pieces of furniture, whereas in the pseudoataxia of hysteria the patient does not benefit by steadying himself in this way, whether he does it spontaneously or is asked to do so.

Postures other than Standing

If the patient is unable to stand or walk (which will of course be noted) his posture in the recumbent or some other position should be observed. The excessively relaxed 'pithed frog' posture when supine does not point to any specific diagnosis, but may be seen with spinal muscular atrophies (Fig. 1), myopathies, and occasionally with scurvy (also characterised by tenderness of the bones and muscles). A similar posture may be encountered in the presence of spinal lesions, although the posture of the typical child with injury of the spinal cord at birth is different as regards the upper extremities (Fig. 2). A footdrop with some contracture of the heelcord is quite common if the patient has spent some time in bed, but flexion contractures of the hips and knees would not be expected except in the presence of spasticity, flexion spasms or other complications.

Patients who are able to stand and walk should also be observed in the sitting and recumbent positions. Truncal ataxia and tremor and deformities of the spine can be adequately evaluated from the sitting posture if the patient is unable to stand without support. When the patient is lying down, a tendency to lie on the side with hyperextension of the spine and retraction of the head (mild degrees of opisthotonos) may give evidence of meningeal irritation. (This posture may also be assumed because of a partially obstructed airway, or sometimes by severely mentally retarded children for no obvious reason.) In the supine position, a tendency for one lower limb to fall into external rotation at the hip with the foot pointing laterally is said to be a sensitive sign of hemiparesis or crural monoparesis.

Gait

Methods of Examination

The ability to walk presupposes standing balance, although patients may be able to walk once they are assisted to the upright posture even if unable to get up unaided.

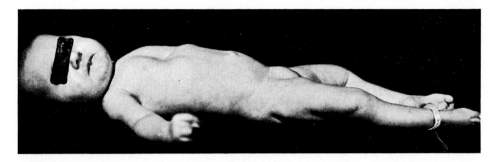

Fig. 1. 'Pithed frog' posture of Werdnig-Hoffman disease. Other noteworthy features are absence of spontaneous movement and the paradoxical pattern of respiration in which each inspiration results in retraction of the chest with bulging of the abdomen.

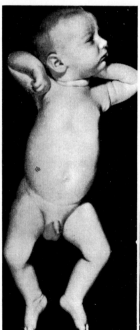

Fig. 2a.

Figs. 2a, b. Abnormal posture in a case of injury to the motor cervical spinal cord at birth. The 'pithed frog' posture is similar to Werdnig-Hoffman disease, as is the pattern of purely diaphragmatic respiration with bulging of the abdomen and retraction of the chest on inspiration. However the posture of the arms is quite different because of spasm of the biceps unopposed by the paralysed triceps (high cervical injuries are usually promptly fatal because of diaphragmatic paralysis).

Fig. 2b.

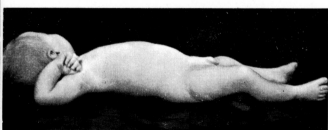

All of the reflexes and integrative mechanisms required in standing are utilised in walking, but walking also requires accurate integration and timing of a number of associated movements and synergisms. In walking, the two lower extremities alternately support the weight of the body and move forward. These two phases of support and progression should be evaluated separately and their relative timing estimated. One should also look at the position of the body as a whole, the freedom of movement, the progressive movements of the lower extremities, the size and speed of the steps and the degree of separation of the feet, and at associated movements of the trunk, upper extremities and head.

The examiner should also listen to the patient walk, possibly closing his own eyes to increase concentration. Slapping, flopping, dragging or scraping noises may be heard. (An asymmetry of footfalls is typical of hemiparesis.) The patient's gait should be observed both while he is barefooted and while wearing shoes and should also be examined during the wearing of any customary braces or apparatus. Gait with support should also be evaluated if a cane or crutches are used. Difficulty in walking may be more obviously brought out if the patient is asked to do heel-to-toe (tandem) walking, placing one heel directly in front of the toes of the other foot. The ability to execute rapid turns and changes of directions should also be noted. Tendency to lateral deviation of gait is more obvious if the patient is asked to walk round a chair first clockwise and then counter-clockwise, slight degrees of drift towards or away from the chair then being easier to see. Ability to climb stairs should be tested, particularly if gluteal weakness or muscular dystrophy is suspected. The ability to rise from a chair and to get up to the standing posture from lying on the floor are also worth observing. The soles and heels of the shoes should be inspected for possible asymmetrical or abnormal wear, or the parents questioned about this if the child happens to be wearing a new pair of shoes.

Interpretation

Different gaits are characteristic of a diversity of neurological and orthopaedic abnormalities. Only certain major varieties with fairly typical clinical features can be considered here. Evaluation and interpretation of abnormal gaits which do not follow any classical pattern, or include combinations of difficulties, is a highly complex matter, although the taking of motion pictures can be helpful, particularly if they are exposed so as to permit projection in slow motion.

The gait of *cerebellar ataxia* is abnormal whether the eyes are closed or open, but the abnormality is often rather more pronounced with the eyes closed. The patient walks on a wide base, staggering and lurching irregularly to either side, or swaying forwards or backwards. Truncal tremor may be present. Heel-to-toe walking and walking along a straight line are particularly difficult. Unilateral cerebellar disease produces predominant swaying or deviation towards the side of the lesion. A child with a tumour of the right cerebellar hemisphere will walk into a chair and stumble over it when walking round it clockwise, and will drift away from it when walking counter-clockwise. If he is asked to take a few steps alternately forwards and backwards he may slowly drift towards the right ('compass deviation'). Abnormal gaits which are almost identical with cerebellar ataxia are seen with dilantin (epanutin) or alcoholic intoxication.

The gait of *sensory ataxia* closely resembles that of cerebellar ataxia in some ways. However, it is much more abnormal with the eyes closed than when they are open, whereas the difference in cerebellar ataxia is only slight. There are several other distinguishing features: the heel is brought down on the floor first, followed by a slapping contact of the toes. The footfalls sound 'split' as the examiner listens to them. The phase of progression is prolonged because of the difficulty in coordinating the movements to place the feet on the floor. (Of course, if the disability is symmetrical, each foot must be involved in static support for as long as the other one is involved in progression. The examiner will then have difficulty in deciding whether the greater difficulty is in static support of body weight or in forward displacement of the progressing limb, but with experience he may be able to gain a useful subjective impression. If a sensory ataxia is unilateral or much more severe on one side than on the other, greater time will be required for forward progression on the affected side and the phase of support which is simultaneous in time will be prolonged on the less affected side.) Patients with sensory ataxia tend to keep their eyes on the floor while walking, in order to watch their feet. In adults, sensory ataxia is most often due to disseminated sclerosis, subacute combined degeneration of the spinal cord, or tabes dorsalis, but in children it more commonly reflects a peripheral neuropathy of some type. Friedreich's ataxia produces a combined sensory and cerebellar ataxia.

The gait of *spastic hemiparesis* is highly characteristic. There is a tendency to an equinus posture of the foot, often with contracture of the Achilles tendon, which makes the lower extremity functionally longer on the paretic side. The patient may compensate for this by circumducting the leg in an arc away from the hip, elevating the pelvic brim on the affected side, and dragging the foot a little, scraping the toes against the floor. Another possible compensation for unequal length is slight flexion of the hip and knee, a posture which may also result from contracture of the hamstrings. The paretic lower extremity shows a prolonged phase of progression and a shorter phase of support. The scraping sound of the toe on the floor and the tendency to wear away the toe of the shoe but not the heel are highly characteristic. The examiner should not lose sight of the involvement of the upper extremity in evaluating the child's gait. There is a paucity of associated movement of the upper extremity on the hemiparetic side; the arm fails to swing to and fro normally, and tends to be held in a posture of flexion and adduction at the shoulder, flexion at the elbow, pronation in the forearm, and usually flexion of the wrist, perhaps with fisting of the hand.

The gait of *spastic paraparesis* is not merely a duplication of the hemiparetic gait. In addition to the equinus position of the ankle, adductor spasm about the hips becomes a major problem. The patient walks with a stiff, shuffling type of gait, scraping his toes but also adducting the lower extremities so as to bump the knees against one another or to cross one foot in front of the other in a 'scissors gait'. The patient may walk on his toes with the lower extremities largely extended if extensor hypertonus predominates, but there is often flexion of the hips and knees (and tight hamstrings) with a crouching manner of walking. The gait of *spastic tetraparesis* is similar except that the upper extremities are also involved, in much the same way as with spastic hemiparesis. However, the upper extremities are usually more severely involved than the lower in hemiparesis, and *vice versa* in most tetrapareses.

The gait of *spastic ataxia* varies according to the relative degree of ataxia and spasticity. Subacute combined degeneration of the cord and disseminated sclerosis are the major causes of spastic ataxic gaits in adults, but in children one would think of ataxic diplegia, or of various uncommon progressive spastic ataxias resulting from spinocerebellar degenerations (of other types than Friedreich's ataxia).

Gaits closely resembling that of *Parkinsonism* in adults are sometimes seen in children with post-encephalitic states or progressive diseases of the central grey matter. The patient's posture and gait are rigid, movements are slow, and there is loss of associated movement. The posture is characteristically stooped, with the head pro-

146

jected forward. There is flexion at the shoulders, elbows and wrists but the fingers are extended in contrast to their posture in most cases of spasticity. The hips and knees are slightly flexed. The patient takes small steps and leans forwards from over his centre of gravity, which leads to increasingly rapid steps to avoid falling forward (festination). The tendency to take short shuffling footsteps, called 'marche à petits pas' and associated with senility or cerebral arteriosclerosis in adults, is rarely encountered in children even in the presence of progressive dementias.

The gaits of *dystonia and athetosis* are protean in their variety. Writhing contortions of the trunk and neck, a tendency to throw the head backwards or from side to side, grimacing of the face, and grotesque and often writhing movements of the extremities, are characteristic of 'athetoid cerebral palsies' or progressive disease of the basal ganglia in which dystonia is a significant component. One sees superimposed on this background the choreatic or athetotic movements in whatever form they are present. During the phase of progression in walking, there is often a characteristic posturing of the lower extremity, which is brought forward with moderate flexion of the hip and knee, slight external rotation of the hip, and with the foot in an equinovarus posture. There may be dorsiflexion of the toes or a Babinski-like posture. This type of prancing step, without other abnormality and without physical signs on examination to explain it, is often the mode of onset of progressive dystonia musculorum deformans. Patients with dystonic gaits, especially at one stage in the evolution of dystonia musculorum deformans, may be able to walk backwards more effectively than forwards. A comparable superiority of backward gait may also be seen in hysteria and in the presence of weakness of the quadriceps muscles (as in femoral neuritis).

The gait of *muscular dystrophy* (the sex-linked recessive pseudo-hypertrophic or autosomal recessive femoral types) is chiefly characterised by weakness of musculature about the pelvis. Lumbar lordosis is marked and there is exaggerated rotation of the pelvis and throwing of the hips from side to side with each step. The side-to-side waddle of the pelvis depends chiefly on weakness of the glutei medii. The patient has much greater difficulty going up steps and in rising from the floor than he does in walking. In getting up from the floor there is difficulty in extending the pelvis on the femora and the patient may give a push on one knee with his hand or may get the trunk erect by a series of movements of the hands up the thighs ('climbing up his legs' — Gower's sign). This last mentioned phenomenon however is by no means specific for muscular dystrophy and can be seen with polymyositis, old poliomyelitis, Guillain-Barré syndrome, or any other condition which happens to include considerable weakness of the glutei maximi.

The gait of *footdrop* results chiefly from weakness of the tibialis anterior muscle. The patient may drag the foot, scraping the toe on the floor, or may attempt to compensate for footdrop by exaggerated lifting of the lower extremity (steppage gait), throwing the foot out and slapping the toe down before the heel strikes the floor (the footfall sounds split, as in the case of sensory ataxia, but the sequence of placing the toe and heel is reversed). Walking is generally somewhat slowed, with a longer phase of progression and shorter phase of support. The peroneal muscles are often affected with the anterior tibial, in which case the foot tends to be inverted, the patient walking on its lateral aspect. Footdrop is the most frequent manifestation of the peripheral

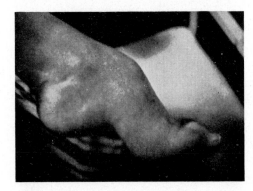

Fig. 3. Typical pes cavus.

neuropathy of lead poisoning in the case of children, who are less likely to develop the wristdrop typical of adults.

A similar gait is of course to be expected with neuropathy of the common peroneal nerve, of traumatic or other origin, and may be seen in the early stage of progressive peroneal muscular atrophy (Charcot-Marie-Tooth disease). When this disease is well developed, however, the foot assumes a cavus posture with some adduction and inversion of the forefoot, hyperextension of the metatarso-phalangeal joints and flexion of the interphalangeal joints, and an overall apparent shortening of the foot in the toe to heel dimension (Fig. 3). It is usually stated that a cavus foot depends on weakness of the intrinsic musculature of the foot, but an important co-factor is probably greater preservation of power in the tibialis posterior muscle than in the tibialis anterior or peronei (Tyrer and Sutherland 1961). A cavus foot is seen not only in Charcot-Marie-Tooth disease, but also in Friedreich's ataxia, some myelodysplasias, and with tumours or other acquired lesions of the lower spinal cord. Spasticity in the lower extremity, of whatever cause, may be associated with a foot which slightly resembles the cavus deformity, but the posture of the spastic foot depends chiefly on tightness of the Achilles tendon, and the degree of inversion, forefoot adduction, and heel to toe shortening is very much less. A true cavus foot should always suggest a possible spinal origin.

The so-called *antalgic gait* is essentially asymmetrical with a shortened phase of support to minimise pain in the affected limb. It may be due to a considerable diversity of painful lesions of the skin, soft tissues, bones or joints.

Weakness of single muscles or of various combinations of muscles, due to past acute anterior poliomyelitis or other causes, may be associated with an enormous variety of abnormal gaits which are very difficult for anyone other than an orthopaedic surgeon to classify.

Psychic disturbances, too, may produce an almost infinite variety of disturbances of gait. Hysterical monoplegia, hemiplegia and paraplegia are all possible. Loss of the ability to stand and walk (astasia abasia) without any other abnormality has already been mentioned. A tendency to walk on the toes or to go round and round in circles is typical of children with infantile autism but it should be remembered that toe walking can also be due to spasticity, even without contracture of the heelcord if there is a strong stretch reflex. Many normal children also do some toe walking for a few weeks or even months at some stage of their early childhood. The presence of wildly exaggerated, bizarre or unclassifiable abnormal movements of the limbs during walking may suggest an hysterical basis, but require at least consideration of the possibility of Sydenham's chorea, dystonia musculorum deformans, etc.

Asymmetrical or otherwise abnormal gaits based on orthopaedic abnormalities are probably nearly as frequent if not more so than those of neurological origin. Paediatricians will need no reminder to consider the possibilities of Legg-Perthes' disease or other aseptic necroses, slipped femoral epiphyses, and the waddling gait of untreated congenital dislocation of the hip. If an abnormal gait is not readily classifiable or is not obviously explained by neurological disease or myopathy, x-rays of the extremity involved and orthopaedic consultation may be wise. Further, neuromuscular disease involving unequal reduction of muscle power or unequal increase in muscle tone may result in orthopaedic problems. An obvious example is the tendency to subluxation of the hip if marked hypertonicity of the adductors accompanies spasticity of the lower extremity.

CHAPTER XI

Motor Function

Muscular Mass

Methods of Examination

Clinical appraisal of muscular bulk is inevitably subjective and must be carried out by inspection and palpation, bearing in mind the standard expected as normal for the patient's size, constitution and build. Estimation of muscle mass is especially difficult in obese patients or in the case of babies who normally have thicker layers of subcutaneous fat. If muscular wasting is suspected it is particularly important to note its distribution, including whether it is predominantly proximal or distal in the limbs, and whether there is any asymmetry. It is usually wise to confirm an impression of asymmetry by actual measurements of the circumferences of the limbs. The largest circumferential measurement obtainable may be taken as a basis for comparison in the case of the calves, but for the thighs, upper arms, and forearms, one should record the circumference at a measured distance from some bony landmark (the anterior superior iliac spine and the olecranon are suggested). In doubtful cases, muscle mass may also be appraised by x-ray, since muscle has a different radiological density to fat. However, the radiologist must be advised that the films are to be made with a view to demonstrating contrast of soft tissues rather than exposed in the routine way.

Interpretation

Atrophy or wasting may be prominent with any affection of the lower motor unit, whether a myopathy, an abnormality of the neuromyal junction, a peripheral neuropathy, or a disease of the anterior horn cells. Wasting also occurs with lesions of the upper motor neurones; in these circumstances it is usually less extreme, but the differences are relative and cannot be used alone for differential diagnosis. Distinction rests rather on other observations such as changes in tone, reflexes, associated sensory changes, the possible presence of fasciculations (which imply an irritative lesion of the lower motor unit) and often on electrical tests. Underdevelopment of bone as well as muscle is seen in many long-standing deficits of motor function acquired early in life, particularly in hemiparetic cerebral palsies (Fig. 1). Undergrowth of bone can often be demonstrated by measurement or by x-ray if desired. The presence of a marked degree of undergrowth in such circumstances is probably to a degree a parietal lobe effect and the large majority of such children will have defective sensation in the affected hand. This is a matter of some importance in planning of rehabilitative measures and training; marked difference in size of the hands implies a probable sensory deficit even if the child is too young, uncooperative or mentally backward to be accurately tested for such functions as stereognosis, 2-point discrimination, and sense of position or passive movement. The other possible causes of atrophy are the uncommon entity, congenital hemiatrophy (which involves not only the muscles but the skin, subcutaneous and

apparent on the finger-to-nose test, figure tracing, etc.

4. Past-pointing is a special case of dysmetria in which the patient in the nose-finger-nose test consistently misses the examiner's finger the same side. This is tested with the patient's eyes closed, the examiner than moving his finger to the point reached by the patient's finger when it has been extended an appropriate distance but has missed contact. If the test is positive, the examiner will find that he has to keep moving his finger each time in the same direction in order to keep up with the patient.

5. Loss of ability to check muscular contraction rapidly, and disability in contracting antagonist muscles immediately after relaxing the agonists, are evaluated in the rebound test of Holmes and in tests of rapid alternating movements. Disability in the latter is called dysdiadochokinesia, but this term properly implies that the disability is presumed to be of cerebellar origin (patients with spastic upper extremities perform alternate pronation and supination of the hands poorly, because of spastic hypertonus of the pronators, but this is not properly dysdiadochokinesia).

6. Intention tremor may be brought out on the finger-to-nose or other test, but this is properly considered an abnormal movement and is discussed in the following section.

7. Ataxia is a more general term for loss of control or coordination and may include any or all of the foregoing. The term 'ataxia,' however, implies in proper usage an incoordination associated with abnormality of the cerebellum or of afferent proprioceptive sensation.

To distinguish true ataxia from mere clumsiness is sometimes difficult. Decision must be made in awareness of the standard of normal coordination for the patient's age and mentality (retarded children are generally clumsier than normal children), and of the range of variation of normal, which is considerable. If objective examination is limited or impossible, the examiner should attempt to appraise separately three types of coordination, by his own observation or by questioning of parents:

1. Coordination of large muscles is considered in terms of whether the patient can walk and run normally, go up and down stairs, ride a tricycle or bicycle, etc.

2. Fine coordination is appraised in terms of ability to tie shoelaces, to cut up food or eat with spoon or fork, to do puzzles, or to use pencil or crayon on paper.

3. The working of puzzles and use of pencil and paper involve visual-motor coordination, which may be selectively affected in chronic cerebral syndromes. Ability to catch a ball in the hands or to kick a ball with the foot are other good criteria readily available.

Abnormal Movements

A wide variety of involuntary (or perhaps, 'unwanted') movements may be observed either with the patient at rest or in attempted activity. Their description and classification is rather difficult but several categories are traditionally accepted. These merge into one another and many patients show combinations of several, yet it is preferable for the examiner to try to describe the patient's difficulties in conventional neurological terms, at least so that others may read his report and gain a similar impression.

165

Methods of Examination

Abnormal movements are detected and classified almost entirely by observation of the patient's motor function at rest and during various activities such as walking, and in carrying out the tests for coordination described in the preceding section. Conventional categories and definitions are as follows:

1. *Fasciculation:* A very quick involuntary contraction of one or more motor units of a muscle, usually insufficient to produce movement of a joint but visible as a brief transient furrow in the skin overlying the muscle and presumed to be due to involuntary discharge of one or more motor units. Fasciculation is difficult to see in skeletal muscle if there is much subcutaneous fat. The entire body should be observed, but the easiest areas in which to recognise fasciculations are the intrinsic muscles of the hands, the deltoids, the musculature of the face and the tongue. Fine fasciculations involve the discharge of single motor units or of only two or three motor units corresponding to two or three lower motor neurones. The discharge from a single motor unit is not repetitive and the next twitch is likely to come from a different one. This type of fine fasciculation suggests disease of the anterior horn cells or bulbar motor neurones, and is often accompanied by the presence of 'giant potentials' of high amplitude on electromyography. Coarse fasciculations are often repetitive in the same motor neurones. These may occur in normal muscles at times, especially in the presence of fatigue; similar coarse fasciculations may be encountered with irritative lesions of nerve roots.

2. *Fibrillation:* Spontaneous contraction of an individual muscle fibre. Some authorities suggest that fibrillations can be seen with the naked eye in surgically exposed muscles or even through the mucous membrane of the undersurface of the tongue, but the more conservative view is that fibrillation is a purely electrical phenomenon demonstrable only on electromyography (see Chapter XV). Fibrillation is characteristic of denervated muscle fibres but is by no means limited to this situation. Fibrillations are encountered in myopathies as well, sometimes in considerable numbers, in the muscles of patients with disturbances of electrolytes, and occasionally in normal muscles, particularly in the case of premature or very young infants.

3. *Myoclonus:* Quick, non-rhythmic contraction of single muscles or small muscle groups, sometimes resulting in a sudden jerky movement of a limb. Myoclonus usually moves about from one area to another but may be rhythmic in the same area, as in myoclonus of the muscles of the palate or pharynx. Myoclonus is enhanced by attempted voluntary activity, emotional stress, and often by a wide variety of sensory stimuli. Myoclonus does not necessarily imply a presumption as to the location of the responsible lesion, although the current view is that this would be in a system including the dentate nucleus, the red nucleus, the olives, the central tegmental tract, and the brain stem reticular formation (projecting hyperexcitability both superiorly to the motor cortex and inferiorly to the bulbar motor nuclei and the anterior horn cells).

4. *Static tremor:* A tremor which is present with the patient lying or seated comfortably and posturally secure, not attempting any activity. Fine or medium rapid tremor (9 or 10 per second) is usually familial or constitutional or due to hyperthyroidism. Medium or coarse slower tremor (3 to 5 per second) usually reflects abnorma-

Fig. 2. Abnormal postures of the hands with excessive dorsiflexion of the fingers and instability of posture are early suggestions of athetosis (patient 15 months old).

lity in the basal ganglia. This type of tremor is at first relatively suppressed on attempted activity but later breaks through in greater amplitude.

5. *Intention tremor:* Tremor not present at rest but brought out by attempted voluntary activity. The finger-to-nose and heel-to-shin test should be used as minimum screening examinations and other tests used when appropriate.

6. *Chorea:* Rapid involuntary jerks or fragments of movement occurring unexpectedly and irregularly. Any muscle or muscle group of the extremities, trunk, head, or face may be involved, but the localisation and intensity are extremely variable and unpredictable. Each hyperkinetic movement is of short duration and separated in time from other episodes. Poor coordination and lack of static support are observed and it is frequently impossible for the patient to maintain uniform posture. Muscle tone is usually diminished. Chorea, like athetosis, is increased by attempted activity, emotional stress, or sensory stimuli. In severe cases of Sydenham's chorea the intensity of the involuntary movement may prevent sleep, or it may continue during sleep and cause the child to fall out of bed. The examiner should merely describe what he observed, but the final diagnostic impression should include the examiner's thoughts as to whether it represents Sydenham's chorea, Huntington's chorea, or a chronic non-progressive brain syndrome. (Chorea and athetosis often occur together. Slight degrees of choreoathetotic movement of the fingers of the extended upper extremities indicate mild disturbance of motor function commonly encountered in children with 'minimal cerebral dysfunction' or 'minimal brain damage.')

7. *Athetosis:* Relatively slow worm-like spasmodic repetitious movements affecting chiefly the peripheral musculature of the limbs and the face. Certain characteristic postures are repeatedly assumed, such as hyperextension of joints (particularly the fingers) and a positive Babinski-like posture of the feet and toes (Fig. 2). Facial expressions are often exaggerated. The muscles are usually hypotonic at rest, although tone is exaggerated during the unwanted movement. The majority of cases also manifest

167

choreiform movements. Many patients with so-called athetoid cerebral palsies suffer chiefly from dystonia and this should not be recorded as 'Athetosis' unless the disorder is observed according to its proper definition.

8. *Dystonia:* Involuntary fluctuations of tone and muscular spasms involving chiefly the muscles of the neck and the trunk and the proximal musculature of the limbs. Strange postures and slow spasmodic rotations (torsions) are characteristic. Muscle tone as appraised by palpation or passive manipulation is at times below and at times above normal. Attempted movement, or the involuntary dystonia, precipitates contractions of muscle groups opposing the original movement. Dystonia usually ceases during sleep but in severe cases may persist, possibly in response to minor sensory stimuli, or may even prevent sleep. (Note that dystonia is used here in its limited sense as a particular type of unwanted movement, not in the general sense of a disturbance of muscle tone, nor as diagnostic of the disease, dystonia musculorum deformans.)

9. *Ballismus:* Large-scale violent tossing or flinging movements which begin suddenly in the proximal muscle groups of a limb, and spread to involve all or the major part of the limb. They may be single or may be repeated over some time but, if so, are irregular both in location and in lack of rhythmicity. The face may also be involved. The movements are so violent and unexpected that the patient may injure himself or fall down. Conventionally, a diagnosis of hemiballismus implies a lesion in the contralateral subthalamic nucleus.

10. *Tic:* An arrhythmic, but usually repeated and stereotyped movement of restricted muscle groups which resembles voluntary movement much more than does myoclonus. In children there is a predilection for the musculature of the face, neck, and upper extremities. The pattern often changes from month to month even though stereotyped at a single time. A yelp or other noise may be uttered. Characteristically, tics do not distort or interfere with voluntary movement, and invariably cease during sleep. Even more than other types of unwanted movement, tics tend to increase in severity while the patient is being watched, or while he is tense or concentrating.

11. *Epilepsia partialis continuans:* Localised rhythmic epileptic discharge, usually without impairment of consciousness, which may be difficult to distingush from myoclonus except that its localisation is more constant and it is more regular.

12. *Abnormal associated movements:* see below.

Associated Movements

Normal associated movements may be lost or suppressed in the presence of abnormality of either the pyramidal or extrapyramidal systems. The most important normal associated movement from the point of view of diagnostic examination is the pendular swinging of the arms during walking. Failure of one arm to swing normally like its opposite is a sensitive clue to the existence of hemiparesis. Actually, associated swinging of the arms is just as characteristically suppressed in extrapyramidal disease, such as Parkinsonsim or the dystonic cerebral palsies, but these entities are usually obvious from other findings on examination and it is in detecting mild degrees of hemiparesis that asymmetry of associated swinging of the arms is particularly helpful.

Other normal associated movements include vivacity of facial expression in talking and in attentive listening, contraction of the frontalis muscle of the forehead on looking upward, turning of eyes, head, and body together in response to sound on one side, contraction of the platysma muscle as the patient opens his mouth to the full range or opposes his chin to the chest, extension of the wrist as the fingers are fisted, and the general body movements accompanying coughing, sneezing, and yawning. All these normal associated movements may be suppressed with disease of either the pyramidal or extrapyramidal systems. Absence of a few types of associated movements may have specific implications as to pyramidal involvement. Associated flexion normally takes place at the patient's elbow when the examiner passively flexes wrist and fingers, and passive flexion of the fingers also produces movement of the thumb in the direction of adduction and opposition. Absence of the former associated movement is referred to as the Leri sign and of the latter as the Meyer sign.

Another sign generally considered to have pyramidal implications depends on inability to achieve muscular fixation of the pelvis on the paretic side: the patient with a hemiparesis can raise either lower extremity separately (the paretic one less effectively of course) when lying in the supine posture but he cannot raise both legs simultaneously, and if he elevates the paretic one first, it falls back as soon as he attempts to raise the normal.

In the phenomenon called 'mirror movement,' voluntary movements on one side of the body, particularly with the hands and fingers, are mimicked in mirror image on the opposite side. A considerable tendency to mirror movement is normal in pre-school children and may persist into adult life, especially when learning or practising unfamiliar patterns of movement. Very strong tendency to mirror movement which cannot be suppressed by attention and effort is abnormal, however. This is conventionally held to accompany some abnormality at the level of the pyramidal decussation in the medulla, but pathological documentation of this is slight. A commoner cause in childhood is hemiparesis, in which mirror movements are seen in one limb when the opposite normal one is moved. This 'overflow' may go in either direction, but is usually more spectacular in the paretic limb when the normal limb is moved than vice versa.

Emergence of a number of abnormal associated movements is also seen with cerebral hemiparesis or tetraparesis (these are less easy to recognise in the latter). Various manoeuvres produce associated pronation and flexion of the wrist; the best known of these is active flexion of the elbow (the pronator sign of Strumpell). If the patient is lying supine and attempts to rise to the sitting position, holding his arms in front of the chest, there may be involuntary associated flexion of the hip in association with the flexion of neck and trunk. In the same posture, voluntary flexion of the hip and knee of a paretic extremity is followed by involuntary dorsiflexion and inversion of the foot. If the patient is standing erect and attempts to bend as far forward as possible by flexing the waist and hips, there will be associated flexion of the hip and knee on the hemiparetic side. Some of the abnormal associated movements referred to probably represent exaggerations of normal tendencies, and apparent abnormalities should be interpreted with caution unless there is definite asymmetry.

Topographical Classification of Motor Disturbances

In addition to describing hypertonus as spastic or to classifying some quality of unwanted movement, it is often customary and desirable to indicate the areas of involvement by terms such as hemiplegia, hemiparesis, paraparesis, etc. Existing terminology in this connexion is somewhat confusing. Properly speaking, a hemiplegia, tetraplegia or paraplegia implies a complete paralysis of sudden onset (and etymologically a stroke). Partial weakness is better categorised as hemiparesis, etc. The following categories are recognised:

1. Hemiparesis: weakness of the upper and lower extremities on the same side of the body, the arm usually being more affected than the leg.

2. Tetraparesis: weakness of all four limbs, which may or may not be symmetrical, the lower extremities usually being more affected than the upper. Diplegia is usually regarded as synonymous, referring to both halves of the body, but a few writers use it to imply a symmetrical spastic tetraparesis, sometimes with microcephaly, and a few use it to mean paraparesis. 'Double hemiplegia' is a term applied now and then to an asymmetrical spastic hemiparesis affecting the upper limbs more than the lower. It is probably preferable to refer to all of these variations as simply 'tetraparesis.'

3. Triplegia or Triparesis: usually, involvement of both lower extremities but asymmetrically, plus the upper extremity on the more severely affected side. Other combinations are possible, the essential feature being the sparing of one limb.

4. Paraparesis: weakness of the lower extremities only, the upper limbs being normal.

5. Monoparesis: weakness of a single limb only. This may be labelled as brachial or crural monoparesis according to whether this is an upper or a lower limb, but the terminology implies an origin in the central nervous system and is best not applied to manifestations of abnormality in the brachial or lumbo-sacral plexuses.

'Quadriplegia' or 'quadriparesis' is an unnecessary word of mixed Latin and Greek derivation, although it is sometimes used (undesirably) to indicate a disability of spinal rather than of cerebral origin. Paraplegia or paraparesis may have either a spinal or a cerebral basis and the examiner should indicate which is suspected. This topographical classification is used chiefly for spastic weakness since the various types of unwanted movement usually involve all four limbs, although hemiathetosis and hemichorea as well as less common possibilities exist.

CHAPTER XII

Reflexes, Responses and Infantile Automatisms

Deep Reflexes

Methods of Examination

The deep reflexes, 'tendon reflexes' or 'tendon jerks' are all tested by producing stretch at the insertion, or less commonly the origin, of the muscle concerned by percussing the tendon or attachment directly with a reflex hammer, by percussing the examiner's finger placed appropriately on the tendon or by percussing the neighbouring structures. Successful examination of reflexes depends chiefly on knowing sufficient anatomy to position the limb optimally and to percuss the correct structure, on being familiar with the normal response, and on having a relaxed patient. This may be difficult to achieve with young children, so it is well to test the reflexes with the patient fully clothed and seated on a chair opposite the examiner or on his mother's lap, planning to follow this preliminary testing with a repeat performance after the child has been undressed.

Almost any variety of reflex hammer may be successfully used and one may even use the edge of a stethoscope head, one's finger, or any moderately heavy object with a distinct but not too sharp edge, if proper hammers are not available. However, reflexes produced with other than standard instruments may have differing standards of normal, usually deviating on the side of hypoactivity, and the examiner must be familiar with these if he is to use them. If reflexes are hypoactive, or if they are extremely difficult to obtain because muscular hypotonia makes it hard to get enough tension on the tendon for it to be stretched by percussion, best results are obtained with the British type of hammer. This has a flexible springy handle attached to the centre of a metal disc, the edge of which is protected by a rubber 'tyre' (Fig. 1, Ch. IV). The large model of this with a wooden or plastic handle 15 or 18 inches long, often referred to as the 'Queen Square Hammer', is designed for adults but is entirely suitable for adolescents and older children. A paediatric model of the same hammer is available (Allen and Hanbury, London) and can be used for infants as well as young children. The head of this model is smaller, the 'tyre' about 3/16 in. thick, and the handle of solid nylon or whalebone. The type of hammer with a metal handle and triangular red rubber head is the common model used in the United States and its standard size is adequate for most applications. Its smaller and lighter version, however, is quite useless in the authors' opinion and frequently gives a false impression of areflexia when normal responses may be obtained with a better and heavier hammer. A folding type of pocket reflex hammer with a small rubber tip about 1/8 in. in diameter can be used for newborn or premature infants but is not adequate at later ages.

When the tendon or other proper structure is percussed, the examiner should note the speed, vigour and amplitude of the response, the range of movement produced and the duration of the contraction. Any duplication of the movement or clonus should also be noted. The response is conveniently graded as follows:

0=absent
± or Tr (trace)=very faint visible or palpable contraction but no movement
1+=hypoactive
2+=normal
3+=hyperactive
4+=hyperactive and reduplicated, inducing clonus.

The reacting muscle should be palpated as well as observed since some reflexes normally produce chiefly a muscular contraction which can be felt, but little or no joint movement. Hypoactive reflexes may also produce palpable contraction even though no movement of the joint is elicited.

The standard deep reflexes which should be included in every routine examination are the biceps jerk, triceps jerk, knee jerk, and ankle jerk. More extensive examination of reflexes should be carried out if there is any reason to suspect neurological abnormality not involving the body as a whole or the entire half of the body, if there is any dissimilarity in the four major reflexes, or if there is doubt as to whether these are normal or not. A more extensive list of deep reflexes is given in Table VI, together with the method of eliciting them, the normal response, and the muscles, nerves and spinal levels involved. Even this list is far from complete and almost any muscle may be tested for reflex contraction if the examiner can devise some way of putting it to stretch.

If reflexes in the lower extremity are quite hypoactive or absent, one should attempt to 'reinforce' them by having the patient execute Jendrassik's manoeuvre of gripping the flexed tips of the fingers of each hand with those of the opposite hand and pulling with one hand against the other. If a child does not understand this, a comparable result can be achieved by having him make a vigorous fist with each hand. Tension of muscles in the head and neck or in the lower extremities may have some action in reinforcing reflexes in the upper extremities but this is less striking. Reinforcement manoeuvres appear by present evidence to have a specific action in increasing the reflex contraction to a given proprioceptive input at a level in the spinal cord, although there is still some debate as to the exact role of the gamma motor fibres in effecting this. Modest increase in tension of the muscle to be tested, or in its antagonist, may enhance the reflex movement. This is particularly true of the finger jerks, which may be unobtainable if the fingers are completely relaxed but can be demonstrated in virtually every normal person if he will flex his fingers slightly against those of the examiner. Further increase in pre-existing flexor tone may give apparently exaggerated finger jerks, and experience is required to evaluate this sign. The Hoffmann reflex (see page 181) is more probably a method of demonstrating hyperactive finger jerks than a pyramidal sign in a sense comparable to the Babinski sign.

The knee jerk is conventionally examined with the patient seated on the edge of an examining table, his legs dangling freely over the side. It is in this position that a pen-

TABLE VI

Deep ('Tendon') Reflexes
(Those clinically most important are in bold type)

Name of Reflex	Tested by Percussion of	Normal Response	PHYSIOLOGICAL BASIS			Comment
			Muscle	Nerve	Spinal Level	
Scapulo-humeral	Vertebral margin of scapula and tip of spine	Retraction of scapula	Rhomboids	Dorsal scapular	C4,5	
Deltoid	Insertion at junction of upper and middle third of humerus on lateral aspect	Elevation of humerus	Deltoid	Axillary	C5, 6	
Pectoral	Examiner's finger on tendon near its insertion on greater tubercle of humerus	Adduction and slight internal rotation of shoulder	Pectoralis major	Lateral and medial anterior thoracic	C5-T1	Patient's shoulder should be slightly abducted at time of testing
Latissimus	Finger on tendon near insertion in intertubercular groove of humerus	Adduction and slight internal rotation of shoulder	Latissimus dorsi	Thoracodorsal (long subscapular)	C6-C8	Test with patient lying prone
Biceps	Finger on biceps tendon	Flexion of elbow (sometimes some supination)	Biceps	Musculocutaneous	C5, 6	Test with forearm semi-flexed and slightly pronated
Triceps	Triceps tendon above olecranon	Extension of elbow	Triceps	Radial (musculospiral)	C6-8	
Brachio-radial	Styloid process of radius or lower lateral edge of radius	Flexion of forearm and supination	Brachio-radialis	Radial	C5, 6	Test with forearm semiflexed and semi-pronated
Finger	Examiner's middle and index fingers placed on volar side of tips of patient's fore-fingers	Flexion of fingers and of distal phalanx of thumb	Long flexors of fingers	Median and ulnar	C6-T1	Test with patients' hands palm up
Costal	Lower ribs or costal cartilages	Deviation of umbilicus upward and laterally	Upper abdominals	Middle intercostals	T5-9	

Table VI (contd.)

Deep ('Tendon') Reflexes
(Those clinically most important are in bold type)

Name of Reflex	Tested by Percussion of	Normal Response	PHYSIOLOGICAL BASIS			Comment
			Muscle	Nerve	Spinal Level	
Deep abdominal	Tongue blade or ruler placed on abdominal muscles	Contraction of abdominal wall and deviation of umbilicus towards stimulus	Abdominals	Intercostals, ilial inguinals, and ilial hypogastric	T5-12	May normally be minimal
Symphysis	Symphysis pubis	Downward movement of umbilicus	Lower abdominal	Ilial inguinal and ilio hypogastric	T11-L1	Test with patient supine and hips slightly abducted
Adductor	Medial epicondyle of femur	Adduction of hip	Adductors	Obturator	L2-4	Test with thigh in slight abduction
Hamstrings	Tendons of medial and lateral hamstrings near insertions	Flexion of knee	Hamstrings	Sciatic, chiefly tibial portion	L4-S2	Test with knee partly flexed and with patient either prone or lying on opposite side
Gluteus	Lower sacrum or posterior ilium	Extension of thigh	Gluteus maximus	Inferior gluteal	L5-S2	Test with patient prone and most of weight on opposite side with some flexion of hip on side to be tested
Tensor	Origin near anterior superior iliac spine	Abduction of hip	Tensor fasciae latae	Superior gluteal	L4-S1	
Knee jerk	Patellar tendon or quadriceps tendon just above patella	Extension of knee	Quadriceps	Femoral	L2-4	See text
Ankle jerk	Achilles tendon	Plantar flexion of foot at ankle	Gastrocnemius and soleus	Tibial	S1, 2	See text
Posterior tibial	Tendon behind medial malleolus	Inversion of foot	Tibialis posterior	Tibial	L4-S1	Test with patient prone and foot over edge of bed. Often normally difficult to obtain

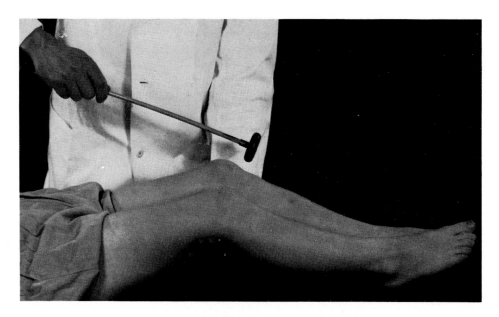

Fig. 1. Posture for comparing knee jerks.

dulous type of knee jerk (associated with hypotonia in the presence of active reflexes, as in cerebellar disease) is best demonstrated. If knee jerks are not obtained in this posture, or if there is some doubt as to their symmetry, better evaluation can be made with the patient in the supine posture and the knees supported in about 30° of flexion over the examiner's arm or over some object such as a medical bag (Fig. 1).

The ankle jerks are often examined with the patient supine and the leg lightly flexed at the hip and knee with the hip in external rotation. Symmetry is not accurately compared in this posture and if there are any doubts the child should be re-examined in one of two other positions. Comparison is also difficult if the ankle jerks are tested while the patient is in a chair with his feet on the floor. One of the appropriate positions for comparison is with the patient kneeling on a chair (Fig. 2), steadying himself with his hands on the back of the chair, and with his feet extended into the air over the front edge of the chair. (He can be told to 'kneel as if at church', assuming that he goes to church and to a kneeling denomination!) The other suitable posture for comparison of ankle jerks is the prone position on a bed or table, with the knees flexed at a right angle and the feet in the air. The examiner's nondominant hand should then be placed against the sole of the foot to steady it and in order to feel as well as to see the reflex contraction (see Fig. 3).

Clonus (Elicitation)

Clonus is a regular repetitive movement of a joint occurring several times per second, set into action by rather rapid mobilisation of the joint by the examiner's hand, or sometimes by testing a tendon reflex. The alternate bringing into action of agonist

175

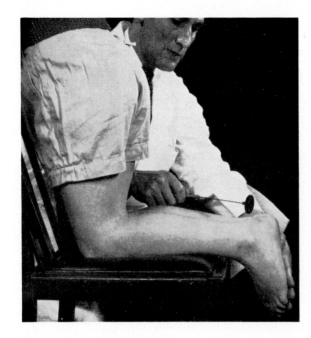

Fig. 2. Posture for comparing ankle jerks.

Fig. 3. Another posture for comparing ankle jerks.

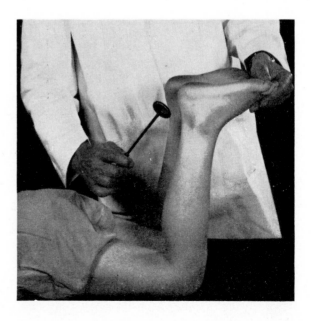

176

and antagonist muscles is a spinal phenomenon emerging with impairment of higher control, and its diagnostic significance is that of a maximal degree of hyperreflexia (in fact, to designate a reflex as 4+ indicates that clonus is induced). Clonus may be suppressed by extreme degrees of spasticity or rigidity, by fixed contractures, or by previous orthopaedic surgery such as a heelcord lengthening operation. If a tonic neck reflex is present, the ability to obtain clonus may be affected by the changes in extensor tone with rotation of the head to one or the other side. It is seldom possible to demonstrate clonus on both sides of the body simultaneously and ankle clonus established on the right will usually be extinguished if another examiner attempts simultaneously to demonstrate it on the left, unless the degree of clonus is extreme. Ankle and patellar clonus are the types usually encountered, but the phenomenon can be obtained from many other muscles in occasional cases.

Interpretation

In order to classify reflexes as normal, exaggerated or depressed, the examiner must of course be familiar with the standard of normal for the different reflexes, some of which involve livelier action than others in the normal condition. For example, the biceps jerk is often more vigorous than the triceps but each would be graded 2+ if considered normal for itself. There is also variation with age. In infants under a month of age the predominant flexor tone of early infancy almost invariably suppresses the triceps jerk entirely, and the ankle jerk may be feeble and difficult to obtain. The strong flexor tone of the upper extremity may also suppress the biceps jerk unless it is repeatedly and patiently tested. Young children are often relatively hypotonic and their reflexes may be depressed by adult standards. If all the reflexes are proportionately hypoactive yet present and symmetrical, one would record the findings as seen (1+ but not 2+) but accept the situation as normal in the absence of other findings. Other children, chiefly older ones, may normally have universal and symmetrical hyperactivity of reflexes, which again may be normal if there are no other findings and if the superficial reflexes and plantar responses are also normal. Hyperreflexia assumes greater significance in the presence of pathological reflexes which are referable to pyramidal abnormality.

The deep tendon reflexes may be somewhat increased in disease of the extrapyramidal systems, but it is with pyramidal involvement (or with the clinically consistent combination of pyramidal and extrapyramidal affection which produces spasticity) that hyperreflexia is most striking. The reflexes may be exaggerated, and additional evidence is provided by their being obtainable from a larger than normal afferent zone or by their spread to include other muscles, such as spread of the knee jerk to include contraction of the adductors of the hip. The knee jerk and adductor jerk may both show a 'crossed' spread to the opposite side up to the age of 8 months or possibly a year, but not normally after that. Some degree of general hyperreflexia may be produced by nervous tension or at certain times in schizophrenia (depressed psychotic patients may also have depressed reflexes). Affections of the upper motor neurones typically produce hyperreflexia, but pure pyramidal lesions or the mysterious group of hypotonic cerebral palsies may be associated with depressed or absent reflexes, as mentioned earlier. Lesions of the anterior lobe of the cerebellum produce hypotonia and hyporeflexia, and certain reflexes are pendulous if elicitable. Certain reflexes are also sometimes absent with cerebellar disease, but this may be because the extreme hypotonia makes it difficult to get the tendon tense enough to stretch it by tapping it with a hammer.

Even laying aside the information usually obtainable by examination of sensation or other functions, comparison of the degree of muscular weakness with the state of the reflexes furnishes valuable hints as to underlying diagnosis. Tendon reflexes are usually depressed in about the same proportion as muscular power in the muscular dystrophies and other myopathies. The principal exceptions to this statement are polymyositis, thyrotoxic myopathy, and the muscular atrophy which occurs about a rheumatic joint; in these conditions reflexes are often hyperactive considering the degree of muscular power, or even slightly hyperactive in comparison with normal. The reflexes may also be rather lively in myasthenia gravis. Peripheral neuropathies, especially if sensory or mixed but even if purely motor, usually depress reflexes to a greater degree than power. This is also true with affections of the anterior or posterior roots (Guillain-Barré syndrome, tabes dorsalis, Friedreich's ataxia, etc.), or if the involvement is in the anterior horn cell itself, as in progressive spinal muscular atrophy, poliomyelitis, etc.

Superficial Reflexes

Methods of Examination

The superficial abdominal reflexes are clinically the most important of the various tests which induce muscular contraction by stroking of the skin. They may be obtained by use of the examiner's fingernail, but better results are obtained with a matchstick, the end of a wooden applicator stick, or an ordinary pin if one scratches lightly enough. A blunt object fails to produce the reflexes and a painful stimulus may result in general tensing of the abdominal muscles in defence. Applying too firm a pressure may elicit the deep abdominal reflexes instead. If critical comparison of the abdominal reflexes on the two sides is desired, the best method of testing is with a tailor's tracing wheel, using very light pressure. The older type of tracing wheel sold by the Singer Sewing Machine Co. 20 years ago is highly satisfactory. The current models have a large number of teeth, closely spaced, and better results are obtained if one files off alternate teeth and sharpens slightly those that remain.

Upper, middle and lower abdominal reflexes may be demonstrated. The direction of stroking is usually not critical but it is conventional to test the upper reflexes by stroking from the xiphoid toward the umbilicus, from the costal margin diagonally toward the umbilicus, or from the xiphoid diagonally outward. The middle reflexes are tested by stroking from the lateral abdominal wall horizontally toward the umbilicus, and the lower reflexes by stimulation diagonally upward from the symphysis pubis. One can also test any of these reflexes by starting laterally and stroking more or less horizontally towards the midline. Normal contraction of the abdominal muscles is obviously visible beneath the skin and there is usually some shift of the umbilicus as well. Depression of the abdominal reflexes is the principal abnormality to be looked for, but an exaggerated response is occasionally seen. If this is suspected, the examiner should run his fingernail or the test object round the abdomen in a circle centered on the umbilicus. The umbilicus may then be seen to 'chase the finger around'. The nerves and segmental levels involved in the superficial abdominal reflexes are roughly the same as those for the deep reflexes (*q.v.*).

The cremasteric reflex is tested in males, and is elicited by upward or downward stroking of the skin on the upper medial aspect of the thigh or by pinching the skin in the same area. Ipsilateral contraction of the cremaster muscle is seen with elevation of the testis. This reflex is subserved through the ilial, inguinal and genitofemoral nerves and the first and second lumbar segments of the cord.

The plantar reflex is tested by stroking the sole of the foot from the heel forward along the outer margin, ending up across the distal ends of the metatarsal bones in the medial direction. Plantar flexion is the normal response and the reflex is innervated through the tibial nerve and the spinal segments L4 through S1 or 2. This response is discussed further in the section on the Babinski sign (page 180).

The anocutaneous reflex is tested by pricking the perianal skin, and the normal response is a visible contraction or 'winking' of the external anal sphincter. The pathway is in the inferior haemorrhoidal nerve and spinal segments S2-4 or 5.

A superficial palmar reflex may be obtained by stroking the skin of the palm from the ulnar side towards the radial or from the proximal distally. The normal reaction is a gentle flexion of the fingers, closing the hand. This response is quite variable and may be absent if the skin on the palm is thick. Its exaggeration in 'forced grasping' is considered in the following section on pyramidal signs. Both median and ulnar nerves are involved (C6-T1). Both palmar and the comparable plantar grasp reflexes are normally obtainable in infants by stroking or by mere contact of the examiner's finger. Their age of disappearance is not sharply defined but the reflexes are not consistently demonstrable after nine months in most babies. Other superficial reflexes which can be demonstrated but which are of limited clinical value are the interscapular reflex, in which the scapula is retracted when the skin is scratched in the interscapular space, and the gluteal reflex in which stroking the skin over the buttock is followed by contraction of the gluteus maximus.

Interpretation

The abdominal reflexes are often unobtainable in infants under 2 to 4 weeks of age because of the normal hypertonus then prevailing, but with luck they may occasionally be demonstrable. Depression of the superficial abdominal reflexes in the presence of exaggerated deep abdominal reflexes and of tendon jerks is an important sign of pyramidal lesions. Exaggeration of the superficial reflexes is usually without significance, accompanying extreme ticklishness, but may also occur with psychogenic disorders. Superficial reflexes are usually unaffected in cerebellar disease. In interpreting the abdominal reflexes one must bear in mind that they may be depressed for other reasons, including poor relaxation of the abdominal muscles, acute surgical abdominal problems, distention of the bladder, and nearness to the site of an old surgical incision. They may also be missing in the very obese and in the presence of a relaxed abdominal wall, as, for example, in the case of a child who has had nephrosis and ascites. In an occasional case, retention of the upper abdominal reflexes with absence of the lower may point to the level of a spinal lesion. Abdominal reflexes become symmetrical again soon after most infantile hemiplegias, and are of less diagnostic value than with young or middle-aged adults.

The cremasteric reflex may be absent if the boy is nervous or cold and has already drawn the tests up. It may also be missing if there is a hydrocele.

It is important to test the anocutaneous reflex of a spinal lesion is suspected or if there is any history of abnormality of function of the sphincter or a problem relating to the bladder. (The external anal sphincter has the same level of spinal representation as the external sphincter of the bladder, although the two are not necessarily involved in parallel in every case.) Its presence in spite of a rather relaxed anus in a child with myelomeningocele is a favourable prognostic sign for eventual continence of faeces on a constipating diet. Congenital imperforate anus is sometimes accompanied by hypoplasia of the sphincter muscle, and the anocutaneous reflex may then be defective after surgical repair of the anomaly. Conversely, in an unoperated infant, the presence of the anocutaneous reflex implies that the sphincter muscle is present and innervated.

Pyramidal Signs
Methods of Examination
There is little doubt that the Babinski sign is the most characteristic sign of disturbance of the function of the pyramidal tract. The plantar surface of the foot is stimulated by scratching with the examiner's fingernail, a key, or other sharp-edged object from the heel forward along the lateral border of the sole, crossing over the distal ends of the metatarsals towards the base of the great toe. Dorsiflexion of the great toe and separation (fanning) of the other toes is seen, sometimes with dorsiflexion of the ankle or withdrawal of the lower extremity as a whole. The examiner should start with a light stimulus, especially in the case of children, but should use a stronger and more noxious stimulus if no response is obtained. The response is difficult to obtain if the patient is very ticklish or fails to relax. It is also difficult to evaluate in the presence of strong withdrawal of the limb. Equivocal movement of the great toe may sometimes be 'reinforced' if the examiner holds the other toes in plantar flexion and then tests as usual, but this of course suppresses the fanning of the toes and permits evaluation of the great toe only. Many other reflexes also produce dorsiflexion of the toes. The sign of Oppenheim is elicited by running the examiner's thumb and forefinger firmly down the anterior edge of the tibia, that of Gordon by squeezing the muscles of the calf, that of Chaddock by blunt stimulation of the skin under and around the lateral malleolus, and that of Gonda by flexing and twisting a toe, maintaining firm pressure on the nail. The medical literature describes many other related reflexes.

There are also abnormal signs referable to the pyramidal tract which are characterised by plantar flexion of the toes. The most important are those of Rossolimo (who actually described two signs, one elicited by tapping the ball of the foot or the plantar surface of the great toe and the other by stroking the balls of the toes or giving a quick lifting snap to their tips) and of Mendel-Bechterew, elicited by tapping the lateral aspect of the dorsum of the foot over the cuboid bone. The 4th or 5th metatarsal bones may also be percussed.

Hoffmann's sign is tested by supporting the patient's hand, palm down, and grasping the middle phalanx of the middle finger between the examiner's index and middle finger, then giving a sharp snap to the nail with the examiner's thumb. If the abnormal Hoffman sign is present this is followed by flexion of the other fingers and flexion and adduction of the thumb under the palm. Another manoeuvre to test the same response is that of Trömner: the examiner grasps the middle phalanx of the patient's middle finger between his thumb and forefinger placed on either side and uses his other hand to flick the fingernail or to tap the volar surface of the distal phalanx of the patient's finger. The abnormal response is in the same manner as the Hoffmann sign.

Counterparts of other pyramidal signs of the foot also exist in the hand. Finger flexion comparable to the Rossolimo or Mendel-Bechterew reflexes may be elicited by percussion of the palmar aspect of the metacarpophalangeal joints or of the dorso-carpal area. The 'Chaddock wrist sign' consists of flexion of the wrist with extension and separation of the fingers following pressure ⁊r scratching on the ulnar side of the tendon of the flexor carpi radialis at the wrist. All these responses are variable and of limited clinical value.

Forced grasping is a more important sign in the upper extremity. The examiner inserts his forefinger or two fingers into the palm of the patient's hand, preferably between the thumb and forefinger, or applies a moving cutaneous stimulus across the palm, and the abnormal response is firm grasp of the patient's fingers, with difficulty in relaxation. Light touch almost anywhere on the patient's hand, particularly between the thumb and forefinger again, or even the sight of the examiner's hand, may be followed by a groping response in which the patient's hand follows the examiner's fingers with a series of reaching movements. A comparable abnormal plantar grasping reflex is also often demonstrable. These are not specifically pyramidal signs, although seen chiefly at a certain stage of recovery from an acute hemiplegia and usually disappearing later. Forced grasping is conventionally held to be associated with lesions in the frontal lobe anterior to the primary motor areas. Pathological forced grasping is not quite the same as the normal palmar grasp response of early infancy. The latter is more a traction response to pressure against the proximal phalanges and is obtained more poorly with a moving stimulus, whereas the reverse is true with abnormal forced grasping.

The signs of Leri and Meyer depend on absence of normal associated movements and have already been discussed in the section on associated movements.

The palmomental reflex is tested by scratching or percussing the thenar eminence of the hand. The abnormal response is contraction of the mentalis and orbicularis oris muscles with retraction of the corner of the mouth on the same side as the stimulus.

Interpretation

An extensor plantar reflex is generally accepted as indicative of disorder of the direct corticospinal (pyramidal) pathway, although this could be at a cortical, subcortical, scapular, brain stem or spinal level. Nathan and Smith (1955) have raised doubts about this, disagreeing with the earlier experiments of Fulton and Keller (1932), but to equate a Babinski sign with pyramidal disease creates no practical

181

problem in clinical work. It is generally accepted that most or all of the responses indicating pyramidal abnormality in older children or adults may normally be present in infancy, an effect probably loosely associated with the rate of myelination of the pyramidal tracts. It is difficult to set an upper limit of normal, even for Babinski's sign. In the authors' experience this may be present (an extensor plantar response) in the majority of children at 1 year of age, and in many even up to $2\frac{1}{2}$ years (Brain and Wilkinson 1959). There is no necessary correlation with the ability to walk independently. A few normal individuals have Babinski signs throughout life but it has been suggested that many of these were late in walking or are clumsy. In such circumstances the response may be brought out or exaggerated by fatigue.

In interpreting an apparent Babinski sign it must be borne in mind that the response is closely mimicked by one phase of athetosis of the foot. A patient with what is thought to be clear extrapyramidal disease should not be said to have a Babinski sign unless the examiner is confident that a more dramatically abnormal response can be demonstrated by stimulation in the conventional manner than the patient produces spontaneously in his writhing, or in response to cutaneous stimulation almost anywhere on the body. One current view is that the Babinski sign involves overlap of the afferent zones for elicitation of the dorsiflexion withdrawal response of the great toe and the withdrawal response of the foot and lower extremity to plantar stimulation. It may thus be considered as an underdevelopment of differentiation of reflex responses in infancy, and as the loss of this differentiation with pyramidal disease. Another view, supported by some electromyographic evidence, is that the extensor response is essentially a hyperactive flexor response with spread to include the extensor hallucis longus (Landau and Clare 1959). A Babinski sign is seen in a significant minority of patients with muscular dystrophy, and this is difficult to explain. It may depend on weakness of plantar flexors of the great toe in comparison with dorsiflexors, in view of the greater involvement of the muscles of the calf in pseudohypertrophic dystrophy. The available power for plantar flexion and dorsiflexion of the great toe should always be objectively tested in the case of patients who 'ought to have a Babinski but don't' or who present the response as an unexpected or inconsistent finding.

The Hoffmann and Trömner signs in the hand are probably merely ways of obtaining the finger jerk and their abnormality may be considered as an exaggerated finger jerk. Just as finger jerks may be quite lively in normal healthy individuals who exert moderate pull against the examiner's hand, a sort of Hoffmann response may also be obtained. Forced grasping is now thought to be a reflex mechanism involving the parietal lobe, in opposition to the opening reflex of the hand to cutaneous stimulation on its dorsum, a frontal lobe response. One view is that lesions of the frontal lobe then suppress the opening response and permit grasping to predominate, but it is perhaps better to consider the forced grasping reflex as exaggeration of the normal cutaneous palmar reflex since the response can be demonstrated without the examiner touching the dorsum of the patient's hand. Forced grasping may be a re-emergence of the normal neonatal palmar grasp, which usually disappears by 8 or 9 months of age, although an upper limit of normal cannot be set because it is gradually covered up by voluntary activity. However, neonatal grasping is best obtained by traction against the base of the fingers, whereas pathological forced grasping is usually better demonstrated by a moving stimulus, applied lightly.

Abnormal Spinal Reflexes

Methods of Examination

Pricking, pinching or scratching the foot may be followed by a jerky automatic withdrawal of the limb, without evidence of appreciation of pain if a pin is used as a stimulus. Crossed extension of the opposite lower extremity may also occur. Stimulation, especially on the inner aspects of the thigh or even on the lower abdomen, may be followed by a mass reflex of general flexion of both lower extremities, and the response may also include sweating, reddening of the skin and a pilomotor response below the level of transection. There may also be emptying of the bladder or bowel, or priapism. In other cases of spinal transection, pressure against the sole of the foot may be followed by extension of the lower extremity.

Flexor spasms may be seen, in which involuntary flexion of the lower extremities occurs after almost any cutaneous stimulus, such as the weight of the bed clothes, or even sudden uncovering of the lower extremities. Secondary contractures in flexion may develop.

Abnormalities of the bladder in the presence of spinal lesions are considered in the section on cystometrograms, Chapter XV.

Interpretation

Abnormal spinal reflex movements of the lower extremities in paraplegia may be confused with voluntary movement by parents or even by physicians, and to avoid confusion the examiner should direct his attention to their stereotyped, automatic, jerky character and the absence of appreciation of pain (judged by the patient's statement or facial expression), in spite of withdrawal to pinprick. It is conventionally stated that paraplegia in flexion results from complete transection of the cord and paraplegia in extension from incomplete, but the newer view is that either may result from complete or incomplete transection (Marshall 1954), and that flexor spasms depend heavily on induction by decubitus ulcers, infections of the bladder, etc. (Boshes 1957).

Except for the automatic withdrawal responses demonstrable in the lower extremities, birth injury of the spinal cord may produce a picture in infancy which closely simulates Werdnig-Hoffmann's progressive spinal muscular atrophy. The lower extremities are atonic and areflexic in many cases, and there is a paradoxical pattern of respiration, with bulging of the abdomen and retraction of the bell-shaped chest on inspiration due to intercostal paralysis (most of the lesions are lower cervical or upper thoracic in location). Analgesia to pinprick below a sensory level is of course a distinguishing point, and the baby with Werdnig-Hoffmann disease can withdraw his legs only feebly, or not at all, in response to pinprick, although he obviously appreciates pain. If the lesion is in the lower cervical cord, there may be an abnormal position of the upper extremities with the shoulders abducted 90° and the elbows fully flexed from biceps spasm in the presence of a paralysed triceps.

Infantile Automatisms

Methods of Examination

Successful examination of the nervous system of infants and of older children with defects of motor maturation depends largely on understanding and proper interpretation of the postural and other automatisms which are peculiar to that period of life. eMost of thse are present in the newborn period (see Peiper 1956, André-Thomas 1960, Paine 1960, Prechtl 1964).

The Moro reflex is the most important of these special responses in that it is always demonstrable with normal newborn infants other than the smaller prematures. The most reliable method of testing is to support the infant's head and shoulders on the examiner's two hands and then allow the head to drop back 20° or 30° in reference to the trunk. If this method is not successful, one should try producing vibration by slapping the bed (Moro's original method), giving the baby a sudden jerk by the feet,

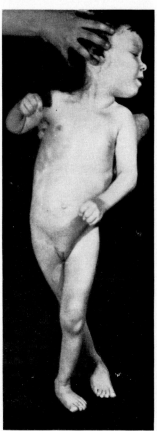

or pulling on the hands to extend the arms and then suddenly releasing them. The response can be reinforced, as it begins to fade with increasing age, by pressure across the infant's knees with the examiner's finger. The positive normal reaction scarcely requires description: sudden extension of the upper extremities followed by drawing them together in front of the baby with the limbs extended in an 'embrace' reaction, the fingers usually being spread. The femora are also flexed on the pelvis in the full reaction seen in newborns. As the response begins to fade away with age, the clasping phase may be lost first and only extension seen.

The asymmetrical tonic neck reflex is the most important infantile automatism in view of its abnormal persistence in cerebral palsies, etc., and of its reappearance following decerebrating catastrophes or with degenerative disease. It is tested by rotating the patient's head to either side, the shoulders being kept horizontal, and can be tested in the supine position, in the sitting posture, or standing supported (Fig. 4), (children who still show marked obligatory tonic neck reflexes are rarely able to stand alone). The positive response is extension of the arm and leg on the side towards which the face is rotated, with flexion of the limbs on the side of the occiput. The upper extremities usually participate more fully than the lower. The examiner should make a mental note of the speed of the reaction, the period of time for which it is maintained and the extent to which the child can 'break through' the pattern by struggling. If the

Fig 4. Obligate tonic neck reflex which is sustained indefinitely in 2½-year-old child with spastic tetraparesis. Patient has no standing balance but is held upright by mother's hands.

184

reaction is only minimally present, the examiner may be able to feel alteration in muscle tone but not to see visible movement of the limbs; similarly, the degree of activity of the tendon reflexes and the ability to obtain ankle clonus may be modified by the tonic neck reaction. Ankle clonus may be either increased or decreased by turning the head towards the side to be tested, depending on whether the pre-existing tone in the leg is such that clonus would be easier or more difficult to obtain with an increase of extensor tone. The examiner should also note the proportion of time which the patient spends with his limbs in a tonic neck pattern. Children may actively assume a tonic neck pattern when it is impossible to impose it on them by passive movement of the head.

The neck righting reflex follows the tonic neck reflex as the latter disappears with age. To test it, the patient must be in the supine posture. The examiner turns the patient's head on one side and this is followed by rotation of the shoulders, then the trunk, and finally the pelvis in the same direction, as if the patient were going to roll over on to his side and then on to the abdomen (Fig. 5a, b). Like the tonic neck reflex, this response may also appear with active rotation of the head by the patient himself.

The placing reaction is tested by suspending the child vertically with the examiner's hands under the axillae and manipulating him so that the dorsa of the feet are brought up against the underside of a table. The child will then plantar flex the ankle and flex the knee and hip, elevating the lower extremity and placing the foot squarely on top of the table. If one foot makes contact with the table edge first, it is normally placed before the other one (if both are stimulated). Even if both feet are stimulated simultaneously, one will be placed before the other in the majority of trials; stereotyped simultaneous placing should be noted if this is obtained.

The positive supporting reaction to bear weight with the lower extremities is tested with the child held in the same way as for placing, and it may conveniently be examined after the placing test. Firm contact of the soles on the table top results in mobilisation of extensor tonus in the lower extremity, from below upward, and sometimes in extension of the trunk as well. The extent to which the child can bear weight must be evaluated by 'feel', and an estimate should be made of how much of his body weight he supports. The examiner should also note whether the supporting reaction is carried out in a crouching position or whether the knee is fully extended and locked.

The stepping and hopping reactions are conveniently tested at the same time as the supporting response. As the examiner shifts the axis of the patient's trunk to one side or the other, or forward or backward, a single step should be taken with one of the lower extremities to maintain a posture of balance with the feet straddling the centre of gravity. Continuing forward displacement of the trunk, particularly if the body is rocked slightly from side to side, may initiate a train of automatic steps in the manner well known to everyone familiar with the newborn. Depression or absence of these reactions is to be noted as well as exaggeration or invariability.

The 'parachute' response is tested with the child suspended horizontally about the waist, face down. He is then let downward by the examiner and as he approaches a table top or other flat surface, the upper extremities are extended in front of him and slightly abducted at the shoulder, the fingers being spread as if to break his fall (Fig. 6).

185

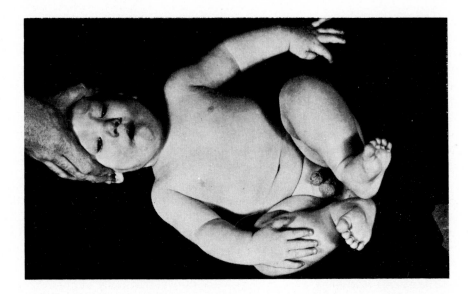

Fig. 5*a*.

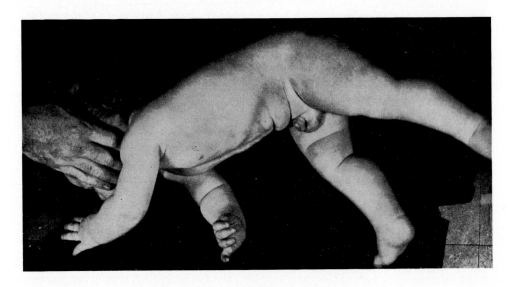

Fig. 5*b*.

Figs. 5*a*, *b*.   Two phases of abnormally strong, obligate and stereotyped neck righting reflex at one year.

Fig. 6. Parachute reflex in normal child of one year. Upper extremities are fully extended and the fingers spread as the child is lowered towards a table top.

The other automatisms tested in the newborn period are of little value in the case of older infants or children. Palmar and plantar grasping do not physiologically disappear at a particular age but are gradually covered up by voluntary activity. The traction response from the supine position, similarly, 'persists' indefinitely if the child desires to get up and is absent if he does not.

In the case of children who are unable to walk, the attitude they assume on suspension in space may furnish valuable information as to the nature of the motor deficit. In vertical suspension, the most important clues to be sought concern early spasticity. The examiner suspends the child with his hands under the axillae and looks chiefly at the posture of the lower extremities. Constant or predominant extension, particularly if the ankles are kept closely together or scissored over one another (Figs. 7, 8), is the most characteristic posture of spastic paraparesis or tetraparesis, and may be suspected from this manoeuvre several months before it becomes obvious from other signs. Another posture in vertical suspension is more difficult to evaluate: small children will sometimes extend both lower extremities in front of them rather than straight down, keeping them separated at an angle of 30° or so. This is often coupled with reluctance to bear weight or to make firm plantar contact with floor or table top. It is sometimes suggested that this posture presages the type of cerebral palsy called ataxic diplegia, and other writers have suggested that it implies psychic disturbance. The phenomenon also occurs in normal children (Paine *et al.* 1964) and is probably without significance unless accompanied by additional convincing abnormalities.

Posture in horizontal suspension is also important. The examiner grasps the child about the trunk, one hand beneath the lower ribs and upper abdomen and the other on the back, and looks especially at the attitude assumed by the head and the lower extremities. Reflex elevation of the head (and of the lower extremities to some

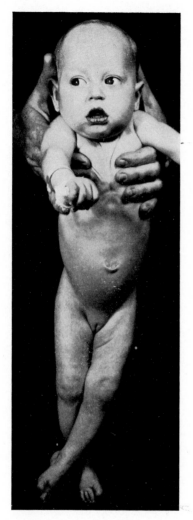

Fig. 7. (left) Adduction and scissoring of the lower extremities of 5-month old baby in vertical suspension (spastic tetraparesis).

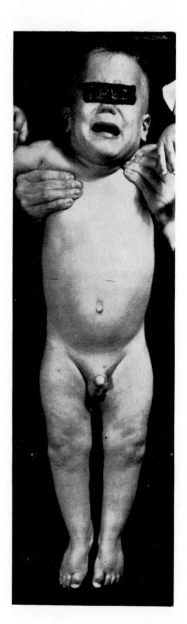

Fig. 8. (right) Adduction and extension of lower limbs without actual scissoring in a somewhat less spastic boy of 13 months.

degree) in this posture is the Landau reflex (Fig. 9a, b). Passive flexion of the neck results in loss of whatever extensor tone has been mobilised in the lower extremities and the legs then drop, but abnormality in this posture consists chiefly in failure to achieve the degree of elevation of head and legs to be expected for age.

The child may also be suspended by the feet, upside down, an attitude in which the head is typically retracted and the upper extremities extended below the child with the fingers spread, as if to break his fall if he were dropped. This test is upsetting to most small children and of rather limited value, and need not be included routinely.

Interpretation

The responses and automatisms described above may be qualitatively abnormal or asymmetrical, and evidence of abnormality may be furnished by their failure to appear at the normal age, or by their persistence after the age at which they ought to have disappeared. The normal range of variation is considerable and has been studied in detail in a group of normal infants reported elsewhere (Paine *et al.* 1964). Table VII shows the percentage of these normal infants who had lost or acquired certain signs at each month of the first year.

Delayed retention of the Moro reflex is occasionally encountered in children with motor disabilities from chronic brain syndromes (i.e. cerebral palsies), but this finding is relatively infrequent and the Moro response is much less valuable than the tonic neck reflex in this connexion. The Moro rarely if ever re-emerges following decerebrating catastrophes, whereas the tonic neck reflex does. The Moro, as indicated in Table VII, is never encountered with normal full term infants after 6 months of age. Flexion of the hips is the last trace to disappear, and if the test is reinforced by gentle pressure with the examiner's hand against the child's knees, it is often possible to feel an attempt at elevation of the femora until a much later age, although movement of the upper extremities should not be seen.

The tonic neck reflex referred to is that which Magnus (1924) called the 'asymmetrical tonic neck reflex'. Magnus' 'symmetrical tonic neck reflex' referred to movement of the extremities as the neck was flexed or extended and is one of the responses previously considered in the section on decerebrate and decorticate postures in Chapter X. The afferent arc of the asymmetrical tonic neck reflex is usually thought to originate in proprioceptive endings on the muscles of the neck (or on the joints of the cervical vertebrae — McCouch *et al.* 1951), and at least in animals it has a representation in the brain stem at about the level of the red nucleus. In dealing with human patients, however, the examiner is not looking for interruption of the anatomical arc of the tonic neck reflex but rather for its presence in a greater than normal degree or for its persistence past the normal age of disappearance.

The asymmetrical tonic neck reflex is infrequently imposable in the neonatal period, whether the baby is normal or not, but a considerable degree of it is actively assumed and also passively imposable to a degree during later months. Its maximum is reached between 2 and 4 months and the imposability of the posture should have disappeared by 7 months at the latest. Sometimes the characteristic posture of the limbs develops immediately when the examiner turns the child's head to one side;

189

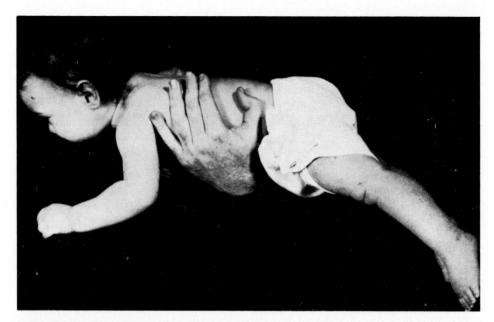

Fig. 9a. Landau reflex with elevation of head, extension of spine and elevation of lower extremities in horizontal suspension in space (normal one-year-old).

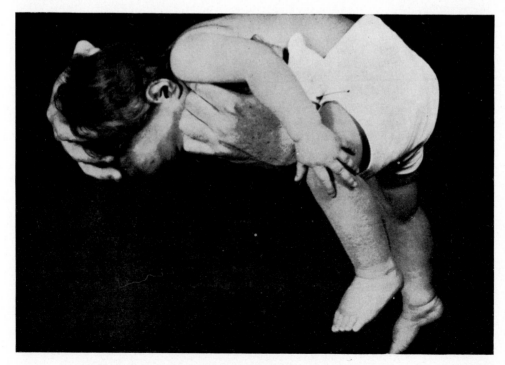

Fig. 9b. Extensor tone is lost when the head is passively flexed (see text).

190

TABLE VII

Percent of Normal Babies Showing Various Infantile Reflexes with Increasing Age

	SIGNS WHICH DISAPPEAR WITH AGE			*SIGNS WHICH APPEAR WITH AGE*				
	Moro	*Tonic Neck Reflex*	*Crossed Adduction to KJ*	*Neck Righting Reflex*	*Supporting Reaction*	*Landau*	*Parachute*	*Hand Grasp*
Degree of sign tabulated	Extension even without flexor phase	Imposable even for 30″ or inconstant	Strong or slight	Imposable but transient	Fair or good	Head above horizontal and back arched	Complete	Thumb to forefinger alone
Age								
1 month	93	67	?*	13	50	0	0	0
2	89	90	?*	23	43	0	0	0
3	70	50	41	25	52	0	0	0
4	59	34	41	26	40	0	0	0
5	22	31	41	38	61	29	0	0
6	0	11	21	40	66	42	3	0
7	0	0	12	43	74	42	29	16
8	0	0	15	54	81	44	40	53
9	0	0	6	67	96	97	76	63
10	0	0	3	100	100	100	79	84
11	0	0	3	100	100	100	90	95
12	0	0	2	100	100	100	100	100

* Divergence of experience and opinion between different examiners

in other instances there may be a delay of 20 or 30 seconds. The time prior to assumption of the posture is not critical, or at least its diagnostic significance has not been worked out. The degree of obligateness and the length of persistence of the pattern are more important. A normal baby of 3 or 4 months may remain in the tonic neck pattern for several minutes if particularly quiet and inactive, but will far more often struggle out of it within half a minute or so. A completely obligate tonic neck pattern, from which the child cannot escape by struggling, is abnormal at any age.

It should be impossible to impose any pattern at all at 7 months or later, and the child ought by then to have lost any tendency to keep himself in a tonic neck pattern for significantly longer than in the reverse or other postures (Gesell and Ames 1950). One suspects, however, that the turning of the head to one side may have some effect on the distribution of tone in the limbs until a much later age, and that this might be demonstrable in the modification of tendon reflexes, ankle clonus, etc., although no detailed study of this has been made. Modest degrees of tonic neck reflex, even at an age at which some degree is normal, should be considered as abnormal if the reaction is consistently asymmetrical in the sense of being more spectacular when the head is turned toward the left than toward the right, or *vice versa*. Whatever degree of tonic neck reflex is present is usually more striking if the patient is lying supine, but it will occasionally be more impressive with the child in the sitting position or even standing supported. Strong degrees of imposable tonic neck reflex are almost always incompatible with independent standing balance or independent walking. They may, however, disappear later and the child may then learn to walk alone.

Unfortunately there is no published information about the ages at which persistence of tonic neck reflexes might predict that the child would never be able to walk. In general, a strongly imposable tonic neck reflex after the age of 6 months, or a completely obligate one at any age, may be taken as evidence of a degree of motor decerebration, but not necessarily of mental deficiency. In the case of a child who is unable to sit unsupported after the latest age to which this might normally be delayed, apparent absence of tonic neck reflexes is a strong argument against the inability to sit being due to a specific motor abnormality (i.e., if the manifestations are those of a chronic non-progressive lesion of the brain, they are more properly classified as general psychomotor retardation than as a cerebral palsy). The examiner would not, of course, hesitate to diagnose cerebral palsy if he were able to demonstrate spastic paresis or athetosis or other dyskinesia. In practice, however, it is quite uncommon to find a child with no sitting balance combined with spasticity, athetosis, etc., who does not also show tonic neck reflexes. The converse is also largely true with some exceptions: consistently imposable tonic neck reflexes in the case of a presumed mentally retarded child usually imply some specific motor disability as well as or instead of uniformly delayed development in all fields of activity, including the acquisition of balance. However, in serial evaluations of a group of young children with delayed motor milestones, the majority of whom had cerebral palsies of various types, 17 had merely general psychomotor retardation; 7 of these 17 retained imposable tonic neck patterns (not completely obligate) past the normal age, and all but one of them past 9 months (Paine 1964).

A phenomenon closely resembling a true neck righting reflex may be demonstrated in the normal newborn infant, in that the examiner can turn the body towards one side by turning the head. However, in the newborn this is a smooth, immediate and almost simultaneous turning based merely on general hypertonus, and on close observation is clearly different from the two-phase neck righting reflex seen later in the first year.

Delayed appearance of the normal neck righting reflex, which sometimes appears immediately after the tonic neck reflex disappears at 4 to 6 months, and is usually easily demonstrable in normals at least by 8 months, is sometimes seen with hypotonic cerebral palsies. Hypertonic cerebral palsies usually produce immediate and entirely mechanical rotation of the body as a whole similar to that seen in the newborn. However, the absence of the normal neck righting reflex is entirely non-specific and its absence with hypotonic cerebral palsy is not in itself different from the absence accompanying general developmental retardation or secondary retardation due to non-neurological disease. The neck righting reflex normally persists in some degree until the child is able to rise directly from the supine position, rather than by rolling over on to the abdomen and getting up first to all fours and then erect. It disappears by degrees, or rather is covered up by degrees by the patient's own voluntary activity, and it is best thought of as the mechanism used by small children to rise from the floor in the quadrupedal fashion. An abnormally obligate neck righting reflex in which the baby can be rolled over and over across the floor like a log, in spite of his most violent struggling, is never normal, and this finding is encountered chiefly with various cerebral palsies.

Abnormally strong tonic neck and neck righting reflexes are frequently seen with cerebral palsies of various types, at the stage before acquisition of sitting and standing balance, but they are in no way specific for dyskinetic types versus spasticity. In extrapyramidal syndromes, one might suspect (although there is no real evidence of this) that the tonic neck and neck righting reflexes would be more prominent in a patient who would later show dystonia rather than merely athetosis chiefly involving the distal part of the limbs. However, this may simply mean that athetosis or choreoathetosis without dystonia are less likely seriously to delay sitting balance, but chiefly affect function of the hands. What Magnus (1924) called the 'asymmetrical tonic neck reflex' may be further asymmetrical in that a more spectacular pattern is produced by rotation of the head to the right than to the left, or *vice versa*. Similar disparity may also exist in the neck righting reflex, or a tonic neck reflex may be elicited when the head is turned to one side and the neck righting response when it is turned to the other. These circumstances suggest that the greatest motor deficit is on the side of the body with the more primitive response.

It is also highly important to remember that tonic neck and neck righting reflexes are in no way diagnostic of cerebral palsies in the sense of non-progressive chronic brain syndromes. These responses, especially the tonic neck reflex, may re-emerge following catastrophes such as cardiac arrest or in the presence of degenerative diseases of a progressive nature. If the progressive disease begins so early in life that the tonic neck reflex has never quite been lost, it continues uninterruptedly and increases in degree. This may give the false impression of a cerebral palsy, a superficial confusion which is particularly easy in the case of Tay-Sachs disease, if the startle reaction to sound is not particularly exaggerated or if the examiner fails to see the cherry red spot at the macula.

The placing and supporting reactions of the lower extremities sometimes furnish useful information in evaluating defects of motor development in infants and very young children. Both are likely to be abnormal in some way with any kind of cerebral palsy affecting the lower limbs. Absence of the normal response, its general disorganisation, or its exaggeration in a stereotyped unvarying way, are the principal abnormalities to be sought. Extrapyramidal involvement usually produces general disorganisation of these responses, and the supporting reaction is usually more poorly developed than the placing. The reverse is true in spasticity, where extensor hypertonus in vertical suspension is an asset in supporting but a liability in placing. Placing in this case is likely to be executed in a stereotyped mechanical fashion, and invariably with both feet at once, regardless of asymmetrical induction by touching only one foot against the underside of the table top. Supporting the weight with the legs closely adducted or by standing on the toes also suggests spasticity. Cerebral hemiparesis produces an asymmetrical placing reflex and sometimes an asymmetrical posture in supporting.

Placing and automatic supporting are both present in the normal neonatal period and an exact age for their disappearance cannot be set because they are gradually covered up by or integrated into voluntary activity. It is probable that something resembling placing can always be obtained if sufficient traction is exerted to produce discomfort, the reaction then becoming a form of withdrawal response. The normal newborn supports weight in a slightly crouching position with the hips and knees flexed, in contrast to the bearing of weight with the knee fully extended and locked, which is characteristic of older children and adults. The two types of supporting reaction may merge into one another without any hiatus, but there is often a period, at 2 to 4 months of age, during which the supporting reaction is less effective than it was in the newborn period in terms of percentage of weight borne. The neonatal form may even disappear and the baby then supports almost none of his weight for a month or two until the more mature fashion of supporting develops. It is well to remember that this apparent regression may be physiological and does not by itself imply progressive disease.

Stepping and hopping are also gradually integrated into voluntary activity and walking, and are of diagnostic value only if absent, asymmetrical or qualitatively abnormal.

The 'parachute reaction' (Fallschirm reaction of Peiper 1956) is a valuable diagnostic sign because its abnormality indicates malfunction of the upper extremities, and may confirm that a supposed cerebral paraparesis is actually a tetraparesis long before a stretch reflex or hyperreflexia can be demonstrated in the arms. The parachute reaction is not present at birth, but may appear around 7 months of age (occasionally earlier) and is present in most normal infants at 9 months, although its absence by itself should not be considered abnormal until one year. An asymmetrical parachute reaction implies greater deficit of function on the more abnormal side; a unilaterally abnormal reaction may be seen with hemiparesis, brachial palsy, or with injuries or other painful lesions of one upper extremity or clavicle. The parachute reaction also has no clearcut age of normal disappearance but is much less automatic and less consistently demonstrable after about 2 years of age. It is more a vestibular reaction than an ocular one, and blindness or bandaging the eyes makes surprisingly little difference in the reaction of extension of the upper limbs and even in the spreading of the fingers. However, there is of course no increase in spreading when the table top is neared if the table cannot be seen. The parachute reaction, comprising not only the extension of the limbs as a whole but the spreading and slight hyperextension of the fingers, tests both proximal and distal function, and should always be compared with the child's ability to grasp small objects since there may be discrepancies between the two. Suppression or distortion of the parachute reaction occurs with both spasticity and extrapyramidal dyskinesia. This type of response, combined with a fisted hand, would probably suggest future spasticity, but the combination of a poor or absent parachute response, or one more abnormal distally than proximally, with delay in acquisition of thumb to forefinger grasp for small objects (normally 9-12 months) might argue more for future athetosis.

Adduction, extension or scissoring of the lower extremities while in vertical suspension in space have already been mentioned as signs of spasticity. Abnormal posture in horizontal suspension, lacking the elevation of head and lower extremities of the Landau reflex, is less specific and merely indicates hypotonia of neck

194

and trunk. Many spastic babies are hypertonic in the limbs while still hypotonic in the trunk, but in the case of future dystonia or choreoathetosis, hypotonus of the trunk is almost universal during infancy once any neonatal rigidity (as that due to kernicterus or an anoxic insult) has worn off. A normal infant, even a neonate if born at term, should not collapse limply across the examiner's hand into the shape of an inverted letter 'U', but the rate at which extension of the neck, spinal column and lower limbs is acquired varies among normals. The degree of elevation of the lower extremities is less critical, but one might demand elevation of the head above the horizontal and arching of the spine so as to be concave upward, as the full Landau reaction. This degree of spinal extension is not seen with every normal infant until about a year of age. Older babies, even those who are not yet too heavy to test in this manner for the average physician, may distort the Landau posture into a wide variety of contortions as they try to get out of it. The response is gradually covered up or integrated into other patterns of movement, and its evaluation should not be attempted unless the child is reasonably relaxed (in the sense of not struggling, not in the sense of a relaxed spinal column!).

Unlike the tonic neck and neck righting reflex, the other early infantile automatisms only occasionally re-emerge or become obligate in the presence of acute cerebral insults or progressive disease. For the most part, too, their abnormality is not specific for one kind of chronic brain syndrome as compared with another (that is, for spasticity versus dyskinesia), except to the degree that some are more disproportionately abnormal than others. Finally, it must be conceded that too little is known about their exact anatomical loci for these infantile responses to be of much value in fixing the level of a lesion. The Moro reflex presumably has a representation in the brain stem and the weight of evidence is that proprioceptive input from the cervical vertebrae and muscles of the neck is more important than vestibular stimuli (Parmelee 1964). Tonic neck and neck righting reflexes have a similar source and level of origin and in animals are most conspicuous after decerebration at the level of the superior colliculi. The supporting reaction, and probably stepping, are spinal mechanisms or synergies which may be utilised from higher levels.

Rademaker (1931) felt that hopping and placing were cortical responses, but one of the authors of the present volume (RSP) has observed a full although not particularly vigorous placing reaction in an infant with complete transection of the lower cervical spinal cord due to injury at birth.

In summary, it may be said that the neonatal and early infantile automatisms and the postures assumed in suspension in space often furnish early diagnostic information in the sorting-out of delayed development of motor function and during the early years of life, particularly under 18 months. These signs may be much more helpful than conventional neurological signs based on alterations of muscle tone, reflexes, etc. They are not, however, in any way specific for a cerebral palsy in the sense of a relatively fixed brain lesion versus progressive disease. All of these signs are best interpreted in conjunction with other findings and with the known history. They are especially useful when the relative abnormality of one is compared with the others, but it is necessary for the examiner to have had enough experience to interpret the responses themselves as well as their diagnostic sum.

CHAPTER XIII

Sensory Function

Superficial or Exteroceptive Sensation (Touch, Pain, and Temperature)

Methods of Examination

Older children may be tested for sense of touch much as adults. The child is asked to close his eyes (or his mother covers them) and various areas of the body are then stimulated by applying a bit of cotton wool or 'kleenex' tissue (these are preferable to a camel's hair brush since clean test objects can be used for each patient). The tip of the examiner's finger may also be used, but, regardless of the test object selected, it must be applied to the patient's skin lightly, so as to avoid stimulating receptors for deep pressure. The child is asked to say 'now' or 'touch' when he feels the stimulus, or if he is shy and reluctant to speak, one may ask him to nod his head or to squeeze the examiner's finger placed in his hand. Light non-moving contact of the test object with the skin is normally sufficient if the child is intelligent and attentive, but when required, one may intensify the stimulus by stroking the skin gently. With children who do not speak because they are very young or for other reasons, one must judge perception by induced movement of the stimulated part of the body, a change in facial expression, or the patient's glance toward the stimulated region. Complete sensory examination of the entire body is rarely indicated unless the history or other physical findings particularly suggest a sensory deficit. As a screening type of examination it is usually sufficient to test the hands and feet and the three divisions of the trigeminal nerve on the face.

Sensory mapping requires testing at least touch and pinprick over the entire body at multiple points placed so as to cover each of the spinal dermatomes, as well as the area of distribution of each of the major superficial nerves. Figures 1 and 2 show the relevant neuroanatomical details. There will be no serious oversight if successive stimuli are applied at intervals of about an inch along imaginary lines drawn down the anterior, posterior, lateral and medial axes of the limbs (and in the case of larger children, down four additional axes placed midway between those mentioned.) The points used for examining the trunk may be more widely spaced. Any area of hypaesthesia or hypalgesia (or of hyperaesthesia if there is exaggerated reaction to sensory stimulation in an area) should be mapped out as completely as possible, marking its boundary on the skin with a pen. Sensory mapping is difficult and time-consuming in children, who are more suggestible and tire more quickly than adults. Errors and misinterpretation arise more readily because of the effect of spatial or temporal summation. Successive stimulations should be made from the hypaesthetic area towards the normal area, but the approach should also be reversed in order to evaluate possible effects of summation.

Appreciation of pain is more easily demonstrated than perception of touch, but as it is upsetting to young children and to apprehensive or retarded older children it is

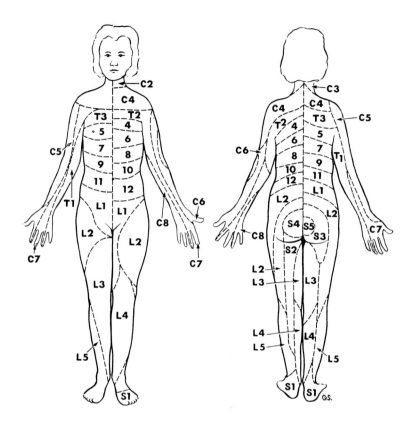

Fig. 1. Sensory innervation of the skin by spinal dermatomes. The usual maximal areas of the odd numbered segments are shown on the right side of the body and of the even numbered segments on the left. There is some individual variation from patient to patient and considerable normal overlapping of dermatomes. Thus, the area of T8 is virtually completely duplicated by the lower part of T7 and the upper part of T9, for example.

usually best left to the end of the examination. An ordinary pin (or the white-headed pin used for testing visual fields) is the usual test object. The pin may be stuck through the end of a tongue blade, which the examiner holds at the other end to give some leverage and control of intensity of pressure, but it is usually just as satisfactory for the examiner to hold the pin between his fingers. If the patient is merely asked to say 'now' when he feels the pinprick, it is difficult for the examiner to decide whether he is testing touch or pain. A better method is to apply the point and head of the pin in irregular sequence, asking the patient to say 'sharp' or 'dull'. This requires cortical discrimination and tests additional functions, but success in sharp-dull discrimination does at least require intact perception of pain.

Movement of the stimulated part, change in facial expression, or looking towards the stimulus, may be used as criteria in young children or infants. In the case of infants, movement of the stimulated limb may be induced by fairly gentle pinprick, but one usually has to prick more forcefully and rely on crying or on a definite change in the

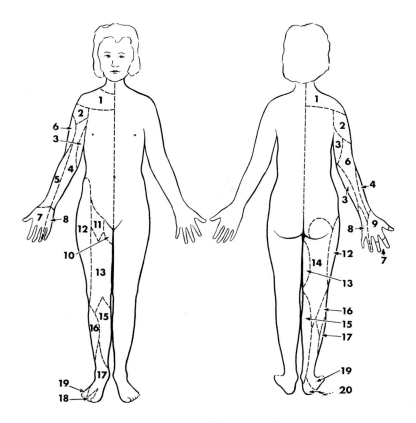

Fig. 2. Sensory innervation of the skin of the upper and lower extremities by cutaneous nerves:
1. Supraclavicular; 2. Axillary; 3. Medial Brachial Cutaneous; 4. Medial Antibrachial Cutaneous;
5. Lateral Antibrachial Cutaneous; 6. Dorsal Antibrachial Cutaneous; 7. Median; 8. Ulnar; 9. Radial;
10. Ilioinguinal; 11. Lumboinguinal; 12. Lateral Femoral Cutaneous; 13. Anterior Femoral Cutaenous;
14. Posterior Femoral Cutaneous; 15. Saphenous; 16. Common Peroneal; 17. Superficial Peroneal;
18. Deep Peroneal; 19. Sural; 20. Tibial.

facial expression as an end point. This usually limits each sensory examination to a
half-dozen or so trials. For this reason, and because pain may be the only sensory
modality which can be tested at a very young age, mapping of areas of analgesia, and
comprehensive evaluation of patients with lesions of the spinal cord such as myelomeningoceles, or with lesions of the peripheral nerves, may require 6 or 8 sensory
examinations over a period of days and the patient may have to stay in hospital.

Perception of temperature is usually tested with two glass test tubes, one of which
contains hot water and the other ice water. However, metal tubes are preferable if
obtainable, as glass is a rather poor conductor of temperature. Very hot and very cold
stimuli may produce responses of pain rather than of temperature. The cold stimulus
may appropriately be at about 40 °F and the warm stimulus at 110 °F but it is not necessary to measure the temperatures exactly unless for research purposes. Adults and
older children can distinguish much smaller differences of temperature, as little as 5 °

or 10°F in the middle ranges, but the examination need not be pushed this far as a routine. Sensations of hot and cold probably originate from separate sensory endings, and if small-tipped test objects are used, normal individuals will make occasional errors, although not consistently over a definable area. Use of extremely hot or especially of extremely cold water may also lead to errors, since ice water may be perceived as hot particularly if a cold stimulus has been presented several times in succession and the patient expects the hot to be next. Correct performance of this test requires reasonable attention on the patient's part and the effect of fatigue or inattention must not be mistaken for anaesthesia. The examiner should also remember that a child may get 50 per cent of the responses correct merely by guessing, and should stimulate each area to be tested enough times to eliminate the effect of chance. In practice, one rarely finds impaired perception of temperature if appreciation of pain is normal, and in this circumstance testing for hot-cold discrimination can safely be omitted. If there appears to be no appreciation of or significant under-reaction to pain over the entire body, one may be dealing with congenital indifference to pain (often but not invariably associated with mental retardation), and testing for temperature then becomes mandatory.

The examiner should also palpate for possible enlargement of the peripheral nerves. This is best done at the olecranon, in the popliteal fossa and (for the peroneal nerve) around the head of the fibula. A marked degree of enlargement would suggest the hypertrophic interstitial polyneuritis of Déjérine and Sottas, but slight enlargement of peripheral nerves may occur under other circumstances.

Interpretation

If screening examination shows any area of anaesthesia or hypaesthesia, or if the history suggests sensory deficit, or if lesions of the peripheral nerves or spinal cord are suspected, a complete sensory examination should be carried out. If detailed sensory mapping is done, the result should be compared with the known distribution of cutaneous nerves and with the arrangement of the spinal dermatomes (see Figs. 1 and 2), in order to try to localise the lesion responsible. However, caution is necessary since there is considerable anatomical variation in the location of the boundaries of peripheral nerve supply and of spinal dermatomes among different normal individuals. For example, the ulnar nerve may supply only the palmar aspect of the 5th finger and ulnar border of the hand, or it may be responsible for half or almost all of the 4th finger with a correspondingly greater extension over the dorsal and palmar surface of the hand. The cutaneous dermatomes also show some variation and there are often surprising differences in drawings of these in different textbooks of neurology! The dermatomes overlap to a considerable degree, possibly so much that the distribution of T4 might be completely duplicated between the inferior distribution of T3 and the superior of T5. Overlapping is less extensive in the case of the peripheral nerves but it is common to find a gradual shading off of anaesthesia into hypaesthesia as one approaches the boundary of an area of sensory deficit.

In attempting to localise spinal lesions, the examiner will of course want to compare the segmental sensory levels with the segmental innervation of any paralysed or paretic muscles and with any localising signs referable to the autonomic nervous system. If these coincide, one's attention is directed to a particular spinal level, but it must be recognised that in the presence of extensive lesions such as myelomeningoceles, the motor and sensory findings are often irregular and inconsistent. In attempting to localise lesions along the vertebral column, it is important to remember that the cord is higher than the bones. In the adult, and in children above about 8 years, the first cervical spinal segment is at the level of the body of the first cervical vertebra, the first thoracic segment slightly above the upper margin of the first thoracic vertebra, the first lumbar spinal segment opposite the top of the body of the 10th thoracic vertebra and the first sacral segment opposite the body of the 12th thoracic vertebra, the cord ending at the lower margin of the first lumbar vertebra. The position of the spinal cord is relatively lower in infants and young children, but even in the newborn the tip of the cord is no farther down than the third lumbar vertebra. Thus, one might reasonably make a downward adjustment of 2 vertebrae in infants up to 6 months and of $1\frac{1}{2}$ or 1 vertebra between that age and 5 years.

Discordant or dissociated deficits with respect to pain, temperature and touch are also important. Loss of appreciation of pain and temperature in some area of the upper extremity, with retention of sense of touch, will make most physicians think of possible syringomyelia, in which the pathways for pain and temperature are interrupted at their decussation in the ventral cord. (The pathways for touch decussate at different levels in the cord, and since some touch may be conveyed as far as the medulla in the posterior columns of the cord, touch is in general much less affected by spinal lesions than are pain and temperature.) Some dissociation of sensory deficit may also occur with insults to peripheral nerves. Nerve fibres may be thought of in order of increasing size, the fibres for slow pain ('second pain') being the smallest, followed by cold, warmth, fast pain, touch and position, the last being of the largest diameter. Chemical agents such as procaine have their greatest effect on the smaller fibres, whereas pressure and anoxia affect the larger fibres to the greatest degree.

A few words need to be said about the interpretation of apparent inconsistencies in sensory examination. Inconsistency from one examination to another is normal to a much greater degree with children than with adults and even greater inconsistency must be anticipated if the examination has had to be carried out by pinprick, using crying as a criterion of sensation. Peripheral neuropathies often involve chiefly the more distal distribution of the nerves and there may be a 'glove and stocking' distribution of analgesia or anaesthesia, fading into an area of hypaesthesia and then into normality without a sharply definable border. This distribution is just as characteristic of polyneuropathy as it is of hysteria, although the latter is thought of first by the inexperienced examiner. Highly inconsistent findings from one examination to another are indeed typical of hysterical anaesthesia, although the borders of the anaesthetic zone are likely to be sharply defined on each individual test. Apparent hemianaesthesia ending precisely at the midline (organic anaesthesia ends a bit short of this line) or a sharp level for absence of vibration sense in the middle of a bone may suggest that the sensory deficit is feigned or hysterical. Children are more guileless than adults and it is usually easy for an experienced examiner to trap a malingering child. However, frank malingering is rare among children, as has already been mentioned in connexion with the evaluation of muscle power, and hysteria often resembles organic disease much more closely than it does malingering. Study of the galvanic skin response and other procedures for evaluating autonomic function of the nerves may aid in evaluating dubious sensory neuropathies.

Hyperaesthesia is an exaggerated and usually unpleasant appreciation of cutaneous stimuli. A zone of hyperaesthesia is frequently encountered just above the anaesthetic level of a case of transverse myelopathy. Hyperaesthesia may be present over a dermatome prior to the eruption of the vesicles of Herpes Zoster. A combination of relative and partial hypaesthesia on one-half the body with an unpleasant or burning reaction to any cutaneous stimulation on the same side (anaesthesia dolorosa) occurs with lesions of the ventral posterolateral nucleus of the thalamus or of its connexions, but this type of thalamic syndrome is extremely rare in childhood. The painful paraesthesiae of sensory neuropathies, such as causalgia of the median or sciatic nerve or meralgia paraesthetica of the lateral femoral cutaneous nerve, are also fortunately almost unknown in paediatric practice.

Deep or Proprioceptive Sensation

Methods of Examination

Proprioceptive sensations originate from the muscles, tendons, ligaments and joints rather than from the skin. The most important pathways originate from the muscle spindles and from spiral and other endings on the muscles and tendons. These are sensitive to the tension and to the degree of lengthening of the muscle fibres, and send their impulses rapidly along large heavily-myelinated 'A' fibres. These fibres constitute the afferent arc of the stretch reflex and of the tendon jerks, but comparable fibres pass up the spinal cord in the spinocerebellar tracts to the cerebellum, and others ascend in the posterior columns to their nuclei and then via the medial lemniscus to the ventral posterolateral nucleus of the thalamus, from whence thalamic radiations pass to the parietal cortex. This system is examined at the level of the peripheral nerve when testing tendon reflexes, and at a peripheral and spinal level in examination for sensory ataxia. Integrity of function of the entire system, including cortical levels, is required for satisfactory function in the usual clinical tests of proprioception.

The most standard test is to ask a patient to close his eyes, after which the examiner moves the child's fingers and toes up or down one at a time, asking him to indicate the direction of movement by saying 'up' or 'down' or by moving an untested finger or hand in parallel direction. This is actually a test of sense of passive movement (kinaesthesia) rather than of position. One may come closer to testing true sense of position at rest by moving the patient's finger rapidly up and down several times and asking the child to indicate whether it comes to rest above or below the horizontal neutral position. This type of testing should be demonstrated to a young child with the eyes open and he should then be allowed to give several correct answers while keeping the eyes open, so that the examiner may be sure that he understands what is desired. Children who do not understand the test or who have deficits of proprioception tend to answer 'up' and 'down' in regular alternation. Thus, the examiner should not alternate regularly but should sometimes produce several upward or downward movements in succession. The examiner's thumb and forefinger should hold the patient's finger by its sides, in testing upward or downward movement (or above and below if movement to right or to left is to be tested, a manoeuvre not usually carried out) in order to avoid giving clues from sensations of pressure. Sense of position may also be tested by asking the patient to touch the tips of his two forefingers together with his eyes closed. Another method is for the examiner to position one of the patient's forefingers in space, and to ask the patient (eyes closed) to put the tip of his other forefinger on the one held by the examiner. Still another method is to arrange the fingers and thumb of one of the patient's hands in a selected posture (the patient's eyes still closed), the patient then being asked to duplicate the same posture with the other hand. The three last tests all require integrity of proprioception, but also depend on motor function, co-ordination, sense of extracorporeal space, and concept of body image.

Appreciation of vibration is tested by holding the stem end of a tuning fork against various body prominences. Testing the finger joints, the great toe, and the medial and lateral malleoli of the ankle is sufficient for screening purposes. A low-frequency tuning fork of 128 vibrations per second (1 octave below middle C) is most suitable, higher frequencies being more difficult to recognise. The test should preferably be carried out with vibration which is not much more than barely perceptible to the examiner. Sense of position or passive movement can rarely be tested with children under 3 years of age, but vibration can often be tested as early as 5 or 6 months under favourable circumstances. The patient must be allowed to keep his eyes open but preferably not to see the tuning fork itself, which should be screened from view. The tuning fork is applied a number of times, sometimes vibrating and sometimes still. The examiner's criterion of perception must be the change in the child's or baby's facial expression, which will usually show a pleased smile (less often an unpleasant reaction) to the vibrating fork and relative indifference to the fork if still. Inability to be sure of differences in facial response does not imply anaesthesia for vibration, although it is usually surprisingly easy to document that vibratory sense is normal. The value of this test depends on the generally held view that vibration and proprioception are carried in identical or closely parallel anatomical pathways. However, it has been suggested that at least a part of vibratory sensation ascends the spinal cord along the medial aspect of the lateral columns (Netsky 1953).

Sensation of pressure originates from subcutaneous Pacinian or Golgi corpuscles in the deeper layers of the skin, in subcutaneous tissues, in fascia and other deep connective tissue, in the periosteum and near tendons and joints. This type of sensation can be tested by firm pressure with the examiner's finger or a blunt object much in the manner used for sense of touch, but the sense of pressure need not be tested in the routine examination. Deep sense of pain is somewhat related to the sense of pressure although its ascending pathway in the spinal cord is in the lateral spinal thalamic tract rather than in the posterior column. Deep pain is tested by forceful squeezing of the muscles or tendons or by pressure on the testes, but may be omitted from routine examination.

Interpretation

Since the tests outlined require for the most part a discriminative answer by the patient, they depend on integrity of the entire proprioceptive pathway including some cortical function in the parietal lobes. Thus, it is not surprising that patients with signs and symptoms referable to the parietal lobes (see Chapter VII) sometimes show defective perception of passive movement or position. The majority of such patients probably suffer from a deficit of cerebral integration and gnosis rather than from impaired proprioception as such. Children with cerebral spastic hemiparesis frequently have defects of cerebral sensory function (see next section) in the affected hand, but stereognosis and 2-point discrimination are affected far more frequently than position or passive movement and the proprioceptive functions are probably never abnormal if the first-mentioned are intact.

Proprioceptive perception is sometimes affected by infiltrating gliomata of the brain stem if these involve the medial lemniscus, although this is rather infrequent. The spinothalamic tract and other modalities of sensation may be spared, but if all other physical signs point to the brain stem, the examiner need not assume a lesion of the opposite parietal lobe. Occlusions of the anterior spinal artery (many cases of transverse myelopathy are based on this) are associated with infarction of the anterior spinal cord, sparing chiefly the posterior root zones, the posterior horns of the grey matter, and the posterior columns. In these circumstances there is dissociated sensory loss with a sharp transverse level of analgesia and thermanaesthesia, with the tactile sensory level somewhat lower or less well defined, but with sparing of sense of position and vibration. It has already been mentioned that the larger proprioceptive fibres in peripheral nerves are more affected by compression than are fibres for touch and pain, so that dissociated sensory signs may also be observed with lesions outside the spinal cord.

In Friedreich's ataxia and other degenerations of the posterior columns, sense of position and passive movement is diminished in the toes earlier than in the fingers. The examiner may need to utilise quite small increments of movement in order to avoid missing a subtle deficit. If sense of position or vibration appears to be absent in the fingers or toes, these sensations should then be tested at the wrist or ankle, or at the elbow or knee if required, in order to follow the progress of the condition in serial examinations, but the earliest involvement of these modalities is always distal. It is well known that perception of vibration may normally diminish after middle age, but this sense should be acute in children of all ages. Presence of normal vibratory sense over the upper tibia may occasionally be encountered when it is absent at the lower end. If at least moderate amplitude of vibration is being used and if there is a rather sharp line of cut-off at some point in the middle of the bone, an hysterical basis should be considered probable. One also occasionally finds alleged anaesthesia for vibration on the medial side of a toe while it is normal on the lateral, or anaesthesia at the medial malleolus with normal vibration sense at the lateral. Because of extensive bony transmission, such situations are also psychogenic. However, a transverse level of anaesthesia over the dorsal processes of the vertebrae is sometimes demonstrable in the presence of organic lesions of the spinal cord or of the innervation of the vertebrae.

Cortical Sensory Functions

Methods of Examination

Cerebral or 'combined' sensory functions include such abilities as stereognosis, discrimination of two points, recognition of textures, recognition of figures written on the skin (graphaesthesia), the ability to localise cutaneous stimuli (topaesthesia or topognosia) and discrimination of size or weight of objects.

Stereognosis in the strict sense can be tested by use of a series of small objects of geometric shape such as spheres, cubes, pyramids, etc. The patient will be asked to close his eyes and to name one of the test objects placed in his hand after manipulating it. A mute person could be asked to give the object back, open his eyes, and then identify its counterpart in a duplicate set of test objects. In clinical practice, stereognosis is usually evaluated with what is actually a test of object recognition, using small blocks, coins, keys and comparable objects of everyday familiarity. One favourite method involves a set of six objects, three of which are a button, a coin, and a Coca Cola bottle cap, all of approximately the same diameter. The three objects last mentioned are presented one at a time without any advance instruction other than to name them, in the case of older children. This produces a more difficult and more critical test and also saves time. If an older child fails by this approach, or routinely in the case of children under 7 or 8, all six objects are shown to the patient and he is asked to name them one by one if there appears any likelihood that he will be unfamiliar with them. He is then told that one of the objects will be placed in his hand and that he is to feel it and name it (or to point its counterpart out in a duplicate set, if he understands but is unable to speak). Actually, only the three closely similar objects (button, coin, and bottle cap) are presented.

Discrimination of two points can be tested with a 2-point discriminator of the caliper type (from which the distance between the points may be read off from a scale on the handle), with points of a compass, or with a bent paper clip or piece of wire. One must first make certain that the patient knows the difference between one and two, and then explain that his skin will be touched with either one or two points and he is to speak the correct number, or hold up the corresponding number of fingers, keeping his eyes closed. One should test with one and two points in mixed irregular sequence, always presenting both points simultaneously if two are used. Testing is begun with the points separated at the distance of the normal threshold, which is two millimetres or less on the fingertips or lips, 10 to 20 mm. on the forehead or face, 20 or 30 mm. on the dorsa of the feet, and an even larger distance on the trunk. Threshold distances are larger in the case of young children or of the mentally retarded or inattentive. Elevations of threshold of less than 100 per cent of the normal value are probably to be ignored, but consistently asymmetrical thresholds warrant thought even if of lesser degree.

Tests of cortical sensory function need not be pursued beyond stereognosis and 2-point discrimination unless these are abnormal, or unless there are signs referable to the parietal lobe or other reasons for which the examiner wishes to pursue special interests. Discrimination of weight or size should ideally be tested with specially constructed test objects, of identical size and shape but differing weight, or of identical weight and shape but different size. Recognition of texture may be tested with various fabrics such as silk, cotton, velvet, corduroy, coarse tweed, or smooth plastic, but the need for familiarity with the materials limits the test to older children or adolescents. To test graphaesthesia, the patient closes his eyes and holds one hand palm upward on his knee or on a table in front of him. The test is explained to him and the examiner then uses the blunt end of a pen, pencil or small stick to 'write' in the patient's palm one of the Arabic numerals from 0 to 9. The figure must be formed in the manner with which the patient is familiar and should be oriented so as to be right side up to him (upside-down to the examiner if seated opposite). Certain confusions are characteristically encountered with normal children under 8 or even 10 years of age. These include confusion of 2 and 6, 4 and 7, and sometimes of 3 and 5; 1, 8 and 0 should always be recognised and 3 and 7 are usually correctly identified.

Tests for displacement or extinction of tactile stimuli should also be carried out when appropriate. The child is asked to close his eyes and the examiner then touches (a brief light touch of the examiner's fingers is as good as any other method) one or both cheeks, one or both hands, the hand and cheek simultaneously, or the foot and hand simultaneously. The child is asked to name or point to (with the other hand) the stimulated point or points.

Interpretation

It is readily apparent that these tests of cerebral sensory function require integration of sensations of touch and pressure, probably involve kinaesthetic information, certainly depend on manipulative ability and also all involve conscious discrimination and association or recognition (gnosis). Abnormal responses may be obtained if a sufficient deficit exists in cutaneous and proprioceptive sensation. Some purists prefer to use the term 'stereoanaesthesia' for inability to recognise objects by manipulation if this is determined at a brain stem, spinal or peripheral level, and reserve 'astereognosis' for a comparable disability based on abnormality in the parietal lobe. In the actual recording of the examination it is preferable to write down what is actually observed (e.g. 'patient is unable to identify a small block, marble, or key by manipulating it in the hand with the eyes closed'), and to elaborate in the statement of diagnostic impression in some such manner as 'chronic brain syndrome presumably associated with meningitis at age 2, manifest by right cerebral spastic hemiparesis and astereognosis in right hand.'

In neurological clinics for children, one encounters defects of cortical sensation chiefly in the presence of cerebral spastic hemiparesis, although it is occasionally seen with bilateral spasticity, or with parietal lobe lesions not producing motor paresis. The hand is usually more severely affected than the foot and the deficit in such functions as 2-point discrimination becomes less as one ascends a limb proximally. The hand is more likely to show a sensory deficit if it is significantly smaller than its opposite, although extensive sensory disability occasionally exists without any obvious undergrowth. Thus, sensory testing should not be omitted merely because the two hands appear of equal size. The extent to which cortical sensory disability might result from disuse alone has been debated, but it seems likely that this is not the sole explanation; existence of sensory disability in the affected hand of a hemiparetic child should certainly be taken into consideration in planning physical therapy or surgical procedures.

'Extinction' may involve imperception of stimuli on one side of the body when both sides are stimulated simultaneously even though a single stimulus is perceived on either side separately. This is also sometimes called tactile inattention, and is fairly common in the presence of contralateral parietal lobe involvement, as in many cases of spastic hemiparesis. Extinction of the more distal of two stimuli on the same side may result in perception of touch on the face or hand, ignoring simultaneous touch on the hand or foot respectively. The inferior stimulus is always the one ignored. The phenomenon may imply abnormality in the contralateral parietal lobe in older children, but findings of this kind are probably normal up to the age of 6 or 7 years. 'Displacement,' in which a single stimulus is falsely identified as coming from a more rostral location on the body, is more abnormal than distal extinction, frequently but not invariably accompanies the latter, and is less common in very young children. If the examiner doubts whether an apparent extinction phenomenon is genuine, he may verify it further by continuing to stimulate the same two areas with his fingers or with cotton wool applicators or sticks. The patient is told that he is being touched in two places, and that one of the stimuli will be withdrawn after a few seconds or minutes. Abnormality is rarely encountered in terms of the patient's failure to perceive that one stimulus has been withdrawn, but occurs more frequently in his saying rather promptly that the more distal stimulus has been withdrawn, while it still remains in place. Observations such as this naturally need repeated testing to determine consistency.

CHAPTER XIV

Autonomic Function

Methods of Examination

Regulation of Vital Signs

The patient's pulse rate, respiratory rate, blood pressure, and temperature are considered in comparison with the figures expected for his age and physiological state at the time. However, constant abnormality of vital signs is less frequent than instability or excessive fluctuation. Paroxysmal violent alterations are particularly important. Recording the pulse rate and blood pressure of a child in an initial or unexplained convulsive seizure has far greater value than retrospective study, as have determinations of sugar and calcium levels in the blood at the same time.

Responses of the Skin

The colour and temperature of the skin are evaluated by inspection and palpation. If the day is warm or the examination room well heated the examiner should try to estimate whether perspiration is appropriate or symmetrical over the body, or at least that areas of greater perspiration are those to be expected (face, hands and axillae). Areas of excessive or defective sweating may be mapped out by painting the areas suspected (not the patient's entire body) with diluted (1 %) tincture of iodine and then testing the region with starch after the iodine solution has dried. The blue colour developed where sweating takes place is dramatic and unmistakable but the residual iodine is difficult to get off, and may be toxic. Abnormal sweating is rarely of sufficient importance to require this type of testing, and seldom provides information which defines abnormality not detectable by other means. Universal deficiency of perspiration is usually based on ectodermal dysplasia and should occasion a look at the teeth, or the making of x-rays if no teeth are seen, since it is the anhidrotic type of ectodermal dysplasia in which the teeth are missing or defective.

The triple response to scratch is tested by scratching the skin moderately with a sharp pin. If the scratch has been adequate, yet not severe enough to draw blood and cover up the reaction, a pale 'blanch' is seen along the line of scratch, soon to be followed by erythematous 'flare' and subsequently by an elevated 'wheal' which can be felt as well as seen. This triple response is used chiefly in determining the level of lesions which may involve the peripheral nerves, and the stimulus should therefore be in the distribution of the nerves suspected. Surprisingly, the response is sometimes abnormal below the level of an acute spinal lesion (see below under 'Interpretation'), and thus should be tested along a line running from above to below the presumed level of involvement.

Salivation and Lacrimation

Saliva from the submaxillary and sublingual glands (7th and 5th nerves) and parotid glands (9th nerve) may be collected and weighed, using previously weighed bits of cotton wool, as mentioned in Chapter IX. However this rather time-consuming manoeuvre rarely if ever gives diagnostic information not otherwise available. Secretion of tears (fibres from 7th nerve via 5th) may be similarly measured, but the abnormality in which the examiner is chiefly interested is inability (complete or nearly complete) to produce tears. This is a feature of all the more complete syndromes of central autonomic dysfunction (Riley-Day syndrome). If the examiner fails to observe tearing, the child's mother should be asked directly whether he ever produces tears. It is usually safe to accept the mother's statement, but reflex lacrimation could be tested by letting the child inhale fumes of ammonia or by placing very highly seasoned food in his mouth.

Sphincters

The anal sphincter should be examined by inspection, and also palpated digitally if it appears excessively relaxed or if there is any history of abnormal function of the bowel or bladder. The anocutaneous reflex is tested by pricking the perianal skin by pin; the normal response is a quick contraction of the external sphincter.

Function of the bladder is more difficult for the examiner to appraise directly, although he may occasionally observe dribbling, or conversely a normally powerful urinary stream. The degree of filling of the bladder should be examined by palpation and percussion. Failure to do the latter at regular intervals frequently results in failure to recognise neurogenic retention of urine in cases of poliomyelitis or Guillain-Barré syndrome. Similar periodic examination should be carried out with all unconscious patients. If the examiner notes no abnormality on palpation and percussion and does not see the patient empty the bladder during his examination, questions should be put to the child's mother. These should cover whether he urinates at normal intervals or excessively frequently or infrequently, whether he is aware of desire to void, whether he can hold back long enough to reach the toilet once he is aware of this need, and finally about the strength of the stream.

A history of more than one urinary tract infection in a girl, or of a single one in a boy, of course makes one think firstly of some anatomical malformation, but may also be associated with stasis of neurogenic origin. The history is in general more important than the physical examination in appraisal of function of the bladder, and if the limited examination together with the routine questions produce no suspicion, the examiner should make some such note as 'no obvious or historical abnormality'. Suspicion of abnormality should be followed up by contrast x-ray studies and/or the making of a cystometrogram.

Interpretation

Vital Signs

Abnormalities of vital signs may indicate that a supposed convulsive fit or non-convulsive syncope (or a fit of which the motor phase was not observed) was due to paroxysmal tachycardia, hypertension, or alternatively to drop in blood pressure (vasodepressor syncope). In the latter instance one would want to test for excessive reflex vagal bradycardia or hypotension in response to pressure on the eyeballs or to digital stimulation of the carotid sinus. Classical carotid sinus syncope, and syncope associated with Stokes-Adams disease, are rare in childhood.

Sudden violent changes in pulse, respiration and blood pressure may be based on an instability of central regulation in the medulla. The pathological basis of this is usually entirely obscure, even at autopsy. Syringobulbia (Duffy and Ziter 1964) has been found in one infant who suffered from paroxysmal bradycardia, apnoeic attacks and laryngeal stridor. An occasional comparable case may be an obscure epileptic equivalent, and putting such a patient on phenytoin (Dilantin, Epanutin) will now and then dramatically stop the attacks. However, evaluation of such treatment is difficult because babies who do not die of acute attacks usually 'outgrow' the tendency after a few months of age. Paroxysmal hypertension is a feature of phaeochromocytoma and also of central autonomic dysfunction (Riley-Day syndrome), but since the latter includes absence of tears as a more constant feature, other causes should be sought if lacrimation is normal.

Responses of the Skin

Generalised anhidrosis has already been mentioned in connexion with ecto-dermal dysplasia. Local anhidrosis may accompany affections of the peripheral nerves. Perspiration is depressed on the involved side of the face in the Horner syndrome of the cervical sympathetic, but miosis and slight ptosis are more constant components. Hypohidrosis may also occur with lesions in the pons, medulla, or cervical cord (List and Peet 1939). The auriculo-temporal syndrome is a phenomenon of misdirected regrowth following trauma to that nerve, with excessive sweating over its cutaneous distribution when food is placed in the mouth.

The triple response to scratch is an axon reflex and is abolished in affections of the nerves distal to the dorsal root ganglia (unless the neuropathy is too slight). In the general view, lesions at or proximal to the posterior roots do not alter the triple response. (Thus, a normal triple response is an unfavourable prognostic sign in brachial palsies, implying avulsion of roots close to the cord.) Acute transverse myelopathies, at least in childhood, are occasionally associated with at least temporary absence of the triple response below the cutaneous level corresponding to the lesion. This is extremely difficult to explain on physiological grounds but is sometimes helpful in the case of babies for whom sensory examination is difficult or limited.

Localised vasomotor instability may reflect lesions of peripheral nerves, or changes confined to a single limb may be of central origin—such as the cold, pale hand in some patients with hemiparesis. (In contrast, Carmichael *et al.* 1935 report normal vasomotor responses in hemiplegic limbs in adults.)

Salivation and Lacrimation

The Riley-Day syndrome of central autonomic dysfunction (Riley 1952) has many possible manifestations, some of which are held to be always present and others acknowledged to be variable:

Features Always Present	*Features Present in 25% to 80% of Cases*
Jewish racial background	Episodic hypertension
Diminished lacrimation	Cyclic vomiting
Blotching of skin	Frequent pulmonary infections
Excessive perspiration	Instability of temperature
Drooling	Breath-holding spells
Emotional lability	Urinary frequency
Depressed tendon reflexes	Convulsions or abnormal EEG
At least relative indifference to pain	Mental retardation
	Corneal ulcers
	Positive family history
	Muscular hypotonia
	Tremor or choreiform movement

Many formes frustes doubtless exist. In dubious cases a histamine test may be carried out as described in Chapter XV. Cases of central autonomic dysfunction have been reported with autopsy findings such as cysts in the hypothalamus, damage to the reticular substance of the pons and medulla (Cohen and Solomon 1955) or with degeneration of the anterior commisure or hypothalamic hamartomata (Haymaker *et al.* 1957). Other autopsies have shown no abnormality. It is probable that none of the various underlying anatomical lesions are surgically correctible, and pneumoencephalography is usually unwarranted in this group of patients, who are rather poor anaesthetic risks.

Except in Riley-Day syndrome, disturbance of salivation is seldom an important clinical sign of neurological disease. Drooling, which is really overflow of a normal amount of saliva or of excess saliva produced in response to its loss from the mouth, is not of the same significance, and usually results from cerebral palsy or mental retardation. The examiner should remember other non-neurological causes of disturbed salivation, such as its excess in mercury intoxication or its depression in atropine intoxication, cystic fibrosis of the pancreas, etc.

Sphincters

Abnormal function of the anal or urinary sphincters may be due to a local structural abnormality, or to disease of the lower motor unit. The abnormality may be in the spinal cord as in myelomeningocele, in the sacral nerves or perhaps in the muscle itself. (Teasdall *et al.* (1964) report myopathic changes in the external anal sphincter in two patients with ocular myopathy.) Loss of control of the sphincters may also be seen with higher spinal involvement and with cerebral disease (either a generalised dementia, or lesions in the hypothalamus, cingulate gyri or other structures).

Abnormality of the sphincters is easily missed in the case of infants and children who are young enough not to be expected to be 'trained'. At later ages, persistence or re-emergence of enuresis or encopresis are usually psychogenic but other possibilities should always be carefully considered. The differential diagnosis of abnormal function of the bladder depends largely on a careful history, as already indicated. The history is considered together with other evidence such as the capacity of the bladder as estimated from a cystogram or cystometrogram, possible presence of ureteral reflux or hydronephrosis, residual urine as measured by catheterisation and a cystometrogram. The last mentioned is the most useful investigation, and the synthesis of findings is therefore discussed in Chapter XV.

Neurogenic incapacity of the anus is not too difficult to identify by inspection, digital examination, and testing the anocutaneous reflex. Unless the sphincter is extremely patulous, most patients with such lesions as myelomeningoceles will eventually become more or less continent of faeces on a fairly constipating diet, and continence may be retained in the presence of an acquired weakness, so that history alone, without examination, should not be accepted as documenting normality. Constipation is rarely organically neurogenic except in the case of Hirschprung's disease, in which there is congenital absence of the ganglion cells of the hind gut. Rectal biopsy is necessary to define this and is used as a means of determining the level of surgical resection, but it is worth remembering that the absence of ganglion cells usually extends so far up the rectum that faeces cannot be palpated by the tip of the examiner's finger. If faeces can be felt thus, faecal impactions with paradoxical diarrhoea almost always prove psychogenic.

Unexplained motor abnormalities in the lower extremities, whether long-standing or more recent, must always raise the possibility of a spinal lesion. In such circumstances the coexistence of abnormalities of sphincter function is usually enough to warrant making a myelogram, unless the diagnosis is obvious from other features. If there is abnormality of either motor power or sphincter function, but not of both, myelography is usually not indicated unless there is also abnormality in one (or more) of the following categories:

1. Abnormality of sensation.
2. Abnormality visible on the skin overlying the spinal column, such as a dimple or tuft of hair.
3. Abnormality of the spine by palpation, preferably confirmed by x-ray.
4. Abnormal findings in plain x-rays of the spinal column (however, the lesion may be a long distance above the abnormal neurological signs and the entire spine should be x-rayed in both A-P and lateral projections).

In doubtful cases, and in most cases of obscure diagnosis for which myelography is not to be performed, a spinal puncture should be made with manometric studies and examination of the spinal fluid for cells and protein (see Chapter XV).

Hypothalamic Syndromes

Hypothalamic lesions must be considered as possible causes of a number of recognised neuroendocrine syndromes as well as of other more vaguely defined conditions. Hypopituitarism may result from tumours involving the hypothalamus or adjacent structures, particularly craniopharyngiomata. X-rays of sella turcica and careful examination of the visual fields are the best tests for intrinsic pituitary tumours. Craniopharyngiomata are sufficiently calcified to be detectable in ordinary skull films in the large majority of cases producing symptoms in childhood, but the characteristic defects of the visual fields are an equally important diagnostic sign. Diabetes insipidus can result from anomalies or tumours involving the supra-optic nuclei, the

211

pituitary stalk or the posterior pituitary itself, but it is more commonly seen following encephalitis, basal skull fractures, or with Hand-Schüller-Christian disease. Lesions in the anterior hypothalamus have been reported with manifestations such as hyperthermia, hyperglycaemia, and hyperphagia (possibly the ventromedial nuclei in the last mentioned), and posterior lesions with hypothermia, somnolence, hypoglycaemia, and excessive or inappropriate rages or laughter. Precocious puberty also accompanies hypothalamic lesions but the location of these is even less well known than for the other manifestations referred to. Many retarded or otherwise neurologically abnormal children are either excessively large or excessively small and one suspects some hypothalamic malfunction in such cases, although contrast x-ray studies and other available investigations are often unrewarding.

CHAPTER XV

Special Investigations

Introduction

Most children with an unexplained neurological syndrome present problems of mental retardation, seizures, or a deficit of motor development which might be some type of cerebral palsy, or combinations of these problems. In planning the investigation of such a case, the physician can choose from a rich but bewildering variety of possible studies. Constantly increasing numbers of chemical tests on the blood, urine and cerebrospinal fluid are known. In addition to electroencephalography, several other electrical tests are possible such as electromyography, measurement of nerve conduction velocities, and electroretinography. Several types of contrast x-rays may be considered, including pneumoencephalography, ventriculography, arteriography and myelography. The brain may also be studied by isotope scanning methods and by ultrasound (ECHO) encephalography. Clinical psychologists, audiologists, urologists, and otolaryngologists have special methods at their disposal, and these are sometimes borrowed by paediatricians and neurologists. Surgeons and pathologists may assist in neurological diagnosis by studying biopsies of muscle, skin, nerve, rectum or brain. The number of possible investigations is staggering, and becomes more so with each month's issues of the medical journals.

This chapter will attempt to consider some of the more important investigations which may add to the history and physical examination in the diagnosis of disorders of the nervous system in childhood, but it will inevitably be incomplete and soon out of date. Each possible test will be approached in terms of the indications for it, the methods available, and its interpretation and especially its limitations. It is impossible to give details of every complicated technique and the physician will have to consult the pertinent medical literature if he wishes to set up a test which is not available to him. New, better and simpler methods are reported from time to time, and the latest literature should be consulted for methods described since the publication of this volume.

Physicians working in large teaching hospitals will usually find that the majority of the special studies discussed are already available to them in the laboratories of clinical chemistry, pathology, electroencephalography or electrophysiology, audiometry or in the department of radiology. Clinical psychologists may be available through the department of psychiatry or are less frequently attached to some other service. Certain tests such as the study of caloric nystagmus and cystometrography may be carried out by an otolaryngologist or a urologist in some hospitals and by paediatricians or neurologists in others. The exact administrative arrangement is less important than that the most experienced person available perform the study. The physician in charge of the patient should be aware of what the test can do and what it cannot, and of its proper interpretation. Paediatricians in private practice or serving as regional consultants not affiliated with teaching hospitals will probably apply only a limited number of the possible investigations. They will thus need to refer certain patients to teaching and research centres, but they should nevertheless be able to understand the special tests which are carried out there and know their interpretation and limitations.

Electroencephalography

Indications

The making of electroencephalograms is now such a common procedure that little comment is required about it. The most important indication is of course a known or suspected seizure disorder. Other diagnostic possibilities on which the electroencephalogram may shed light include expanding intracranial lesions, degenerative diseases of the brain, and head injuries. It may also have prognostic value following acute cerebral problems such as anoxic episodes, cardiac arrest or encephalitis.

In certain other situations, the usefulness of electroencephalograms is more debatable. They are often recorded in a 'full-scale' routine study of mental retardation and behaviour problems. In these circumstances, the electroencephalogram very occasionally reveals an unsuspected seizure disorder responsive to medication. However, unless a seizure disorder is suspected, it is doubtful whether an electroencephalogram ought to be ordered as part of the routine investigation of cases of mental retardation. It is true that such tracings are frequently abnormal if retardation is associated with the consequences of a traumatic or other cerebral insult, but electroencephalographic abnormality is highly non-specific. Records are also abnormal in many biochemically determined disorders such as phenylketonuria, and it is well to remember that the EEG is normal in most cases of Down's syndrome (mongolism), while many patients with cerebral palsy and epilepsy have very abnormal tracings in spite of normal intelligence.

Unless a seizure disorder is suspected, the principal indication for making an EEG in a case of mental retardation is that the question has been raised by a parent or by the referring physician and the test must then be carried out for everyone's peace of mind. Even then, the EEG must be carefully interpreted to the parents so that they neither assume that a normal electroencephalogram rules out mental retardation nor come to believe that an abnormal one indicates a hopeless situation, or on the other hand, a brain injury from which the patient may recover. Similar arguments apply to the making of EEG's in the evaluation of behaviour problems. Tracings from such children are more frequently abnormal than would be expected by random chance, but the significance of this in terms of practical management is debatable. Some psychiatrists require EEG tracings as an essential preliminary to psychotherapy, and a few are reluctant to undertake psychotherapy when there is evidence of an organic neurological problem.

In the management of seizure disorders it is usually wise to obtain an electroencephalogram. Even if a classical petit mal is observed, one may find that the EEG shows isolated spikes as well as the expected 3 per second spike-wave complexes. This may suggest the likelihood of grand mal fits as well (and possibly their precipitation by giving trimethadione) and thus affect the choice of medication. In the case of what appear to be uncomplicated febrile convulsions in early childhood, it may not be necessary to make electroencephalograms routinely, but only to make them if the fits are prolonged beyond 10 minutes, have some focal feature or a post-ictal hemiplegia, or continue despite the administration of phenobarbitone along with antipyretic measures.

Methods

The placing of the scalp electrodes is now quite standard and little need be said about it. Both monopolar (that is, with some other area, usually the ears or mastoids, as the reference point) and bipolar recordings should be made, the latter measuring the differences in potential between two adjacent electrodes. The monopolar record is sometimes more revealing of a general cerebral dysrhythmia, which is more frequent in children than in adults, but the bipolar recording system is indicated for the localisation of focal discharges or to search for focal slowing as an indication of an expanding lesion.

It is customary to attempt to activate electrical abnormality of the brain by having the patient take 100 or more deep breaths and by stimulating him with a regularly flickering light at various frequencies, in an effort to bring out abnormalities which may not be present in the resting record. Sleep, however, is probably the most valuable activator for children and sleep-recordings should be obtained when possible. Patients with nocturnal seizures, those with temporal lobe attacks and also those with supposed diencephalic discharges (14 and 6 per second positive spikes), frequently have abnormal electroencephalograms only during sleep. Unfortunately, every hypnotic in common use, whether barbiturates, choral hydrate, paraldehyde or other preparations, tends to produce medium voltage fast activity as an artifact in many patients. This sedation artifact may cover up the very abnormalities to be sought and natural sleep is therefore much to be preferred. This will sometimes require admitting the patient to the hospital and keeping him up all night before the tracing is made.

Interpretation

Electroencephalograms are usually 'read' by an electroencephalographer attached to the department although many neurologists read themselves the records made for their patients. The report submitted to the physician in charge usually contains a description of the record, and, if it is abnormal, a statement that the electroencephalographic findings are 'consistent with a diagnosis of . . . ' if such is the case. The diagnosis of epilepsy, even petit mal, has to be a clinical one using the electroencephalogram as only one piece of evidence. The physician should remember that many people have considerably abnormal EEG's without ever having seizures. For example, patients with spastic cerebral palsies are seen from time to time who have very frequent spike-wave discharges in the EEG but have never taken any fits. Individuals who are entirely normal may also have electroencephalographic abnormalities. Conversely, it must be remembered that the EEG is merely a 20- or 30- minute sample of the electrical activity of the patient's brain. Even if recorded for longer periods of time, the inter-seizure records of epileptics may be repeatedly normal. This is particularly true in the case of temporal lobe seizures and in idiopathic grand mal, but children with all types of seizures show electroencephalographic abnormalities in a higher percentage of cases than do adults. Petit mal is the only type of epilepsy in which one can almost always obtain a typical electroencephalographic discharge in a resting record, or at least on hyperventilation or photic stimulation.

Slow wave foci, best localised in bipolar recordings, may be encountered with intracranial tumours, cysts, abscesses, or subdural haematomata. These lesions have in common local expansion with local increase in pressure; similar slow wave foci may be seen with infarcts. Focal slowing is not seen in all patients with the lesions mentioned. Perhaps 80 per cent of brain abscesses have corresponding focal slowing in the EEG but the percentage of positive EEG's is less with the other lesions mentioned. Generalised slowing is non-specific and may be based on deep coma of whatever cause, deep anaesthesia, very deep sleep (in the case of young children), cerebral oedema, encephalitis, hypoglycaemia, and a diversity of other causes. Activity of very low voltage, at times almost a flat record, is sometimes seen over the cerebral hemisphere opposite a hemiplegia, and general flattening over a somewhat smaller area may accompany subdural haematoma (but many subdural haematomata or effusions fail to produce any electroencephalographic abnormality). Recently performed subdural puncture sometimes results in the leakage of subarachnoid fluid under the scalp; under these circumstances the EEG may show generalised or localised slowing or flattening. A generally or locally slowed or flattened EEG tracing is to be expected for a few days or sometimes as long as 10 days following a convulsion (for this reason electroencephalography is best postponed for 10 days following the initial fit unless an acute lesion is suspected). If a child has undergone cardiac arrest, an acute anoxic episode or some other potentially catastrophic cerebral insult, it is of some prognostic value to make an electroencephalogram three days or more after the event. A relatively normal or mildly slowed tracing has some correlation with good recovery, whereas a very flat or grossly slowed record implies either eventual death or considerable residual damage if the patient survives. Frequent spike wave discharges under these circumstances are sometimes said to argue for survival but with residual encephalopathy.

The various types of electroencephalographic abnormality which accompany various types of seizures are fully described in the standard books on electroencephalography and on epilepsy (e.g. Lennox and Lennox 1960, Hill and Parr 1963, Fois 1963).

Electromyography

Indications

Electromyograms are recorded chiefly to investigate patients with muscular weakness (local or generalised) suspected to be due to a disorder of the lower motor unit. Thus, study of the electrical activity of affected muscles is indicated for children suspected of myopathies, peripheral neuropathies or of diseases of the lower motor neurones in the spinal cord or brain stem. The electromyogram is abnormal in a non-specific way in cases of spasticity, dystonia, athetosis, etc., but is not of differential diagnostic value for suprasegmental spinal or cerebral disease in our present state of knowledge. Electromyography may also be used to test existent muscle power of individual muscles in such cases as infants with myelomeningoceles, where the usual clinical testing of muscle power is limited or technically difficult. The presence or absence of electromyographic evidence of denervation has some prognostic value in peripheral neuropathies such as Bell's palsy.

Methods

Complete electromyographic units may be purchased fully assembled, but many EMG laboratories use combinations of amplifiers, oscilloscopes, and speakers assembled according to the special interests of the person in charge for research or clinical work. All involve the use of concentric needle electrodes from which the changes in electrical potential associated with activity of the muscles are recorded, amplified and displayed by an electron beam moving across the screen of the cathode ray oscilloscope. The same amplified input is also usually fed into a loudspeaker, producing the noise-pattern of normal muscle action or the pips of fibrillation which the experienced examiner can identify by ear just as accurately as he can the potentials visible on the screen. Some sort of camera is usually attached for photographing the oscilloscope screen, but this is not essential unless permanent records are desired for publication or other purposes.

The electrical potential associated with muscle activity may be recorded from needle electrodes or from pairs of disc electrodes (such as for EEG's) placed on the skin overlying the muscle to be tested, using an ordinary EEG apparatus set for the larger voltages involved and with the muscle filtres switched out. In electromyography using an EEG machine, the response of the equipment is too slow to permit the recording of fibrillation or for detailed study of the action potentials in suspected myopathies, and is limited to a search for fasciculations coming from irritated anterior horn cells or nerve roots. The application is largely restricted to investigation of the level of slipped invertebral discs and is thus infrequent in paediatrics.

Interpretation

A detailed discussion of electromyographic abnormalities is inappropriate here, for paediatricians or neurologists who do this work will be familiar with it. For other physicians it is sufficient to mention the principal abnormalities which may be reported to them (see Fig. 1a-f).

1. *Insertion potentials.* A small amount of electrical activity is normally produced when the needle is inserted. This is increased in hyperirritable muscles, as for example in polymyositis, and is prolonged in myotonia congenita and in myotonic dystrophy.

2. *Movement potentials.* Moving the needle about has a similar effect to its original insertion described above.

3. *Activity at rest.* Normal resting muscle is silent. The most characteristic finding in denervation, whether from a peripheral neuropathy or from disease of the anterior horn cells, is the presence of fibrillations which represent the spontaneous contraction of individual denervated muscle fibres.

217

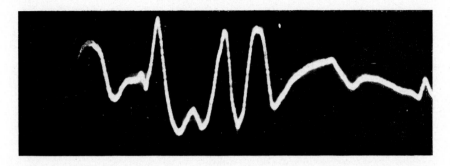

Fig. 1a. Normal action potentials during moderate voluntary contraction of quadriceps muscle of 12-year-old girl.

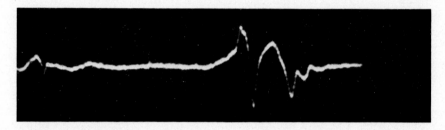

Fig. 1b. Electromyogram showing slow polyphasic action potentials from patients with muscular dystrophy. More rapid biphasic potentials are seen in Figure 1c.

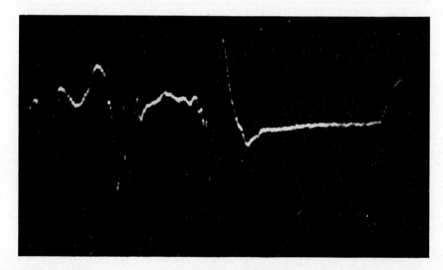

Fig. 1c. Rapid splintered or polyphasic action potentials from muscle of a patient with muscular dystrophy.

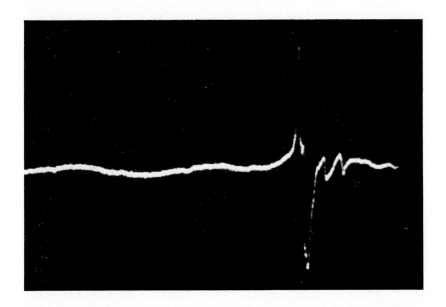

Fig. 1d. Normal high potential representing contraction of a single motor unit. Slight 'splintering' in the middle of the downward phase is not abnormal.

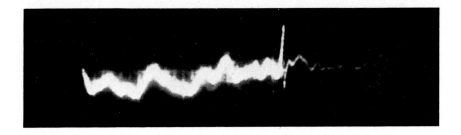

Fig. 1f. Fibrillation potential in a denervated muscle. The amplitude is approximately 50 microvolts and the duration less than one millisecond. This represents the spontaneous contraction of a single isolated muscle fibre.

Fibrillations are lightning-quick and of small amplitude (50 to 100 microvolts). The characteristic sharp pip of fibrillations as heard from the loudspeaker is unmistakable. *Fasciculations* represent the discharge of a motor unit (all the muscle fibres innervated by a single lower motor neurone), and have amplitudes (100-500 µv) comparable to normal trains of action potentials seen in slight voluntary effort in normal muscle. They can occur from irritation of a nerve root or, in childhood, more frequently from active irritative disease of the anterior horn cell or bulbar motor neurone. Fasciculations are of much greater amplitude than fibrillations.

4. *Slight voluntary activity.* In normal muscle a slight, suitably graded sustained voluntary contraction results in a train of action potentials occurring more or less regularly. These are similar to fasciculations in amplitude and in their appearance on the oscilloscope screen, except that they occur in a regular series and only on voluntary effort, rather than irregularly at rest. Giant action potentials as high as 1000 to 3000 microvolts may be seen in Werdnig-Hoffmann's progressive spinal muscular atrophy; potentials of this magnitude are abnormal and suggest disease of the anterior horn cells rather than of peripheral nerves. In muscular dystrophy and other myopathies the action potentials are smaller and are splintered or polyphasic. Increasing voluntary effort results in recruitment of additional motor units in normal muscle. Myopathies are likely to result in greater than normal recruitment at modest voluntary effort. Disease of the anterior horn cells frequently causes hypersynchrony of the additional action potentials in simultaneous recordings from different regions of the muscle. (This is uncommon with peripheral neuropathy.)

5. *Maximal voluntary contraction.* In normal muscle maximal contraction results in an 'interference pattern' of continuous activity of rather uniform amplitude. This is less strong, less well developed, and of irregular amplitude in myopathies, whereas in neuropathies it is more uniform but of lower than normal amplitude. Electrical activity ceases promptly on relaxation in normal muscle, but in myotonia congenita and myotonic dystrophy relaxation is delayed and is easily seen on the oscilloscope screen.

As has been mentioned, electromyography is of limited use in suprasegmental disease, except to differentiate it from disease of the lower motor unit. In spasticity, there may be normal-appearing action potentials in a muscle supposedly at rest; attempted activity or passive movement produce increased activity. The stretch reflex is easily displayed in this manner. Very similar increased electrical activity is seen with dystonia, chorea, athetosis and other types of adventitious movements which differ only in the fluctuation of the interference pattern, in its timing, and in the activation of antagonist as well as agonist muscles in dystonia.

Studies of Nerve Conduction

Indications

The velocity of motor or sensory conduction along a peripheral nerve may be measured using the same equipment as for electromyography, provided it is anatomically possible to apply electrodes to the nerve at 2 points on the skin, separated by

220

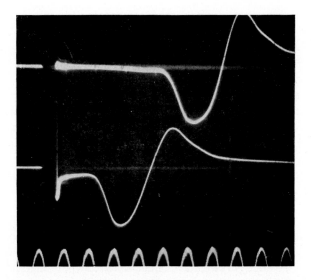

Fig. 2. Photograph of cathode ray oscilloscope tube showing measurement of conduction velocity of median nerve. Upper trace: stimulation in antecubital space just medial to brachial artery. Lower trace (tested subsequently but exposed on same film): stimulation at wrist, between tendons of flexor carpi radialis and palmaris longus. The time signal at the bottom was then exposed on the same film. The distance between the points of stimulation on the skin is measured, and divided by the difference between the two conduction times to calculate the conduction velocity.

10 cm. or more. In other situations it may be possible to determine conduction time from a single pair of electrodes, comparing the time from stimulus to muscle contraction with normal standards for the individual electrode placement and individual muscle. The principal indication for nerve conduction studies is in suspected peripheral neuropathies as part of the investigation of apparent disease of the lower motor unit. Motor and sensory conduction velocities may be measured separately and one can thus determine whether a neuropathy is motor, sensory or mixed in nature.

Methods

To study, for example, the motor conduction velocity of the median nerve, paired stimulating electrodes are placed a centimetre or two apart over the nerve at the wrist, where it lies between the tendons of the flexor carpi radialis and palmaris longus, and recording electrodes are placed over the thenar eminence (See Fig. 2). The time which elapses between the stimulus and the muscle contraction can then be measured on a photograph of the oscilloscope screen or by various timing devices which move a reference point across the screen, usually by the examiner's turning a dial bearing a time scale. The stimulating electrodes are then placed farther up the median nerve, usually in the antecubital space in which the nerve lies just medial to the brachial artery. The conduction time is again determined and the examiner measures with a tape the distance between the two points of stimulation. Dividing this distance by the difference in conduction time gives a conduction velocity in metres per second.

Conduction velocities are similarly readily measured for the ulnar and peroneal nerves, which are the ones commonly studied. If an injury or neuropathy of other individual nerves is suspected, it is usually possible, with ingenuity, to measure the conduction velocity or at least to determine the conduction time from a single point of stimulation, comparing this with normal standards in milliseconds.

Sensory conduction velocities may also be determined both for the median and ulnar nerves. For the median nerve, a 'ring electrode' is put around the forefinger. This type of electrode is easily made from a piece of flexible wire using electrocardiographic paste for contact, or a pipe cleaner moistened in saline solution may be used. Stimulation is applied at this point, where the nerves are purely sensory, and the ascending potential recorded from the 2 pairs of electrodes used for stimulation in studying motor conduction velocity.

Interpretation

The abnormalities found are slowing of conduction times in various neuropathies, which differ little from one another in this respect. The normal conduction velocity in adults is 50 to 70 metres per second. Conduction in newborn infants is much slower, 20 to 30 metres per second, but the speed of conduction increases rapidly with age and by the age of 3 years has reached adult standards. Most neuropathies are more severe distally and the reduced conduction velocity is thus readily measured. If the involvement is chiefly proximal, as in Guillain-Barré syndrome, there may be little or even no reduction of peripheral conduction speed. Most neuropathies of childhood are mixed in nature, although certain toxins such as lead produce a pure motor neuropathy, and a few rare sensory neuropathies exist. Slowing of nerve conduction velocities has been described in 7 children with metachromatic leukodystrophy (Fullerton 1964), and indicates involvement of the peripheral nerve in that disease, which is not surprising in view of the longer-recognised presence of metachromatic material in nerve biopsies.

Electroretinography

Indications

Electroretinography is principally a research tool for ophthalmologists, but if available it may be useful in the early detection of macular degeneration. It may show abnormality in cases of cerebral macular degeneration, particularly the Spielmeyer-Vogt type, before any abnormality can be detected on examining the macula with an ophthalmoscope.

Special Studies of the Blood

The number of possible chemical studies of the blood is almost limitless, and the physician must use his interpretation of the patient's history and physical findings to decide which investigations will be carried out in an attempt to establish the suspected diagnosis and to rule out other possibilities. Some of the more useful tests will be considered here under headings of the disease categories to which they are applicable.

Convulsive Disorders

The levels of sugar, calcium, phosphorus and frequently of urea nitrogen or nonprotein nitrogen in the blood are often determined routinely as part of the 'fit work-up.' Little comment is needed except to note that the fasting blood sugar and serum calcium and phosphorus should be measured on several occasions if abnormality of these is seriously suspected, since they fluctuate from one occasion to another. The level of glucose in the blood should also be measured 2 hours after a meal because of the possibility of hypoglycaemia induced by protein intake (leucine-sensitive hypoglycaemia). Glucose tolerance tests, leucine tolerance tests, and other special studies of carbohydrate metabolism are usually not indicated unless hypoglycaemia is actually demonstrated on some occasion, or unless postprandial rebound is suspected from the timing of the patient's hypoglycaemic symptoms.

Developmental Retardation

The fasting blood sugar is usually measured as part of the work-up for mental retardation. It is reasonable to determine the calcium and phosphorus in the blood as well, but these should be done on several occasions if hypercalcaemia is suspected from the patient's facial appearance, since in many cases the serum calcium is not abnormal except intermittently. Determinations should be made of the protein-bound iodine and butanol-extractable iodine in the blood if there is any reason to suspect hypothyroidism. These tests are done almost routinely in some clinics. Any previous medication with thyroid alters the patient's appearance and renders the physician's clinical diagnosis less exact. Both determinations are falsely elevated (and any hypothyroidism concealed) by previous medication with thyroid or iodine, or by the use of iodine compounds for radiography, such as in the making of bronchograms or intravenous pyelograms. In such circumstances, critical measurement of the PBI or BEI in the blood cannot be made until the patient has had a period of 6 weeks or more free from conflicting medication.

Muscular Dystrophy and other Myopathies

Measurement of the levels of various enzymes in the blood may assist in the differential diagnosis of muscular weakness. The serum glutamic oxalacetic transaminase (SGOT) is usually elevated in active myopathies and also in neuropathies with active breakdown of muscle tissue. It is quite non-specific and may reflect cellular breakdown in many areas (myocardial infarction, hepatic disease, etc.). Lactic dehydrogenase is also rather non-specific. Aldolase is often elevated in the blood even in early cases of pseudohypertrophic muscular dystrophy (Aronson 1960), and is more strikingly elevated in this type of dystrophy than in others. However, creatine phosphokinase is the most specifically elevated enzyme in muscular dystrophy (Swaiman and Sander 1963). It is constantly high in the sex-linked pseudohypertrophic type, and smaller elevations may be noted in limb girdle and facio scapulo humeral dystrophy as well as in myotonic dystrophy (Pearce *et al.* 1964*a*). These authors state that creatine kinase is normal in the blood in acquired myopathies, including polymyositis, except that it may be elevated in cases of polymyositis in childhood. Pearce *et al.* (1964*b*) have also reported that the level of creatine kinase may be elevated in the sera of female carriers of pseudohypertrophic muscular dystrophy, which may prove to be a valuable tool in genetic counselling.

Lead Intoxication

Patients with encephalopathy due to lead intoxication usually have elevated levels of lead in the blood. If this laboratory procedure is readily and quickly available. it may be the quickest means of substantiating the diagnosis. Anaemia, glycosuria, coproporphyrinuria, and elevated protein levels in the cerebrospinal fluid are the other most important laboratory findings.

Galactosaemia

If galactosaemia is suspected from the finding of galactose in the urine, the diagnosis may be confirmed by demonstrating absence of galactose-1-phosphate-uridyl transferase in the red blood cells (Anderson *et al.* 1957, Nordin *et al.* 1961). This test is also the method of choice for establishing or ruling out galactosaemia in a newborn baby whose parents are known to carry genes for galactosaemia.

Phenylketonuria

The Guthrie test for phenylalanine in the serum is based on inhibition of bacterial growth and can be done reasonably economically on a very large scale as a screening procedure. It is now required by law in several areas in the United States and has the obvious advantage that samples of blood can be collected from all new babies before they leave the hospital. However, it is not reliable if infants go home with their mothers at 2 days of age, and subsequent testing of blood or urine is then required. Guthrie (1963) recommends that an apparent level of 6 mg. per cent or more of phenylalanine be considered positive. This should be re-checked by a second determination of phenylalanine by a more exact quantitative method, of which several are available. In patients with proven phenylketonuria, phenylalanine levels in the blood should be measured quantitatively at regular intervals, preferably every one to two months. Excessively low levels are dangerous and high levels will suggest the diet is not effective. These serial tests are the only practical way to regulate prescribed intake of phenylalanine.

Maple Syrup Urine Disease

Dancis (1963) has suggested that an early and specific approach to the diagnosis of maple syrup urine disease in the newborn period can be made by demonstrating that the white blood cells of patients with this disease can transaminate leucine, isoleucine and valine, but cannot decarboxylate them (leukocytes of normal newborns can do both).

Caeruloplasmin

Abnormally low levels of caeruloplasmin in the blood are usual in Wilson's Disease, even in early stages, and this is one of the standard confirmatory tests.

Gargoylism (Hurler's Disease) and Other Storage Diseases

Metachromatic cytoplasmic inclusions in leukocytes are usually present in cases of gargoylism, and it has been suggested (Muir *et al.* 1963) that this test is as reliable as the determination of urinary mucopolysaccharides. Vacuoles in the cytoplasm of leukocytes are also frequently encountered with Niemann-Pick's and Gaucher's diseases, but bone marrow as well as blood should be examined if these entities are suspected.

Glycogen Storage Disease

Quantitative determination of the glycogen concentration in the red blood cells may make it possible to distinguish different types of glycogenosis. Progress in this field is proceeding so rapidly that the physician must consult the latest literature or refer his patient to a research centre working in this field.

Serologic Tests

Congenital syphilis is now so rare in many parts of the world that it is hardly considered as a cause of neurological disease in childhood. Such classical syndromes as juvenile tabes or taboparesis and syphilitic optic atrophy are now very seldom encountered in most areas, but some standard serologic test for syphilis should be performed in every case of suspicious or otherwise unexplained neurological disease. The Wassermann reaction should be tested in the spinal fluid as well as in the blood since the former is occasionally positive while the latter is negative. Other serologic tests which may be considered in appropriate cases include reactions for typhoid and other specific fevers, for toxoplasmosis (rarely diagnostic unless there is either chorioretinitis in the eye grounds or intracranial calcification in skull films), determination of the mother's and of the child's major blood groups and of any anti-D titre in suspected cases of kernicterus, and the Paul Bunell reaction for infectious mononucleosis.

Chromosomal Studies

Indications

The technical methodology of preparing chromosomal karyotypes from cultures of leukocytes in peripheral blood is now well developed and cytogenetic laboratories doing this type of work exist in most teaching hospitals. However, these laboratories are usually tied up with their own research projects and are often reluctant to perform this time-consuming and expensive study for routine clinical purposes. This is unfortunate because one cannot otherwise determine whether a case of mongolism is based on trisomy or on translocation in order to advise the parents whether they are likely to have a second mongol child. In cases of mental retardation other than mongolism, study of chromosomes is statistically very unfruitful unless there are clues suggesting this type of study. The situations which ought to alert the clinician to make the considerable effort often required to get a karyotype are:

1. The presence, in addition to some degree of mental retardation, of a structural anomaly of some non-ectodermal structure, especially of the musculoskeletal system, heart, or kidneys.

2. A history that the mother has had several spontaneous abortions or anatomically abnormal stillbirths.

3. Resemblance of the patient to the clinical features of one of the chromosomal

anomalies already reported.

4. The 'hunch' of an experienced investigator in cytogenetics that a particular child looks as though he 'might not have all his chromosomes' or might have too many.

Methods

For details, the interested reader is referred to one of a number of readily available reviews such as that of Hamerton (1962). Most methods involve some technique for setting leukocytes in tissue culture and subsequently arresting mitosis in metaphase with colchicine. Enlarged photomicrographs are made and the individual chromosomes are cut out and arranged in pairs in descending order of size according to the known normal karyotype. Several such preparations are made and counts are also done of a considerably larger number of cells to determine the average number of chromosomes and to consider whether the tissue studied might be mosaic.

A buccal smear is usually made and stained to determine the number of sex chromatin bodies on the nuclear membrane, if an anomaly of the X-chromosomes is suspected. If there is any reason to suspect that the patient may be a chromosomal mosaic, karyotypes may also be prepared from cells of tissue cultures of other tissues such as skin or fibroblasts. If the possibility of hereditary transmission of a chromosomal anomaly is not generally known from the literature, karyotypes should also be prepared of the patient's parents (the mother is the carrier in almost all hereditary types).

Interpretation

The identification and classification of chromosomal anomalies and the determination of their implications as to heredity are so complicated, and changing so constantly, that the clinician must rely on the advice of the investigator who did the work for him, or refer all the material elsewhere for further consultation.

Special Studies on Urine

Many special chemical tests may be carried out on the urine; a number of these should be considered in cases of neurological abnormality in childhood, particularly in mental retardation. These will be considered test by test rather than by disease category suspected.

Reducing Substances

The clinician is interested chiefly in glucose and galactose although several other substances reduce copper. A point which physicians sometimes overlook is that some tests routinely used for glucose are specific for it. Glucose oxidase test papers do not react to galactose and the Benedict test should be performed (its convenient adaptation, the Clinitest tablets, are also satisfactory).

Ferric Chloride Test

This cheap and convenient test is easily carried out by adding a few drops of 5 or

10 per cent ferric chloride solution to fresh urine previously acidified with 5 per cent sulphuric acid (other acids are less satisfactory), or by putting a few drops of the ferric chloride solution on to a really fresh soaking-wet diaper. A dark green colour results if phenylpyruvic acid is present. A similar green colour results from the presence of imidazolepyruvic acid in the urine of patients with histidinaemia (La Du *et al.* 1953) and a blue colour follows the addition of ferric chloride if the patient suffers from maple syrup urine disease. While the percentage of false negatives in occasional specimens from patients with phenylketonuria is probably somewhat greater than is the case with the Guthrie test on blood, the performance of a ferric chloride test on 2 or 3 specimens of fresh urine is generally believed to be a sufficient screening test for phenylketonuria and has the advantage of screening for histidinaemia and maple syrup urine disease as well. False negative tests result if the patient is on a very low dietary intake of protein, if he is taking very large doses of vitamin C, or if the urine specimen is not fresh. The test may remain positive even after the specimen has been stored under refrigeration for a week or more but it is safer to use fresh urine. The ferric chloride test gives a red to purple colour in the urine of patients who have been taking aspirin or other salicylates. Phenothiazine drugs produce a grey-green to blue-black colour reaction.

DNPH Test

To one ml. of urine, the examiner adds 0.2 ml. of 0.5 per cent solution of 2, 4-dinitrophenylhydrazine in 2N hydrochloric acid. In a positive test a yellow precipitate or cloudiness forms within a minute. The test is positive in phenylketonuria, maple syrup urine disease, histidinaemia, tyrosyluria and in hyperglycinaemia.

Nitroprusside Test

Children with homocystinuria usually have dislocated lenses of the eyes, and often genu valgum and sparse blond hair in addition to mental retardation. Routine screening may be easily carried out by mixing 5 ml. of urine with 2 ml. of 5 per cent sodium cyanide solution. The mixture is allowed to sit for 10 minutes at room temperature and a few drops of 5 per cent sodium nitroprusside solution are added. A magenta colour results from the presence of cysteine or homocysteine.

Amino-Acids

Many syndromes of mental retardation and other neurological signs and symptoms involve some genetically-transmitted metabolic error, and are associated with abnormal urinary outputs of one or more amino-acids, or with generalised amino-aciduria. Even the commonest of these, phenylketonuria, accounts for only one per cent of institutionalised mental defectives; the others are individually much rarer. Procedures for studying urinary amino-acids are complicated, time-consuming and expensive and usually require hospitalisation in order to collect a complete 24-hour urine specimen from an uncooperative or incontinent child. (Van Gelderen and Dooren (1964) have recently claimed that early morning specimens are equally good, at least above the age of 2 years, but this requires further confirmation). Large outputs of a single or of two or three amino-acids, or the presence of an amino-acid not normally found in the urine (such as argininosuccinic acid) is best demonstrated by 2-

dimensional paper chromatography. Ghadimi and Shwachman (1959) have described a very simple screening test using filter paper discs, but many laboratories have found this method unreliable for screening purposes. A better method has recently been described by Efron and her associates (1964) and other simplified methods will doubtless be developed in the future.

Accurate but expensive quantitative determinations of each individual amino-acid may conveniently be carried out on a Moore and Stein column analyser if one is available and if screening tests or other features of the case suggest the probability of a positive result. This type of column analyser also readily detects a generalised aminoaciduria in which all the amino-acids of the blood appear in the urine in excess of the smaller qualities of a smaller number of amino-acids which are normally present. Unless the aminoaciduria is quite marked, however, it may be difficult to be sure of a quantitative generalised excess by paper chromatography. Several methods are available for measuring total alpha-amino-nitrogen in a 24-hour urine collection and an older method (Van Slyke *et al.* 1943) can even be carried out using the Van Slyke apparatus available in almost every laboratory for clinical chemistry. Decision on whether or not the total amount of alpha-amino-nitrogen is abnormal is best made by comparing it with other parameters (Ghadimi and Shwachman 1960):

	Mean Value	*Range of Normal*
Alpha-amino-Nitrogen/Total Urinary Nitrogen	0·72%	0·31-1·76%
Alpha-amino Nitrogen/Creatinine	11%	3·9 -37%
Alpha-amino Nitrogen/Kg. body weight/24 hrs.	1·86 mg.	0·84-3·18
Alpha-amino Nitrogen/100 ml. urine	9·42 mg.	3·42-14·73

Increased urinary excretion of amino-acids (some more than others) is physiological in the newborn period (Armstrong *et al.* 1964) and may continue up to a month or two of age. Increased aminoaciduria also results from a state of negative nitrogen balance in which the patient breaks down his own body proteins, and it may have this basis in the case of any debilitated infant. Deficiencies of certain vitamins also cause aminoaciduria. An aminoaciduria is secondary to a toxic effect on the renal tubules, as seen with several conditions producing mental retardation, including Wilson's disease, galactosaemia and lead poisoning. Finally, there are several known genetically-determined aminoacidurias which are not accompanied by mental retardation (tyrosinosis, most cases of glycinaemia, and the syndrome of Luder and Sheldon in which glucose and amino-acids are both defectively reabsorbed by the renal tubules).

The difficulties of technique and interpretation should be considered when selecting patients for studies of amino-acid metabolism. The principal indications are:

1. Diffuse and non-lateralised disease of the central nervous system, if not explained on the basis of an abnormal birth history or thought to be to a known anatomical congenital defect or to cerebral dysgenesis accompanying other visible congenital anomalies. This category includes most cases of severe mental retardation in children born to intelligent parents, whose retardation is not otherwise explained.

2. A family history positive for a condition similar to the patient's.

3. Acidosis, hypoglycaemia or early unexplained inanition.

4. Convulsions in the neonatal period unexplained by birth history, infection or ordinary neonatal tetany.

5. Possible infantile spasms or electroencephalographic hypsarrhythmia. If evidence of an abnormal aminoaciduria is obtained, the examiner may wish to make further investigations such as determination of the amino-acids in the blood or in the cerebrospinal fluid, examination of the urine for keto-acids, performance of a tryptophane loading test, examination of the urine for xanthurenic acid, or other special tests.

Creatine

It has been known for many years that muscular dystrophies usually cause increased excretion of creatine in the urine, resulting in reversal of the creatine/creatinine ratio in a 24-hour urine specimen. Pathological creatinuria depends on the presence of active muscular wasting ; it is also non-specific for muscular dystrophy since it occurs with acute or sub-acute polymyositis, rapidly progressing spinal muscular atrophy and other conditions. Measuring the creatine/creatinine ratio in cases of suspected muscular dystrophy has become outmoded since the development of tests for certain enzymes in the blood (see p.223).

Metachromatic Material

The centrifuged sediment of a random urine specimen may contain renal tubular cells with inclusions giving a metachromatic pink or red colour when stained with toluidin blue. However, the fluff test of Austin (1957) is much more reliable and the most suitable test for screening purposes, although it must be performed on a 24-hour urine specimen collected into a chilled bottle. The test is appropriate whenever metachromatic leukodystrophy is suspected; as, for example, in a child under five years of age whose development has stopped or regressed, or who has ataxia or developing spasticity. Biopsy of a peripheral nerve may also show metachromatic material in this disease.

Mucopolysaccharides

There are several available methods of measuring the excretion of mucopolysaccharides in the urine of patients suspected of gargoylism (Hurler's disease), such as those of Steiness (1961), Denny and Dutton (1962) and Clausen et al. (1963). Terry and Linker (1964) have differentiated four types of gargoylism according to their patterns of excretion of chondroitin sulphate B and heparitin sulphate. A simplified screening test has been used satisfactorily at the Children's Hospital, Washington, D.C., for several years but its origin is obscure: approximately ·05 ml. of urine is 'spotted' on Whatman number 1 filter paper to make a spot about 1 cm. in diameter, using fractional spotting if required. The filter paper is immersed for 45 seconds in toluidin blue solution (1 gram to 400 ml. of acetone and 100 ml. of water). The paper is then dried between other pieces of filter paper or even on a cloth towel. It is then washed for four minutes in 10 per cent acetic acid, again dried, and washed a second time in another saucer containing 10 per cent acetic acid. Chondroitin sulphate appears as a persistent blue spot. (If feasible, a normal control specimen should be tested at the same time, 'matched' as to creatinine content by the amount used.)

Gargoylism is often suspected before the patient's facial appearance is striking enough to be diagnostic and before the liver and spleen are markedly enlarged; under these circumstances examination of the urine for mucopolysaccharides is extremely helpful.

Vanimandelic Acid

A semi-quantitative method for measuring urinary excretion of vanimandelic acid has recently been described (Young *et al.* 1963) and may be used in connexion with the initial diagnosis or suspected post-operative recurrence of neuroblastomata or ganglioneuroblastomata. Phaeochromocytoma may cause increased urinary excretion of the VMA and ganglioneuroma appears to do so inconsistently.

Coproporphyrins

Coproporhyrins I and III, protoporphyrin and porphobilinogen may be determined individually by complex chemical methods if the tests can be arranged in a research laboratory, but a simple screening test for coproporphyrins in a random urine specimen is readily performed. The urine is acidified with a few drops of glacial acetic acid and shaken up briefly in a tube test with an equal quantity of ether. When the ether and aqueous layers have separated, the tube is examined under an ultraviolet light, a pink fluorescence in the ether layer constituting a positive test. If there is no fluorescence the specimen should be re-examined after 20 minutes before concluding it is negative. This test is almost always positive in the urine of children with acute lead encephalopathy, and is frequently positive in chronic lead intoxication without acute symptoms. It is not specific for lead poisoning, however, since coproporphyrins are also present in the urine in certain types of anaemia and with tumours of the brain, encephalitis, poliomyelitis, and other conditions. Nevertheless, a negative test for coproporphyrins, competently done, argues strongly against lead intoxication being the basis of unexplained coma or convulsions.

Lead

Determination of the level of lead in the blood is probably a more satisfactory screening test for lead intoxication, but use may also be made of the lead content of a 24-hour urine collection (in the case of children, the concentration of lead in micrograms per litre is a less satisfactory criterion because normal children suddenly hospitalised and restrained for 24-hour collections usually have poor fluid intakes and small outputs of urine, which are concentrated with respect to lead as well as to other components). In doubtful cases one may wish to check the amount of increase of lead excretion after infusion of calcium disodium versenate (EDTA). Emmerson (1963) suggests one gram in 250 ml. of 5 per cent glucose solution, but points out that the 24-hour urinary excretion of lead may go up to 600 micrograms in healthy subjects.

Copper

Increased urinary excretion of copper (measured in a 24-hour collection) is characteristic of Wilson's disease, and the test may be used for diagnostic purposes together with or in place of the measurement of caeruloplasmin in the blood. When testing lead and copper in the urine, comparison should be made with standards of normal in the laboratory performing the analyses.

Cerebrospinal Fluid

Indications

Although the cerebrospinal fluid is likely to be examined in any patient with disease of the central nervous system if the diagnosis is not obvious, it is of course particularly indicated when meningitis or encephalitis are suspected or when there is a possibility of expanding mass lesions involving the brain or spinal cord. A detailed listing of indications for this examination is scarcely possible and would not be necessary for paediatricians or neurologists. Fluid may be obtained by lumbar, cisternal or ventricular puncture and it may be well to consider the indications for each.

Lumbar Puncture

The routine technique is well known and need not be described. Infection or maceration of the overlying skin are contraindications, as is presence of a meningocele or myelomeningocele. Lumbar puncture should be performed with extreme caution if there is evidence of increased intracranial pressure or of a suspected expanding lesion in the posterior fossa. The danger from lumbar puncture in the presence of papilloedema has probably been overrated, but if a spinal tap is to be done under these circumstances it should be performed by an experienced operator after carefully weighing the pros and cons, and in a hospital at which a neurosurgeon is available if needed. In such situations, the patient should lie on his side and the lumbar puncture be performed with the bevel of the needle upwards so as to slit the dura along its vertical axis. A needle of small diameter should be used, and once puncture is accomplished, the needle should be connected by a three-way stop cock to a manometer already filled with sterile physiologic saline solution, in order to measure the pressure without allowing any fluid to escape. Turning the stop cock will then permit escape of the few drops of fluid required for cell count and determination of protein content, after which the needle should be withdrawn. Leakage of fluid through the hole in the dura is a greater danger than the puncture itself. Apprehensive or uncooperative children should be sedated both before and after the procedure and kept in the recumbent posture afterwards.

Measurements of pressure may reasonably be omitted in routine spinal puncture in young children unless there is reason to believe that pressure or mechanics will be abnormal. Small children almost always struggle or tense up sufficiently to elevate the pressure and make its measurement useless, unless they are heavily sedated prior to the procedure. Once the opening pressure has been measured, it should be possible to produce a sharp rise in pressure by compressing either jugular vein or by compression of the abdomen. Failure to get such a rise in pressure suggests a block to circulation of the cerebrospinal fluid, usually at or below the foramen magnum. A rise from compression of one jugular vein but not of the other is supposed to be an indication of thrombosis of a lateral sinus, but the size and connexions of the lateral sinuses are sufficiently variable to make interpretation difficult. The indication for jugular or abdominal compression is the suspicion of a block, usually at a spinal level, and it cannot be over-emphasized that these tests should never be performed if there is reason to suspect intracranial tumour or increased pressure. Injudicious use in these circumstances may result in sudden death of the patient.

Cisternal Puncture

Cisternal puncture may be performed to get spinal fluid for examination when there are contraindications to the lumbar route, particularly local lesions of, or over, the spine. Its advantage in not producing post-spinal headache is not of major importance, and cisternal puncture is not significantly safer than lumbar puncture if the intracranial pressure is increased (it may be less safe if there is medullary or cerebellar herniation through the foramen magnum). The technique is seldom needed in work with children and is not described here since it should not be undertaken by other than an experienced operator (the distances involved are considerably shorter in children than in adults and the risk correspondingly greater).

Ventricular Puncture

Ventricular puncture is safer than cisternal puncture and is to be preferred to lumbar puncture if one is unable to obtain spinal fluid by the lumbar route. It is also preferable in most cases where intracranial pressure is increased. Ventricular puncture must be performed by a neurosurgeon, except in the case of an infant with an open fontanelle, or of a young child with separated cranial sutures.

Leukocyte Content

The cerebrospinal fluid normally contains no more than 5 or 6 leukocytes per cubic millimetre, although a higher figure is sometimes given. All leukocytes present are normally mononuclear and the presence of even one segmented form is probably abnormal, although it might be produced by non-specific meningismus or by a previous spinal puncture. If more than 1,000 white blood cells per cubic millimetre are present these will usually be polymorphonuclear and an indication of bacterial meningitis. Cell counts of less than 1,000 or particularly less than 500 may indicate a viral aseptic meningitis or encephalitis if the large majority of the cells are mononuclear (in mumps meningoencephalitis the number of cells may be even higher, but they are nearly 100 per cent mononuclear). It is the cell count of 500 per cubic millimetre or less, with a mixture of mononuclear and polymorphonuclear cells, which offers the greatest diagnostic difficulty. This count may be due to an early or partially treated bacterial meningitis, to a viral infection, to tuberculous meningitis, cryptococcosis or other unusual infection, to intracranial or spinal tumour, to abscess, to venous or arterial infarction, to a wide variety of degenerative conditions, or to toxic agents, especially lead. The differential diagnosis rests on other clinical and laboratory findings, and especially on changes in the cerebrospinal fluid with respect to red blood cells, protein and sugar content. The parainfectious encephalopathies (neuro-allergic meningo-encephalitides) such as accompany the common childhood diseases, possibly as some types of reaction of hypersensitivity ('measles encephalitis' does not involve direct invasion of the brain by measles virus), usually produce some cellular reaction in the spinal fluid. Counts of 300 or fewer white blood cells, some polymorphonuclear and some mononuclear, are common but a small proportion of authentic·cases fail to show any abnormal number·of cells in the spinal fluid even on several taps. On the other hand, a diagnosis of a type of encephalitis involving viral invasion of the central nervous system is probably untenable if there is no leukocytosis in the spinal fluid.

Erythrocytes

Red blood cells may be introduced into the spinal fluid traumatically during the performance of the puncture, usually by the needle striking one of the veins near the posterior surfaces of the bodies of the vertebrae. The operator may be aware that he has gone too far and has struck bone but it is not difficult to nick a vein without doing this. The obtaining of pure blood, which clots, is almost always due to a traumatic tap, but, short of this, the physician who feels that he has performed a clean puncture should not too quickly ignore a bloody fluid, especially if it fails to clear as it is collected in serial' tubes. The possibility of subarachnoid haemorrhage and of its various potential causes should not be too lightly dismissed. Even if the fluid is grossly bloody, its content of both red and white cells should be counted and compared. Contamination with blood seems somehow to produce a slight relative excess of leukocytes in many instances, but one would be suspicious about leukocytes present in more than twice the number calculated from the white and red counts of the circulating blood. Whether the erythrocytes in the spinal fluid are crenated or not is of no value in deciding how long they have been there. A better criterion is the presence or absence of xanthochromia in the supernatant fluid of the centrifuged specimen. Xanthochromia requires at least several hours to develop and rules out a bloody tap as the sole cause of erythrocytes in the spinal fluid, unless a previous traumatic puncture has been performed. The presence of large numbers of erythrocytes in the spinal fluid, without a significant excess of leukocytes, suggests subarachnoid haemorrhage first and foremost, although subdural haematoma or thrombosis of venous sinuses may produce lesser numbers of red blood cells without much of a leukocytic reaction in some cases. More often, a mixture of red and white blood cells, if anything, will be encountered with these conditions as well as with haemorrhagic infarction of the brain. It is well to bear in mind that the number of cells in the spinal fluid in association with any lesion in the brain varies inversely with its depth from the surface, and that the presence of erythrocytes in the fluid requires a haemorrhagic lesion.

Protein

The fluid in the lumbar space normally contains more protein than that from the cisterna or ventricles. There is considerable variation in the standard of normal in different laboratories; this may be 25 mg. per cent at one hospital and 45 or 50 mg. per cent at another. Protein levels are higher in adults than in children, except that in the newborn period the spinal fluid may normally contain as much as 125 mg. per cent of protein. This should fall to 60 mg. per cent by 2 months and reach normal values soon after. Most of the pathological situations causing leukocytosis in the cerebrospinal fluid also produce proportionate or disproportionate elevation of the protein content. Tumours, lead poisoning, and certain unusual infections such as cryptococcosis or toxoplasmosis, typically produce elevations in protein which are much higher than the cell counts. However, it cannot be stated that intracranial tumours invariably lead to elevated protein levels in the cerebrospinal fluid. Acoustic neuromata are probably the only tumour of which this is practically always true, and this type of tumour is very rare in childhood unless accompanying neurofibromatosis. On the other hand, an acute encephalopathy with coma or convulsions, if due to lead intoxication, will be accompanied by elevated levels of protein in all or nearly all cases. Protein levels of 100 mg. per cent or more with little or no cellular reaction may accompany a block due to a spinal lesion; otherwise they usually reflect Guillain-Barré syndrome or a radiculitis or polyneuritis (conditions which overlap one another), or a tumour.

Electrophoretic studies may show an abnormally high content of gamma globulin in disseminated sclerosis. The gold sol test is an older method of studying the globulins in the cerebrospinal fluid and involves precipitation of colloidal gold in serial dilutions. Ten tubes are customarily used, and are graded from 0 (unchanged) to 5 (complete precipitation of colloid). A 'first zone curve' such as 5532100000 is supposed to be characteristic of general paresis of the insane (tertiary syphilis) and is sometimes called a 'paretic curve' (Lange curve), while a second zone curve such as 0012443100 is usually held more typical of tabes dorsalis. The third zone is that most precipitated in meningitic infections but is not needed to diagnose these. A first zone curve is characteristic of Dawson/Van Bogaert subacute encephalitis. Fifty per cent or more of patients with disseminated sclerosis show normal gold sol tests in the spinal fluid but a minority show either first or second zone curves. This may be helpful in distinction from progressive leukoencephalopathies such as Schilder's disease, since the latter usually produce no alteration in the colloidal gold test. A midzone gold sol curve has been reported in one case of metachromatic leukodystrophy, however (Allen *et al.* 1962).

Glucose

The content of glucose in the cerebrospinal fluid is normally about 60 per cent of that in the blood. It lags behind any fluctuations which take place in the blood sugar, so that the fall and subsequent recovery of blood sugar in the case of hypoglycaemic convulsions may leave the glucose content of the cerebrospinal fluid higher than that of the blood for a brief period. The extent to which glucose levels in the cerebrospinal fluid (and in the blood as well) are influenced by a severe convulsion alone is surprisingly obscure, and it is unwise to take the glucose content of the spinal fluid as the sole criterion for establishing or ruling out hypoglycaemia as the cause of a convulsion. The blood sugar should be determined as closely as possible to the time of the lumbar puncture. Bacterial meningitis (including tuberculous) is the major cause of depression of glucose levels, which are valuable in differentiating viral infections in which the sugar is normal. Cryptococcosis also depresses the sugar content, as do leukaemic meningitis, disseminated medulloblastomata or sarcoidosis of the central nervous system.

Chlorides

The chloride content of the cerebrospinal fluid has been thought for years to be specifically depressed in tuberculous meningitis, but the general opinion is now that this depression reflects the level of chlorides in the blood and, indirectly, the amount and duration of vomiting which has taken place, and is therefore a sign of no specific diagnostic value.

Cultures

Both aerobic and anaerobic cultures are routinely planted. Cultures should be ordered for tuberculosis on appropriate special media when indicated, and a culture should be planted on a Sabouraud's medium if cryptococcosis is suspected. When appropriate, attempts may be made to isolate viruses from cerebrospinal fluid, blood, stool, or nasopharyngeal washings.

Stained Smears

If an excess of leukocytes is present in the cerebrospinal fluid or if meningitis is suspected, examination should always be made of a Gram-stained smear of the sediment of a centrifuged sample of fluid. Another slide should be examined for acid-fast forms if a tuberculous infection is to be considered. If cryptococcosis is suspected, microscopic examination of a mixture of spinal fluid with a drop of Indian ink may make the budded forms visible.

Ethanol

Cryptococcosis (torulosis) is the principal cause of the presence of ethanol in the spinal fluid in children. A test for this has been described, and may be of diagnostic value (Dawson and Taghavy 1963).

Enzymes

Levels of glutamic oxalacetic transaminase and lactic dehydrogenase have been reported as elevated in the cerebrospinal fluid in infants who have had traumatic births (Ianniruberto 1961, Lending *et al.* 1963) and with cerebral infarction (Green *et al.* 1957). However, they do not necessarily parallel the levels in the blood. Creatine phosphokinase has been found in the cerebrospinal fluid in levels up to 5 units (normal below ·06 units) from patients with various intracranial tumours, symptomatic epilepsy, progressive hydrocephalus and in benign intracranial hypertension (Herschkowitz and Cummings 1964). The finding is clearly non-specific and the authors suggest that brain tissue contains more of this enzyme than do tumours, so that increased levels of creatine kinase in the cerebrospinal fluid probably reflect breakdown of brain tissue. At present, the determination of enzyme content in the cerebrospinal fluid is a tool for research, but the clinical application of these methods will doubtless become more usual in the near future.

Subdural Taps

Indications

Every paediatrician is familiar with the indication and method for performing

235

subdural taps in infants with open fontanelles and sutures. The same technique may be used with older children if the sutures are separated, as from increased intracranial pressure, and even without increased pressure sufficient force will often produce passage of a stout needle up to the age of 2. Otherwise, suspected subdural haematoma or effusion requires neurosurgical intervention and the making of burr holes at appropriate locations. This is usually done only if the suspicion of subdural fluid is raised by abnormality in an arteriogram.

X-Ray and Contrast X-Ray Studies

Indications

X-rays of the skull and other relevant areas should be studied before considering further measures (Fig. 3). The signs of increased intracranial pressure are somewhat different in children and adults. Intracranial calcification (Fig. 4) may point to an expanding lesion such as a tumour, but the causes of calcification are again rather different in children and adults. In childhood, calcification is most likely to be due to toxoplasmosis, cytomegalic inclusion disease, tuberose sclerosis, Sturge-Weber syndrome, old meningitis or haemorrhage, or to certain types of tumours such as a craniopharyngioma. Calcification may normally occur in childhood just as it does in adult life in such structures as the choroid plexuses, the falx or tentorium, but the pineal does not calcify in childhood and this indication of the location of the midline structures is therefore not available for diagnostic purposes.

Since the brain and the cerebrospinal fluid in its ventricles and cisterns and over its surface have the same radiological density, it is obvious that more radiological information can be obtained by the replacement of this fluid by air or by injection of the cerebral circulation with a contrast medium.

The principal indications for making contrast x-rays of the head are as follows:

1. Suspicion of an intracranial tumour.

2. Suspicion of a porencephalic or leptomeningeal cyst.

3. Suspicion of subdural haematoma or effusion.

4. Investigation of possible obstruction of flow of cerebrospinal fluid, such as hydrocephalus or aqueductal stenosis.

5. Suspected intracranial vascular malformation.

6. Suspected congenital anomaly, cortical atrophy or ventricular dilatation, if the examiner believes that evidence of incurable defects of this kind will be valuable generally and in interpretation to the parents, who should have been told of the arguments pro and con before the procedure is carried out.

The clinical signs and symptoms pointing to the above diagnostic categories are far too numerous to describe even in outline. However, it is worth emphasising that while focal epilepsy is much less frequently associated with tumour in children than in adults, focal seizures which are not promptly controlled by standard anticonvulsant drugs usually warrant contrast radiography, particularly if there are also localising signs or a focally abnormal EEG. Nevertheless, most children with focal epilepsy prove to have atrophic rather than expanding lesions.

236

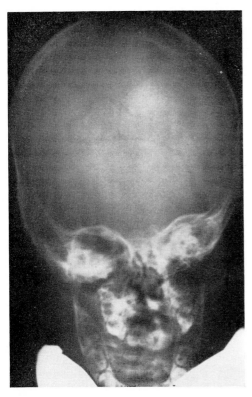

Fig. 3a. Large fused biparietal foramina may appear as a single bony defect in the skull.

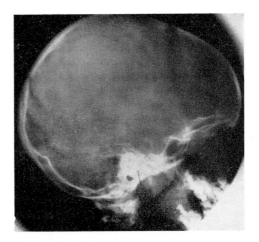

Fig. 3b. Erosion of posterior clinoids as a result of increased intracranial pressure. This is the principal radiological manifestation of increased intracranial pressure of some duration in the adolescent or older child, just as it is in the adult, but in younger children the cranial sutures usually separate instead. (Sutures are also separated, in this case.)

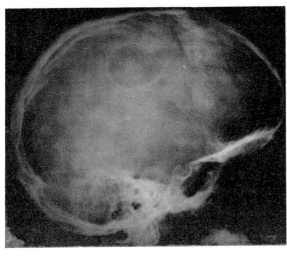

Fig. 3c. Bony defect in skull with eburnated edge of increased radio density which suggests that the lesion is an epidermoid tumour.

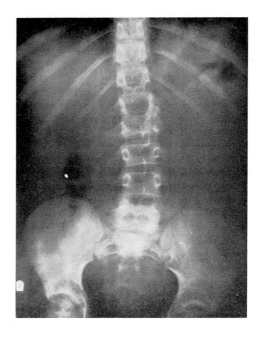

Fig. 3d. Anomalous spicule of bone extending from the body of the second lumbar vertebra and transfixing the spinal cord (diastematomyelia). There is also partial fusion of the upper lumbar vertebrae.

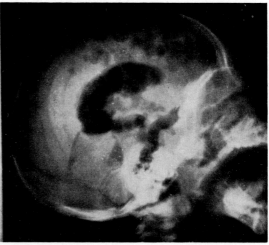

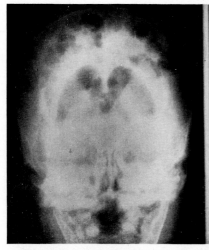

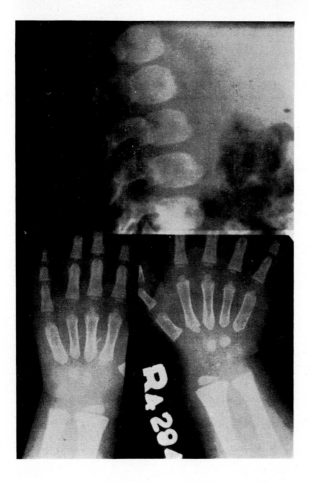

Fig. 3*e*. (above) X-ray of skull showing increased intracranial pressure but without direct evidence of its cause. Note particularly the abnormally separated sutures. There is also erosion of the dorsum sellae, although in children the changes in the sella are usually less striking than in adults, and separation of the sutures is the major sign of increased intracranial pressure in childhood. Increased convolutional markings of the inner table of the skull ('beaten silver appearance') may be normal in childhood and do not indicate increased intracranial pressure by themselves, unless much more extreme than those seen here.

Fig. 3*f*. (left) Lateral x-ray of lumbar spine in gargoylism, in which there is underdevelopment of the upper ossification centre, resulting in a lipped appearance of the anterior edge of the vertebrae. At bottom, broad metacarpal and phalangeal bones in the hand of a child with gargoylism. The hands are broad with short fingers.

238

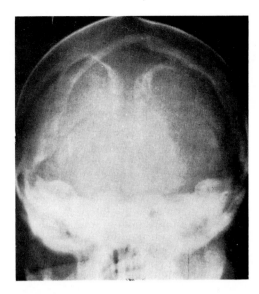

Fig. 4a. Intracranial calcification in cytomegalic inclusion body disease. Note that the deposits of calcium are just beneath the ependyma so as to form almost a perfect cast of the ventricular system.

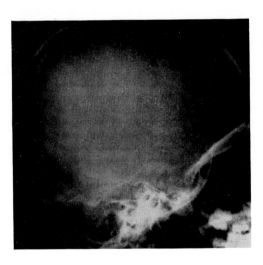

Fig. 4b (above). Intracranial calcification of 'mothball' type, in tuberose sclerosis.

Fig. 4c (left). Calcification in craniopharyngioma.

Fig. 4d (right). Intracranial calcification in Sturge-Weber syndrome. The double lines (sometimes called 'railroad tracks)' reflect greater radiologic density of subpial calcification at the sulci, at which the deposit is oriented perpendicular to the x-ray film. The appearance is not due to calcification around blood vessels, as is sometimes erroneously stated.

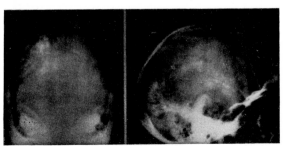

A *ventriculogram* should usually be made in preference to a lumbar pneumoencephalogram, if there is any reason to suspect increased intracranial pressure or a tumour. Lumbar pneumoencephalography is particularly dangerous in the presence of tumours in the posterior fossa of the skull (other than intrinsic gliomata of the brain stem). Except under these circumstances, lumbar pneumoencephalography is usually less drastic than ventriculography since the latter requires shaving the head and the making of burr holes in the skull. Pneumoencephalography also gives more information since it permits easier filling of the various cisterns and of the subarachnoid pathways over the convexity of the brain. Arteriography is of course to be preferred if a vascular malformation is suspected, and is also best for the demonstration of subdural haematoma. The above are only general guidelines, however, and the type of contrast x-ray chosen depends upon what type of lesion is anticipated and where it is. Proper selection often requires consultation between the physician in charge, the neurosurgeon and the radiologist.

In *myelography*, a few millilitres of a contrast medium such as pantopaque (Myodil) are introduced into the lumbar subarachnoid space by spinal puncture. Under fluoroscopy, the patient is examined in various positions on a tilt table to outline the spinal subarachnoid space from its lower extremity up to the foramen magnum. The indication for this is suspicion of an intraspinal lesion such as a tumour, vascular anomaly or diastematomyelia. The immediate problem is usually an unexplained paraparesis accompanied by at least one other finding such as a sensory deficit, dysfunction of bowels or bladder, a tuft of hair or a cutaneous lesion overlying the spine, or abnormalities of plain x-rays of the spine; however, motor signs alone may be a sufficient indication if one is convinced that the paraparesis is progressive.

Methods

In many hospitals, pneumoencephalography, myelography, ventriculography and arteriography are all performed by neurosurgeons. In other centres, either paediatricians or neurologists perform pneumoencephalography and the latter may also do arteriography. In still other centres, an experienced staff member in the department of radiology will perform all these procedures. Local custom is probably the most important determining factor, together with the obvious need for the procedure to be done by a physician experienced with it. In general, contrast x-rays should not be made for patients suspected of having surgical lesions unless they are done by or at least with the approval of the surgeon who will have to decide whether or not to operate on the basis of the evidence produced. The same applies to the making of myelograms. Detailed techniques need not be described here, for any physician attempting these procedures will have had training and experience with them.

Interpretation

Figures 5, 6, 7 and 8 show a few examples of various abnormalities which may be encountered with pneumoencephalography, ventriculography, arteriography and myelography. Interpretation of the films is clearly a matter for a radiologist experienced in such work. If a radiologist is not available, the physician who performed the contrast study will of course wish to interpret the films himself, and in any event a consultation with the radiologist is advisable.

Other Special Procedures which are Substitutes for Contrast X-Rays

Brain Scans using Radioisotopes

Just as with an adult, a child's head may be scanned with a counter after intravenous administration of serum albumin tagged with radioactive iodine (RISA) or isotopes of mercury or other substances. Standards of normal are in general less well developed for children than for adults, and the procedure has the obvious disadvantage that children frequently will not lie still for the period of time required for the scan. The method depends chiefly on the alterations in blood supply which accompany lesions within the skull. The venous sinuses are naturally conspicuously demonstrated. Relatively avascular tumours are difficult to demonstrate by this method, and it is often stated that lesions in the posterior fossa show up less well than supratentorial lesions, although this is not necessarily true.

Ultrasound (ECHO) Scans

Ultrasound equipment has recently been introduced which makes it possible to locate a boundary between soft tissue and fluid. The method is chiefly applicable to localisation of the midline structures of the brain, and its usefulness roughly compensates for the failure of the pineal to calcify sufficiently to be visible in x-rays in children's skulls. However, as the most innocuous of all of the procedures described, it might have considerable application in screening for subdural haematoma or other expanding lesions. Sometimes, but not always, other structures such as the basal ganglia may be defined.

Pharmacologic Tests

A great variety of drug tests are available but only a few are sufficiently common to justify description here.

Tests for Myasthenia Gravis

Edrophonium (Tensilon (R)) is the drug of choice for a diagnostic test for untreated myasthenia gravis, since it produces a much more easily recognisable endpoint than does neostigmine. It is available in a solution of 1 mg. per ml. The test dose for an adult is 10 mg. given intravenously. One would use half this amount for a 6-year-old child and 1 mg. as the total test dose for a newborn infant. Before beginning the test the proper dose of atropine sulphate for the patient's size should be available and drawn up in a syringe ready for injection if a severe reaction to the edrophonium occurs. One-tenth of the planned test dose is then given, followed by the remainder after a minute if no adverse reaction has taken place. In a positive test, dramatic improvement in ptosis and in extraocular movements is readily visible by inspection or on routine testing. If the weakness is chiefly in the skeletal muscles, some objective test should be used if possible. Such tests may take the form of timed climbing of steps or

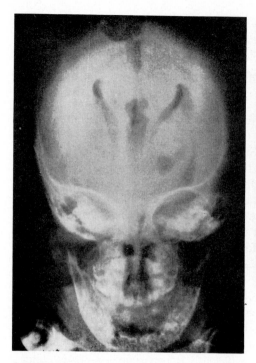

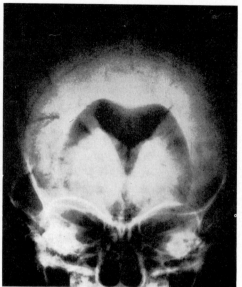

Fig. 5b. Absent septum pellucidum.

Fig. 5a. Aplasia of corpus callosum. Note separated lateral ventricles and elevation of third ventricle between them to give a 'bat-wing' appearance.

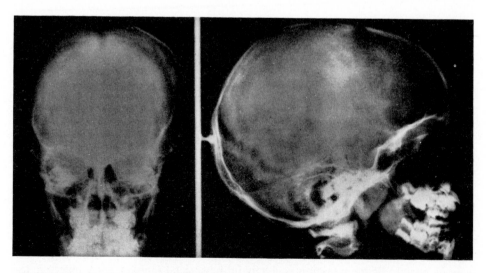

Fig. 5c. Generally dilated ventricles and widened sulci with excessive subarachnoid air in pneumoencephalogram of patient with cerebral and cortical atrophy.

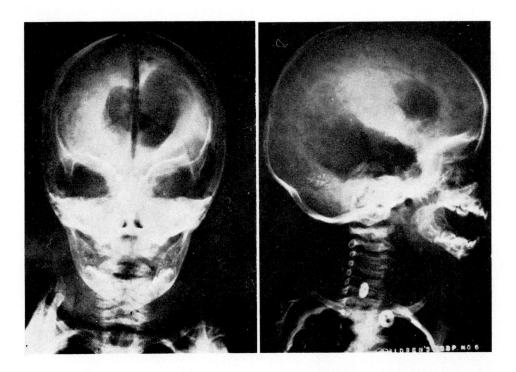

Fig. 5*d*. Bilateral ventricular dilatation, chiefly on left with local areas of disproportionate dilatation which are difficult to distinguish from porencephaly.

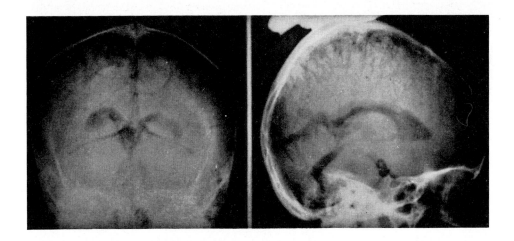

Fig. 5*e*. Posterior displacement and distortion of fourth ventricle, due to pontine glioma.

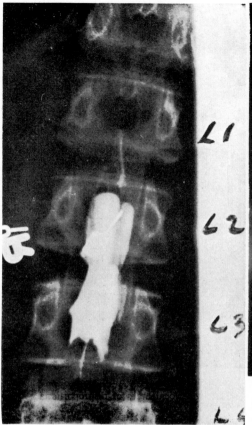

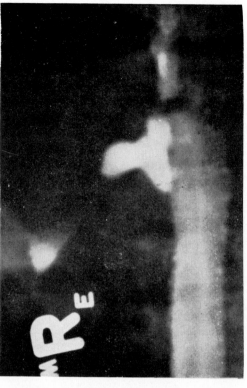

Fig. 6b. Myelogram of 10 year old girl who fell from a truck and sustained an almost complete right sided paralysis from C6 through T1. Myelogram showed contrast medium out into the neural sheaths of the nerve roots and also extradurally, indicating probable complete avulsion of roots. This type of study can also be carried out for cases of brachial palsy. Clear evidence of avulsion of roots is usually a contraindication to surgical exploration of the brachial plexus and is a prognostic sign of very poor significance

Fig. 6a. Myelogram demonstrating complete block at level of the lower part of the third lumbar vertebra, due to a medulloblastoma. Pantopaque (myodil) was injected at the site of the needle opposite the second lumbar vertebra but was unable to pass below the third.

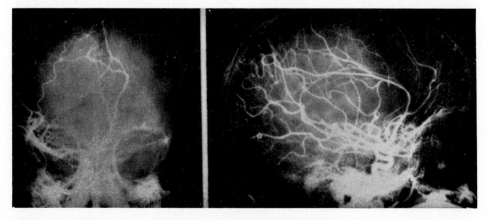

Fig. 7a. Arteriogram showing displacement of ant. cerebral circulation by right parietal cystic glioma.

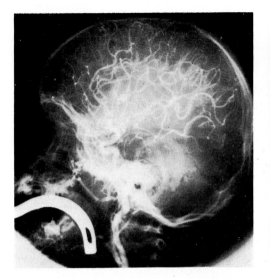

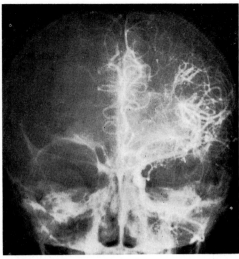

Fig. 7*b* (i) and (ii). Normal left carotid arteriogram, arterial phase.

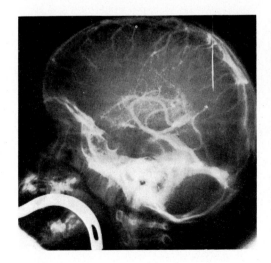

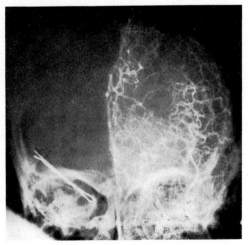

Fig. 7*c*. Normal left carotid arteriogram, venous phase.

Fig. 7*d*. Late arterial phase of arteriogram of child with left subdural haematoma. The anterior cerebral artery is displaced toward the right, indicating an expanding lesion in the left hemicranium. The fact that the terminal vessels do not reach the inner table of the skull indicates a superficial lesion pushing the cortex away from the skull.

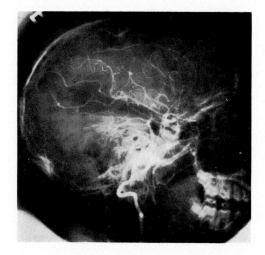

Fig. 7e. Arteriogram of 14-year-old boy with tumour of posterior fossa (the same patient as Fig. 6a; some air from the previous ventriculogram can still be seen). The injection was made in the right brachial artery. Note the marked bowing and displacement anteriorly of the basilar artery. The pericallosal artery is considerably elevated, reflecting dilatation of the lateral ventricles.

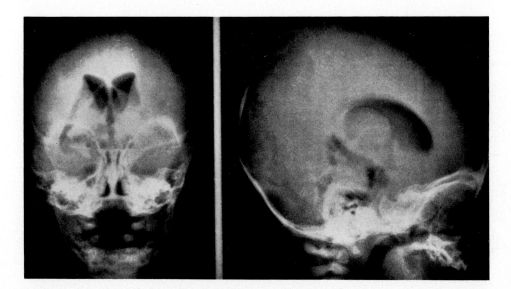

Fig. 8a. Pneumoencephalogram showing cavum veli interpositi, an innocuous congenital anomaly. Not all malformations which may be seen by pneumoencephalography have implications for cerebral malfunction.

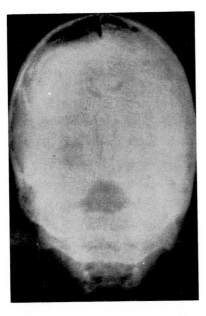

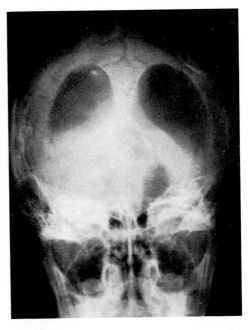

Fig. 8*b*. Pneumoencephalogram of a patient with bilateral subdural haematomata. Note displacement of brain away from inner table of skull. Considerable cortical atrophy is also present (note enlarged sulci).

Fig. 8*c*. Ventriculogram of 14-year-old boy with cystic astrocytoma in posterior fossa. The tumour is chiefly in the right cerebellum and the fourth ventricle is greatly displaced toward the left. There is also obstructive hydrocephalus with marked dilatation of the third, fourth and both lateral ventricles.

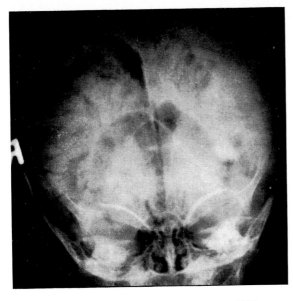

Fig. 8*d* (left). Pneumoencephalogram in which most of the injected air has entered the subdural space. The air may have been injected subdurally at the level of the spinal puncture or may have entered the subdural space through some higher opening in the arachnoid. The clear outline of the falx and the failure to visualise convolutional markings of sulci and gyri indicate that the air is subdural rather than subarachnoid in location. In such circumstances, large amounts of air may enter the subdural space but do not imply cortical atrophy, as does excessive subarachnoid air, which may demonstrate widened sulci and atrophic gyri.

247

TABLE VI

Pupillary Pharmacodynamics

ABNORMALITY	REACTIONS TO				
	Eserine	Mecholyl	Epinephrine (Adrenaline)	Cocaine	Atropine
Normal pupil	constriction	little reaction	slight dilatation	dilatation	dilatation
Parasympathetic denervation					
Postganglionic	no response	exaggerated constriction			no reaction
Preganglionic	constriction	little reaction			
Sympathetic denervation					
Postganglionic			exaggerated dilatation	little reaction	
Preganglionic			only slight dilatation	strong dilatation	
Argyll-Robertson pupil	=normal	little reaction	=normal	=normal	only slight dilatation
Adie pupil	=normal	exaggerated constriction	=normal	=normal	=normal

of power of grip as measured with a dynamometer before and after the tensilon, remembering that the effect of the tensilon may wear off in a few minutes. Side effects are chiefly referable to the autonomic system and include vomiting, abdominal cramps, diarrhoea and sometimes prostration. Mild side effects indicate that a therapeutic dose of tensilon has been given even if the patient has not responded to it and confirm that the test is negative. Severe reactions can be controlled with atropine, as already mentioned. Myasthenia gravis, in addition to being uncommon in childhood, is often clinically atypical and difficult to recognise at an early age, and is also often atypical in its response to tensilon or neostigmine.

In a recognised case of myasthenia already under treatment, it is sometimes difficult to determine whether weakness is due to the inadequacy of oral dosage of neostigmine or mestinon (R), or whether it is due to the paralytic effect of excess medication. In these circumstances a test dose of tensilon (using for this purpose 1/10 of the dose for a diagnostic test in an untreated case) will usually resolve the dilemma by making the patient better or worse, according to whether his medication was previously inadequate or excessive.

Histamine Test for Familial Dysautonomia (Riley-Day Syndrome)

With normal subjects, intradermal injection of 0·1 ml. of 1-1000 solution of histamine is followed by a painful sensation over an area an inch or two in diameter. Within 5 minutes a wheal of about 1 cm. diameter appears, surrounded by 1 to 3 cm. of erythema. Children with dysautonomia feel pain only at the immediate site of injection, and have smaller wheals which are surrounded only by one to two mm. of erythema deeper in colour than the normal flare (Smith and Dancis 1963).

Pharmacological Tests on the Pupil

Abnormally large or small pupils may be due to either paralytic or irritative affections of either sympathetic or parasympathetic fibres, and are sometimes part of syndromes such as those of Argyll-Robertson or Adie. A variety of pharmacological tests (Table VI) are described, based on instillation into the eye of epinephrine, cocaine, or other substances. Most depend on the principle that post-ganglionic denervation of a structure innervated by the autonomic nervous system renders this structure hypersensitive to the normal chemical mediator involved (epinephrine or acetylcholine), and that this effect is much less if the denervation is pre-ganglionic. Physicians wanting to use these tests will wish to check the details and dosages in an appropriate reference book of ophthalmology before undertaking such studies, or may prefer to refer the patients to ophthalmologists. Actually, these tests are infrequently required in clinical work.

Caloric Nystagmus

Methods of testing vestibular nystagmus and their interpretation have been considered in the section on the 8th cranial nerve in Chapter IX. For routine testing of caloric nystagmus the simplest method is to inject 10 ml. of ice water over a period of 1 minute, a small piece of plastic or rubber tubing being attached to the end of the syringe to conduct the cold water as close to the ear drum as possible.

Carmichael *et al.* (1954) have developed a quantitative method. The patient is positioned on his back as usual, with the head supported on a pillow at about 30° above the horizontal, to bring the horizontal semicircular canal as nearly into the vertical plane as possible. Thermostatically controlled reservoirs of warm and cold water (30° and 44°C) are required, and 300 ml. or more are run in over a period of 40 seconds. The time is recorded from the beginning of irrigation until the end of visible nystagmus, disregarding the latent period. Lesions of the frontal lobes produce no deficit of caloric nystagmus but temporal lesions are said to cause a preponderance of the fast component towards the side of the lesion by decreasing nystagmus to the opposite side. Lesions of the angular and supramarginal gyri, on the other hand, produce the same preponderance by increasing nystagmus towards the side of the lesion. For example, a lesion of the left temporal lobe should produce directional preponderance of nystagmus to the left, the nystagmus being longer following irrigation of the left ear with warm water than of the right. Correspondingly, nystagmus from irrigation of the left ear with cold water would be briefer than with cold irrigation of the right. Such comparisons are impossible with unstandardised use of 10 ml. of ice water.

Cerebral Circulation Time

Most methods of studying the cerebral circulation time in man have involved use of radio-isotopes such as radio-iodinated serum albumin injected intravenously (Thompson 1961). Gotham *et al.* (1962) have described a method in which 5 ml. of 5 per cent fluorescein are injected into an antecubital vein. The pupils have previously been dilated and the examiner watches for the appearance of fluorescein in the retinal vessels with an ophthalmoscope, using a blue filter. The authors found a sudden end point after 8 to 14 seconds in normal individuals, the mean time being 10·3 seconds. The end point was delayed in the presence of carotid occlusion or stenosis and appeared abnormally early in one patient with an angioma of the carotid distribution. Results with intracranial tumours were variable. At present, studies of cerebral circulation time are of research rather than clinical application, and are more interesting with adults than with children.

Psychometric Tests

Some consideration has already been given in Chapter VII to the patterns of irregularity which are commonly encountered in the presence of organic cortical encephalopathies. These depend on disproportionate depression, in comparison with full scale I.Q., of performance on such tests as design perception and copying, block design assembly, mazes, coding, arithmetical concepts (more than memory) and abstraction in general, and usually result in a verbal I.Q. which is considerably higher than the performance I.Q. The reverse pattern may also occur. The question of possible regression due to progressive neurological disease is best settled by comparing recent tests with previous scores if available. Very often however, no previous testing will have been done; under these circumstances a resourceful clinical psychologist may nevertheless be able to get suggestive evidence in such fields as impairment of recent memory and immediate recall and from discrepancies between what the patient has learnt in the past and still retains, in comparison with what new material he can be taught. Recall of previously learnt material may be very patchy, or the child may pass the 7-year items in a particular subtest yet be unable to do the 5-year items.

The indications for psychometric testing are usually quite clear if the physician suspects and wants to document an organic encephalopathy, or to measure it in order to plan schooling, or if progressive dementia is suspected. Psychological evaluation is also frequently necessary when the physician is not certain whether a child's difficulties are purely or primarily organic, or whether a functional emotional component of greater or lesser proportionate severity may be involved. Projective tests such as the Rorschach and the Thematic Apperception Test (TAT) are then used. These must usually be preceded by some psychometric test such as the Binet or the Wechsler Intelligence Scale for Children (WISC) and, as is desirable with all psychological referral, the physician should acquaint the testing psychologist with the nature of the problem and particularly with what type of information is desired, and, if possible, with the result of any previous tests done. Results of previous tests are especially important if any progressive disease or dementia is suspected, or if the psychological test is to be made to evaluate, for instance, the progress of a child with phenylketonuria who has been withdrawn from the therapeutic diet deficient in phenylalanine.

A more routine reason for psychometric testing is to determine whether a particular child is mentally retarded and if so, how severely, and whether he is equally retarded in all types of learning and reasoning. Such testing is usually necessitated by some imminent decision such as school placement. Psychometric testing of valid predictive value as to educability and occupational potential is rarely if ever possible in infancy or even up to 3 or 4 years, except in the case of children whose retardation is obvious to any experienced physician. Testing in doubtful cases is usually better deferred unless it is essential for the parents to know the results, or unless, again, some decision depends on it, such as adoption or institutional placement. There is sometimes considerable pressure from relatives or other physicians to carry out psychometric testing fairly early after some potentially devastating cerebral insult such as a head injury, an anoxic episode or an attack of encephalitis. Recovery usually proceeds gradually and slowly in these circumstances, for a child must not merely get back to his prior intellectual level but must catch up with what his age-mates have accomplished in the meantime. Results of psychological tests are usually inaccurate and discouraging in the early months after events of this type and are sometimes best deferred as long as circumstances permit. In other cases, however, comparison between the degree of recovery and competence after a couple of months and the situation 3 or 6 months later can be very useful in giving a prognosis and making plans.

Audiometry

Indications

It is wise to include an audiogram as part of the routine investigation of any child past $2\frac{1}{2}$ years of age who has no speech, and such testing is appropriate for many children with suspected mental retardation or autism. An audiogram is also indicated for any child with neurological disability believed to be based on neonatal jaundice, since a hearing loss for high frequencies is one of the most constant manifestations of kernicterus and may exist in the absence of other clinical abnormality. A mother's statement that she is not sure whether her child hears normally or not should always be received with respect, and formal testing of auditory acuity should then usually be carried out. A skilled audiologist will usually be able to assure himself whether or not a particular child has sufficient hearing for the development of speech, even when the child is 2 years of age, although a pure tone audiogram with construction of a graph for different frequencies is often impossible. Even more limited testing is much more difficult and less accurate in the case of mentally retarded or uncooperative children, or children suspected of the various types of developmental aphasias (see Chapter VI). It is precisely these children that the physician wishes most earnestly to test, but the results of such testing should be considered with great caution.

Method

The methods of audiometry to be employed will depend on the resources and interests of the clinic to which the patients are referred, and need not be discussed in detail here except to say that it is wise for the paediatrician or neurologist to have first-hand contact with the audiological centre used, and to be familiar with the interpretation and limitations of its methods. Cooperative and intelligent children may be tested with pure tones of different frequencies either by asking them to press the button when they hear a sound, in the conventional type of examination, or by some kind of play testing. If several loudspeakers are placed in different parts of the room, the child may be observed to turn his face towards the one from which the sound comes, but this test of localisation involves other abilities in addition to simple hearing.

251

Electrodermal audiometry is based on continuous monitoring of the electrical resistance of the skin, and on its alterations in what was formerly called the psycho-galvanometric skin resistance response (PGSR). A sound of a chosen frequency and intensity is presented, followed shortly by an electric shock. The latter is associated with increased perspiration and with a brief drop in the skin resistance. A comparable drop can be obtained with the sound alone, if this is heard and perceived, after a series of paired stimuli. Conditioned reflexes are usually held to be cortical but even if this were true of the electrodermal skin response, it would of course not prove that phonemes or words were necessarily reaching the temporal cortex without excess distortion, nor that they were properly perceived and correlated at a cerebral level. Actually, there is some evidence that, at least in animals, the electrodermal skin responses may be mediated at a level in the brain stem. In man, this type of audiometry is inconsistent and difficult even with normal children under a year of age, and similar difficulties exist to a much later age in subjects with developmental aphasias, mental retardation or 'brain injury.'

Several approaches to electroencephalographic audiometry are currently being developed. A simple approach is to present various sounds of differing intensities and to look for a startle reaction or a K complex in the EEG. In the case of babies, it is frequently but not always possible to obtain a visible evoked spike-like response to a click stimulus, which can readily be identified by inspection of the EEG tracing, although the resultant change in potential is more likely to be recorded from the vertex than over either temporal lobe. This phenomenon is seen up to a few months of age, but after that is suppressed either by increased background electrical activity in the brain or by greater thickness of skull and scalp. At later ages, including older children and adults, evoked potentials may nevertheless be demonstrated by averaging, in a computer, the activity during a one-second period following 20, 50, or 100 successive sound stimuli. At present this method involves expensive equipment and is a research instrument, but its early practical clinical use can be foreseen. Again, the presence of evoked electrical activity in the electroencephalogram following sound stimuli probably merely indicates that the stimulus reaches the brain in some form, and does not necessarily imply that this form can be appropriately analysed nor that it is perceived and correlated with past experience and with input in other sensory modalities.

Interpretation

Regardless of which method of audiometry is used, one frequently finds that there is difficulty in obtaining a reproducible record or that serial tests over a period of nine months or a year are highly inconsistent. Such a situation suggests some central defect in transmission of auditory input, or one of the developmental aphasias, and should not be considered to imply lack of skill on the part of the audiologist. If consistent curves are obtained, severe hearing losses (more than 50 decibels), especially if the loss is greater for high frequencies than for low, are characteristic of nerve deafness or of a deficit more centrally located but at present difficult to define. Hearing losses of conductive types involve less severe diminution of auditory acuity and show bone conduction to be better than air conduction. This is the reverse of the situation in the

252

normal individual or in cases of nerve deafness. The reader is referred again at this point to the description of clinical methods of testing hearing in Chapter IX (page 132). The methods there described (which are admittedly rather crude) will sometimes give clear evidence of hearing in the case of children who are thought profoundly deaf by more sophisticated audiometry.

Neither type of evidence should be disregarded, but all available information should be considered together in attempting to arrive at a clinical diagnosis.

Cystometrograms

Indications

The primary indications for making a cystometrogram are incontinence or retention of urine, situations in which the physician wishes to determine whether or not the basis is neurological, and if possible whether it reflects a lesion of the sacral nerves or one in the spinal cord or at a higher level. Occasionally, if there is an obscure motor deficit in the lower extremities without any accompanying findings to point to a spinal lesion, a cystometrogram may be performed to seek further evidence of spinal involvement.

Method

Several types of equipment are available, some using a water manometer and some using mercury. All have in common the principle of serial determinations of intravesical pressure in relation to the volume of sterile saline solution introduced, preferably at a uniform rate, and the construction of a graph of pressure against vesical content. The test may be performed by a paediatrician, neurologist, general surgeon, or urologist, perhaps best by the urologist in the average hospital. The physician in charge of the patient must, however, be familiar with the method and with the typical normal tracing obtained with the equipment available. During the making of the cystometrogram, several points are to be noted:

1. The slope of the pressure-volume curve up to the initiation of micturition (Fig. 9). A relatively flat curve with little or no increase in pressure and with increased capacity for filling is classically held to represent a 'neurogenic bladder' of the atonic type, but there is some reason to dispute this view. Plum (1962) has assembled considerable evidence that the 'tone' of the bladder is largely non-neurogenic and depends on elastic qualities of the smooth muscle itself; he suggests that the large vesical capacity and failure of pressure to increase with filling reflect excessive stretching of the smooth muscle of the bladder between the time of the acute neurological illness and the making of the first cystometrogram. Conversely, the 'small irritable bladder,' with its rapid rise in pressure and low threshold for reflex micturition, may be the result of infection and hypertrophy of the wall of the bladder, or of its shrinkage after decompression by continuous catheter drainage.

2. Rhythmic waves of contraction appear as brief increases in pressure as additional increments of fluid are introduced. These probably also originate autonomously in the smooth muscle without necessarily requiring normal innervation, although they have been observed to be absent in some instances of spinal shock.

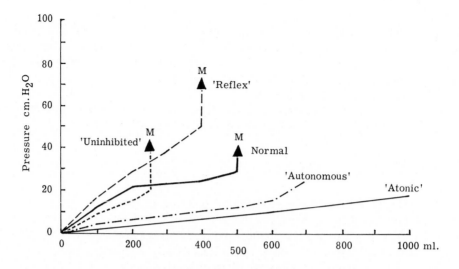

Fig. 9. Various types of cystometrograms in which the intravesical pressure in centimetres of water is plotted against the content of the bladder in millilitres. See discussion in text.

3. Sensation of fullness and subsequently of urgency are subjective findings which the patient describes during the performance of the cystometrogram, and the examiner customarily marks these points on the graph. Lack of any sensation of fullness or urgency suggests a lesion of the sacral nerves or dorsal roots. The sensation of distention is traditionally held to be transmitted in the pelvic nerves (S2, 3, 4).

4. Reflex micturition normally results from a rapid build-up of rhythmic waves of contraction, with involuntary emptying of the bladder during tetanus of the detrusor muscle. Plum (1962) suggests that each rhythmic contraction accompanying stretching the wall of smooth muscle results in transmission of an afferent burst to the sacral spinal segments. At that level, reflex efferent neural discharge may be produced, depending on the sum of descending inhibitory and facilitatory influences acting on the sacral reflex arc. (A difficult point in attempting to apply this hypothesis to voluntary micturition is that the latter chiefly requires 'letting go,' without any sense of positive contraction, and is quite different from the induction of reflex emptying of the bladder by increasing intravesical pressure through the Crédé manoeuvre). Reflex micturition is usually held to be absent during the stage of spinal shock following acute cord lesions, and does not develop if the bladder is separated from its afferent and efferent innervation to the sacral cord. An excessively strong micturition reflex which cannot be restrained voluntarily produces precipitate micturition, with lesions of the spinal cord above the sacral level or lesions of the frontal lobes and other cerebral areas. Other spinal reflexes such as tendon jerks are also usually exaggerated under these circumstances.

5. The capacity of the bladder may be measured by the amount of fluid introduced before micturition occurs. Excessively large capacity is conventionally equated with atonic denervation resulting from lesions in the nerve roots, although a lesser

254

TABLE VII

Traditional Concept of Types of Neurogenic Bladder

Type	Presumed Site of Lesion	Sensation of Fullness	Capacity	Residual	Micturition	Cystometrogram
Atonic	Post. roots or columns (or Spinal Shock)	Absent	Much increased	+++	Overflow incontinence and dribbling	Flat Curve
Autonomous	Cauda Equina or Conus (or at one stage in higher injury)	Absent	Increased	+	,,	Normal Slope but Increased Capacity
Reflex	Cord above S1 (except soon after injury)	Vague Fullness	Diminished	0 or ±	Sudden and uncontrollable	Steep Slope, Reduced Capacity
Uninhibited (similar to Infantile)	Brain	Normal	Diminished	0	,,	Normal Slope, Reduced Capacity

(This table may be incorrect in part; see text and article by Plum 1962)

degree of increased capacity is acknowledged with the 'autonomous bladder'. Diminished capacity (Table VII) is, in the classical view, the late stage of the atonic and autonomous bladders when these are followed by a reflex type of bladder function with sudden uncontrollable micturition. As already mentioned, it is perhaps more accurate to consider the bladder of small capacity as the probable result of infection, prolonged constant catheter drainage with shrinkage of the muscular wall, or hypertrophy and trabeculation of the wall.

Interpretation

Interpretation of the cystometrogram should be made in combination with other historical facts (abnormality may escape notice in patients who are not old enough to be expected to be toilet trained), and with physical findings referable to the nervous system in general and in particular to its sacral level (Table VII). Malfunctions of the bladder are more difficult to detect in children, who are frequently unable to give accurate description of sensations of fullness or urgency and who frequently struggle during making of the cystometrogram so as to raise intra-abdominal and intravesical pressures. As already mentioned in the chapter on Autonomic Function, much information may be obtained by asking the patient's mother about frequency of micturition, force of urinary stream, etc. The amount of residual urine in the bladder, as determined by catheterisation soon after voiding, is also important. Traditionally, a large residual is to be expected with the atonic denervated bladder and a lesser degree with the autonomous bladder, but obstruction of the bladder neck is too frequent with small, irritable bladders for residual alone to be diagnostic. Many different cystometrograms may be obtained from children with ordinary enuresis and there is no consistent pattern (the tracing is frequently normal). It is ordinarily not worthwhile to make cystometrograms for patients with purely nocturnal enuresis unless there is also daytime incontinence, and the procedure may aggravate accompanying psychological disturbances.

Biopsies of Muscle

Indications

While there may be minimal and subtle changes in the histological appearance of muscles accompanying disease above the level of the lower motor neurone, muscle biopsy is chiefly used for investigation of presumptive disease of the lower motor unit. The 'lower motor unit' comprises the lower motor neurone, the ventral and dorsal roots, the peripheral nerve, the neuromyal junction and the muscle itself; muscle biopsy and electrical studies of muscle and nerve are the principal aids to differential diagnosis of the site of disease at this level.

Methods

Muscle biopsy is all too frequently a disappointing procedure and too often non-diagnostic, but this can be avoided by careful planning and proper technique. It is the responsibility of the physician in charge of the patient to select which muscle shall be biopsied. This should be a muscle with significant weakness but not one which is so atrophic as to be almost totally replaced by fat, with little histological evidence of its original disease. A muscle which rates 3+ or 4+ on the M.R.C. scale (see Chapter XI) is usually the best choice. Muscles recently studied by electromyography should not be selected for biopsy. Standards of normal are better developed for some muscles than for others, and the biopsy of a quadriceps or gastrocnemius is easier to interpret than that of one of the glutei or of a muscle less frequently sampled.

The biopsy should be performed by a competent surgeon who knows what is desired and should not be delegated to the most junior house surgeon. A sufficiently large sample of muscle should be taken and the specimen should be promptly fixed and sent to the Department of Pathology without delay. It may be desirable to freeze part of the specimen in liquid nitrogen for special histochemical methods or stains for cellular enzymes, but if these are not available the biopsy should still be carried out if clinically indicated. It is most important that the specimen be properly oriented on the block before the microscopic sections are cut in order to obtain a true longitudinal and especially a true cross section of the prevailing direction of the muscle fibres. As a minimum, material which has been fixed in formalin should be stained with haematoxylin and eosin and with some trichrome stain, but other techniques may be applied as desired, such as the PAS strain on material fixed in Lilly's solution if glycogen storage disease of muscle is suspected.

Interpretation

Many pathologists in general hospitals have only limited knowledge and experience of muscle biopsies but slides may be sent away for consultation if necessary.

Colour Figures 1—14

1. Muscle biopsy in pseudohypertrophic muscular dystrophy. Note disparity in size of muscle fibres. Fibres of large and small diameters are mixed at random rather than in separate areas corresponding to motor units. There is also considerable replacement with fat.

2. Advanced muscular dystrophy in which the muscle is almost entirely replaced by fat and collagen.

3. Werdnig-Hoffmann disease. Note large areas of atrophic fibres and other areas of fibres of normal diameter.

4. Muscle biopsy in a low-grade neuropathy. Areas of atrophy by motor units are not seen but there are small triangular fibres (in cross section) which stain deeply.

5. Muscle biopsy in central core disease (courtesy of Dr. W. K. Engel, National Institute of Health, Bethesda, Md.)

6. Polymyositis. Note intensity of inflammatory reaction in muscle.

7. 'Onion skin' hypertrophy of Schwann cells in hypertrophic interstitial polyneuritis of Déjérine-Sottas.

8. Distended Purkinje cell in cerebellum in patient with Batten's amaurotic familial idiocy.

9. Distended 'foamy' neurones in the brain of a patient with gargoylism (other storage diseases are similar in haematoxylin and eosin stained sections).

10. Biopsy of brain in metachromatic leukodystrophy. Metachromatic material is contained in microglial phagocytes but is difficult to reproduce in photographs, the metachromatic colour is seen best in the cell in the midline at 12 o'clock.

11. Multinucleate cell characteristic of Krabbe's leukodystrophy.

12. Intranuclear inclusion in brain biopsy from case of Dawson's subacute inclusion encephalitis.

13 and 14. These two pictures emphasize the difficulties of interpretation of rectal biopsies. Fig. 14 is from a case of Hirchsprung's disease with an absent nerve plexus, and in 13 a normal rectal biopsy is shown for comparison. The inexpert eye may have difficulty in picking out the ganglion cells, which are arrowed.

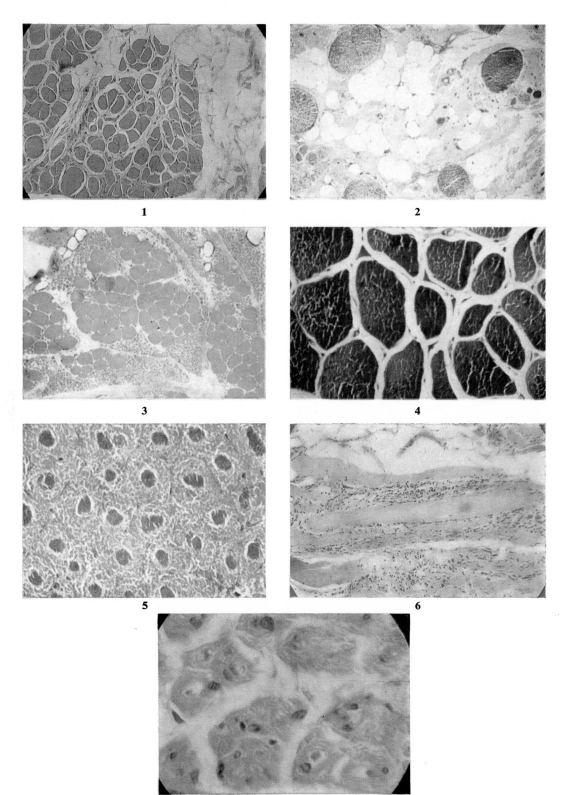

1

2

3

4

5

6

7

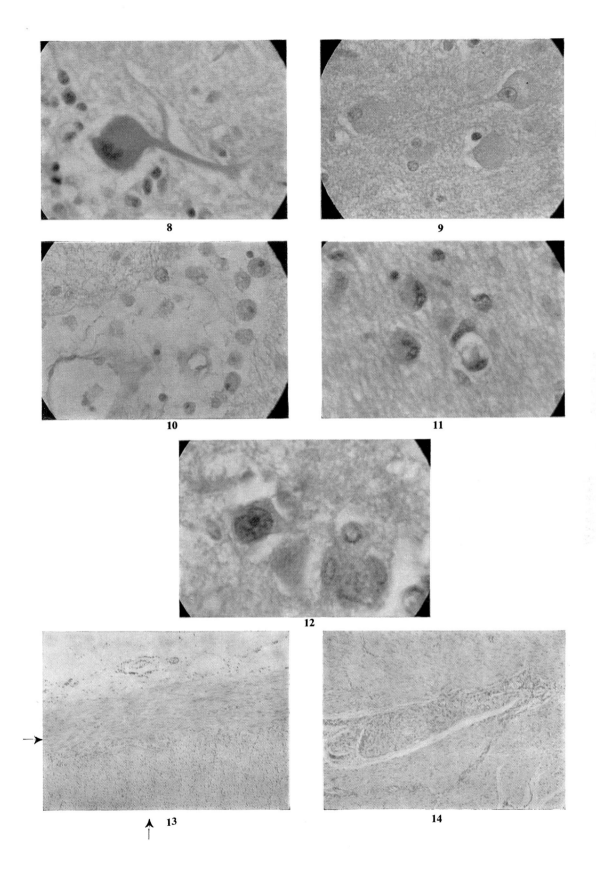

Otherwise they must be interpreted by an experienced pathologist or by a paediatrician or neurologist with special knowledge of this field. Only a limited number of conditions can be differentiated by muscle biopsy. The chief distinction is drawn between a *myopathy*, disease of the muscle itself, and *denervation*, but in most cases it is not possible to determine whether denervation is based on disease of the peripheral nerve or of the lower motor neurone itself. In addition, certain types of myopathy may be differentiated with some confidence, such as the distinction between muscular dystrophy (less reliably between different types of this), myositis, and the various relatively benign congenital myopathies, etc. (see Colour Figures 1-6).

Biopsies of Skin

It is quite easy to obtain a small specimen of skin for microscopic examination at the time that a muscle biopsy is performed. This is indicated especially if there is any reason to suppose that a presumed polymyositis might be in fact dermatomyositis. Biopsy of skin may also help to identify adenoma sebaceum in doubtful cases of tuberose sclerosis. Levin (1960) has described what he believes to be a characteristic skin lesion in gargoylism, consisting of local deposits of chondroitin sulphate as 'peau d'orange'. Carlisle and Good (1960) report induction of an inflammatory cycle by abrasion of the skin as a simpler method of producing leucocytes containing characteristic basophilic metachromatic granules in gargoylism.

Biopsies of Nerve

A small piece of sural nerve can be conveniently obtained when a biopsy of the gastrocnemius muscle is performed. Other nerves may also be studied, although it is obviously impossible to sacrifice a segment of any important motor, sensory or mixed nerve. The principal abnormality to be sought is thickening and reduplication of the Schwann cells to produce an 'onion skin' appearance (Colour Fig. 7) in the hypertrophic interstitial polyneuritis of Déjérine and Sottas. Metachromatic material is also accumulated as a result of demyelination of peripheral nerves in metachromatic leukodystrophy. (Hagberg *et al.* (1962) also mention the existence of a non-functioning gall bladder, shown by x-ray, as another diagnostic sign, although this may be late to develop.)

Biopsies of Rectum

Indications

The neurones of the submucous and myenteric plexuses of the rectum are more easily obtained for microscopic examination than the neurones of the brain. They are often comparably affected in degenerative diseases of the grey matter, and the procedure (suggested by Nakai and Landing in 1960) is diagnostically reasonable although sometimes difficult to explain to parents of patients. The proper indication is a suspicion of some disease of neurones resulting in abnormal intracellular storage of some substance which is histochemically identifiable. Rectal biopsy will be negative in the case of disease of the white matter (leukodystrophies, etc.) and the responsible physician must therefore attempt to decide whether grey or white matter is chiefly affected in each case. This differentiation must be made on clinical grounds, drawing on history and physical findings. In general, progressive polioencephalopathies tend to be earliest manifest by dementia, fits, electroencephalographic abnormalities or ataxia, whereas these manifestations are relatively late in the leucoencephalopathies, which tend to begin with cortical blindness or deafness (somewhat overrated in the literature as to frequency) or with evidence of involvement of the corticospinal or other long tracts.

Methods

The cooperation of a competent and understanding surgeon is essential, since a fairly large specimen of rectal wall must be obtained and this must be deep enough to contain the myenteric plexus (neurones in the submucous plexus are not numerous and often difficult to find under the microscope in sufficient numbers). As with muscle biopsies, it is most important that the specimen be properly oriented on the block before the cutting of microscopic sections. The specimen must be arranged so as to permit the cutting of radial rather than tangential sections, since the neurones in the myenteric plexus are difficult enough to find at best and are often impossible to locate except in a true radially-oriented section. Fresh frozen material (preferably in liquid nitrogen) should be sectioned in a cryostat and stained with Sudan, Scarlet R, or other stain for neutral fat. Material fixed in Lilly's solution should be stained with PAS, and as a minimum there should also be formalin-fixed material stained with haematoxylin and eosin. A considerable variety of histochemical stains are also available. Proper interpretation of slides requires time, patience and experience as well as the application of special histochemical methods when indicated (Colour Figures 13, 14).

In the cases of Niemann-Pick's disease and Gaucher's disease, the examiner's suspicions are usually aroused by enlargement of the patient's liver and spleen or by the finding of abnormal 'foam cells' on examination of the bone marrow. Rectal biopsy is chiefly useful when no such clues exist. It can be expected to be positive in the cerebral lipidosis and in other storage diseases, and there is one report that the type A intranuclear inclusions of Dawson's subacute encephalitis may be seen in rectal ganglion cells (Bodian and Lake 1963).

Biopsies of Brain

Indications

If the suspected disease is primarily of the cerebral white matter (and perhaps in the case of Dawson's encephalitis), biopsy of the brain is the preferred method of establishing a definitive diagnosis. This is of course a biopsy procedure of some magnitude and would have to be carefully interpreted to the patient's parents. One should also mention in honesty that there is little or no likelihood of any conceivable treatment resulting from the procedure and that it is rather an attempt to establish a definite diagnosis for purposes of giving a prognosis and genetic counselling. Also, as is true

261

with any biopsy, the examiner is gambling on being able to obtain a representative sample of typically affected tissue. The sample taken is relatively small, and while a definitively positive specimen results in a definitive diagnosis, the converse is not true of a negative biopsy.

Methods

A sufficiently large sample of brain should be obtained, preferably several grams. This is usually taken from the right frontal lobe but other areas without identifiable vital function may be chosen, or one may select an area of prime importance if its function has already been eliminated by the disease process. Both frozen and formalin-processed material should be studied as already described. Proper orientation of the specimen is important so that a cut perpendicular to the surface of the cortex may be made. Both frozen material (in liquid nitrogen) and formalin-fixed material should be studied, and at least by the same stains recommended for biopsies of the rectum (neutral fat, PAS, and haematoxylin and eosin). Ideally a separate specimen should be divided into grey and white matter and both subjected to chemical analysis for lipids.

Interpretation

If the severity of the patient's situation warrants a biopsy of the brain, arrangement should have been made ahead of time for the specimen to be subjected to sophisticated chemical analysis and to histological examination by an experienced neuropathologist. The question of interpretation is therefore beyond the scope of this book, but a few examples of possible abnormalities are shown in Colour Figures 8, 9, 10, 11 12.

Anaesthesia for Contrast X-Ray and Biopsy Procedures

Electromyography and studies of nerve conduction may be carried out even with small children by use of heavy sedation. Contrast x-rays and the various biopsy procedures usually require general anaesthesia in the case of young, mentally retarded, or thoroughly frightened children. Various mixtures of secobarbital (quinalbarbitone), meperidine (pethidine), and chlorpromazine (thorazine or largactil), sometimes with atropine, are currently being used in different centres and are sometimes stated to be satisfactory and sufficient for pneumoencephalography with children. The personal experience of the authors is that this is not sufficiently analgesic or reassuring to eliminate the violent struggling which usually takes place under these circumstances, and general anaesthesia is felt to be preferable at least under the age of adolescence.

General anaesthesia in young sick children is, of course, a hazardous procedure, and an anaesthetist with special experience in this field will supervise the anaesthetic.

References

Allen, R. J., McCusker, J. J., Tourtellotte, W.W. (1962) 'Metachromatic leukodystrophy: clinical, 'histo-chemical, and cerebrospinal fluid abnormalities.' *Pediatrics*, **30**, 629.

Altrocchi, P. H., Menkes, J. H. (1960) 'Congenital ocular motor apraxia,' *Brain*, **83**, 579.

Amidon, H. (1941) A Statistical Study of Relationships among Articulation Errors Made by One Hundred First-Grade Children. M.A. Thesis, University of Iowa, Iowa City.

Anderson, E. P., Kalckar, H. M., Kurahashi, K., Isselbacher, K. J. (1957) 'A specific enzymatic assay for the diagnosis of congenital galactosemia; the consumption test.' *J. lab. clin. Med.*, **50**, 469.

André-Thomas, Chesni, Y., Saint-Anne Dargassies, S. (1960) The Neurological Examination of the Infant. Little Club Clinics No. 1. London: Nat. Spastics Society.

Arieff, A. J., Tigay, E. L., Kurtz, J. F., Larman, W. A. (1961) 'The Hoover sign. An objective sign of pain and/or weakness in the back or lower extremities.' *Arch. Neurol. Psychiat.*, **5**, 673.

Armstrong, M. D., Yates, K. N., Connelly, J. P. (1964) 'Amino acid excretion of newborn infants during the first twenty-four hours of life.' *Pediatrics*, **33**, 975.

Aronson, S. M. (1960) 'Enzyme determinations in neurologic and neuromuscular diseases of infancy and childhood.' *Pediat. Clin. N. Amer.*, **7**, 527.

Austin, J. H. (1957) 'Metachromatic form of diffuse cerebral sclerosis. 1. Diagnosis during life by urine sediment examination. 2. Diagnosis during life of metachromatic lipids from urine.' *Neurology (Minneap.)*, **7**, 415, 716.

Baker, A. B. (ed.) (1962) Clinical Neurology. 4 Vols. New York: Hoeber-Harper.

Bender, L. (1946) Instructions for the Use of the Visual Motor Gestalt Test. New York: Amer. Orthopsychiat. Ass.

—— (1955) 'Organic brain conditions producing behaviour disturbance.' *In* Modern Trends in Child Psychiatry, ed. by Lewis and Pacilla, Psychopathology of Children with Organic Brain Disorders, Springfield, Ill.: C. C. Thomas.

Benton, A. L. (1959) Right-left Discrimination and Finger Localization. New York: Hoeber.

——, Elithorn, A., Fogel, M. L., Kerr, M. (1963) 'A perceptual maze test sensitive to brain damage.' *J. Neurol. Neurosurg. Psychiat.*, **26**, 540.

Bergès, J., Lézine, I. (1963) Test d'Imitation de Gestes: Techniques d'Exploration du Schema corporel et de Praxis chez l'Enfant de 3 à 6 ans. Paris: Masson.

Birch, H. D. (ed.) (1964) Brain Damage in Children. The Biological and Social Aspects. Baltimore: Williams and Williams.

Birch, H. G., Belmont, L. (1964) 'Auditory-visual integration in normal and retarded readers'. *Amer. J. Orthopsychiat.*, **34**, 852.

Bland, J. (1964) 'Eyeing the eye'. *N. Y. State J. Med.*, **64**, 1313.

Bodian, M., Lake, B. D. (1963) 'The rectal approach to neuropathology.' *Brit. J. Surg.*, **50**, 702.

Bond, E. D., Appel, K. (1931) The Treatment of Behavior Disorders Following Encephalitis; an Experiment on Re-education. New York: Commonwealth Fund.

Boshes, B. (1957) *In* 'Symposium of inquiry: the pyramidal tract.' *Neurology (Minneap.)* **7**, 496.

——, Myklebust, H. R. (1964) 'A neurological and behavioral study of children with learning disorders.' *Neurology (Minneap.)*, **14**, 632.

Bosma, J. A. (1965) Personal Communication.

Boyd, J. A., Eyzaguirre, C., Matthews, P. B. C., Rushworth, J. (1964) The Role of the Gamma System in Movement and Posture. New York: Assn. for the Aid of Crippled Children.

Brain, Lord R. (1961) Speech Disorders; Aphasia, Apraxia and Agnosia. London: Butterworth.

Brain, W. R., Wilkinson, M. (1959) 'Observations on the extensor plantar reflex and its relationship to the functions of the pyramidal tract.' *Brain*, **82**, 297.

Cameron, K., Lewis, M., Stone, F. H. (1961) 'Is there a syndrome of brain damage in children?' *Cerebral Palsy Bull.*, **3**, 74, 75, 76. (Letters).

Carlisle, J. W., Good, R. A. (1960) 'The inflammatory cycle. A method of study in Hurler's disease.' *Amer. J. Dis. Child.*, **99**, 193.

Carmichael, E. A., Dix, M. R., Hallpike, C. S. (1954) 'Lesions of the cerebral hemispheres and their effect upon optikokinetic and caloric nystagmus.' *Brain*, **77**, 345.

Clare, M. H., Landau, W. M. (1964) 'Fusimotor function. V. Reflex reinforcement under fusimotor block in normal subjects.' *Arch. Neurol.*, **10**, 123.

Clausen, J., Dyggve, H. V., Melchior, J. C. (1963) 'Mucopolysaccaridosis; paper electrophoretic and infra-red analysis of the urine in gargoylism and Morquio-Ullrich's disease.' *Arch. Dis. Childh.*, **38**, 364.

Cogan, D. G., Adams, R. D. (1953) 'A type of paralysis of conjugate gaze (ocular motor apraxia).' *Arch. Ophthal.*, **50**, 434.

Cohen, P., Solomon, N. (1955) 'Familial dysautonomia. Case report with autopsy.' *J. Pediat.*, **46**, 663.

Creak, M., *et al.* (1961) 'Schizophrenic syndrome in childhood. Progress report of a working party.' *Cerebral Palsy Bull.*, **3**, 501.

Dancis, J., Hutzler, J., Levitz, M. (1963) 'The diagnosis of maple syrup urine disease (branch-chain ketoaciduria) by the in vitro study of the peripheral leucocyte.' *Pediatrics*, **32**, 234.

Dawson, D. M., Taghavy, A. (1963) 'A test for spinal fluid alcohol in torula meningitis.' *New Engl. J. Med.*, **269**, 1424.

De Jong, R. N. (1958) The Neurologic Examination, 2nd. ed. New York: Hoeber.

De Lange, C. (1934) 'Congenital hypertrophy of the muscles, extrapyramidal motor disturbances and mental deficiency: A clinical entity.' *Amer. J. Dis. Child.*, **48**, 243.

Denhoff, E., Laufer, M. W., Holden, R. H. (1959) 'The syndromes of cerebral dysfunction.' *J. Oklahoma med. Ass.*, **52**, 360.

Denny, W., Dutton, G. (1962) 'Simple urine test for gargoylism.' *Brit. med. J.*, **i**, 1555.

Denny-Brown, D., Adams, R. D., Fitzgerald, P. J. (1944) 'Pathologic features of herpes zoster; a note on 'geniculate herpes'.' *Arch. Neurol. Psychiat.*, **51**, 216.

—— (1964) 'The cerebral control of movement.' *Clin. Pharmacol. Ther.*, **5**, 812.

De Renzi, E., Vignolo, L. A. (1962) 'The token test: A sensitive test to detect receptive disturbances in aphasics.' *Brain*, **85**, 665.

Dodge, H. W. (1956) 'Cephalic bruits in children.' *J. Neurosurg.*, **13**, 527.

Duffy, P. E., Ziter, F. A. (1964) 'Infantile syringobulbia. A study of its pathology and a proposed relationship to neurogenic stridor in infancy.' *Neurology (Minneap).*, **14**, 500.

Efron, M. L., Young, D., Moser, H. W., MacCready, R. A. (1964) 'A simple chromatographic screening test for the detection of disorders of amino metabolism: a technic using whole blood or urine collected on filter paper.' *New Engl. J. Med.*, **270**, 1378.

Eisenson, J. (1954) Examining for Aphasia. A Manual for the Examination of Aphasia and Related Disturbances. New York: Psychological Corp.

Emmerson, B. T. (1963) 'Chronic lead nephropathy: the diagnostic use of calcium EDTA and the association of gout.' *Aust. Ann. Med.*, **12**, 310.

Farmer, T. W. (ed.) (1964) Pediatric Neurology. New York: Hoeber-Harper.

Fois, A. (1963) Clinical Electroencephalography in Epilepsy and Related Conditions in Childhood. Springfield, Ill: C. C. Thomas.

Ford, F. R. (1960) Diseases of the Nervous System in Infancy, Childhood and Adolescence. 4th ed. Springfield, Ill.: C. C. Thomas.

Frostig, M., Lefever, D. W., Whittlesey, J. R. B. (1961) 'A developmental test of visual perception for evaluating normal and neurologically handicapped children.' *Percept. Mot. Skills*, **12**, 383.

Fullerton, P. M. (1964) 'Metachromatic leucodystrophy: peripheral nerve conduction measurement.' *J. Neurol. Neurosurg. Psychiat.*, **27**, 100.

Fulton, J. F., Keller, A. D. (1932) The Sign of Babinski: a Study of the Evolution of Cortical Dominance in Primates. Springfield. Ill.: C. C. Thomas.

Garfield, J. G., (1964) 'Motor impersistence in normal and brain-damaged children.' *Neurology (Minneap.)*, **14**, 632.

Gesell, A., Ames, L. B. (1950) 'Tonic-neck-reflex and symmetro-tonic behavior, developmental and clinical aspects.' *J. Pediat.*, **36**, 165.

Ghadimi, H., Shwachman, H. (1959) 'A screening test for aminoaciduria.' *New Engl. J. Med.*, **261**, 998.

——, —— (1960) 'Evaluation of amino-aciduria in infancy and childhood.' *J. Dis. Child.*, **99**, 457.

Goldstein, K. (1942) After-effects of Brain Injuries in War. New York: Grune and Stratton.

Gorman, J. J., Cogan, D. G., Gellis, S. S. (1957) 'An apparatus for grading the visual acuity of infants on the basis of opticokinetic nystagmus.' *Pediatrics*, **19**, 1088.

Gotham, J. E., Gilroy, J., Meyer, J. S. (1962) 'Studies on cerebral circulation time in man. I. Normal values and alterations with cerebral vascular disease and tumour in arm-to-retina circulation times.' *J. Neurol. Neurosurg. Psychiat.*, **25**, 292.

Graham, F. K., Kendall, B. S. (1960) 'Memory-for-designs test.' *Percept. Mot. Skills*, **11**, 147.

Green, J. B., O'Doherty, D. S., Oldewurtel, H. A., Forster, F. M. (1957) 'Cerebro-spinal fluid transaminase concentrations in clinical cerebral infarction.' *New Engl. J. Med.*, **256**, 220.

Guthrie, R., Susi, A. (1963) 'A simple phenylalanine method for detecting phenylketonuria in large populations of newborn infants.' *Pediatrics*, **32**, 338.

Hagberg, B., Sourander, P., Svennerholm, L. (1962) 'Sulfatide lipidosis in childhood. Report of a case investigated during life and at autopsy.' *Amer. J. Dis. Child.*, **104**, 644.

Halstead, W. C. (1947) Brain and Intelligence. Chicago: Univ. Chicago Press.

Hamerton, J. L. (ed.) (1962) Chromosomes in Medicine. Little Club Clinics in Develop. Med. No. 5. London: Heinemann/Nat. Spastics Society.

Hanvik, L. J., Nelson, S. E., Hanson, H. B., Anderson, A. S., Dressler, W. H., Zarling, V. R. (1961) 'Diagnosis of cerebral dysfunction in child as made in a child guidance clinic.' *Amer. J. Dis. Child.*, **101**, 364.

264

Haymaker, Webb, Stevens, H. (1957) 'Familial dysautonomia.' Presented at Amer. Acad. of Neurology, April 26.

Hermann, K. (1959) Reading Disability. A Medical Study of Word-blindness and Related Handicaps. Springfield Ill: C. C. Thomas.

Herschkowitz, N., Cumings, J. N. (1964) 'Creatine kinase in cerebrospinal fluid.' *J. Neurol. Neurosurg. Psychiat.*, **27**, 247.

Hill, D., Parr, G. eds. (1963) Electroencephalography. New York: Macmillan.

Hines, M. (1937) 'The "motor" cortex.' *Bull. Johns Hopk. Hosp.*, **60**, 313.

Hsia, D. Y-Y., Litwack, M., O'Flynn, M., Jakovcic, S. (1962) 'Serum phenylalanine and tyrosine levels in the newborn infant.' *New Engl. J. Med.* **267**, 1067.

Ianniruberto, A. (1961) 'L'attivita transaminasica glutammico-ossalacetica nel liquido cerebro spinale di neonati in condizioni fisiologiche e patologiche.' *Arch. Ostet. Ginec.*, **66**, 363.

Illingworth, R. S. (1966) The Development of the Infant and Young Child, Normal and Abnormal. 3rd ed. Edinburgh: Livingstone.

Ingram, T. T. S. (1964) 'Late and poor talkers'. *In* The Child Who Does Not Talk, Ed. Renfrew, C. and Murphy, K. Little Club Clinics in Developmental Medicine No. 13. London: Spastics Society/ Heinemann.

Kang, E., Paine, R. S. (1963) 'Elevation of plasma phenylalanine levels during pregnancies of women heterozygous for phenylketonuria.' *J. Pediat.*, **63**, 283.

Kanner, L, (1943) 'Autistic disturbances of affective contact'. *Nerv. Child*, **2**, 217.

Kinsbourne, M., Warrington, E. K. (1962) 'A disorder of simultaneous form perception.' *Brain*, **85**, 461.

——, —— (1964) 'Disorders of spelling.' *J. Neurol. Neurosurg. Psychiat.*, **27**, 224.

Knobloch, H., Pasamanick, B. (1959) 'Syndrome of minimal cerebral damage in infancy.' *J. Amer. med. Ass.*, **170**, 1384.

Kugelberg, E., Welander, L. (1956) 'Heredofamilial juvenile muscular atrophy simulating muscular dystrophy.' *Arch. Neurol. Psychiat.*, **75**, 500.

La Du, B. D., Howell, P. R., Jacoby, G. A., Seegmiller, J. E., Sober, E. K., Zannoni, V. G., Canby, J. P., Ziegler, L. K. (1963) 'Clinical and biochemical studies on two cases of histidinemia.' *Pediatrics*, **32**, 216.

Landau, W. M., Clare, M. H. (1959) 'The plantar reflex in man, with special reference to some conditions where the extensor response is unexpectedly absent.' *Brain*, **82**, 321.

——, Weaver, R. A., Hornbein, T. F. (1960) 'The effect of gamma efferent blockade in man.' *Trans. Amer. neurol. Assn.*, **85**, 61.

——, Clare, M. H. (1963) 'An experimental review of reflex reinforcement and fusimotor function in man.' *Trans. Amer. neurol. Assn.*, **88**, 136.

——, —— (1964) 'Fusimotor function. IV. H reflex, tendon jerk, and reinforcement in hemiplegia.' *Arch. Neurol.*, **10**, 128.

Laufer, M. W., Denhoff, E. (1957) 'Hyperkinetic behaviour syndrome in children.' *J. Pediat.*, **50**, 463.

Lending, M., Stone, M. L., Slobody, L.B., Mestern, J. (1963) 'Glutamic oxalacetic transaminase and lactic dehydrogenase in pregnancy. III. Enzyme activity in the newborn infant.' *Amer. J. Obstet. Gynec.*, **85**, 41.

Lennox, W. G., Lennox, M. A. (1960) Epilepsy and Related Disorders. Boston: Little, Brown.

Levin, S. (1960) 'A specific skin lesion in gargoylism.' *Amer. J. Dis. Child.*, **99**, 444.

List, C. F., Peet, M. M. (1939) 'Sweat secretion in man.' *Arch. Neurol. Psychiat.*, **42**, 1098.

Lorber, J., Emery, J. L. (1964) 'Intracerebral cysts complicating ventricular needling in hydrocephalic infants: a clinico-pathological study.' *Develop. Med. Child Neurol.*, **6**, 125.

McCouch, G. P., Deering, I. D., Ling, T. H. (1951) 'Location of receptors for tonic neck reflexes.' *J. Neurophysiol.* **14**, 191.

McDonald, E. T. (1964) Articulation Testing and Treatment. A Sensory-Motor Approach. Pittsburgh: Stanwix.

McIntyre, A. K., Robinson, R. G. (1959) 'Pathway for the jaw-jerk in man.' *Brain*, **82**, 468.

Magnus, R. (1924) Körperstellung. Monographien aus dem gesamtgebiet der Physiologie der Pflanzer und der Tiere, 6 Band, Berlin: Julius Springer.

Magoun, H. W., Rhines, R. (1947) Spasticity: The Stretch-reflex and Extra-pyramidal Systems. Springfield, Ill.: C. C. Thomas.

Marshall, J. (1954) 'Observations on reflex changes in the lower limbs in spastic paraplegia in man.' *Brain*, **77**, 290.

Medical Research Council, War Memorandum No. 7. (1943) Aids to the Investigation of Peripheral Nerve Injuries. London: H. M. Stationery Office. 2nd ed. 1963.

Meyer, J.S., Herndon, R. M. (1962) 'Bilateral infarction of the pyramidal tracts in man.' *Neurology*, **12**, 637.

Mitchell, R. G. (1962) 'The Landau reaction (reflex).' *Develop. Med. Child Neurol.*, **4**, 65.

Morley, M. E. (1957) The Development and Disorders of Speech in Childhood. Edinburgh: Livingstone.

Mudd, S. H., Finkelstein, J. D., Irreverre, F., Laster, L. (1964) 'Homocystinuria, an enzymatic defect.' *Science*, **143**, 1443.

Muir, H., Mittwoch, U., Bitter, T. (1963) 'The diagnostic value of isolated urinary mucopolysaccharides and of lymphocyte inclusions in gargoylism.' *Arch. Dis. Child.*, **38**, 358.

Murphy, K. (1964) 'Development of normal vocalisation and sound.' *In* The Child Who Does Not Talk, ed. Renfrew, C. and Murphy, K. Little Club Clinics in Developmental Medicine No. 13. London: Spastics Society/Heinemann.

Nakai, H., Landing, B. H. (1960) 'Suggested use of rectal biopsy in the diagnosis of neural lipidoses.' *Pediatrics*, **26**, 225.

Nathan, P. W., Smith, M. C. (1955) 'The Babinski response: a review and new observations.' *J. Neurol. Neurosurg. Psychiat.*, **18**, 250.

Netsky, M. G., (1953) 'Syringomyelia: a clinicopathologic study.' *Arch. Neurol. Psychiat.*, **70**, 741.

Nordin, J. H., Bretthauer, R. K., Hansen, R. G. (1961) 'Development and application of a simplified calorimetric method for detecting carriers of galactosemia.' *Clin. chim. Acta*, **6**, 578.

Norris, F. H. Jr., Fawcett, J. (1965) 'A sign of intracranial mass with impending uncal herniation.' *Arch. Neurol.*, **12**, 381.

O'Reilly, S. (1962) 'A modified oxidase assay for low concentrations of ceruloplasmin in serum and other biological fluids.' *Neurology (Minneap.)*, **12**, 460.

Paine, R. S. (1957) 'Facial paralysis in children, review of the differential diagnosis and report of ten cases treated with cortisone.' *Pediatrics*, **19**, 303.

—— (1960) 'Neurologic examination of infants and children.' *Pediat. Clin. N. Amer.*, **7**, 471.

—— (1962) 'Minimal chronic brain syndromes in children.' *Develop. Med. Child. Neurol.*, **4**, 21.

——, Brazelton, T. B., Donovan, D. E., Drorbaugh, J. E., Hubbell, J. P., Jr., Sears, E. M. (1964) 'Evolution of postural reflexes in normal infants, and in the presence of chronic brain syndromes.' *Neurology. (Minneap.)*, **14**, 1036.

—— (1964) 'The evolution of infantile postural reflexes in the presence of chronic brain syndromes.' *Develop. Med. Child Neurol.*, **6**, 345.

Parmelee, A. H. Jr. (1964) 'A critical evaluation of the Moro reflex.' *Pediatrics*, **33**, 773.

Pearce, J. M. S., Pennington, R. J., Walton, J. N. (1964a) 'Serum enzyme studies in muscle disease. Part II. Serum creatine kinase activity in muscular dystrophy and in other myopathic and neuropathic disorders.' *J. Neurol. Neurosurg. Psychiat.*, **27**, 96.

——, ——, —— (1964b) 'Serum enzyme studies in muscle disease. Pt. II. Serum creatine kinase activity in relatives of patients with the Duchenne type of muscular dystrophy.' *J. Neurol. Neurosurg. Psychiat.*, **27**, 181.

Peiper, A. (1956) Die Eigenart der Kindlichen Hirntätigkeit, 2nd ed. Leipzig: Georg Thieme.

Plum, F. (1962) 'Bladder dysfunction.' *In* Modern Trends in Neurology, No. 3. D. Williams (ed.) London: Butterworth, p. 151.

Pond, D. (1960) 'Is there a syndrome of brain damage in children?' *Cerebral Palsy Bull.* **2**, 296.

Prechtl, H., Beintema, D. (1964) The Neurological Examination of the Full-term Newborn Infant. Little Club Clinics no 12. London: National Spastics Society.

Rademaker, G. G. J. (1931) Das stehen, statische Reaktionen; gleichgewichts reaktionen, und Muskeltonus unter besonderer Berücksichtigung ihres Verhaltens bei kleinhirnlosen Tieren. Berlin: J. Springer.

Riley, C. M. (1952) 'Familial autonomic dysfunction.' *J. Amer. med. Ass.*, **149**, 1532.

Rimland, B. (1964) Infantile Autism. New York: Appleton-Century-Crofts.

Rochford, F., Williams, M. (1964) 'The measurement of language disorders.' *Speech Path. Ther.*, **7**, 3.

Roe, V., Milisen, R. (1942) 'The effect of maturation upon defective articulation in elementary grades.' *J. Speech Dis.*, **7**, 37.

Rushworth, G. (1961) 'The gamma system in Parkinsonism.' *Int. J. Neurol.*, **2**, 34.

—— (1964) 'The nature and management of spasticity. The pathophysiology of spasticity.' *Proc. roy. Soc. Med.*, **57**, 715.

——, Somekh, D. E. (1965) 'The ankle jerk in thyroid disease and in cerebral palsy.' *Develop. Med. Child Neurol.*, **7**, 65.

Shank, K. H. (1964) 'Recognition of articulatory disorders in children'. *Clin. Pediat.* **3**, 333.

Sheridan, M. D. (1960) Developmental Progress of Infants and Young Children. London: H. M. Stationery Office.

—— (1964) 'Development of auditory attention and language symbols in young children.' *In* The Child Who Does Not Talk, ed. Renfrew, C. and Murphy, K. Little Club Clinics in Developmental Medicine. London: Spastics Society/Heinemann.

Sidbury, J. B. Jr., Cornblath, M., Fisher, J., House, E. (1961) 'Glycogen in erythrocytes of patients with glycogen storage disease.' *Pediatrics*, **27**, 103.

Smith, A. A., Dancis, J. (1963) 'Response to intradermal histamine in familial dysautonomia—a diagnostic test.' *J. Pediat.*, **63**, 889.

Sogg, R. L., Hoyt, W. F., Boldrey, E. (1963) 'Spastic paretic facial contracture. A rare sign of brain stem tumor.' *Neurology (Minneap.)*, **13**, 607.

Steiness, I. (1961) 'Acid mucopolysaccharides in urine in gargoylism.' *Pediatrics*, **27**, 112.

Stillhart, H. (1954) 'Uber die klinische Bedeutung des sogenannten reflexartigen Phänomens der untergehenden Sonne beim Neugeborenen.' *Helv. Paediat. Acta.*, **9**.

Strauss, A., Lehtinen, L. (1947) Psychopathology and Education of the Brain-Injured Child. New York: Grune and Stratton.

Sturup, G., Bolton, B., Williams, D. J., Carmichael, E. A. (1935) 'Vasomotor responses in hemiplegic patients'. *Brain*, **58**, 456.

Swaiman, K. F., Sander, B. (1963) 'The use of serum creatine phosphokinase and other serum enzymes in the diagnosis of progressive muscular dystrophy.' *J. Pediat.*, **63**, 116.

Teasdall, R. D., Schuster, M. M., Walsh, F. B. (1964) 'Sphincter involvement in ocular myopathy.' *Arch. Neurol.*, **10**, 446.

Terry, K., Linker, A. (1964) 'Distinction among four forms of Hurler's syndrome.' *Proc. Soc. exp. Biol. (N. Y.)*, **115**, 394.

Teuber, H. L., Rudel, R. G. (1962) 'Behaviour after cerebral lesions in children and adults.' *Develop. Med. Child Neurol.*, **4**, 3.

Thompson, S. W. (1961) 'A radioisotope method for studying cerebral circulation.' *Arch. Neurol.*, **5**, 580.

Tiefnsee, K. (1925) 'Die Reflexe an den oberen Extremitaten.' *Arch. Psychiat.*, **74**, 62.

Tower, S. W. (1940) 'Pyramidal lesions in the monkey.' *Brain*, **63**, 36.

Tremble, G. E., Penfield, W. (1963) 'Operative exposure of the facial canal with removal of a tumor of the greater superficial petrosal nerve.' *Arch. Otolaryng.*, **23**, 573.

Tyrer, J. H., Sutherland, J. M. (1961) 'The primary spino-cerebellar atrophies and their associated defects, with a study of the foot deformity.' *Brain*, **84**, 289.

Van Gelderen, H. H., Dooren, L. J. (1964) 'The excretion of free alpha amino-acids in children.' *Arch. Dis. Childh.*, **39**, 261.

Van Slyke, D. D., MacFadyen, D. A., Hamilton, P. B. (1943) 'The gasometric determination of amino acids in urine by the ninhydrin-carbon dioxide method.' *J. biol. Chem.*, **150**, 251.

Wadia, N. H. (1960) 'Venous signs in cerebral angioma.' *Brain*, **83**, 425.

Walton, J. N., Ellis, E., Court, S. D. M. (1962) 'Clumsy children: developmental apraxia and agnosia.' *Brain*, **85**, 603.

Wartenburg, R. (1953) Diagnostic Tests in Neurology. Chicago: Yearbook Publishers.

Weisenburg, T., McBride, K. A. (1935) Aphasia, A Clinical and Pathological Study. London: Commonwealth Fund, Oxford University Press.

Werner, H., Strauss, A. (1941) Pathology of figure-ground relation in the child.' *J. abnorm. soc. Psychol.* 36, **58**.

Wigglesworth, R. (1961) 'Minimal cerebral palsy.' *Cerebral Palsy Bull.*, **3**, 293. (Letter).

Williams, M., Jambor, K. (1964) 'Disorders of topographical and right-left orientation in adults compared with its acquisition in children.' *Neuropsychologia*, **2**, 55.

Wilson, S. A. Kinnier (1954-55) Neurology. 2nd. ed. Bruce, A. N. (ed.) 3 vols. London: Butterworth.

Worster-Drought, C. (1956) 'Congenital suprabulbar paresis.' *J. Laryngol.*, **70**, 453.

Yasuna, E. R. (1963) 'Hysterical amblyopia in children.' *Amer. J. Dis. Child.*, **106**, 558.

Young, R. B., Steiker, D. D., Bongiovanni, A. M., Koo, C. E., Eberlain, W. R. (1963) 'Urinary vanimandelic acid (VMA) excretion in children: Use of a simple semiquantitative test.' *J. Pediat.*, **62**, 845.

ZuRhein, G. M., Eichman, P. L., Puletti, F. (1960) 'Familial idiocy with spongy degeneration of the central nervous system of van-Bogaert-Bertrand type.' *Neurology (Minneap.)*, **10**, 998.

Index

A

Abdominal reflexes: 179, 179.
Abnormal movements: 165 *et seq.*
Achondroplasia: 27, 41.
Acute lymphocytic meningitis: 34.
Adams, R. D.: 115.
Adenoids: 26.
Adenoma Sebaceum 26.
Adie's syndrome: 121, 249.
Affect: 30, 46 *et seq.*
Agraphia: 61.
Acalculia: 61.
Alexia: 61.
Altrocchi, P. H.: 115.
Amaurotic Family Idiocy: 42.
Amblyopia: 100, 116.
Ames, L. B.: 191.
Amino acids: 227 *et seq.*
Amidon, H.: 53.
Anaemia: 21.
Anderson, A. S.: 67.
Anderson, E. P.: 224.
André-Thomas, C. Y.: 158, 184
Anencephalic: 8.
Angiomata: 26.
Anhidrosis: 209.
Ankle jerk: 172, 175, 176.
Anocutaneous reflex: 179, 180.
Anosmia: 98, 130.
Anoxia: 18.
Antalgic gait: 148.
Apert's syndrome: *See Craniostenosis.*
Aphasia: 52, 57, 58, 60, 61, 69, 70, 134.
Aphonia: 54.
Apraxia: 61.
Arachnodactyly (Marfan's syndrome): 27.
Argyll-Robertson pupil: 121.
Arieff, A. J.: 154.

Armstrong, M. D.: 228.
Aronson, S. M.: 223.
Arteriography: 240 *et seq.*
Articulation: 46,
Associated movements: 168 *et seq.*
Asymmetrical tonic neck reflex: 184. 189, 191, 192, 193.
Asynergia: 164.
Ataxia: 10, 30, 71, 142, 146, 147, 165. *See also Friedreich's Ataxia.*
— cerebellar: 145, 148.
— diplegic: 187.
— sensory: 145.
— telangiectasia: 42, 104, 105, 106, 107.
Athetoid speech: 55.
Athetosis: 10, 128, 131, 141, 147, 164, 167, 168, 182, 192, 193.
Audiometry: 22, 50, 60, 133, 134, 251.
Auditory agnosia: 61.
Auriculo-temporal syndrome: 209.
Auscultation of skull: 93.
Austin, J. H.: 229.
Autism: 45, 46, 54, 57, 58, 64.

B

Babinski sign: 160, 172, 179, 180, 181, 182.
Backwardness: 38 *et seq. See also Mental retardation.*
Bacteraemic shock: 34.
Ballismus: 168.
Barány chair: 134.
Barber's chair sign: 96.
Beintema, D.: 184.
Bell's Palsy: 128, 217.
Bell's phenomenon: 129.
Belmont, L: 70.

Bender, L.:   67, 80.
Bender Test: 82.
Benedikt's syndrome: 123.
Benign congenital hypotonia: 14.
Benton, A. L.:   71.
Bergès, J: 51, 71, 80.
Bertrand, cerebral degeneration of: 87.
Biceps jerk: 172.
Bielchowski, cerebromacular degeneration of: 109.
Birch, H.:   67, 70.
Bitter, T. H.:   189.
Bland, J.:   110.
Blindness: 99 *et seq.*, 129.
Blink reflex: 99.
Blood tests: 222 *et seq.*
Body image: 70.
Boldrey, E.:   128.
Bonnevie-Ullrich syndrome: 95.
Bodian, M.:   261.
Boshes, B.:   67, 183.
Bosma, J. A.:   55.
Boyd, J. A.:   160.
Brachycephaly: 87, 88.
Brain biopsy: 261 *et seq.*
Brain, W. R.:   182.
Brain scars: 241.
Brazelton, T. B.:   182.
Breath-holding spells: 19.
Bretthauer, R. K.:   224.
Brudzinski's sign: 162.
Bruits: 26, 93.
Brushfield's dots: 42, 104, 106, 107.
Byrne's reflex: 121.

C

Caeruloplasmia: 224.
Café-au-lait patches: 24, 27, 28, 42.
Calcification, intracranial: 37, 239.
Canby, J. P.:   227.
Carotid sinus reflex: 138.
Carlisle, J. W.:   260.
Carmichael, E. A.:   135, 209, 249.
Canavan, cerebral degeneration of: 87.
Cataracts: 108.

Catatonic rigidity: 162.
Cavus foot: 148.
Cerebral abscess: 14, 34.
Cerebral circulation time: 249 *et seq.*
Cerebral hypotonias: 13.
Cerebral malaria: 34.
Cerebral palsies: 10, 14, 42, 55, 66, 139, 168, 189, 192, 195, 215.
Cerebral tumour: 34.
Cerebroside lipidosis: 43.
Cerebro-spinal fluid: 37, 231 *et seq.*
Cerebro-vascular accidents: 34.
Chaddock sign: 180, 181.
Charcot-Marie-Tooth disease: 6, 148.
Cherry-red spot: 24, 109, 193.
Chicken pox: 34.
Chondro-ectodermal dysplasia: 27.
Chorea: 11, 153, 164, 167.
Choreoathetosis: *See Athetosis.*
Chorioretinitis: 36, 104, 108.
Chromosomes: 8, 225 *et seq.*
Chvostek sign: 129.
Cisternal puncture: 232.
Clare, M. H.:   161, 182.
Clausen, J.:   229.
Cleidocranial dysostosis: 41.
Cleft palate: 42.
Clonus: 175 *et seq.*
Clonus, ankle: 185.
Clumsiness: 10, 67.
Cogan, D. G.:   115.
Cohen, P.:   210.
Coloboma: 104, 121.
Colour blindness: 70.
Colour vision: 101.
Coma: 33 *et seq.*, 120.
Congenital dislocation of the hip: 149.
Convulsive disorders: *See Epilepsy.*
Coordination: 163, 167.
Copper: 231.
Corneal reflex: 125.
Cortical blindness: 66.
Cough: 17, 138.
Court, S. D. M.:   67.
Cracked pot sign: 26.

Cranial nerves:	27, 30.
— (1)	98 *et seq.*
— (2)	99 *et seq.*
— (3)	99, 110 *et seq.*
— (4)	96, 110 *et seq.*
— (5)	124 *et seq.*, 196, 207.
— (6)	110 *et seq.*
— (7)	127 *et seq.*, 207.
— (8)	132 *et seq.*,
— (9)	136 *et seq.*, 208.
— (10)	136 *et seq.*
— (11)	138 *et seq.*
— (12)	140 *et seq.*
Craniopharyngiomata:	103, 211, 239.
Craniostenosis:	24, 42, 43.
Creak, M.:	46.
Cremasteric reflex:	179.
Cretinism:	*See Hypothyroidism.*
Cri du Chat syndrome:	8.
Cribriform plate fractures:	98.
Cummings, J. N.:	235.
Cystometrograms:	253 *et seq.*
Cytomegalic inclusion disease:	108, 236, 239.

D

Dancis, J.:	224.
Dawson, D. M.:	235.
Deafness: 22 *et seq.* 51, 56, 57, 58, 66.	
—, central:	56.
Decerebrate rigidity:	161.
Deering, I. D.:	189.
Dejerine-Sottas: 14, 199. 257, 258, 260.	
De Jong, R. N.:	153.
Demyelinating diseases:	38.
Denhoff, E:	67.
Denny, W.:	229.
Denny-Brown, D.:	131, 160
Dentition:	3.
DeRenzi, E.:	48.
Dermal sinuses:	92.
Dermoid tumours:	92.
Developmental articulary dyspraxia:	56.
Developmental examination:	39.

Developmental milestones:	10.
Diabetes insipidus:	211.
Diabetes mellitus:	33, 35, 36.
Diplopia:	116.
Disarticulation:	55.
Disseminated sclerosis:	114, 145, 146.
Dix, M. R.:	119, 209, 135, 249.
Dodge, H. W.:	93.
Dolichocephaly:	89.
Donovan, D. E.:	187, 189.
Dooren, L. J.:	227.
Down's syndrome:	8, 14, 27, 42.
D.P.N.H. Test:	227.
Drawing:	10, 40, 73, 74, 79
Dressing:	9, 10, 26, 40, 142.
Dressler, W. H.:	67.
Drorbaugh, J. E.:	187, 189.
D trisomy:	8.
Duane's syndrome:	123.
Duffy, P. E.:	209.
Dutton, G.:	229.
Dyggve, H. V.:	229.
Dysarthia:	49, 54, 57, 61.
Dysdiadochokinesia:	165.
Dyskinesia:	13.
Dyslalia:	55.
Dyslexia:	63, 67, 69..
Dysmetria:	164.
Dysphasia:	51, 137.
Dysprosody:	61.
Dysrhythmia:	56.
Dystonia:	11, 141, 147, 168.
Dystonia musculorum deformans:	149.
Dystrophic nails:	27.

E

Echolalia:	64.
Ectodermal dysplasia:	27.
Efron, M. L.:	228.
Eichman, P. L.:	87.
Eisenson test:	52, 61.
Elective mutism:	57.
Electroencephalography:	13, 18, 37, 45, 60, 214 *et seq.*

EEG audiometry: 133, 252.
Electromyography: 163, 166, 216 *et seq.*
Electroretinograms: 222.
Ellis, E.: 67.
Encephalitis: 14, 22, 126, 212, 214, 233.
Encephaloceles: 92, 95.
Encopresis: 20.
Enophthalmos: 122.
Enteric fever: 14.
Enuresis: 18, 20 *et seq.*, 255.
See also Toilet training.
Environment: 9.
Epidermal tumours: 92.
Epilepsia Partialis Continua: 11, 168.
Epilepsy: 9, 16 *et seq.*, 33, 34, 46, 66, 98, 111, 128, 208, 214, 222, 229.
Epileptic boy: 78.
Epiphora: 130.
Esophoria: 115.
Etrisomy: 8.
Exanthemata: 34.
Exophthalmos: 122.
Eye movements: 99, 110 *et seq.*, 112 *er seq.*
Eyzaguirre, C.: 160.

F
Facies: 26, 89., *et seq.*
Fainting: 18.
Fallschirm reaction: 194.
Fasciculation: 166.
Fawcett, J.: 96.
Feeding: 3, 44.
Fibrillation: 166.
Finger agnosia: 71.
First words: 3.
Fits: *See Epilepsy.*
Fitzgerald, P. J.: 131.
Flexor spasms: 183.
Floppy baby: 13.
Following reaction to light: 99.
Footdrop: 143, 147.
Forster, F. M.: 235.

Foville's syndrome: 123.
Friedreich's ataxia: 21, 97, 146, 148. 159, 178, 203.
Frostig, M.: 70.
Fullerton, P. M.: 222.
Fulton, J. F.: 160, 181.
Fundal examination: 23, 36, 108 *et seq.*

G
Gag reflex: 137.
Gait: 142 *et seq.*
Galactosaemia: 224, 228.
Gamma system: 160.
Gargoylism: 24, 42, 90, 91, 224, 229, 238.
Gaucher's Disease: *See Cerebroside lipidosis.*
Genetic disorders: 4 *et seq.*
Gerhardt's syndrome: 123.
Gerstmann syndrome: 71.
Gellis, S. S.: 99, 117.
Gesell, A.: 39, 191.
Gestures, imitation of: 51, 80.
Ghadimi, H.: 228.
Gilroy, J.: 249.
Gnosis: 69.
Goldstein, K.: 83.
Golgi corpuscles: 202.
Gonda sign: 180.
Good, R. A.: 260.
Goodenough test: 79, 80.
Gordon sign: 180.
Gordon Holmes test: 164.
Gorman, T. J.: 99, 117.
Gotham, J. E.: 249.
Gower's sign: 147.
Grace Arthur Mannequin Assembly: 80.
Gradenigo's syndrome: 122.
Graham, F. K.: 80, 81.
Graphaesthesia: 70, 204.
Green, J. B.; 235.
Griffiths, R.: 39.
Guillain-Barré syndrome: 54, 132, 147, 153, 159, 178, 208, 222, 234.
Guthrie, R.: 224.

H

Hagberg, B:	260.
Hallpike, C. S.:	119, 135, 209, 249.
Halstead, W. C.:	70.
Hamilton, P.B.:	228.
Hamerton, J. L.:	226.
Hand-Schuller-Christian disease:	212, 234.
Hansen, R. G.:	224.
Hanson, H. B.:	67.
Hanvik, L. J.:	67.
Hare-lip:	42.
Haymaker, W.:	210.
Head:	85. *et seq.*
Headache:	14 *et seq.*, 96.
Head circumference:	26, 41, 85, 86.
Head injury:	33, 34, 45, 214.
Hearing:	30, 50, 132, *See also Deafness.*
Height:	26.
Hemiparesis (hemiplegia):	43, 145, 146, 150, 154, 159, 170, 181, 193, 203, 205.
Hepatolenticular degeneration:	38.
Hepatomegaly:	27.
Hermann, K.:	62, 67, 71.
Herndon, R. M.:	160.
Herpes Zoster:	131, 201.
Herschkowitz, N.:	235.
Heterochromia:	108, 120.
Heterozygous:	5 *et seq.*
Heterophoria:	115.
Hines, M.:	160.
History:	1 *et seq.*
— developmental:	3.
— family,	4 *et seq.*
— medical:	2.
Hippus:	121.
Hirschprung's disease:	211, 257, 258.
Hoffmann's reflex:	172.
Hoffmann's sign:	181, 182.
Homocystinuria:	227.
Homozygous:	6.
Hoover's sign:	154.
Hopping:	194.
Hopping reaction:	185.
Horner's syndrome:	120, 122, 209.
Housing:	9.
Howell, P. R.:	227.
Hoyt, W. F.:	128.
Hubbell, J. P. Jr.:	187, 189.
Hunt, Ramsey:	131.
Huntington's chorea:	6, 167.
Hurler's syndrome:	*See Gargoylism.*
Hutzler, J.:	224.
Hydranencephaly:	41, 94.
Hydrocephalus:	24, 41, 74, 87, 93, 98, 111, 112.
Hypaesthesia;	196.
Hypalgesia:	196.
Hyperactive child:	84.
Hyperacusis:	129.
Hyperaesthesia:	196, 201.
Hyperbilirubinaemia:	23.
Hyperosmia:	98.
Hypertension:	15, 16.
Hyperthyroidism:	120, 122.
Hypertropha Musculorum Vera:	151.
Hypoglycaemia:	18, 34, 216, 229.
Hypopituitarism:	211.
Hypophonia:	54.
Hypothyroidism:	35, 42, 43, 90, 151.
Hypotonic cerebral palsy:	13, 14, 177.
	See also Cerebral palsy.
Hysteria:	98, 104, 126, 143, 148, 154, 161, 200.

I

Ianniruberto, A.:	235.
Illingworth, R. S.:	39.
Infantile automatisms:	171 *et seq.*, 184.
Infectious mononucleosis:	14.
Influenza:	14.
Ingram, T. T. S.:	55.
Inner language:	51.
Institutionalised child:	64.
Intelligence:	30, 38 *et seq.*
Intelligence tests:	30, 68, 83, 250.
Intention tremor:	165, 167.
Internuclear ophthalmoplegia:	122.
Interpeduncular Space syndrome:	124.
Intracranial hypertension:	96.

Involuntary movements: 11.
Isselbacker, K. J.: 224.

J

Jacoby, G. A.: 227.
Jawjerk: 55, 124, 126.
Jendrassik's manoeuvre: 172.

K

Kakosmia: 98.
Kalckan, H. M.: 224.
Kanner, L.: 46, 64.
Kayser-Fleischer ring: 42, 104, 106, 107.
Keller, A. D.: 160, 181.
Kendall, B. S. 80, 81.
Kernicterus, eye movement in: 112.
Kernig sign: 162.
Kingsbourne, M.: 63, 70.
Klinefelter's syndrome: 8.
Klippel-Feil syndrome: 23, 95.
Knee jerk: 172, 175, 177.
Knoblock, H.: 67.
Kufs: 109.
Kugelberg and Welander spinal muscular atrophy: 153.
Kurahashi, K.: 224.
Kurtz, J. F.: 154.
Kyphosis: 97, 142.

L

Lacrimation: 207.
La Du, B. D.: 227.
Lake, B. D.: 261.
Landau, W. M.: 161, 182.
Landau reaction: 189 *et seq.* 194.
Landing, B. H.: 260.
de Lange syndrome: 42.
Language: 9, 50.
Larman, W. A.: 154.
Lasègue's sign: 162.
Laufer, M. W.: 67.
Laurence-Moon-Beidl syndrome: 42, 109.

Laxatives: 3.
Lead: 34.
Lead intoxication: 21, 35, 38, 98, 224, 228, 230.
Lefever, D. W.: 70.
Lehtinen, L.: 67, 70.
Lending, M.: 235.
Leri sign: 169, 181.
Leukaemia: 15, 34.
Levin, S. 260.
Levitz, M.: 224.
Lézine, I.: 51, 71, 80.
Ling, T. H.: 189.
Linker, A.: 229.
Lipomata: 92.
Lisp: 54.
List, C. F.: 209.
Lordosis: 97, 142.
Lowe's syndrome: 42.
Lumbar puncture: 37, 231 *et seq.*

M

MacFadyen, D. A.: 228.
Magnus, R.: 189, 193.
Magoun, H. W.: 160.
Malaria: 14.
Malingering: 154, 200.
Mandibulo-facial dysostosis: 23.
Maple syrup urine disease: 224, 227.
Marcus Gunn phenomenon: 122, 125.
Marshall, J.: 183.
Matthews, P. B. C.: 160.
McBride, K. A.: 60.
McCarthy's reflex: 129.
McCouch, G. P.: 189.
McDonald, E. T.: 47, 48, 53.
McIntyre, A. K.: 127.
Measles: 34.
Medical Research Council Muscle Tests: 152.
Medulloblastomata: 143.
Melchior, J. C.: 229.
Memory: 68.
Mendel-Bechterew reflex: 180, 181.
Menière's syndrome: 119, 136.

Meningitis: 14, 22, 23, 44, 98, 126, 153, 232, 236.
—, tuberculous: 43.
Meningoceles: 97, *See also Myelomeningoceles.*
Menkes, J. H.: 115.
Menstruation: 19.
Mental retardation: 10, 13, 14, 38, 43, 57, 58, 66, 92, 223, 228.
Mental state: 33 *et seq.*
Mestern, J.: 235.
Metachromatic leukodystrophy: 38, 87, 109, 222.
Meyer, J. S.: 160, 249.
Meyer sign: 169, 181.
Microcephalia Vera: 41, 85.
Microcephaly: 13, 85.
Migraine: 9, 15, 104.
Milisen, R.: 53.
Millard and Gubler's syndrome: 123.
Minimal cerebral dysfunction: 10, 66 *et seq.*, 167.
Mirror movement: 169.
Mittwoch, U.: 224.
Moebius' syndrome: 54, 123, 131, 91. *See also Nuclear agenesis.*
Mongolism: *See Down's syndrome.*
Monoparesis: 170.
Morley, M. E.: 56.
Moro reflex: 184, 189, 191, 195.
Mothers: 2, 3, 25, *See also Parents.*
Motor function: 150 *et seq.*
Muco-polysaccharidoses: 23, 24.
Muir, H.: 224.
Multiple sclerosis: 21.
Murphy, K.: 52.
Muscle atrophy: 150.
Muscle biopsy: 256 *et seq.*
Muscle power: 30, 152.
Muscular dystrophy: 4, 12, 14, 147, 150, 151, 159, 182, 218, 220, 223, 229.
Muscular hypertrophy: 151.
Muscle mass: 150.

Muscular tone: 17, 37, 158 *et seq.* 167, 168.
Musical agnosia: 61.
Myasthenia gravis: 14, 91, 114, 153, 159, 241.
Myelography: 240 *et seq.*
Myelomeningoceles: 8, 20, 97, 154, 180, 211.
Myklebust, H. R.: 67.
Myoclonus: 11, 166, 128.
Myotonia: 162, 163.
Myotonia congenita: 140, 151.
Myxoedema: 151.

N
Nakai, H.: 260.
Nathan, P. W.: 181.
Neck-righting reflex: 185, 186, 191, 192, 193.
Nelson, S. E.: 67.
Neonatal jaundice: 43, 251.
Nephritis: 24, 35.
Nerve biopsy: 260.
Nerve condition: 220 *et seq.*
Netsky, M. G.: 202.
Neurofibromatosis: 23, 24, 28, 42, 97.
Neurolipidoses: 38.
Niemann-Pick disease: 43, 109, 201.
Nordin, J. H.: 224.
Norris, F. H.: 96.
Nothnagel syndrome: 124.
Nuclear agenesis: *See Moebius' syndrome.*
Nystagmus: 99, 100, 115, 116 *et seq.*, 134, 135, 136, 249.

O
Oculomotor apraxia: 115.
O'Doherty, T. S.: 235.
Oldenwurter, A. A.: 235.
Opisthotonos: 143.
Optic atrophy: 36, 104, 106, 107, 110.
Optic neuritis: 104, 106, 107, 109.
Opticokinetic nystagmus: 99.
Oppenheim sign: 180.

Otitis media: 23.
Ototoxic drugs: 23.

P

Pacinian corpuscles: 202.
Pain: 196 *et seq.*, 202.
Paine, R. S.: (*specific references*) 50, 67, 130, 184, 187, 189, 192.
Palmar grasp: 187.
Palmar reflex: 179.
Palmomental reflex: 181.
Papilloedema: 36, 106, 107, 109.
Parachute response: 185, 187, 191, 194.
Paraparesis: 146, 170, 187.
Paraphrasia: 61.
Paraplegia: 170, 183.
Parents: 1, 4, 5, 9, 30.
Parinaud's syndrome: 112, 114, 122.
Parkinsonism: 119, 131, 146, 158, 159, 161,168.
Parmelee, A. H.jr: 195.
Pasamanick, B: 67.
Past-pointing: 165.
Pearce, J. M. S.: 223.
Peet, M. M. 209.
Peiper, A.: 184, 196.
Penfield, W.: 130.
Pennington, R. J.: 223.
Perception: 70.
Periodic syndrome: 16, *See also Migraine.*
Perthes' disease: 149.
Pica: 21.
Pithed frog posture: 143.
Phenylketonuria: 43, 91, 224, 227.
Phonemes: 48.
Phonation: 47, 54.
Photogenic epilepsy: 19.
Photophobia: 14.
Placing reaction: 185, 193.
Plagiocephaly: 42, 87, 88, 90.
Plantar grasp: 187.
Plantar reflex: 179.
Plum, F.: 253, 254.

Pneumoencephalography: 123, 214.
Poliomyelitis: 147, 178, 208, 220, 229.
Polymyositis: 14, 97, 147, 230, 257, 258.
Porencephaly: 95.
Porphyria: 12.
Porphyrins: 230.
Positive supporting reaction: 185.
Posture: 142 *et seq.*
Prader's syndrome: 42.
Praxis: 71.
Prechtl, H.: 184.
Premature synostosis: 87.
Progressive spinal muscular atrophy: 14, 178.
Proprioceptive sensation: 201.
Pseudohypertrophic muscular dystrophy: 151.
Pseudohypoparathyroidism: 27.
Psychogalvanometric skin resistance test: 133, 252.
Psychometric tests: *See Intelligence tests)*
Ptosis: 121 *et seq.*
Puletti, F.: 87.

R

Rademaker, G. G. J.: 195.
Radiology: 37.
Raised intracranial pressure: 15, 37.
Raymond-Cestan's syndrome: 123.
Reading: 51, 69, *See also Dyslexia.*
Rectal biopsy: 211, 260.
Reflexes: 171 *et seq.*
Regression: 45.
Respiration and speech: 47.
Retinal haemorrhage: 109.
Retinitis pigmentosa: 24, 36, 42, 104, 109. *See Laurence-Moon-Biedle syndrome.*
Retrolental fibroplasia: 108.
Rhines, R.: 160.
Rickettsial infection: 34.
Riley, C. M.: 209.
Riley-Day syndrome: 203, 209, 210, 248.
Rimland, B.: 64.

Rinné test: 133.
Robinson, R. G.: 127.
Rochford, F. : 53, 63.
Romberg sign: 143.
Rossolimo sign: 180, 181.
Rubella syndrome: 23, 24, 108, 136.
Rüdel, R. G.: 70.
Running: 40.
Rushworth, G.: 160.

S

Saint-Anne Dargassies, S.: 158, 184.
Salivation: 207.
Sander, B.: 223.
Scanning speech: 56.
Scaphocephaly: 89.
School phobia: 15.
Schizophrenia: 79, 177.
Schuster, M. M.:' 210.
Schwachman, H.: 228.
Scoliosis: 97.
Scotomata: 104.
Sears, E. M.: 187, 189.
Sedatives: 3.
Seegmiller, J. E.: 227.
Seizures: See Epilepsy.
Sensory function: 196 et seq.
Sensory function, cortical: 204.
Setting sun sign: 111, 112.
Sex-linkage: 5.
Shank, K. H.: 52.
Sheridan, M. D.: 39, 53, 100.
Sinusitis: 15.
Sitting: 3, 143.
Skin biopsy: 260.
Sleep: 9, 43.
Sleep states: 33.
Slobody, L. B.: 235.
Smiling: 3.
Smith, M. C.: 181.
Sneezing: 138.
Snellen test: 100.
Sober, E. K.: 227.
Sogg, R. L.: 128.
Solomon, N.: 210.

Sourander, P.: 53, 63.
Spasmus nutans: 118.
Spastic speech: 55.
Specific developmental speech dis-
    orders: 55.
Speech: 40, 47 et seq., 137, 69.
Spielmeyer-Vogt, cerebral macular
    degeneration: 109, 222.
Spina Bifida: 20, 97, See also Myelomen-
                    ingocele.
Spinal reflexes: 163, 171 et seq.
Splenomegaly: 27.
Standing: 3, 142 et seq.
Station: 142.
Steiness, I.: 229.
Stepping: 194.
Stepping reaction: 185.
Stereoanaesthesia: 205.
Stereognosis: 150, 204.
Stevens, H.: 210.
Stokes-Adams' syndrome: 18.
Stone, M. L. : 235.
Strabismus: 100, 111, 114, 115 et seq.
Strauss, A.: 67, 70.
Strumpell, pronator sign of: 169.
Stupor: 33.
Sturge-Weber syndrome: 42, 236, 239.
Stuttering: 56.
Subacute combined degeneration of
    spinal cord: 146.
Subacute inclusion body encephalitis:
                    38.
Subarachnoid haemorrhage: 96.
Subdural haematoma: 24, 87, 95, 233,
                    236, 247.
Superficial reflexes: 178 et seq.
Supporting reaction: 191, 193.
Susi, A.: 224.
Sutherland, J. M.: 148.
Svennerholm, L.: 260.
Swaiman, K. F.: 223.
Swallowing: 138.
Sweating: 207.
Sydenham's chorea: 13, 149, 159, 167.
Symmetrical tonic neck reflex: 189.

Syphilis: 24.
Syringobulbia: 141, 209.
Syringomyelia: 200.

T

Tabes dorsalis: 146, 159, 178.
Tactile agnosia: 61.
Taghavy, A.: 235.
Taste: 130, 138.
Tay-Sachs disease: 14, 109, 129, 193.
Tears: 130.
Teasdall, R. D.: 210.
Telangiectasia: 27, 42, 104, 105. *See also Ataxia telangectasia*
Temperature sense: 198.
Tendon reflexes: 13, 33, 171 *et seq.*
Terry, K.: 229.
Tetraparesis: 146, 170.
Tetraplegia: 170.
Teuber, M. L.: 70.
Thalidomide embryopathy: 23.
Thompson, S. W.: 249.
Tics: 11, 128, 139, 168.
Tigay, E. L.: 154.
Tinnitus: 136.
Toilet training: 3, 9, 20 *et seq. See also Enuresis.*
Tonic neck reflexes: 13.
Tone: *See Muscle tone.*
Tongue: 128, 140.
Tongue-tie: 54.
Topaesthesia: 204.
Topognosia: 204.
Torticollis: 139.
Torticollis, infantile: 96.
Touch: 196.
Tower, S. W.: 160.
Toxoplasmosis: 23, 24, 42, 108, 230.
Transillumination: 87, 94 *et seq.*
Treacher-Collins syndrome: 92.
Tremble, G. E.: 130.
Triceps jerk: 172.
Triparesis: 170.
Triple response: 207.
Triplegia: 170.

Trömner sign: 181, 182,
Tuberose sclerosis: 24, 28, 42, 106.
107, 108 ,236, 239, 260.
Tumour, intracranial: 87.
Turner's syndrome: 8, 42, 95.
Twins: 5.
Two-point discrimination: 30, 150, 204.
Tyrer, J. H.: 148.

U

Ultra sound scans: 241.
Urinalysis: 37, 45, 226 *et seq.*

V

Vaccinia: 34.
Van Bogaert: 87.
Van Gelderen, H. H.: 227.
Van Slyke, D. D.: 228.
Ventricular puncture: 232.
Ventriculogram: 240.
Vertigo: 18, 136.
Vestibular function: 134 *et seq.*
Vibration: 202.
Vignolo, L. A.: 48.
Viral meningoencephalitis: 34.
Vitamins: 3.
Vision: 30, 99.
Visual acuity: 100.
Visual agnosia: 61.
Visual fields: 101 *et seq.*
Vocabulary: 53.
Von Hippel-Lindau disease: 106, 107,
108.

W

Waardenburg's syndrome: 24.
Wadia, N. H.: 96.
Walking: 3, 26. 143 *et seq.*
Walton, J. N.: 67.
Walsh, F. B.: 210.
Warrington, E. K.: 63, 68, 70.
Wartenburg, R.: 128.
Weakness: 11.
Weber's syndrome: 123.
Weber Test: 133

Weight: 26.

Weisenburg, T.: 60.

Werdnig-Hoffman infantile spinal
progressive muscular atrophy: 13,
14, 141, 144, 153, 183, 220, 257, 258.

Werner, H.: 70.

Whittlesey, J. R. B.: 70.

Wigglesworth, R.: 66.

Wilkinson M.: 182.

Williams, M.: 53, 63.

Wilson's disease: 42, 104, 224, 228, 231.

Winking-jaw phenomenon: 125.

Worster-Drought, C.: 55.

Writing: 51, 62.

X

X-ray studies: 89, 236 *et seq.*

Y

Yasuna, E. R.: 100.

Z

Zannoni, V. G.: 227.

Zarling, V. R.: 67.

Ziegler, L. K.: 227.

Ziter, F. A.: 209.

Zu Rhein, G. M.: 87.

Printed in England by THE LAVENHAM PRESS LTD., Lavenham, Suffolk.